THE COMPLETE BOOK OF
SOCCER

CLIVE GIFFORD & JOHN MALAM

Firefly Books

A FIREFLY BOOK

Published by Firefly Books Ltd. 2016
Copyright © 2016 Moseley Road Incorporated
Text copyright © 2016 Clive Gifford, John Malam
All photography © Action Images Ltd

First printing

Publisher Cataloging-in-Publication Data (U.S.)

Names: Gifford, Clive, author. | Malam, John, 1957-, author.
Title: The complete book of soccer / John Malam & Clive Gifford.
Description: Richmond Hill, Ontario, Canada : Firefly Books, 2016. | Includes index. | Summary: "This book tells the story of soccer's origins and its evolution around the world. It includes player biographies, facts and statistics, the world's major championships and the most important competitions" — Provided by publisher.
Identifiers: ISBN 978-1-77085-765-0 (hardcover)
Subjects: LCSH: Soccer – History. | Soccer players. | Soccer – Miscellanea.
Classification: LCC GV943.G544|DDC 796.334 – dc23

Library and Archives Canada Cataloguing in Publication

Malam, John, author
The complete book of soccer / John Malam & Clive Gifford.
Includes index.
ISBN 978-1-77085-765-0 (hardback)
1. Soccer. 2. Soccer—Rules. 3. Soccer—Tournaments. 4. Soccer teams. 5. Soccer players. I. Gifford, Clive author II. Title.
GV943.M35 2016   796.334   C2016-903722-3

Published in the United States by
Firefly Books (U.S.) Inc.
P.O. Box 1338, Ellicott Station
Buffalo, New York 14205

Published in Canada by
Firefly Books Ltd.
50 Staples Avenue, Unit 1
Richmond Hill, Ontario L4B 0A7

Printed in China

CONTENTS

THE BEAUTIFUL GAME

THE SPECIAL ONE

Football is a universal language that needs no translation. Give a group of people a ball, and before you know it they've divided themselves into two teams and are running around kicking it the length of a makeshift pitch, each trying to score a goal. It's taken a long time to get to this.

Football. The word is a special one. You'll find it in the Oxford English Dictionary, sandwiched between the obsolete "footback" (traveling on foot, as opposed to riding on horseback), and the scientific "footballene" (a roughly spherical-shaped molecule). It's been in the English language a long time and has gone through many spelling variations, from fut ball (1424), fotebal (1486), foote balle (1531) and foot-ball (1663), until finally arriving at the one we know – football.

The dictionary has this to say about it:

Football noun
1. An inflated ball used in the game [of the same name].

2. An open-air game played with this ball by two sides, each of which endeavors to kick or convey the ball to the goal at the opposite end of the field.

It seems like a good place to start.

The modern game of football has been with us for little more than 150 years. Those first matches came too soon to be caught on film, but chances are we would recognize them as the game we know and love. However, there were ball games long before our game of football took over the park, and it's to these games that football's family tree can ultimately be traced. Whether we would recognize them as football is another matter.

Opposite page: An artist's impression of the 1891 FA Cup Final.

Above: A depiction of a football game from the early 18th Century

THE BEAUTIFUL GAME

Made in China

The earliest known record of a game resembling something like football was played 2,000 years ago in ancient China, in the Han Dynasty period (206BC–220AD). It was known as Tsu Chu, which roughly translates as "kicking a ball with the feet": sounds a lot like "football."

The aim of Tsu Chu was to kick a leather ball filled with feathers and hair through a small hole into a net. Players needed plenty of skill (and probably a fair amount of luck), as the hole they aimed at was only 30cm-40cm wide. If that wasn't a tough enough call, the net was held between a tall pair of bamboo "goalposts," with the target hole raised high off the ground.

Ancient Chinese records reveal that Tsu Chu was used for exercise by soldiers, that touching the ball with the hands was not allowed, and that the emperor was a fan. A game of Tsu Chu was played in celebration of his birthday and, according to legend, the winners were treated to a banquet while the losers were put to death.

Ball-juggling in Japan

An early foot and ball game was played in Japan, though the game of Kemari has more to do with today's "keepie uppie" than scoring goals and winning games. Originating in China, Kemari became popular in Japan some 1,400 years ago, where it was the game of nobles, samurai warriors, priests and the Imperial Japanese court.

Above: "Mob football" was popular in medieval England. It involved an unlimited number of players, a pig's bladder and very few rules. Due to its destructive nature, it was banned by King Edward II in 1314

There were no winners or losers in this non-competitive ball-juggling game, in which the objective was to keep the ball in the air as long as possible.

Kemari survived unchanged for centuries, but as Japan opened its doors to outside (Western) contacts after 1868, the game rapidly fell into decline. In 1903, the Kemari Preservation Society was formed in Japan to preserve the ancient game, and it's largely because of this that it has survived and is played to this day, especially at Kemari festivals held annually at some shrines.

Ball games in the ancient West

We owe our knowledge of early ball games played in the West to the Greek and Roman writers of antiquity. It's thanks to Julius Pollux, a Greek writer who lived about 180AD, that we know about the game of episkyros, which, he says, was the most important ball game of them all. By another name it was known as epikoinos, which literally means "the team game."

The game, says Pollux, was played by two teams of equal numbers, made up of youths between the ages of seventeen and eighteen. He doesn't say how many were in each team. The young men played on a pitch marked out with a center line and goal lines at either end. A ball was placed on the center line, and the game began. But, from hereon, the comparison with our game of football ends, as the ball was picked up and thrown over and beyond the opposing team, whose task was to catch it and throw it back until one side was finally forced back over its own goal line.

Pollux's description of this ancient ball game was brought vividly to life in 1922, when a carved marble panel showing two teams of lads playing episkyros was found in Athens. The panel, which dates from c.500BC, revealed a detail overlooked by Pollux – the muscular players with their well-honed bodies played the game in the nude.

If depictions in ancient art are anything to go by, then it's clear that the sport-loving Greeks enjoyed their ball games as much as we do. The difficulty comes in trying to make sense of them, especially where the ancient writers are frustratingly silent.

What, for example, are we to make of a naked male athlete, carved in relief in marble, shown skillfully balancing a large ball on his right thigh, while standing on tiptoes on his left leg, hands behind his back? Is he about to flick the ball up and catch it on his left thigh, then back again to his right? With no written clues to guide us, we can only imagine what's really happening, but whatever this athlete is doing, it must have been important and well-known enough for an artist to record it for prosperity in stone.

RULES OF KEMARI

Number of players: 6 or 8, men and women.

Court: A 15m x 15m area of flat ground with a pine, cherry, willow and maple tree at the corners of the square (a protective spirit is believed to live in each tree).

Ball: White deerskin, about 25cm in diameter and weighing 100–150g.

Costume: Traditional, aristocratic dress of the Heian period (794-1186) – cap, loose-fitting jacket, a wide divided skirt and long boots.

Game play: The game begins with the players standing in a circle, about 3m in diameter. The ball is kicked high into the air with the right foot, and players move freely around the court as they try to keep the ball in the air, not letting it touch the ground. When a player kicks the ball, he calls out "Ari," "Ya" or "Oh" – the names of the game's protective spirits. A game ends when a player loses control of the ball and it touches the ground. Players then resume the circle position and a new game begins.

Duration: Games last 15–20 minutes.

1876 Football Association of Wales is formed. Scotland play Wales for the first time.

1877 The London Association and Sheffield Association agree to use the same rules.

1878 The whistle is introduced by referees.

1879 First international between England and Wales takes place at Kennington Oval. England win 2-1.

1880 The Irish FA is formed.

1882 The two-handed throw-in is introduced.

1883 First British Home Championship is staged and won by Scotland.

1885 Professionalism is legalised in England. Arbroath beat Bon Accord 36-0, a record for a first-class match.

1886 The awarding of caps for international appearances is approved by the FA.

1887 Preston North End beat Hyde United 26-0 to record the biggest FA Cup score. Football introduced in Russia.

1888 The Football League is formed.

1889 Preston North End win first league and cup "double."

1890 The Scottish League is formed.

1891 Devised by Liverpool engineer John Alexander Brodie, goal nets are introduced. The taking of penalties from a penalty line is also introduced.

1893 Genoa, Italy's oldest football club, is formed by British diplomat Sir Charles Alfred Payton and nine of his contemporaries. The club is originally named Genoa Football and Cricket Club.

THE BEAUTIFUL GAME

The forbidden game

Something akin to football eventually emerged in the streets and on the fields of western Europe – though where and when is unknown. Suffice to say, the medieval game of football was anything but orderly and is frequently referred to by modern commentators as "mob football," with good reason.

Opposing teams of seemingly unlimited numbers pushed, shoved, wrestled and barged their way in pursuit of the ball, each side attempting to be the first to get it to a marker post. Given that the "pitch" might be the public highway through town, is it any wonder that the authorities took a dim view on this rowdy game? Take, for example, what happened in London.

At the turn of the 14th century, London had a population of around 80,000, crammed into timber and stone buildings along a patchwork of narrow streets. It was a bustling city of traders and merchants, carts and ships, noise, stench and grime, and where high-spirited groups ran amok as they chased and kicked footballs.

Concerns were raised about this rough and tumble practice affecting trade, and matters came to a head in 1314 when Edward II issued a royal proclamation that decreed:

"Forasmuch as there is great noise in the city caused by hustling over large balls, from which many evils may arise, which God forbid, we command and forbid on behalf of the King, on pain of imprisonment, such game to be used in the city in future."

It was the first attempt to impose authority on an activity enjoyed by the masses – not just to regulate or control it, but to stamp it out (in London, at least). Needless to say, it didn't work.

A further ban in England was brought in during the reign of

Top: A game of Kemari at Tanzan Shrine

Bottom: The Romans also played a form of football which could more accurately be described as a cross between soccer and rugby, but with a great deal more brutality involved.

1902 The maximum wage of £4 per week is brought in. Real Madrid are founded. Austria beat Hungary 5-0 in Vienna in the first European international between countries outside of Britain.

1904 World governing body FIFA is formed in Paris.

1905 Goalkeepers ordered to stay on goal line for penalties. The first £1,000 transfer sees Alf Common move from Sunderland to Middlesbrough.

1908 England play Austria in Vienna — their first international against a non-British side. The transfer fee limit is fixed at £350. England win the first official Olympic football gold, beating Denmark in the final.

1910 Argentina win the first unofficial South American championship, in a three-team tournament that also includes Uruguay and Chile.

1912 Goalkeepers banned from handling outside the box.

1916 The founding of the South American Football Confederation.

1919 The four British football associations withdraw from FIFA after refusing to play against any of their recent wartime enemies. They extend their boycott to any nation prepared to play against these countries.

1920 Players cannot be offside from throw-ins.

1921 THe Football Association bans women's football from being played at the grounds of its member clubs.

Top: A team from Harrow public school in the 19th Century

Bottom: Preston, the first double-winners in 1889

THE BEAUTIFUL GAME

Edward III who, in 1349, condemned football as distracting men from practicing archery – a necessary skill for the conduct of war and the defense of the country. Medieval monarchs knew where their priorities lay, and allowing the population the pleasure of football was certainly not one of them.

There were similar worries in Scotland, where the Football Act of 1424 announced in crystal clear terms:

"It is decreed and the King forbids any man to play at football on pain of 4d to be paid to the lord of the land as often as he is convicted, or to the sheriff of the land or to his agents, if the lords are unwilling to punish such trespassers."

The king in question was James I of Scotland, and by these few words football was outlawed throughout his realm. Just as in England, Scotland's powers-that-be wagged their collective fingers at the common man, telling him to stop his unruly, disruptive behavior and take up his bow instead. Football had no practical use, unlike archery, which had obvious military advantages.

It was, of course, a forlorn hope, and despite three further similar Acts passed in Scotland before the 15th century was over, football was here to stay.

Football at English public schools

By the early 16th century, football was being played at English public schools, and in 1519, William Horman, headmaster at both Eton and Winchester College, wrote "We wyll playe with a ball full of wynde" – one of the earliest references to football being played at public schools.

Like street football of the time, the game played by the sons of the aristocracy was rough and physical, although for these young men it formed part of their education, instilling in them an understanding and appreciation of teamwork and leadership. These games were competitive, keenly played and much anticipated throughout the school by staff and scholars. In time, England's public schools devised rules for their versions of football, and it is to these that the modern rules of football can be traced.

Above: Part of a 14th century misericord at Gloucester Cathedral depicting an early example of ball game players.

THE ETON WALL GAME

Played at Eton College, Windsor, since at least 1766, the Eton Wall Game, is played on a narrow strip of grass about five metres wide, running alongside a high brick wall about 110m long.

The Wall Game sees two teams of no more than 10 players in each team try to kick the ball to the far end of the pitch and score a goal. Players are not allowed to handle the ball, not allowed to let any part of their bodies except feet and hands touch the ground, and not allowed to strike or hold their opponents. There are strict "offside" rules (no passing back and no playing in front), but apart from that, almost anything goes in the hour-long game. Inevitably, it turns into an almost continuous scrum – known in Eton slang as a "bully" – as the players try to push toward the other's end. If they manage to do that, a team must try to raise the ball and put it against the wall to score a "shy," worth one point. The scoring team can then try to throw the ball against a door at one end, and a tree stump at the other, in a bid to score a goal, worth nine points. However, that's easier than it sounds – the last time a goal was scored in the annual St Andrew's Day match was in 1909.

BOY'S OWN TALES OF THE BEAUTIFUL GAME ON THE WESTERN FRONT

FOOTBALL AT WAR

As British troops headed off to war in August 1914, they were sure they would be home by Christmas. Their German foe expected to be home even sooner, by the time the leaves fell from the trees. But by December 1914, the Race to the Sea – the first phase of World War I – was over, and both sides were dug in to long lines of trenches, stretching south from the North Sea coast through Belgium and into France. Only a strip of "no man's land" separated them, so narrow in places the combatants could sling insults across to each other.

THE FOOTBALL CHARGE

A similar story comes from the first day of the Battle of the Somme. Knowing they would be going "over the top" into the teeth of the Germans, Captain W.P. "Billie" Nevill supplied footballs to the men as a distraction . On one ball was written "The Great European Cup Tie Final. East Surreys v. Bavarians. Kick off at zero". Another read "No Referee", as in "anything goes." It became known as "the football charge." One ball was recovered and made its way to the Surrey Infantry Museum in the basement of Clandon Park, Guildford, Surrey. It was lost in a devastating fire in 2015.

THE LOOS FOOTBALL OF 1915

As the war progressed, footballs were again kicked around on no man's land, but this time in anger. In September 1915, the Battle of Loos became the first major British offensive, and men of the London Irish Rifles were to be first out of the trenches. The battalion was well known for its footballing prowess, and some of the men hatched a plan to dribble six footballs across the killing zone to the German lines. They were rumbled by their commanding officers, who shot five of the balls before the attack began. The sixth ball remained hidden. It was launched with a goalkeeper's throw, then dribbled all the way across the battlefield, until it was impaled on German barbed wire. The Loos Football survived the war, and is today proudly preserved at the London Irish Rifles Museum.

Top left: Captain Nevill's regiment celebrates the return of one of the Somme footballs.

14

Top right: A bronze statue of Francis Edwards, the "'footballer of Loos", who took the ball over the top stuffed into his coat. It was found later wedged in barbed wire and taken back to headquarters.

Above: September 1915. Soldiers of the London Irish Rifles kick footballs as they charge into German lines in the Battle of Loos.
Illustration: Lady Elizabeth Butler

Left: The Christmas Truce, 1914. Enemy soldiers on the Western Front enjoyed a few hours of respite from battle when they spontaneously met on No Man's Land to exchange rations and cigarettes, and play pick-up football. More than a century later, it is a story that still inspires.
Illustration: Alamy (Originally published in The Illustrated London News, January 9, 1915.)

Right: Captain "Billie" Nevill, who had bought two footballs, was among those who charged into German lines in the Battle of the Somme. Unfortunately the losses were huge and quick, and included Nevill.

FOOTBALL IN NO MAN'S LAND

Men, who only days before had been bitter enemies, emerged from the safety of their trenches and exchanged gifts and greetings amongst the shell holes and entanglements of no man's land. For a few brief hours it really was "all quiet on the Western Front." There can be no doubt that football was played on Christmas Day 1914 – troops' diaries and letters make this clear. Kickabouts took place behind the lines as men relaxed in those rare moments of calm. This much is historical fact. But it's what happened in front of the lines that is the stuff of legend. There wasn't a single organized football match between German and British troops. Instead, games took place at several locations, such as the one in the area of Frélinghien–Houplines, Flanders, recorded by a German, Johannes Niemann, saying "The game ended 3–2 for Fritz." It seems to have been this game noted in an anonymous letter to The Times, 1st January 1915, "[The regiment] … had a football match with the Saxons, who beat them 3–2." There was to be nothing like it again for the duration of the war.

"IF HE'S NOT INTERFERING WITH PLAY THEN WHAT'S HE DOING ON THE PITCH?"
BRIAN CLOUGH ON THE OFFSIDE RULE

THE LAWS OF

THE GAME

PLAYING BY THE RULES

It is to the public schools and universities of England that the global game of football can ultimately be traced. With their in-built love of order and rule-making it was a natural step for these institutions to impose the first codes upon the game – but they were anything if uniform.

If the 18th century and earlier had been a time of "anything goes" for football, the 19th century sought to take the emerging game by the scruff of the neck and shape it into something with rules. It began with a banning order about where the game was not to be played.

As the pace of Britain's red-hot Industrial Revolution increased, towns and cities expanded, canals then railways linked them together, and the importance of maintaining the nation's road network became obvious. To that end, the Highway Act 1835, banned certain activities from the highway – a term defined as "roads, bridges, carriageways, cartways, horseways, bridleways, footways, causeways, churchways, and pavements."

The new law cracked down hard on football, saying: "If any person shall play at football or any other game on any part of the said highways, to the annoyance of any passenger or passengers … every person so offending shall for each and every such offence forfeit and pay any sum not exceeding 40 shillings" (about five times the average weekly wage of the time). It was designed to rid the streets of the unruly mobs that had characterized football until then – and it did what it set out to do, as case law records.

Football goes to court

In 1860, a game of mob football involving several hundred people clad in nailed boots and padded clothing was played on the streets of Ashbourne, Derbyshire, "prepared mostly as if for a deadly struggle." It was the town's annual Shrove Tuesday football game, which had been played in the streets for longer than anyone could remember. Despite being outlawed by the Highway Act, the townsfolk of Ashbourne turned out in numbers determined to enjoy their game of football, as their ancestors had done before them.

Not surprisingly, the game brought traffic to a halt. Amongst those involved, a certain George Woolley made himself conspicuous and was arrested.

At his trial, Woolley was convicted under the Act of obstructing the passage of two horse-drawn carts in Ashbourne marketplace, and was duly fined by the magistrates. Woolley refused to pay, appealed against the decision, and raised £200 by public subscription for the services of a barrister.

The case went to the Court of Queen's Bench, where Woolley's counsel freely admitted that his client had played football, but objected to the failure of the prosecution to present any evidence of "annoyance to passengers," as the law demanded. To add weight to their case, Woolley's counsel noted how the obstruction had been witnessed by a police constable who had even joined in with the game.

The judge, Lord Cockburn, was dismissive. In an infamous summing up, he ruled there was no requirement "that the parties who were actually annoyed by the obstruction of the highway should be called to give evidence of the annoyance." In other words, he wasn't about to allow a pair of horses – the annoyed parties – to be trotted in to his court. It was sufficient for the court to presume annoyance despite evidence to the contrary. And with this, it seemed the suppression of folk football was complete and the game was destined for extinction. The practice of "footballing" was outlawed as the authorities took control of the streets.

Lord Kinnaird, who presided over the first ever international match.

THE LAWS OF THE GAME

The inhabitants of Ashbourne resented Lord Cockburn's decision, and satirical broadsheets were quickly circulated, one of which declared:

Death of The Right Honourable Game Football

"It becomes our painful duty to record the death of the Right Honourable Game Football, which melancholy event took place in the Court of Queen's Bench on Wednesday Nov. 14, 1860. The deceased Gentleman was, we are informed, a native of Ashbourne, Derbyshire, at which place he was born in the Year of Grace, 217, and was consequently in the 1643rd year of his age. For some months the patriotic Old Man had been suffering from injuries sustained in his native town, so far back as Shrove-tide in last year; he was at once removed (by appeal) to London, where he lingered in suspense till the law of death put its icy hand upon him, and claimed as another trophy to magisterial interference one who had long lived in the hearts of the people. His untimely end has cast a gloom over the place, where the amusement he afforded the inhabitants will not soon be forgotten."

Despite the court's ruling, the residents of Ashbourne ignored the law and on Shrove Tuesday 1862 a sizeable crowd once again played the game. The police moved in and made arrests, leading to a decision that all future games were to be played on fields outside the town – not on the public highway.

While the Act was used successfully to extinguish street football from many towns across Britain, the game stubbornly refused to die, and in some places Shrove Tuesday games continue the age-old tradition to this day. Ashbourne's game is alive and well and has even assumed the title "Royal," since the Prince of Wales, later to become King Edward VIII, "turned up" the ball in 1928, as did his great-nephew, HRH Prince Charles, who threw the ball to the crowd in 2003.

Same game, different rules

While Britain's authorities were busy clearing football from the streets, the game was flourishing at the nation's public schools, where it was enthusiastically played at Eton, Harrow, Westminster, Rugby, Charterhouse, Marlborough, Shrewsbury and many others. Each school had its own set of rules devised by the boys themselves. There was ample scope for confusion, misunderstanding and disobedience, with games frequently descending into brute force and violence.

At Eton, two games of football evolved – the Wall Game and the Field Game, the latter notable for having football's first written rules, issued in 1815, well before any other school took the trouble to document theirs. Eton's Field Game, like the games played at other public schools, had similarities with both football and rugby, showing how the two games share common origins.

From the 1850s, school masters took a growing interest in the game's administration, and the rules governing their particular school's game began to appear in print. It was a move toward formalizing the game, and with written rules to refer to, issues of interpretation could be overcome and disputes easily resolved (in theory, at least). But, having written rules highlighted the obvious differences between how each school played the game, effectively preventing them from playing against each other.

Cambridge University, birthplace of football

The differences became even more apparent as the boys went up to university and mixed with their counterparts from other public schools. Henry de Winton and John Thring, from Shrewsbury School, went up to Cambridge University and in 1846

Above: The FA Cup Final at Crystal Palace 1897.

Opposite: The original laws of the game.

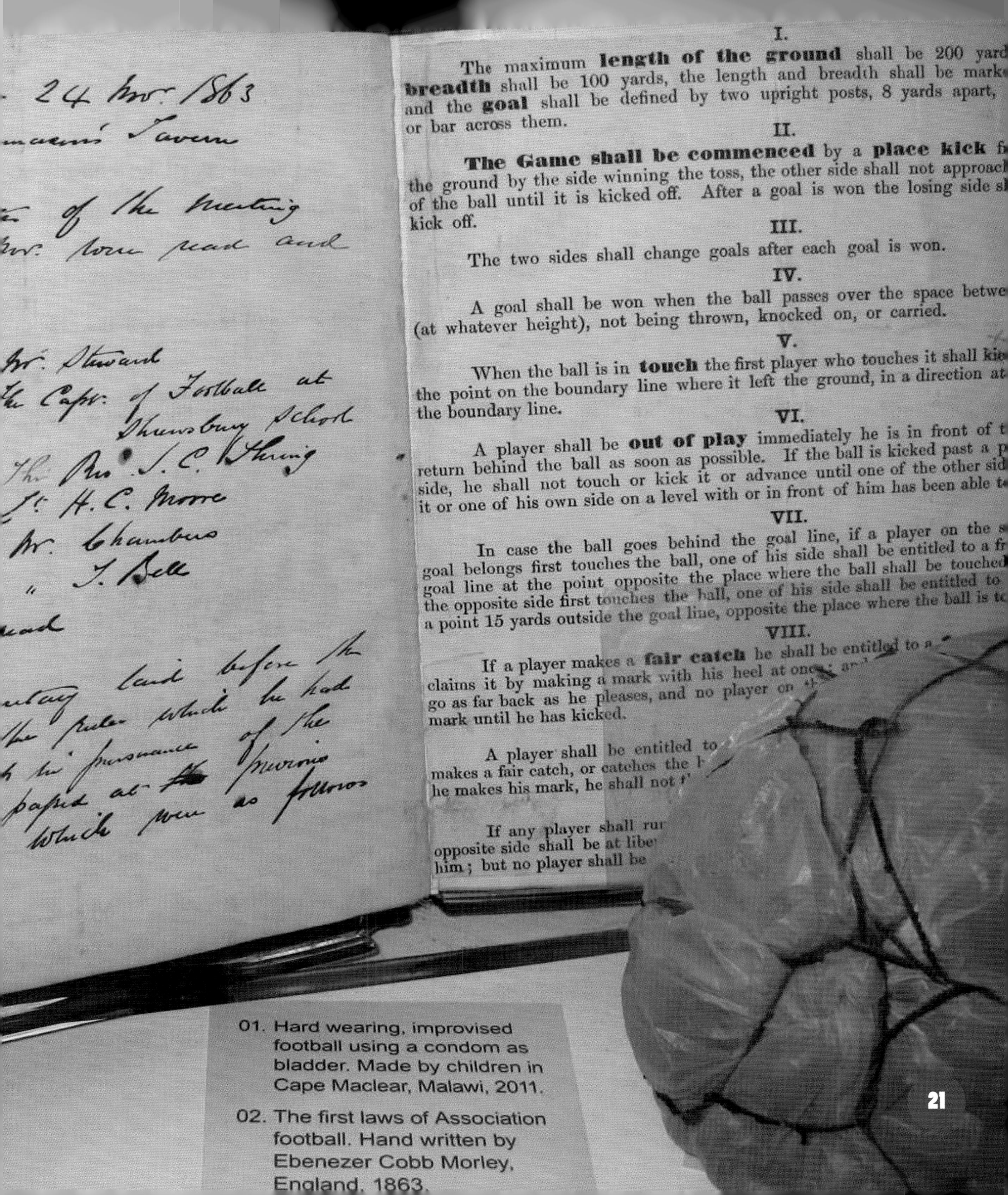

I.

The maximum **length of the ground** shall be 200 yard
breadth shall be 100 yards, the length and breadth shall be marke
and the **goal** shall be defined by two upright posts, 8 yards apart,
or bar across them.

II.

The Game shall be commenced by a **place kick** f
the ground by the side winning the toss, the other side shall not approac
of the ball until it is kicked off. After a goal is won the losing side sl
kick off.

III.

The two sides shall change goals after each goal is won.

IV.

A goal shall be won when the ball passes over the space betwe
(at whatever height), not being thrown, knocked on, or carried.

V.

When the ball is in **touch** the first player who touches it shall kie
the point on the boundary line where it left the ground, in a direction at
the boundary line.

VI.

A player shall be **out of play** immediately he is in front of t
return behind the ball as soon as possible. If the ball is kicked past a p
side, he shall not touch or kick it or advance until one of the other sid
it or one of his own side on a level with or in front of him has been able te

VII.

In case the ball goes behind the goal line, if a player on the s
goal belongs first touches the ball, one of his side shall be entitled to a fr
goal line at the point opposite the place where the ball shall be touched
the opposite side first touches the ball, one of his side shall be entitled to
a point 15 yards outside the goal line, opposite the place where the ball is to

VIII.

If a player makes a **fair catch** he shall be entitled to a
claims it by making a mark with his heel at once; and
go as far back as he pleases, and no player on
mark until he has kicked.

A player shall be entitled to
makes a fair catch, or catches the k
he makes his mark, he shall not t

If any player shall run
opposite side shall be at liber
him; but no player shall be

01. Hard wearing, improvised
football using a condom as
bladder. Made by children in
Cape Maclear, Malawi, 2011.

02. The first laws of Association
football. Hand written by
Ebenezer Cobb Morley,
England, 1863.

1960 The Soviet Union win the first European Championship, beating Yugoslavia 2-1 in the final. Uruguayan side Per arol become the first winners of the Copa Libertadores. Real Madrid win the European Cup for the fifth consecutive time, beating Eintracht Frankfurt 7-3. They also win the first World Club Cup, beating Peñarol 5-1 on aggregate.

1961 CONCACAF is founded in North and Central America. Juventus become the first Italian side to be awarded a gold star following their tenth title victory. Tottenham win England's first domestic "double" of the 20th Century. Fulham's Johnny Haynes becomes the first British player to earn £100 per week. The first British £100,000 transfer sees Denis Law move from Manchester City to Torino. Fiorentina win the first European Cup Winners' Cup, beating Rangers 4-1 on aggregate. Aston Villa are the first League Cup winners.

1963 The West German Bundesliga begins. Prior to this German football had been regional. Tottenham win the Cup Winners' Cup against Atletico Madrid.

1964 Oryx Douala of Cameroon win the first African Champions Club Cup. George Best makes his debut for Manchester United. Alfredo Di Stefano scores his 49th European Cup goal.

SHROVETIDE FOOTBALL – AN ENGLISH CUSTOM

Despite the Highway Act 1835 banning football from Britain's highways, the will of the people is such that the street game has survived as an annual custom in some towns in England, traditionally played in February or March on Shrove Tuesday ("Pancake Day"). The games were – and still are – mob football, with few rules, physical contact and high spirits. A Frenchman who observed one of these riotous games in 1829 said: "If this is what they call football, what do they call fighting?"

• Alnwick, Northumberland – Scoring the Hales: the game caused so much devastation in the streets that it's now played on a meadow, with more than 100 players taking part.

• Ashbourne, Derbyshire – Royal Shrovetide Football: teams of Up'ards and Down'ards kick, carry and throw a cork-filled ball along streets and a stream as they attempt to score a "goal" by banging the ball against one of two stone plinths some 5km (3 miles) apart.

• Atherstone, Warwickshire – the Atherstone Ball Game: a heavy leather ball decorated with ribbons is thrown from a window at 3:00pm and the game begins. The object of the game is simple – be the person holding the ball when the game finishes at 5:00pm.

• Corfe Castle, Dorset: Members of the Company of Marblers and Stone Cutters of Purbeck kick a football through the town, keeping alive an ancient tradition of preserving a right of way for the transportation of Purbeck marble. Once at the wharfage, the ball is kicked into the water.

• Sedgefield, County Durham – the Ball Game: originally contested between farmers and tradesmen, the game is now open to all-comers who battle for possession of a small ball in order to pass it through an iron ring on the village green.

• St. Columb Major, Cornwall – Hurling the Silver Ball: the game starts at 4:30pm and for the next hour "townsmen" and "countrymen" snatch and tackle as they compete for the honor of scoring a goal by hurling a small, solid ball toward goals set 3km (2 miles) apart

The 1st Royal Engineers AFC, the first passing side

persuaded some Old Etonians to join them in forming the first university football club. However, with students staying loyal to the school rules they knew, the prospect of any sort of competition was impossible, let alone playing on the same side, especially as some schools permitted handling the ball whereas others placed an emphasis on kicking and running with the ball (dribbling). If the game was to be enjoyed by all, order had to be made from the chaos that existed, and in 1848 Winton and Thring called a meeting of representatives from different schools. It was the first attempt at unifying the game with a standard set of rules, and compromises were inevitable, given the scale of the task, before all parties could agree to a code. After nearly eight hours of deliberation, the patchwork of conflicting school rules had been reduced down to eleven, which became known as the Cambridge Rules.

Unfortunately for historians of the game, no copy of the historic 1848 Cambridge Rules – football's birth certificate – is known to exist, the earliest surviving set dating from about eight years later and preserved at Shrewsbury School. The Cambridge Rules make interesting reading today, and as handling the ball was allowed, the connections of this early version of the game to rugby are all too clear.

Sheffield Rules

Beyond the closed world of Britain's public school and university system, the common man was addressing a similar problem – the need to impose rules on his game of football.

In 1857, Sheffield Football Club was founded in the industrial northern English city of Sheffield. Known for its steelworks, Sheffield couldn't have been further removed from the ivory towers of Cambridge, but it was here, in 1858, that Sheffield F.C. formed the Sheffield Rules. Originally intended for teams playing in and around Sheffield to follow, the eleven Sheffield Rules were taken up in the

THE LAWS OF THE UNIVERSITY FOOT BALL CLUB (CAMBRIDGE RULES, 1856)

- This club shall be called the University Foot Ball Club.

- At the commencement of the play, the ball shall be kicked off from the middle of the ground: after every goal there shall be a kick-off in the same way.

- After a goal, the losing side shall kick off; the sides changing goals, unless a previous arrangement be made to the contrary.

- The ball is out when it has passed the line of the flag-posts on either side of the ground, in which case it shall be thrown in straight.

- The ball is behind when it has passed the goal on either side of it.

- When the ball is behind it shall be brought forward at the place where it left the ground, not more than ten paces, and kicked off.

- Goal is when the ball is kicked through the flag-posts and under the string.

- When a player catches the ball directly from the foot, he may kick it as he can without running with it. In no other case may the ball be touched with the hands, except to stop it.

- If the ball has passed a player, and has come from the direction of his own goal, he may not touch it till the other side have kicked it, unless there are more than three of the other side before him. No player is allowed to loiter between the ball and the adversaries' goal.

- In no case is holding a player, pushing with the hands, or tripping up allowed. Any player may prevent another from getting to the ball by any means consistent with the above rules.

- Every match shall be decided by a majority of goals.

Queens' College Cambridge football team 1900-1901,

1965 Stanley Matthews is the first footballer to be knighted. The Football League agree to one substitute per team in the event of injury. Arthur Rowley retires with a record 434 goals in the English Football League.

1966 The Oceania Football Confederation is founded.

1969 Pele scores the 1,000th goal of his career for Santos against Vasco da Gama at the Maracana Stadium.

1970 Brazil win the World Cup for a third time and retain the Jules Rimet Trophy outright. Red and yellow cards, devised by referee Ken Aston, are used at the World Cup for the first time.

1971 Tostao is voted the first South American Footballer Of The Year.

1972 The Fairs Cup changes its name to the UEFA Cup and Tottenham are the first winners in an all-English final, beating Wolverhampton Wanderers 3-2 on aggregate.

1973 The first million transfer sees Johan Cruyff move from Ajax to Barcelona. The Football League opts for a three-up and three-down system of promotion and relegation.

1974 A Cruyff-led Holland introduce "Total Football" to the World Cup in Germany.

1976 Diego Maradona makes his debut for Argentina Juniors as a 15-year-old.

THE LAWS OF THE GAME

1860s and 1870s by teams playing in the north and midlands of England.

In one way the Sheffield Rules hark back to the days of folk football, where some handling of the ball was permitted, but they also acknowledge the game played at public schools (Rules 3, 4 and 7). However, Rule 6, which punishes illegal play with a free-kick, was completely unknown in any public school code. Crucially, the Sheffield Rules were to have a major influence on the development of the modern game, introducing the concepts of corners, throw-ins, and free-kicks for fouls.

The Simplest Game

A further development in the evolution of football's rules came in 1862, and John Thring was again involved. By then he was assistant master at Uppingham School, Rutland, where he amended the Cambridge Rules to come up with a set of ten rules he termed "The Simplest Game" (also known as "Uppingham Rules"). The rules were to regulate football played at Uppingham, where they were immediately popular with the boys, resulting in a greater interest in the game played there.

In October 1862, Eton and Harrow Old Boys played an eleven-a-side match at Cambridge University, using rules that closely paralleled the Simplest Game. It led the following year to a modified set of Cambridge Rules which forbade handling the ball and hacking (kicking below the knee).

The Football Association is formed

The rules of football had a life of their own, refusing to conform to a nationally agreed code. They were, in a word, fragmented. A meeting was called on 26th

SHEFFIELD RULES, 1858

01. Kick off from the middle must be a place kick.

02. Kick out must not be more than 25 yards out of goal.

03. Fair catch is a catch from any player provided the ball has not touched the ground or has not been thrown from touch and is entitled to a free-kick.

04. Charging is fair in case of a place kick (with the exception of a kick off as soon as a player offers to kick) but he may always draw back unless he has actually touched the ball with his foot.

05. No pushing with the hands or hacking or tripping up is fair under any circumstances whatsoever.

06. Knocking or pushing on the ball is altogether disallowed. The side breaking the rule forfeits a free-kick to the opposite side.

07. No player may be held or pulled over.

08. It is not lawful to take the ball off the ground, except in touch, for any purpose whatsoever.

09. If the ball be bouncing it may be stopped by the hand, not pushed or hit, but if rolling it may not be stopped except by the foot

10. No goal may be kicked from touch, nor by free-kick from a fair catch.

11. A ball in touch is dead. Consequently the side that touches it down must bring it to the edge of the touch and throw it straight out at least five yards from touch.

Above: Sheffield Football Club in 1890

Opposite: Mob football; Thames vs Townsend in 1846

October 1863 at the Freemasons' Tavern (present-day New Connaught Rooms), Great Queen Street, London, "for the purpose of forming an association with the object of establishing a definite code of rules for the regulation of the game."

At the meeting were representatives from eleven London and suburban football clubs – Barnes, War Office, Crusaders, Forest (Leytonstone), No Names (Kilburn), Crystal Palace, Blackheath, Kensington School, Perceval House (Blackheath), Surbiton, Blackheath Proprietory School and Charterhouse.

Most of the clubs were in favor of the modified Cambridge Rules, in which football was defined as a dribbling game played largely with the feet. But there was strong resistance from Blackheath, who wanted to keep catching and hacking, arguing that it showed courage. The meeting had two immediate results. The clubs agreed to the formation of the Football Association and they agreed to the need for a definitive set of rules for the game of football.

The major public schools where football was played were invited to join the new Football Association, but one by one they indicated their wish to keep to their own rules. Uppingham School, on the other hand, accepted the invitation, and on 8th December 1863, less

THE SIMPLEST GAME (UPPINGHAM RULES, 1862)

01. A goal is scored whenever the ball is forced through the goal and under the bar, except it be thrown by hand.

02. Hands may be used only to stop a ball and place it on the ground before the feet.

03. Kicks must be aimed only at the ball.

04. A player may not kick the ball whilst in the air.

05. No tripping up or heel kicking allowed.

06. Whenever a ball is kicked beyond the side flags, it must be returned by the player who kicked it, from the spot it passed the flag line, in a straight line toward the middle of the ground.

07. When a ball is kicked behind the line of goal, it shall be kicked off from that line by one of the side whose goal it is.

08. No player may stand within six paces of the kicker when he is kicking off.

09. A player is "out of play" immediately he is in front of the ball and must return behind the ball as soon as possible. If the ball is kicked by his own side past a player, he may not touch or kick it, or advance, until one of the other side has first kicked it, or one of his own side has been able to kick it on a level with, or in front of, him.

10. No charging allowed when a player is out of play; that is, immediately the ball is behind him.

1992 Late replacements Denmark win the European Championship. The European Cup is relaunched as the Champions League.

1993 Manchester United are the inaugural winners of the FA Premier League. The backpass rule is introduced to prevent defenders time wasting.

1994 The World Cup is decided on penalties for the first time as Brazil beat Italy.

1997 English goalkeeper Peter Shilton retires from football, following 1005 first-class appearances.

1998 A record 32 teams compete in the World Cup finals in France.

1999 Lazio beat Mallorca to become the last winners of the European Cup Winners' Cup.

2001 Zinedine Zidane smashes world transfer record when he joins Real Madrid from Juventus for £47 million.

2002 Real Madrid win the European Cup for a record ninth time. Rio Ferdinand joins Manchester United from Leeds for £30 million, smashing the British transfer record.

2003 AC Milan lift the European Cup for a sixth time, beating Juventus 4-2 on penalties following a 0-0 draw.

2005 Rai-A becomes the first player to score 50 European Cup goals.

2006 Italy win the World Cup for the fourth time.

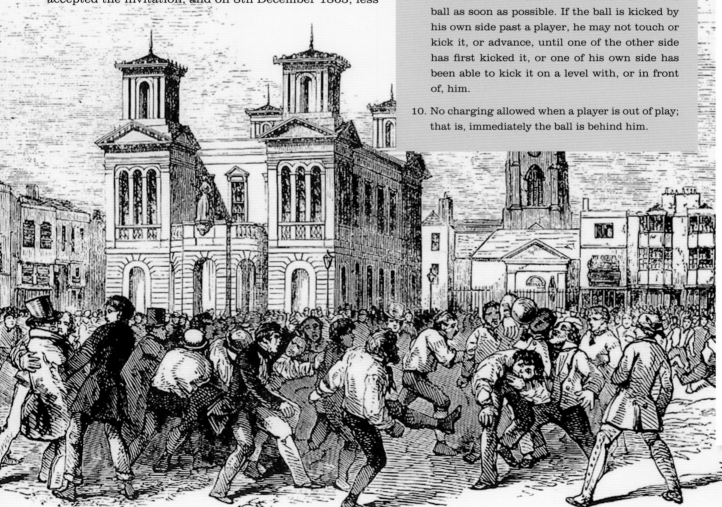

THE LAWS OF THE GAME

2006 A major match-fixing scandal erupts in Italy, with five Serie A teams implicated. Egypt record victory for the fifth time in the African Cup of Nations. The Women's World Championship, with an increased age limit of 20, takes place in Russia, won by Korea DPR.

2007 FIFA Women's World Cup is held in China and won by Germany. On 9 November Étoile Sportive du Sahel became the first African squad to have won all official club competitions recognized by CAF after defeating Al-Ahly 3–1 in the CAF Champions League final in Susa.

2008 CONCACAF Champions Cup is replaced by the CONCACAF Champions League.

2009 Spain achieves two world records: most consecutive wins (15) and most matches without a loss (35, with Brazil). Barcelona achieves a sextuple: La Liga, Copa del Rey, Supercopa de España, UEFA Champions League, UEFA Super Cup and FIFA Club World Cup.

2010 The FIFA World Cup is held in South Africa, the first African nation to host the tournament. Spain win the FIFA World Cup for the first time, becoming the first European nation to win the tournament outside of Europe. The FIFA Ballon d'Or is awarded for the first time (to Lionel Messi) after France Football's Ballon d'Or and the FIFA World Player of the Year award were merged.

FOOTBALL ASSOCIATION RULES, 1863

01. The maximum length of the ground shall be 200 yards, the maximum breadth shall be 100 yards, the length and breadth shall be marked off with flags; and the goals shall be defined by two upright posts, 8 yards apart, without any tape or bar across them.

02. The winner of the toss shall have the choice of goals. The game shall be commenced by a place kick from the centre of the ground by the side losing the toss, the other side shall not approach within 10 yards of the ball until it is kicked off.

03. After a goal is won the losing side shall kick off and goals shall be changed.

04. A goal shall be won when the ball passes between the goal posts or over the space between the goal posts (at whatever height), not being thrown, knocked on, or carried.

05. When the ball is in touch the first player who touches it shall throw it from the point on the boundary line where it left the ground, in a direction at right angles with the boundary line and it shall not be in play until it has touched the ground.

06. When a player has kicked the ball any one of the same side who is nearer to the opponent's goal line is out of play and may not touch the ball himself nor in any way whatever prevent any other player from doing so until the ball has been played; but no player is out of play when the ball is kicked from behind the goal line.

07. In case the ball goes behind the goal line, if a player on the side to whom the goal belongs first touches the ball, one of his side shall be entitled to a free kick from the goal line at the point opposite the place where the ball shall be touched. If a player of the opposite side first touches the ball, one of his side shall be entitled to a free kick (but at the goal only) from a point 15 yards from the goal line opposite the place where the ball is touched. The opposing side shall stand behind their goal line until he has had his kick.

08. If a player makes a fair catch he shall be entitled to a free kick, provided he claims it by making a mark with his heel at once; and in order to take such kick he may go as far back as he pleases, and no player on the opposite side shall advance beyond his mark until he has kicked.

09. No player shall carry the ball.

10. Neither tripping nor hacking shall be allowed and no player shall use his hands to hold or push his adversary.

11. A player shall not throw the ball or pass it to another.

12. No player shall take the ball from the ground with his hands while it is in play under any pretence whatever.

13. No player shall wear projecting nails, iron plates, or gutta percha on the soles or heels of his boots.

Illustration of a public school game of football in the 1860's

THE LAWS OF THE GAME: SIMPLIFIED PRESENT DAY RULES OF FOOTBALL

Law 1: The Field of Play: Football can be played on natural or artificial surfaces, which must be green and rectangular in shape. The long sides are touch lines and the short sides are goal lines. A halfway line divides the field in half.

Law 2: The Ball: Must be spherical, made of leather (or similar) 68–70cm in circumference and of a certain pressure.

Law 3: The Number of Players: Two teams of no more than 11 players in each team. The minimum number of players in a football team is seven.

Law 4: The Players' Equipment: Players must wear a jersey, shorts, socks, shin guards and boots.

Law 5: The Referee: The referee ensures the rules are respected and upheld.

Law 6: The Assistant Referees: There may be at most two assistant referees.

Law 7: The Duration of the Match: The game is played in two halves of 45 minutes each with a half-time interval of no longer than 15 minutes. At the referee's discretion time can be added to allow for any stoppages during play.

Law 8: The Start and Restart of Play: A kick-off starts a game and restarts it at the second half or after a goal is scored. The team which kicks off at the start of the match is determined by a coin toss.

Law 9: The Ball In and Out of Play: The ball is out of play when a goal has been scored or when the referee has stopped the game. The ball is in play at all other times.

Law 10: The Method of Scoring: A goal is scored if the ball crosses the goal line between the two goalposts and under the crossbar, as long as no violation of the rules has taken place.

Law 11: Offside: A player is in an offside position if, when the ball is played by a teammate, he is nearer to the opposition's goal line than both the ball and the second last opponent. He is not offside if he is in line with his opponents.

Law 12: Fouls and Misconduct: It is an offence to use excessive force or to handle the ball (other than the goalkeeper). The referee may show the yellow card to caution a player and the red card for serious offences resulting in the player being sent off. Two yellow cards are equivalent to one red card.

Law 13: Free Kicks: A direct free kick can be kicked into the opposition's goal. An indirect free kick must be played by a second player before being kicked into the opposition's goal.

Law 14: The Penalty Kick: A penalty kick is awarded if a defender commits a foul inside his own penalty area. The kick is taken from the penalty spot and all players (except kicker and goalkeeper) must be outside the penalty area.

Law 15: The Throw-In: Used to restart play after the whole of the ball has crossed the touch line.

Law 16: The Goal Kick: Used to restart play after the whole of the ball has crossed the goal line.

Law 17: The Corner Kick: A corner kick is awarded to the attacking team if an opposing player is the last to touch the ball before it crosses the goal line.

2011 Japan defeat the United States in the FIFA Women's World Cup final to win the tournament for the first time.

2012 Spain wins the 2012 European Championship: for the first time the trophy was won by the same team twice in a row. Lionel Messi scores 91 goals, establishing the new world record for most goals scored in a single calendar year, surpassing Gerd Müller's record of 85 set in 1972.

2014 German Miroslav Klose becomes the all time FIFA World Cup top scorer with 16 goals.

2015 Chile claim their first Copa America title after defeating Argentina 4-1 on penalties. The U.S. Women's National Team win the Women's World Cup, a 5-2 victory over Japan. Cristiano Ronaldo enters the record books for becoming Real Madrid's most prolific scorer of all time, surpassing Madrid legend Raul's goal tally of 323. May 2015 goes down as possibly one of the most iconic moments in world football's recent history. After months of speculation and accusation, moves are set in motion to finally uncover FIFA's corrupt and unlawful dealings, as FIFA officials are finally arrested on money laundering, and racketeering charges. The arrests lead to a chain of events which eventually see the likes of FIFA president Sepp Blatter and UEFA president Michel Platini banned from football for eight years.

than two months after the Football Association was formed, it published its thirteen rules of football. They were not met with universal approval, and later that month the games of rugby and football went their separate ways, the split becoming permanent in 1871 with the formation of the Rugby Football Union.

The first FA rules – laws as they became termed – were far from perfect. For example, there was nothing about the number of players in a team or how long a match should last. Despite this, the FA rules gradually reached out to clubs across Britain and when, in 1878, Sheffield clubs agreed to move away from their Sheffield Rules to follow "London rules" (as they were perceived), a single, standardized code was within sight.

The laws of the game have continued to evolve, with notable milestones including the introduction of the position of goalkeeper (1871), penalty kick (1891), substitutes (1958), red and yellow cards (1970) and the back-pass rule (1992). After more than 150 years of gradual change, the modern game is now governed by a grand total of seventeen laws, though with referees expected to use their judgment and common sense in applying them, an unwritten eighteenth law is said to exist!

LIKE THE RULES OF FOOTBALL, THE GAME'S EQUIPMENT HAS ALSO STEADILY EVOLVED OVER TIME, AND NONE MORE SO THAN THE MOST BASIC COMPONENT – THE FOOTBALL.

"From bladder to ball"

Richard Lindon 1816-1887

Stories about medieval mobs kicking severed heads through the streets of English towns are probably just that, stories concocted for dramatic effect. Whatever the truth, these ancient, unruly precursors to the modern game of football had to have something to kick, though it was more likely to be an inflated animal bladder, probably a pig's, held inside a leather case.

Bladder balls were anything but reliable, and were prone to bursting, losing shape and veering off course, but in the years of mob football, players were hardly concerned about the quality of the ball they kicked and handled.

Enter the round ball

It was a self-taught chemist from the USA who introduced the spherical football to the world. In 1839, Charles Goodyear had discovered how to make rubber harder when he accidentally spilled rubber mixed with sulphur onto a hot stove. The result was vulcanized rubber, which Goodyear patented for use with numerous products, many in the medical sector. He saw potential for durable, hard-wearing rubber in the world of sport, and came up with ideas for inflatable boxing gloves and a skating hat. He proposed rubber wheelbarrow tires, washable rubber bank notes, and a rubber globe that could double as a football when not teaching geography in the classroom!

In 1855, Goodyear created the first vulcanized rubber football, with panels glued together at the seams. Despite keeping its round shape, being easier to kick and with a greater ability to bounce than all previous balls, the Goodyear ball was not the finished product. That task fell to Richard Lindon, a boot and shoemaker from Rugby, who made the breakthrough that transformed the ball into one that became instantly successful.

Amongst Lindon's customers were the boys of Rugby School, who came to him for their leather footballs inflated with pigs' bladders. It was a family business, and while Richard made the balls, Rebecca, his wife, inflated them – by mouth, through the snapped stem of a clay tobacco pipe. Herein lay a health hazard, as there was no way of knowing if the bladder was from a healthy or a diseased pig. Tragically, and perhaps inevitably, Mrs Lindon succumbed to lung disease and died.

Perhaps motivated by the death of his wife, in 1862 Lindon created an artificial bladder made from vulcanized rubber. He also created a brass pump, based on the design of a syringe, to inflate the bladder. For the first time it became possible to make leather footballs with a standardized, spherical size. Sadly, for Lindon, he didn't patent his ball, his bladder or his pump.

A football made from leather and a pig's bladder, found behind paneling at Stirling Castle, Scotland, in the 1970s, is believed to be around 500 years old, making it the world's oldest. It has a diameter of 14–16cm (5.5–6.3in) and weighs 125g (4.4oz) and might even be one of the balls ordered in 1497 by King James IV of Scotland, who paid two shillings for a bag of "fut ballis."

Above: How would modern players of today feel about playing on a pitch like this? Here, two Preston players leaving the pitch at half-time during a match against Charlton at The Valley in 1937.

Improving the ball

The first footballs with rubber bladders were made with two leather "buttons" that concealed the stitching where the ends of the panels met at the ball's "north" and "south" poles. Entirely made by hand, they were works of great skill, but there was always room for improvement.

From the 1880s, balls started to be made with interlocking leather panels which did away with the button ends. Balls became rounder and generally smoother. Stronger rubber bladders were introduced, which allowed the ball to be struck with greater force, and in the 1940s, when the leather case was made water-repellant, the ball no longer became heavier in wet weather. At around the same time, a valve for inflating the bladder replaced the laced slit on the side of the ball, improving its aerodynamics.

THE MODERN BALL

1974 Telstar

2006 Teamgeist

2010 Jambulani

The ball most commonly seen today is made entirely from synthetic material. Polyurethane or PVC has replaced leather, and the bladder is of butyl or latex. Since the 1960s, balls have been made with different combinations of panels. The 32-panel ball, for example, is composed of 20 hexagonal and 12 pentagonal panels. This iconic black and white ball – the Adidas Telstar – made its debut at the 1968 European Football Championship, and on the world stage at the World Cup Finals in Mexico in 1970. Adidas has continued to innovate ball design, with the 14-panel Teamgeist ball introduced at the 2006 World Cup Finals in Germany, and the 8-panel Jabulani design showcased at the 2010 World Cup Finals in South Africa.

THE
WORLD
CUP

"FIRST AND FOREMOST, THE WORLD CUP SHOULD BE A FESTIVAL OF FOOTBALL."

FRANZ BECKENBAUER

A festival of football

Since the inaugural tournament was staged in 1930, the football World Cup has become the biggest single-event sporting competition in the world, unmatched by any other sport – but it got off to a slow start.

The founding in 1863 of the Football Association in England paved the way for others to follow, and by the close of the century a further thirteen national associations had been established. As international interest in football grew, the idea of a single governing body to oversee the game's global development gathered pace.

On 21st May, 1904, representatives from seven footballing nations met in Paris, at the headquarters of the Union Française de Sports Athlétiques. The nations were France, Belgium, Sweden, Spain, Switzerland, the Netherlands, and Denmark. Of those, Sweden, Spain, and the hosts, France, were without their own national associations (not formed until December 1904, 1909 and 1919, respectively).

The meeting established the Fédération Internationale de Football Association (FIFA) as football's world governing body, with the authority to organize an international football tournament.

England was a notable absentee from FIFA's founding meeting. The Football Association had been invited, and there were hopes that England, as the senior member, would play a leading role in the new federation. However, the FA declined to attend. The response from Frederick Wall, Secretary of the FA, was: "The Council of the Football Association cannot see the advantages of such a Federation, but on all matters upon which joint action was desirable they would be prepared to confer." It was a short-lived absence and the following year, 1905, the Football Association was persuaded to become affiliated to FIFA.

Football at the Olympics

Saying it was going to organize an international football tournament was one thing, actually making it a reality was an entirely different matter. The world had to wait 26 years, until 1930, before the first festival of football – the World Cup – was held. Until then, football's international stage was the Olympic Games, where it was included from the very beginning with an appearance at the first modern Games, in Athens, in 1896.

At the Paris Games of 1900 and the St Louis Games of 1904, football was featured as a demonstration sport, but at the London Games of 1908, it made it to the main program of events. When the Olympics returned to Paris in 1924, no fewer than 22 nations were represented, including for the first time a South American nation, Uruguay, who went on to win the gold medal.

World Cup awarded to Uruguay

The success of football at the Olympics was a wake-up call for FIFA, who had been discussing a world tournament since 1904. In 1921, Jules Rimet had become FIFA's third president, and he was determined that FIFA should assert control over the global game during his presidency. In 1926, FIFA's Secretary, Henri Delaunay, who was Secretary of the French Football Federation, put it this way: "Today international football can no longer be held within the confines of the Olympics."

At its 1927 Congress in Zurich, FIFA established a commission to examine the feasibility of organizing a football World Cup tournament, and at its 1928 Amsterdam Congress, FIFA agreed to stage the tournament every four years, starting in 1930.

With Uruguay retaining the Olympic crown at the 1928 Amsterdam Games, the South American nation put itself forward to host the first football World Cup. Italy, Sweden, the Netherlands, Spain and Hungary also lodged applications to host the event. A vote was to be held at FIFA's 1929 Barcelona Congress, but it never came to that, as nations withdrew their bids until only Uruguay remained. The double Olympic champions were awarded the inaugural 1930 World Cup, promising to build a new stadium, pay the travel and hotel costs for competing nations, and take on any deficit should one arise.

Current tournament format

The World Cup has been staged every four years since 1930, except in 1942 and 1946 when it was not held due to World War II. The current format begins with the preliminary competition, staged over three years and designed to determine which teams make it through to the World Cup Finals in the fourth year. The host nation is guaranteed a place in the Finals, in which 32 teams compete.

FOOTBALL WORLD CUP HOST NATIONS

- 1930 Uruguay • 1934 Italy • 1938 France • 1942 not held
- 1946 not held • 1950 Brazil • 1954 Switzerland • 1958 Sweden
- 1962 Chile • 1966 England • 1970 Mexico • 1974 West Germany
- 1978 Argentina • 1982 Spain • 1986 Mexico • 1990 Italy
- 1994 United States • 1998 France • 2002 South Korea and Japan
- 2006 Germany • 2010 South Africa • 2014 Brazil • 2018 Russia

Opposite Top Left: Jules Rimet, photographed in 1920. Top Right: Italy's Roberto Baggio (C) stares at the ground after missing the penalty kick which cost his team the World Cup. Bottom Right: Henri Delaunay – Founder of the European Championship. Bottom Left: South Africa 2010 – Brazil's Michel Bastos (L) fouls Holland's Arjen Robben

When FIFA awarded the inaugural World Cup to Uruguay, there was every hope the tournament would be supported by the 41 member nations of the Federation.

URUGUAY 1930

In the days before transatlantic flights, it was a lengthy trip by liner to cross the ocean from Europe to South America. Even though the hosts had offered to pay travel costs, most European nations were reluctant to travel to faraway Uruguay, and the tournament was ultimately played out by just thirteen teams – seven from South America, four from Europe and two from North America.

1930 was a significant year for Uruguay as the nation was celebrating the one-hundredth anniversary of its independence. However, the appropriately-named Estadio Centenario (Centenary Stadium), in the capital Montevideo, which the hosts had built for the tournament, wasn't ready in time for the opening games. Instead, eight group matches, played during the first five days, were switched to two other stadiums in the city.

1930 WORLD CUP FINALS

Host country	Uruguay
Dates	13–30 July 1930 (18 days)
Teams	13
Venues	3 (in 1 host city)
Matches played	18
Goals scored	70
Top scorer	Guillermo Stábile, Argentina (8)
Attendance	590,549 (32,808 per match)
Champions	Uruguay (1st title)
Runners-up	Argentina
Third place	United States
Fourth place	Yugoslavia

Official 1930 Poster

Opposite: Uruguay team line up.
Above Top: Uruguay celebrate at the final whistle
Above Center: Hector Castro of Uruguay scores the Final's match-winner, this despite having only one arm
Bottom: The opening ceremony 1930

THE FINAL

4 (1) URUGUAY
DORADO 12
CEA 57   IRIARTE 68
CASTRO 89

COACH
ALBERTO SUPPICCI

2 (2) ARGENTINA
PEUCELLE 20
STÁBILE 37

COACH
FRANCISCO OLAZAR

Date: 30 July 1930
Attendance: 68,346
Venue: Estadio Centenario, Montevideo

It was a fitting match with which to conclude the first World Cup Finals – a re-run of the 1928 Olympic Final in which Uruguay had beaten arch-rivals Argentina 2–1 in a replay. The following year, Argentina had been crowned champions of South America, winning the Copa América for a fourth time.

In the years before official match balls, both sides turned up with a ball of their own. The Belgian referee made the obvious decision – to play with a different ball in each half. A coin-toss determined that the Argentinian ball would have the first half, and when half-time was called, it had been pulled from the back of the Uruguayan net twice.

Uruguay had everything to play for, and soon after the break they equalized, and then took the lead with a third. It stayed that way until the final seconds, when the hosts headed home a fourth and entered the history books as the first winners of the World Cup. The following day was declared a national holiday in Uruguay.

Estadio Centenario, Montevideo, opened 1930

The success of the inaugural World Cup encouraged more teams to enter the second tournament, only this time a preliminary competition was needed to determine who the finalists would be.

ITALY 1934

Thirty-two nations entered the qualification round, mostly from Europe, competing for the 16 places in the Finals in Italy. Uruguay, the reigning champions, declined to enter, still upset over the reluctance of European teams to play in "their" competition four years previously. This is the only time in which World Cup winners have not defended their title.

The Finals began with all 16 teams in action on the opening day, playing eight knockout matches simultaneously in eight Italian cities. The hosts, Italy, met the United States in the national stadium in Rome, and ran out 7–1 winners, the biggest margin in any first round match. For Argentina and Brazil, the only South American teams represented, they were on the boat home after playing one game each, knocked out by Sweden and Spain respectively. The surviving eight teams were all from Europe.

The quarter-finals pitched Italy against Spain in Florence, where a crowd of 35,000 watched as the game finished 1–1 after extra time. Replayed the next day, the home nation proceeded to the semi-finals with a 1–0 victory.

1934 WORLD CUP FINALS

Host country	Italy
Dates	27 May–10 June (15 days)
Teams	16
Venues	8 (in 8 host cities)
Matches played	17
Goals scored	70
Top scorer	Oldřich Nejedlý, Czech (5)
Attendance	363,000 (21,353 per match)
Champions	Italy (1st title)
Runners-up	Czechoslovakia
Third place	Germany
Fourth place	Austria

COPPA DEL MONDO · COUPE DU MONDE · WORLD'S CUP · WELTMEISTERSCHAFT · COPA DEL MUNDO

ITALIA
A. XII

CAMPIONATO MONDIALE DI CALCIO
27 MAGGIO 10 GIUGNO

F.I.F.A.

Official 1934 Poster

Above: Italy coach Vittorio Pozzo (L) with the players before the match
Opposite Top: Italy coach Vittorio Pozzo (top) celebrates with the players after the match. Center: The Brazil team and entourage at the airport. Bottom: Italy's Giuseppe Meazza scores the only goal in the opening round to edge past Spain.

THE FINAL

2 (1) ITALY
ORSI 82
SCHIAVIO 95

COACH
VITTORIO POZZO

1 (1) CZECHOSLOVAKIA
PUČ 70

COACH
KAREL PETRU

Date: 10 June 1934
Attendance: 55,000
Venue: Stadio Nazionale del Partito Nazionale Fascista, Rome

Semi-final defeats for Austria and Germany brought Italy and Czechoslovakia together in the final of the second World Cup, played in stifling heat with temperatures soaring above 40°C. It was also played against the backdrop of fascist propaganda, and in the presence of Italian dictator Benito Mussolini, who saw how the tournament could be used to broadcast his political ideology. And with Italy in the final, Mussolini called the nation to a standstill in anticipation of a resounding national triumph. Czechoslovakia had other ideas.

The game was evenly matched, and when the sides came out for the second half the battle was on to break the 0–0 deadlock. With twenty minutes left on the clock, Czechoslovakia struck first through a shot from Antonin Puc. It looked like an upset was on the cards, until Raimondo Orsi equalized eight minutes from time, and when the whistle went the sides were level. The game went into extra-time, and Angelo Schiavio's goal clinched victory for home nation Italy.

Stadio Nazionale del Partito Nazionale Fascista, Rome, opened 1911

It was only the third World Cup, but some nations felt a pattern had been established, alternating hosts between different continents. But, when France was awarded the 1938 tournament, it meant a second successive World Cup for Europe, which outraged the nations of South America who expected it to come their way.

FRANCE 1938

Perhaps it was no great surprise. FIFA's membership had grown to 57 nations, most of which were in Europe. Mindful of the difficulties European nations had faced in traveling to Uruguay in 1930, and wishing to acknowledge the work of founding father Jules Rimet, the award was made to France. Argentina had applied to host the competition, but when they didn't get it, the reigning South American champions, five times winners of the Copa América, refused to attend. Brazil was the only South American nation to travel to France.

For the first time the title holders (Italy) and the hosts (France) were given automatic qualification and escaped the preliminary knockout stage of the tournament. Fourteen other nations qualified to join them, but when Austria pulled out due to the political turmoil in Europe, FIFA invited England to be country number 16. However, the Football Association completed a hat-trick of World Cup no-shows by again declining to take part. England would not be in the competition, and the tournament was left a team short. The absence of Austria/England was to Sweden's advantage who, with no first round opponents to play, went straight through to the quarter-finals, and then on to the semi-finals, where Hungary overcame them 5–1. In the other semi-final, Italy defeated Brazil 2–1.

1938 WORLD CUP FINALS

Host country	France
Dates	4–19 June (16 days)
Teams	15
Venues	10 (in 10 host cities)
Matches played	18
Goals scored	84
Top scorer	Leônidas, Brazil (7)
Attendance	375,700 (20,872 per match)
Champions	Italy (2nd title)
Runners-up	Hungary
Third place	Brazil
Fourth place	Sweden

Official 1938 Poster

Top Left: The Italian team celebrate victory.
Top Right: Italy's Silvio Piola scores against Hungary
Opposite Top: President Albert Lebrun presents the trophy to Italy's Giuseppe Meazza
Opposite Bottom: Italy's Giuseppe Meazza and Hungary's György Sárosi before the match

THE FINAL

4 (3) ITALY
COLAUSSI 6, 35
PIOLA 15, 80

COACH
VITTORIO POZZO

2 (1) HUNGARY
TITKOS 8
SÁROSI 70

COACH
KÁROLY DIETZ

Date: 19 June 1938
Attendance: 45,000
Venue: Stade Olympique de Colombes, Paris

Italy entered the record books as the first nation to play in a World Cup Final twice, and the reigning champions quickly showed their superiority with a sixth minute goal from Gino Colaussi. Within two minutes, the scores were level, but by half-time the Italians had taken a two-goal lead.

Although Hungary pulled one back in the second half, a fourth from Italy sealed the underdog's fate. Italy were the first back-to-back World Cup winners, and the first non-host nation to become champions.

But, as Europe readied itself for World War II, the 1938 World Cup was the last for twelve long years. The festival of football was on hold.

Olivieri
Foni • Rava
Serantoni • Locatelli
Andreolo
Meazza • Ferrari
Biavati • Piola • Colaussi

Sas • Titkos
Sarosi
Vincze • Zsengeller
Szucs
Szalay • Lazar
Polgar • Biro
Szabo

Stade Olympique de Colombes, Paris, opened 1907

Getting to the Finals

In today's game, the route to the World Cup Finals is a long one, with some 200 nations competing in a three-year qualification round. Hundreds of games are played to decide which nations are eliminated, and which will join the hosts to make the final 32 – but it wasn't like this in the early days.

The inaugural World Cup, played in Uruguay in 1930, stands apart from all subsequent tournaments as it is the only one not to have had a preliminary competition. Instead, FIFA sent invitations to its 41 Federation members, and 13 accepted. For Italy 1934, the process of qualification was introduced, and the field of 32 entrants was slimmed down to the 16 who made it through to the Finals. This set the pattern for all subsequent tournaments.

As FIFA's membership steadily increased, the qualification phase intensified as more nations competed for places in the last 16 – a number that remained constant through to Argentina 1978, the first tournament to have more than 100 teams in the qualifiers. The number of places in the Finals has been increased twice since then, to take into account the growing numbers of football nations from Africa and Asia who want a place on the world stage. For Spain 1982, there were 24 places in the Finals, and from France 1998 the number has risen to 32.

FIFA's confederations

Qualifying tournaments are held in each of FIFA's six continental zones, organized by their respective confederations. Before the qualifiers begin, FIFA decides how many places in the Finals each confederation will compete for, and the teams battle it out through a series of home and away matches. The confederations are:

- Asia – Asian Football Confederation (AFC)
- Africa – Confédération Africaine de Football (CAF)
- North and Central America and the Caribbean – Confederation of North, Central American and Caribbean Association Football (CONCACAF)
- South America – Confederación Sudamericana de Fútbol (CONMEBOL)
- Oceania – Oceania Football Confederation (OFC)
- Europe – Union of European Football Associations (UEFA)

Since Germany 2006, the defending champions have had to qualify for the Finals; prior to this tournament the champions were given free passage through to the last round. The only team that does not have to qualify is the host nation, who receives an automatic place in the Finals.

NATIONS ENTERED INTO WORLD CUP QUALIFIERS

Year	Host	Entered	Year	Host	Entered
1930	Uruguay	—	1986	Mexico	121
1934	Italy	32	1990	Italy	116
1938	France	37	1994	United States	147
1950	Brazil	34	1998	France	174
1954	Switzerland	45	2002	South Korea & Japan	199
1958	Sweden	55	2006	Germany	198
1962	Chile	56	2010	South Africa	205
1966	England	74	2014	Brazil	203
1970	Mexico	75	2018	Russia	208
1974	West Germany	99			
1978	Argentina	107	Note: Some teams withdrew before playing		
1982	Spain	109			

Above: Spain's Álvaro Negredo fights for the ball with Georgia's Dato Kvirkvelia
Opposite Top: Wayne Rooney scores the third goal for England against Kazakhstan.
Center: Australia score against Bahrain in the 2010 qualifier. Bottom: England's Michael Carrick holds off Montenegro's Mirko Vučinić and Dejan Damjanović.
Far Right: Belgium's internationals celebrate their victory as they walk past the scoreboard displaying 10-1 against San Marino.

World War II (1939–45) had left Europe in ruins, but FIFA wasted no time in restarting the World Cup. At its 1946 congress, held in Luxembourg, the fourth tournament was awarded to Brazil – the only nation to submit a bid.

BRAZIL 1950

Brazil had previously made a bid for the 1942 tournament, and had war not stopped play, it would have been a head-to-head against Germany for the honor. When FIFA called for bids for the first post-war competition, Brazil dusted down its 1937 application and sent it in, with a condition attached – that it should be staged in 1950, not 1949 as FIFA had planned. Apart from the choice of host nation, FIFA's 1946 congress made another key decision – to re-admit the four British associations to football's growing family. The football associations of England, Scotland, Wales and Ireland had initially withdrawn from FIFA in 1920, partly out of unwillingness to play against countries they had so recently fought in World War I (1914–18), but had soon rejoined. Then a new rift developed over the status of amateur players and, in 1928, the four associations once again resigned from FIFA – and missed out on the first three World Cup tournaments.

The 1950 World Cup tournament would welcome British teams for the first time, added to which FIFA made an unprecedented offer – the winners and runners-up in the 1950 British Home Championship would be guaranteed places at the Finals.

FIFA was prepared to treat Britain's series of home internationals as World Cup qualifiers, with two of the four British teams making it through to Brazil. However, Scotland managed to contrive a plot twist of staggering arrogance, saying they would only accept FIFA's offer if they finished as British champions – second place just wouldn't do. And that's how England booked a place in their first World Cup, and Scotland, as runners-up in the Home Championship, missed out.

FIFA offered Scotland's place to France and then Ireland, runners-up in their groups, but both declined the invitation. The Finals would go ahead with just 13 teams.

Above: 1950 World Cup Uruguay line up before a game.
Opposite Top: England team depart from London Airport for the 1950 World Cup Finals in Brazil. Bottom: USA striker Joe Gaetjens scores the only goal as England loses 1-0 in the 1950 World Cup.

1950 WORLD CUP FINALS

Host country	Brazil
Dates	24 June – 16 July (23 days)
Teams	13
Venues	6 (in 6 host cities)
Matches played	22
Goals scored	88
Top scorer	Ademir, Brazil (8)
Attendance	1,045,246 (47,511 per match)
Champions	Uruguay (2nd title)
Runners-up	Brazil
Third place	Sweden
Fourth place	Spain

IV CAMPEONATO
MUNDIAL DE
FUTEBOL
-TAÇA JULES RIMET-

JUNHO DE 1950
BRASIL

Official 1950 Poster

THE FINAL

2 (0) URUGUAY
SCHIAFFINO 66
GHIGGIA 79

COACH
JUAN
LOPEZ

0 (0) BRAZIL

COACH
FLÁVIO
COSTA

Date: 16 July 1950
Attendance: 199,854
Venue: Maracanã Stadium, Rio de Janeiro

In a break with tradition, there was no final match at Brazil 1950. Instead, the four group winners played against each other to decide the final places, with the winner of the group lifting the World Cup trophy. It came down to the very last game, with Brazil, leading the table by one point, favorites to beat arch-rivals Uruguay.

It was a thriller, with Brazil launching 30 shots on the Uruguayan goal and a world record crowd of some 200,000 looking on. Brazil struck first, then Uruguay leveled, and with about ten minutes to go the Uruguayans took the lead, giving them a famous victory.

Máspoli
González
Gambetta   Tejera   Andrade
Varela
Pérez   Schiaffino
Ghiggia   Miguez   Morán

Chico   Ademir   Friaça
Jair   Zizinho
Danilo   Bauer
Bigode   Juvenal   Augusto
Barbosa

Maracanã Stadium, Rio de Janeiro, opened 1950

43

Switzerland's choice as host nation of the 1954 World Cup was a formality. The announcement had been made at FIFA's 1946 congress, and with no other bidders to consider, the tournament would be played on "home ground." The Swiss had eight years to prepare.

Switzerland 1954

FIFA had relocated its headquarters from Paris to Zurich in 1932. It was a shrewd move, as Switzerland's famous neutrality accorded well with FIFA's own philosophy. The country had escaped the ravages of World War II, was in good shape to mount the tournament and, added to this, FIFA would be celebrating its half-century in 1954.

Following the pattern set by previous editions, there was the usual number of places in the Finals (16). Switzerland (hosts) and Uruguay (defending champions) received automatic spots, leaving 14 places on offer in the qualification round.

Germany, banned from the 1950 contest because of World War II, was re-admitted to the fold. Now a divided nation, teams from West Germany and East Germany could enter the tournament, creating the potential for a Germany vs. Germany match. As it turned out, only West Germany entered the 1954 competition.

The Golden Team

Hungary came to the Finals as Olympic Champions and red-hot favorites, unbeaten in 27 matches stretching back to May 1950 (won 23, drawn 4). The crowning glory was the 6–3 defeat of England in November 1953. It was the first time a foreign team had beaten England at Wembley Stadium, London, their home ground, in a match that went down in history as the Match of the Century. Six months later, Hungary did the double, beating England 7–1 in Budapest (England's biggest margin of defeat). Not surprisingly, the Hungary "Golden Team" was known variously as the Magnificent, the Magical, the Mighty, and the Marvellous Magyars.

In the group stage, Hungary dismissed South Korea 9–0 and West Germany 8–3. Brazil were dispatched 4–2 in the quarter-final, and Uruguay went for the same score in the semi-final.

Above: 1954 World Cup Hungary line up before a game.
Opposite Top: West Germany's Helmut Rahn scores past Hungary's Gyula Grosics. Center: Tom Finney get a head to the ball for England against Uruguay. Bottom: Hungary's Ferenc Puskás in action against Brazil

1954 WORLD CUP FINALS

Host country	Switzerland
Dates	16 June – 4 July (19 days)
Teams	16
Venues	6 (in 6 host cities)
Matches played	26
Goals scored	140
Top scorer	Sándor Kocsis, Hungary (11)
Attendance	768,607 (29,562 per match)
Champions	West Germany (1st title)
Runners-up	Hungary
Third place	Austria
Fourth place	Uruguay

Official 1954 Poster

THE FINAL

3 (2) WEST GERMANY
MORLOCK 10
RAHN 18, 84

COACH
VINCENTE FEOLA

2 (2) HUNGARY
PUSKÁS 6
CZIBOR 8

COACH
GUSZTAV SEBES

Date: 4 July 1954
Attendance: 60,000
Venue: Wankdorf Stadium, Berne

In what became known as the Miracle of Berne, the 1954 World Cup Final was a replay of the Hungary vs. West Germany group match. Hungary set the pace, and within ten minutes were 2–0 ahead. It all seemed to be going to form, but West Germany replied with two quick goals, and the sides went in at half-time as equals. There was deadlock in the second half until, with six minutes to play, West Germany took the lead. Seconds later and the ball was in the net at the other end of the field. The Hungarians were convinced they had equalized, but the referee thought otherwise and ruled the strike offside.

At the final whistle, the magic was over for Hungary as their unbeaten run came to an unexpected end, not in a game that would soon be forgotten, but in the unforgettable Final of the World Cup. Runners-up for a second time.

Wankdorf Stadium, Rio de Janeiro, opened 1925

Fifty-five nations entered the 1958 World Cup qualifying tournament, and by the time the 16 finalists had been decided, some big names had failed to qualify. Italy and Uruguay, both previous winners, would not be going to Sweden, and neither would Spain or the Netherlands.

SWEDEN

The Soviet Union were there for the first time, encouraged by their triumph in the final of the 1956 Olympic Games. Joining them were all four British teams, the only time England, Scotland, Wales and Northern Ireland have made it through to the Finals together. But this wasn't to be their tournament.

The show-stealers came to Sweden with World Cup form. Brazil, runners-up to Uruguay eight years earlier, were determined to put that painful memory behind them, and with their South American rivals staying at home, one obstacle had already been cleared.

Brazil arrived in Sweden with a 22-man squad, one of whom was an unknown 17-year-old mid-fielder, Édson Arantes do Nascimento. The youngest player in the tournament, he played in four of Brazil's six matches, and scored six goals including a hat-trick. By the end of the tournament the world knew him by his childhood nickname – Pelé.

1958 WORLD CUP FINALS

Host country	Sweden
Dates	8–29 June (22 days)
Teams	16
Venues	12 (in 12 host cities)
Matches played	35
Goals scored	126
Top scorer	Just Fontaine, France (13)
Attendance	819,810 (23,423 per match)
Champions	Brazil (1st title)
Runners-up	Sweden
Third place	France
Fourth place	West Germany

Official 1958 Poster

Above: Brazil line up before the game against Sweden
Opposite Top: Just Fontain scores for France
Center: Brazil celebrate at the final whistle after beating Sweden 5 - 2 to win World Cup
Bottom: Pelé and King Gustaf Adolf before the start of the match in Stockholm.

THE FINAL

5 (2) BRAZIL
VAVÁ 9, 30
PELÉ 55, 89
ZAGALO 68

COACH
VINCENTE FEOLA

2 (1) SWEDEN
LIEDHOLM 4
SIMONSSON 80

COACH
GEORGE RAYNOR

Date: 29 June 1958
Attendance: 49,737
Venue: Råsunda Stadium, Stockholm

It was a dream final, the hosts Sweden against the rising power of Brazil. And with all eyes on Pelé, there were expectations of a high-scoring game. The capacity crowd, and millions watching on televisions around the world, were not to be disappointed. Heavy rain had left the surface of Stockholm's Råsunda Stadium slippery, and after only four minutes the home side took the lead, to deafening cheers from the stands. It was the first time Brazil had gone behind in the tournament, but that was as good as it got for Sweden.

Within five minutes Brazil were level with a goal from Vavá, who struck a second into the Swedish net just before half-time. Brazil owned the second half, slotting home three more goals, two scored by Pelé, who burst into tears at the final whistle. The 5–2 scoreline holds the record for the most goals scored in a World Cup Final. For the first time, a non-European team lifted the World Cup trophy on European soil. It marked the coming-of-age of Brazil.

Gilmar
Orlando Peranha   Bellini
Djalma Santos   Nilton Santos
Zito   Didi
Garrincha   Zagallo
Vavá   Pelé
Simonsson
Skoglund   Hamrin
Liedholm   Gren
Børjesson
Axbom   Bergmark
Gustavsson   Parling
Svensson

Råsunda Stadium, Stockholm, opened 1937

CHILE 1962

In 1956, at FIFA's Lisbon congress, Carlos Dittborn, president of the Chilean football federation, famously summed up his country's bid to host the 1962 World Cup Finals: "Porque nada tenemos, lo haremos todo" ("Because we have nothing, we will do everything").

They were portentous words. On 22 May 1960, the most powerful earthquake ever recorded struck Chile, killing thousands and damaging the country's infrastructure and World Cup stadiums. The competition, which was just two years away, could have been switched to Argentina, the beaten favorites, but Dittborn pleaded to keep it in Chile. It went ahead as planned, and Dittborn's inspirational words became its unofficial slogan. Unfortunately, the tournament didn't live up to expectations. Brazil won the cup but Chile was also victorious. It staged an exciting event despite the challenges. Sadly, Dittborn did not see his dream; he died just one month before kick-off.

Battle of Santiago

World Cups should be remembered for classic matches, star players and stunning goals. The 1962 contest in Chile served up few of these. Teams played it safe with an ultra-defensive style of football, and empty seats could be seen at many games (the Czechoslovakia–Yugoslavia semi-final was watched by fewer than 6,000, in a ground with an 18,000 capacity). Worst of all, games were marred by problems on the pitch, none worse than when hosts Chile met Italy on 2 June 1962 in an infamous game that became known as the Battle of Santiago.

Trouble began before the game, when Italian journalists made derogatory comments about the hosts. Their unwise words fueled the atmosphere inside the National Stadium, and the 60,000 home crowd was in a hostile mood.

Just seven minutes into the game, Italy's Giorgio Ferrini was sent off for kicking an opponent. The Italians protested, the ball was booted away, and with matters threatening to get out of hand, the referee called for help. Even with armed police and officials on the pitch, it was ten minutes before Ferrini headed back to the dressing room. A second Italian (Mario David) was sent off just before half time for felling Leonel Sánchez with a flying kick. Minutes before, Sánchez had escaped the same punishment, despite landing a left hook that broke Humberto Maschio's nose. As for the game, it ended 2–0 to Chile, although the after-match analysis was an inquest, not a celebration.

1962 WORLD CUP FINALS

Host country	Chile
Dates	30 May – 17 June (19 days)
Teams	16
Venues	4 (in 4 host cities)
Matches played	32
Goals scored	89
Top scorer	Flórián Albert, Hungary
	Garrincha, Brazil
	Valentin Ivanov, Soviet Union
	Dražan Jerković, Yugoslavia
	Leonel Sánchez, Chile
	Vavá, Brazil (8 goals each)
Attendance	893,172 (27,912 per match)
Champions	Brazil (2nd title)
Runners-up	Czechoslovakia
Third place	Chile
Fourth place	Yugoslavia

CAMPEONATO MUNDIAL DE FUTBOL
WORLD FOOTBALL CHAMPIONSHIP
CHAMPIONNAT MONDIAL DE FOOTBALL
COUPE JULES RIMET
CHILE 1962

Opposite Top: Chile vs Italy. Italy's Giorgio Ferrini is removed from the pitch by police after being sent off
Above: Mauro lifts the cup after victory

THE FINAL

3 (1) BRAZIL
AMARILDO 17
ZITO 68
VAVÁ 77

COACH
AYMORÉ MOREIRA

1 (1) CZECHOSLOVAKIA
MASOPUST 15

COACH
RUDOLF VYTLAČIL

Date: 17 June 1962
Attendance: 68,679
Venue: Estadio Nacional, Santiago

Defending champions Brazil lined up against Czechoslovakia, hoping to claim their second title. They were odds-on favorites, but it was the Czechs who took an early lead, only for it to be wiped out two minutes later by Amarildo, playing in place of the injured Pelé.

Brazil piled on the pressure, and with just over 20 minutes remaining, took the lead. Nine minutes later, Brazil had a third, and as the best game of a troubled tournament ended, the Jules Rimet Cup was set to stay in South America for another four years.

Maracanã Stadium, Santiago, opened 1938

1966 WORLD CUP FINALS

Host country	England
Dates	11–30 July (20 days)
Teams	16
Venues	8 (in 7 host cities)
Matches played	32
Goals scored	89
Top scorer	Eusébio, Portugal (9)
Attendance	1,563,135 (48,848 per match)
Champions	England (1st title)
Runners-up	West Germany
Third place	Portugal
Fourth place	Soviet Union

Official 1966 Poster

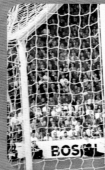

West Germany and England were rivals to host the 1966 World Cup, and at FIFA's 1960 congress delegates voted 34 to 27 in favor of England. The nation that had given football to the world began to plan for the best tournament to date.

ENGLAND 1966

More nations than ever before tried to qualify for the Finals, and as England (hosts) and Brazil (defending champions) had automatic places, it left 74 teams to compete for the 14 coveted spots. There was controversy from the start, as FIFA had grouped Africa with Asia-Oceania to compete for just one place at the Finals. The African countries felt they should have had a direct route to the Finals, guaranteeing an African nation a place. It wasn't to be, and all 15 African nations eligible to play in the qualifiers boycotted them in protest over the organization of their group.

North Korea, the surprise team

World Cups have a habit of throwing up surprises, and with African nations absent, one of the three Asia-Oceania teams knew they would be going to England. But then South Korea withdrew, leaving Australia and North Korea to contest the place. A 9–2 aggregate win saw North Korea on their way to England, where they produced one of the greatest upsets of all time by knocking Italy out to gain a spot in the quarter-finals, where they met in-form Portugal.

It looked like the North Koreans were about to pull off another sensational win, taking a 3–0 lead in the first 25 minutes. But then normal service resumed, and Portugal's star striker Eusébio struck four into the North Korean goal to make it 4–3 for Portugal. With ten minutes to go, the Portuguese made it 5–3, setting up a semi-final place against England.

Above Left: A victorious England side celebrate after winning the World Cup
Above: West Germany's goalkeeper Hans Tilkowski makes a save against Uruguay
Opposite Top: 1966 FIFA World Cup mascot World Cup Willie
Bottom: Eusébio in action against Hungary.

THE FINAL

4 (1) ENGLAND
HURST 18, 101, 120
PETERS 78

COACH
ALF RAMSEY

2 (1) WEST GERMANY
HALLER 12
WEBER 90

COACH
HELMUT SCHÖN

Date: 30 July 1966
Attendance: 93,000
Venue: Wembley Staium, London

The England manager, Alf Ramsay, had a lot to live up to. On taking the job on after England's exit from the 1962 World Cup, he'd rashly promised that England would win the next tournament. And now the England team had made it through to the Final (defeating Portugal 2–1 in the semi-final), they were one game away from fulfilling the manager's promise.

England's opponents were West Germany who, like England, had won four and drawn one to reach the Final (conquering the Soviet Union 2–1 in their semi-final). The sides were evenly matched, and after 90 minutes it was 2–2. The game went into extra-time, and in the 101st minute, England's Geoff Hurst struck the ball onto the underside of the bar – but which side of the line did it come down on? The referee was uncertain, but the linesman had no doubt it had bounced down over the line. It was – and still is – a controversial decision: 3–2 England.

Any hopes that West Germany might have had disappeared when Hurst scored England's fourth, and his third, the first player to score a hat-trick in a World Cup Final.

Wembley Stadium, London, opened 1925

WORLD CUP RECORDS – FIRST HALF

Miroslav Klose

TOP GOALSCORERS IN WORLD CUP FINALS

Player	Team	Tournaments	Goals
Miroslav Klose	Germany	1	16
Ronaldo	Brazil	3	15
Gerd Müller	West Germany	2	14
Just Fontaine	France	1	13
Pelé	Brazil	4	12
Sándor Kocsis	Hungary	1	11
Jürgen Klinsmann	Germany	3	11
Helmut Rahn	West Germany	2	10
Gary Lineker	England	2	10
Gabriel Batistuta	Argentina	3	10
Teófilo Cubillas	Peru	2	10
Thomas Müller	Germany	2	10
Grzegorz Lato	Poland	3	10

Gerd Müller

Gary Lineker

TOTAL GOALS SCORED IN WORLD CUP FINALS

Tournament	Goals
1930	70
1934	70
1938	84
1950	88
1954	140
1958	126
1962	89
1966	89
1970	95
1974	97
1978	102
1982	146
1986	132
1990	115
1994	141
1998	171
2002	161
2006	147
2010	145
2014	171
Total	2,379

Ronaldo

1954 Austria 7–5
Switzerland

HIGHEST SCORING MATCHES

1954	Austria 7–5 Switzerland
1938	Brazil 6–5 Poland
1954	Hungary 8–3 Germany
1982	Hungary 10–1 El Salvador
1958	France 7–3 Paraguay
1930	Argentina 6–3 Mexico
1954	Hungary 9–0 South Korea
1954	West Germany 7–2 Turkey
1958	France 6–3 West Germany
1974	Yugoslavia 9–0 Zaire

FASTEST SENDINGS OFF IN WORLD CUP FINALS

Sent off	Player	Match	
56 secs	José Batista	(Uruguay) vs. Scotland	1986
8 min	Giorgio Ferrini	(Italy) vs. Chile	1962
14 min	Zezé Procópio	(Brazil) vs. Czechoslovakia	1938
19 min	Mohammed Al-Khilaiwi	(Saudi Arabia) vs. France	1998
19 min	Miguel Bossio	(Uruguay) vs. Denmark	1986
21 min	Gianluca Pagliuca	(Italy) vs. Rep of Ireland	1994

José Batista

Giorgio Ferrini

WORLD CUP FIRSTS

First goal: Lucien Laurent, of France, against Mexico, in the 19th minute of the first World Cup match, 13 July 1930.

First own goal: Manuel Rosas of Mexico, against Chile, 16 July 1930.

First penalty: Mexico's Manuel Rosas, against Argentina, 19 July 1930.

First penalty miss: Brazil's Waldemar de Brito, against Spain, 27 May 1934.

First penalty miss in the Final: Italy's Antonio Cabrini, against West Germany, 11 July 1982.

First hat-trick: Bert Patenaude of the United States, against Paraguay, 17 July 1930.

First goal by a substitute: Juan Basaguren of Mexico, against El Salvador, 7 June 1970.

First sending off: Plácido Galindo of Peru, against Romania, 14 July 1930.

First red card sending off: Carlos Caszely of Chile, against West Germany, 14 June 1974.

YOUNGEST PLAYERS

Youngest player
Norman Whiteside (Northern Ireland), 17 years, 1 month, 10 days
Northern Ireland vs. Yugoslavia, 17 June 1982

Youngest player, Final
Pelé (Brazil), 17 years, 8 months, 6 days
Brazil vs. Sweden, 29 June 1958

Youngest goalscorer, Finals
Pelé (Brazil), 17 years, 8 months, 1 day
Brazil vs. Wales, 19 June 1958

Youngest player, qualifying match
Souleymane Mamam (Togo), 13 years, 10 months, 6 days
Togo vs. Zambia, 6 May 2001

Pelé

Lucien Laurent

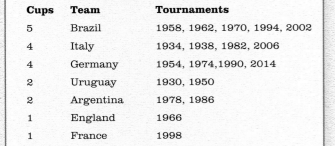

Bert Patenaude

Norman Whiteside

OLDEST PLAYERS

Oldest player
Faryd Mondragón (Colombia), 43 years, 3 days
Colombia vs. Japan, 24 June 2014

Oldest player, Final
Dino Zoff (Italy), 40 years, 4 months, 13 days
Italy vs. West Germany, 11 July 1982

Oldest goalscorer, Finals
Roger Milla (Cameroon), 42 years, 1 month, 8 days
Cameroon vs. Russia, 28 June 1994

Oldest player, qualifying match
MacDonald Taylor (US Virgin Islands), 46 years, 5 months, 22 days
US Virgin Islands vs. St. Kitts and Nevis, 18 February 2004

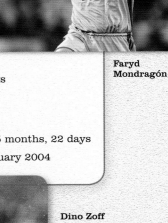

Faryd Mondragón

Roger Milla

MOST WORLD CUP VICTORIES

Cups	Team	Tournaments
5	Brazil	1958, 1962, 1970, 1994, 2002
4	Italy	1934, 1938, 1982, 2006
4	Germany	1954, 1974,1990, 2014
2	Uruguay	1930, 1950
2	Argentina	1978, 1986
1	England	1966
1	France	1998
1	Spain	2010

Dino Zoff

One of the teams at the rain-soaked Finals of the 1974 World Cup was about to make history, as the first to win the competition's new trophy which, in keeping with the tournament's official name, was simply called the "FIFA World Cup."

WEST GERMANY 1974

Ninety-nine countries took part in the qualifying tournament, all hoping for a place in the last 16. Several leading footballing nations from Europe failed to reach the Finals, including Spain, France and England. The Soviet Union was disqualified for refusing to play the second leg of their contest against Chile. Its military had transformed the National Stadium into a detention camp where 7000 political prisoners were tortured and executed, and the Soviets refused to play on a field "stained with blood."

With so many big-name absentees, the Finals welcomed several nations for the first time. Australia, Zaire and Haiti all traveled to West Germany, but it was the first-timers next door East Germany who set up the most anticipated game: the Cold War clash of Germany vs. Germany in the opening round, and on German soil, no less.

Total football

The 1974 World Cup Finals are remembered for the emergence on the international stage of Holland playing "total football," pioneered at home by the league club Ajax. It was a style of football in which players switched positions all over the field, as defenders suddenly appeared as strikers, and strikers pulled back to midfield and defense. A mould-breaking style of football, total football took players away from the rigidity of fixed positions.

With Holland notching up five wins and a draw, conceding only one goal and scoring 14, their exciting brand of football took them all the way to the Final and a meeting with hosts and favorites, West Germany.

1974 WORLD CUP FINALS

Host country	West Germany
Dates	13 June – 7 July (25 days)
Teams	16
Venues	9 (in 9 host cities)
Matches played	38
Goals scored	97
Top scorer	Grzegorz Lato, Poland (7)
Attendance	1,865,762 (49,099 per match)
Champions	West Germany (2nd title)
Runners-up	Holland
Third place	Poland
Fourth place	Brazil

Official 1974 Poster

THE FINAL

2 (2) WEST GERMANY
BREITNER (PEN) 25
MÜLLER 43

COACH
HELMUT SCHÖN

1 (1) HOLLAND
NEESKENS (PEN) 2

COACH
RINUS MICHELS

Date: 7 July 1974
Attendance: 78,200
Venue: Olympic Stadium, Munich

West Germany made it to the Finals after a run of five wins and an unexpected defeat against East Germany. They came to the Finals as favorites, but with Holland on form, the match seemed set to be a classic. It didn't disappoint, and with Holland awarded a penalty in the second minute, Johan Neeskens made history by scoring the fastest ever goal in a World Cup Final. The Germans hadn't even touched the ball.

Holland's lead lasted until mid-way through the first half, when they surrendered it cheaply with a penalty, and just before the interval the Germans took the lead – and that's the way it stayed. West Germany were world champions for a second time, their victory all the sweeter for winning at home and becoming the first team to lift the new FIFA World Cup.

Olympic Stadium, Munich, opened 1972

Opposite Top: West Germany captain Franz Beckenbauer (with teammates L–R Sepp Maier, Paul Breitzner, Jurgen Grabowski) holds the cup aloft after his side wins the cup for the second time. Top: Johan Cruyff (C) playing against Germany. Center: West Germany's Franz Beckenbauer and East Germany's Bernd Bransch, shake hands. Bottom: Johan Neeskens (L) of the Netherlands scored the first-ever penalty kick in a FIFA World Cup final match.

Argentina had 12 years to prepare for the 1978 World Cup Finals, but by the time the show arrived, the country was in the grip of a military dictatorship following a coup only two years before.

For Argentina it was fifth time lucky, having lost out in bids to host the Finals of 1938, 1962, 1970, and the cancelled tournament of 1942. However, the political situation in the country was of concern to many nations, most notably Holland who agonized over whether to pull out or not. Argentina's military government, knowing the eyes of the world would be on them, promised the tournament would run smoothly, and in the end no teams stayed away.

The World Cup was becoming a crowded place, and for the first time in its history, more than 100 nations (107 in total) competed in the qualifying tournament for the 14 available slots in the Finals; West Germany, as defending champions, and Argentina, as hosts, being given automatic places in the last 16. With odds like these, the 1978 World Cup Finals were statistically the hardest to date to qualify for.

Controversial match

Argentina wanted success, and hoped to match their South American neighbors Uruguay and Brazil in winning football's greatest prize. And then came the crunch match: Argentina vs. Peru. It would determine who would be in the Final – Argentina or Brazil.

For Argentina, it meant beating Peru by at least four clear goals – a tall order at any time. Anything less than this and Brazil would go through. The result? Argentina 6 Peru 0. Argentina had booked their place in the Final in a match quickly overshadowed by accusations of match fixing, though nothing was ever proved.

1978 WORLD CUP FINALS

Host country	Argentina
Dates	1–25 June (25 days)
Teams	16
Venues	6 (in 5 host cities)
Matches played	38
Goals scored	102
Top scorer	Mario Kempes, Argentina (6)
Attendance	1,545,791 (40,679 per match)
Champions	Argentina (1st title)
Runners-up	Holland
Third place	Brazil
Fourth place	Italy

Official 1978 Poster

THE FINAL

3 (1) ARGENTINA
KEMPES 37, 104
BERTONI 115

COACH
CÉSAR LUIS MENOTTI

1 (0) HOLLAND
NANNINGA 82

COACH
ERNST HAPPEL

Date: 25 June 1978
Attendance: 71,483
Venue: Estadio Monumental, Buenos Aires

Argentina had played in the first ever World Cup Final in 1930 and now, after a wait of 48 years, they were back – and on home soil. Their opponents were the much-fancied Holland, playing in their second successive Final. The "visitors" were kept waiting five minutes before the Argentinians emerged from the tunnel to an ear-splitting roar from what was effectively a home crowd, who launched a streamer and confetti storm that fluttered down from the stands and littered the pitch.

Argentina took the lead mid-way through the first half, and so it stayed until eight minutes from the end when the Dutch equalized and the partisan crowd lost its voice.

Games are so often remembered for near-misses, and if Holland's last minute strike had not hit the post, World Cup history would be very different. Instead, the game went into extra time, and with two goals for the hosts, Argentina's dream of winning the World Cup at home was fulfilled.

Estadio Monumental, Buenos Aires, opened 1936–38

Opposite Top: Argentina vs Holland 1978 line-up. Above Top: Argentina fans celebrate in front of the scoreboard. Center: Mario Kempes in action. Bottom: France play in green & white stripes vs Hungary.

1982 WORLD CUP FINALS

Host country	Spain
Dates	13 June – 11 July (29 days)
Teams	24
Venues	17 (in 14 host cities)
Matches played	52
Goals scored	146
Top scorer	Paolo Rossi, Italy (6)
Attendance	2,109,723 (40,572 per match)
Champions	Italy (3rd title)
Runners-up	West Germany
Third place	Poland
Fourth place	France

Official 1982 Poster

Left: Italy's Paolo Rossi celebrates with Marco Tardelli after scoring the first goal.
Opposite Top: Paolo Rossi scores for Italy in the World Cup final
Center: Italy (L) and Germany line up before the match
Bottom: Italy players celebrate and parade the World Cup trophy

It was a new-look World Cup Finals for the tournament's twelfth edition. The number of places was increased from 16 to 24, with the customary two places set aside for the hosts and defending champions. Spain 1982 promised to be the biggest and most exciting Finals to date.

SPAIN 1982

By adding eight extra places, FIFA hoped to improve the qualification chances of countries outside of Europe and South America, who had dominated the competition from the start. It worked, with first-timers from Africa (Cameroon and Algeria), Asia (Kuwait), Oceania (New Zealand), and North/Central America (Honduras) all qualifying for the first time. Concerns that these new nations would hinder the tournament by playing dull, defensive football turned out to be wrong. This tournament lived up to FIFA's founding hopes of a truly worldwide sporting event open to all.

Algeria eliminated

West Germany went to the 1982 World Cup Finals as reigning European Champions. They'd won all eight of their qualifying games, scoring 33 goals and conceding just three, and were widely tipped to

win. But, in one of the most surprising matches in World Cup history, they lost their first match of the tournament 2–1 to rank outsiders Algeria. It was enough to raise Algerian hopes of progressing to the next round, but it didn't work out like that.

West Germany had to play Austria, in a match that kicked off after Algeria had beaten Chile. The Germans and Austrians went into their match knowing that a 1–0 win for West Germany would send both of them through to the next round at the expense of Algeria.

The Germans scored the only goal, after 10 minutes, and the rest of the match was played out as if it was a friendly, to boos and shouts of "fuera, fuera" ("out, out"). West Germany and Austria were through, Algeria went out on goal difference, and FIFA made sure that in future crunch matches started at the same time as each other, thus preventing teams from going into a game with an unfair advantage.

THE FINAL

3 (0) ITALY
ROSSI 57
TARDELLI 69
ALTOBELLI 81

COACH
ENZO BEARZOT

1 (0) WEST GERMANY
BREITNER 83

COACH
JUPP DERWALL

Date: 11 July 1982
Attendance: 90,000
Venue: Santiago Bernabéu Stadium, Madrid

Despite West Germany's first round slip-up against Algeria, they made it to the Final, and a contest with Italy, who had disposed of defending champions Argentina and favorites Brazil. It was not the Final many had hoped for. Italy's Antonio Cabrini wrote himself into the record books by shooting wide and becoming the first player to miss a penalty in a World Cup Final, and the first half concluded without a single shot on target. The second half was a different story with four goals in 26 minutes, three of them for Italy, who lifted the World Cup for a third time.

Zoff
Scirea
Gentile   Collovati   Bergomi   Cabrini
Oriali
Tardelli
Conti   Graziani
Rossi

Littbarski   Fischer   Rummenigge
Matthäus   Dremmler
Briegel   Kaltz
B. Förster   K. Förster
Stielike
Schumacher

Santiago Bernabéu Stadium, Madrid, opened 1947

1986 WORLD CUP FINALS

Official 1986 Poster

Host country	Mexico
Dates	31 May – 29 June (30 days)
Teams	24
Venues	12 (in 9 host cities)
Matches played	52
Goals scored	132
Top scorer	Gary Lineker, England (6)
Attendance	2,394,031 (46,039 per match)
Champions	Argentina (2nd title)
Runners-up	West Germany
Third place	France
Fourth place	Belgium

Left: Gary Lineker, England, in action vs Morocco. He went on to be the competition's top scorer. Opposite Top: Diego Maradona beats England's Peter Shilton to the ball to score the first goal with his hand, now known as the Hand of God goal. Center: Argentina's José Luis Brown heads at goal against West Germany. Bottom: Argentina's Diego Maradona kisses the World Cup trophy.

Back in 1974, Colombia, the only bidder, had been awarded the 1986 World Cup Finals. Then, with four years to go, the Colombians had second thoughts as the competition they'd applied to host would have had 16 teams, but the new-look tournament now had 24.

In late 1982, Colombia announced it would host the Finals, but only on condition that FIFA reverted to the old 16-team format. Not surprisingly, FIFA refused. When Colombia pulled out, Canada, the United States and Mexico put bids in, and Mexico emerged as winner – the first country to have hosted the World Cup twice.

With only 16 years between tournaments, much of the infrastructure was already in place, but then, in September 1985, a devastating earthquake rocked Mexico. FIFA wondered if the tournament should be moved, but the Mexican government insisted it go ahead as planned.

The Golden Boy

Argentina came to Mexico 1986 with Diego Maradona their star player and captain, his second outing to the Finals. Four years earlier, his tournament had ended early when he was sent off for kicking a Brazilian opponent. Now at the peak of his abilities, "El Pibe de Oro" ("The Golden Boy") was about to shine like never before. It happened in the quarter-final against England.

The first half had been goalless, but six minutes into the second half the match came alive in spectacular, controversial fashion. A miskicked England clearance saw the ball balloon up toward Peter Shilton in goal. He tried to punch it away but was beaten by a high-jumping Maradona who, the England players protested, had punched it with his hand. The referee ignored their pleas and gave the goal, thinking Maradona had headed it into the net. TV replays clearly showed that Maradona had handled the ball and he himself later claimed that it was "a little with the head of Maradona and a little with the hand of God."

Four minutes after the infamous "Hand of God" goal, and with England still reeling, Maradona dribbled half the length of the field past five England players to score his second. It was a goal that left no one in any doubt of his genius, and in 2002 it was selected by FIFA as the Goal of the Century.

England managed a consolation goal, but it was too little, too late to stop Argentina from progressing to the semi-finals and a victorious meeting with Belgium.

THE FINAL

3 (1) ARGENTINA
BROWN 23
VALDANO 55
BURRUCHAGA 83

COACH
CARLOS BILARDO

2 (0) WEST GERMANY
RUMMENIGGE 74
VÖLLER 80

COACH
FRANZ BECKENBAUER

Date: 29 June 1986
Attendance: 114,600
Venue: Azteca Stadium, Mexico City

Argentina were clear favorites to win the World Cup, and their superior skill showed against West Germany, who had made it to their fifth Final. After 55 minutes, the South Americans had a two goal lead, and only then did German determination set in with two goals in six minutes leveling the score. With five minutes to go, who else but Maradona should set up the winning goal for Argentina, who lifted the World Cup for the second time.

Azteca Stadium, Mexico City, opened 1966

The 1990 World Cup Finals created a clutch of new records, but not the sort the Italian organizers would have wanted. The tournament holds the record for the fewest goals per game (2.21), the first sending-off in a Final, and a then record number of red cards (16 – twice as many as any previous competition).

ITALY 1990

From a field of eight it had become a two-horse race between Italy and the Soviet Union to host the 1990 Finals. The vote went in Italy's favor, who became hosts for the second time. Three teams reached the Finals for the first time: Costa Rica, the Republic of Ireland and the United Arab Emirates, while France, Denmark, Poland and Hungary failed to qualify. Mexico and Chile were also missing, both having been disqualified by FIFA (Mexico for fielding an over-age player in an earlier youth tournament; Chile for cheating in a qualifier against Brazil).

Italy, playing on home soil, were the favorites, winning all three group matches without conceding a goal, and their goalkeeper, Walter Zenga, setting a record of five consecutive clean sheets. Italy's dream of being crowned world champions ended after extra time in a semi-final penalty shoot-out against Argentina, the South Americans winning 4–3. It was the same score in the other semi-final, where England played West Germany in a memorable match that ended 1–1 after extra time, and then 4–3 to West Germany on penalties in favor of West Germany.

1990 WORLD CUP FINALS

Host country	Italy
Dates	8 June – 8 July (31 days)
Teams	24
Venues	12 (in 12 host cities)
Matches played	52
Goals scored	115
Top scorer	Salvatore Schillaci, Italy (6)
Attendance	2,516,215 (48,389 per match)
Champions	West Germany (3rd title)
Runners-up	Argentina
Third place	Italy
Fourth place	England

Official 1990 Poster

Above: Argentina vs West Germany, Stadio Olympico, Rome. Teams line up before the match. Opposite Top: Roger Milla shoots at goal in England vs Cameroon. Center: West Germany's Lothar Matthäus and Pierre Littbarski celebrate with the trophy. Bottom: Paul Gascoigne in tears after England's defeat by West Germany.

THE FINAL

1 (0) WEST GERMANY
BREHME 85

COACH
FRANZ BECKENBAUER

0 (0) ARGENTINA

COACH
CARLOS BILARDO

Date: 8 July 1990
Attendance: 73,603
Venue: Olympic Stadium, Rome

It was a repeat of the 1986 Final – West Germany vs. Argentina – the first time this had happened. For the Germans it was their third successive Final. It failed to live up to expectations, and is widely regarded as the worst Final on record. Both teams were sapped of energy after their epic semi-finals, and it came down to a controversial spot-kick for West Germany in the closing minutes. Argentina, already down to 10 men after the first-ever sending-off in a Final, suffered the ignominy of having a second man sent off shortly after West Germany had scored their World Cup winning penalty.

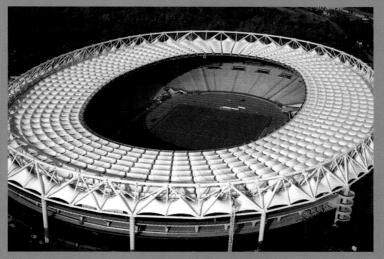

Olympic Stadium, Rome, opened 1937

1982 World Cup, Spain
mascot Naranjito

WORLD CUP MASCOTS

Tournament	Mascot	Description
England 1966	World Cup Willie	A lion wearing a Union Jack football shirt.
Mexico 1970	Juanito	A boy wearing a sombrero.
West Germany 1974	Tip and Tap	Two boys wearing West Germany uniforms.
Argentina 1978	Gauchito	A boy in a gaucho hat.
Spain 1982	Naranjito	A smiling orange, a typical fruit of Spain.
Mexico 1986	Pique	A jalapeno pepper, typical of Mexican food.
Italy 1990	Ciao	A stick figure player with a football head.
United States 1994	Striker	A cartoon dog.
France 1998	Footix	A cockerel, a national symbol of France.
South Korea/Japan 2002	Ato, Kaz and Nik	Three manga-style cartoon characters.
Germany 2006	Goleo and Pille	A lion in a German shirt and a talking football.
South Africa 2010	Zakumi	A leopard, a common animal in South Africa.
Brazil 2014	Fuleco	A three-banded Brazilian armadillo.

The South Africa official 2010
mascot, a leopard known as
Zakumi, during a launch in
Auckland Park, Johannesburg

UNBEATEN GOALKEEPERS IN THE WORLD CUP FINALS

Goalkeeper	Minutes unconceded	Tournament
Walter Zenga (Italy)	517	Italy 1990
Peter Shilton (England)	502	Mexico 1986–Italy 1990
Iker Casillas (Spain)	476	South Africa 2010–Brazil 2014
Sepp Maier (West Germany)	475	West Germany1974–Argentina 1978
Gianluigi Buffon (Italy)	460	Germany 2006
Émerson Leão (Brazil)	458	Argentina 1978
Gordon Banks (England)	442	England 1966

Spain's Iker Casillas
makes a save.

Italy's Walter Zenga

MOST GOALS CONCEDED IN ONE WORLD CUP

Goals conceded	Team	Tournament	Matches played
16	South Korea	Switzerland 1954	2
15	Sweden	Brazil 1950	5
15	France	Sweden 1958	6
15	Belgium	Mexico 1986	7
14	Brazil	Brazil 2014	7
14	Zaïre	West Germany 1974	3
14	Haiti	West Germany 1974	3
14	West Germany	Sweden 1958	6
14	West Germany	Switzerland 1954	6
13	El Salvador	Spain 1982	3
13	Mexico	Uruguay 1930	3

South Korea line-up
1954

PLAYERS IN THE MOST TOURNAMENTS

Player	Number of tournaments	
Antonio Carbajal (Mexico)	5	1950, 1954, 1958, 1962, 1966
Lothar Matthäus (Germany)	5	1982, 1986, 1990, 1994, 1998
Gianluigi Buffon (Italy)	5	1998, 2002, 2006, 2010, 2014
Nílton Santos (Brazil)	4	1950, 1954, 1958, 1962
Carlos Castilho (Brazil)	4	1950, 1954, 1958, 1962
Djalma Santos (Brazil)	4	1954, 1958, 1962, 1966
Uwe Seeler (W. Germany)	4	1958, 1962, 1966, 1970
Karl-Heinz Schnellinger (W. Germany)	4	1958, 1962, 1966, 1970
Bobby Charlton (England)	4	1958, 1962, 1966, 1970
Pelé (Brazil)	4	1958, 1962, 1966, 1970

England's Stanley Matthews in action with Brazil's Nílton Santos

West Germany's Lothar Matthäus celebrates

TEAMS WHO HAVE SCORED MORE THAN 100 GOALS IN ALL WORLD CUP FINALS

Team	Total goals
Germany/West Germany	224
Brazil	221
Argentina	131
Italy	128
France	103

TEAMS WHO HAVE NEVER SCORED AT THE WORLD CUP FINALS APPEARANCES

Team	Total goals
Germany/West Germany	224
Brazil	221
Argentina	131
Italy	128
France	103

PLAYERS WITH THE MOST CARDS IN WORLD CUP FINALS

Player	Total cards	Yellow	Red	Tournaments	Matches played
Zinédine Zidane (France)	6	4	2	1998, 2002, 2006	12
Rafael Márquez (Mexico)	6	5	1	2002, 2006, 2010, 2014	16
Cafu (Brazil)	6	6	0	1994, 1998, 2002, 2006	20
Rigobert Song (Cameroon)	5	3	2	1994, 1998, 2002, 2010	9
Tim Cahill (Australia)	5	4	1	2006, 2010, 2014	8
Diego Maradonna (Argentina)	5	4	1	1982, 1986, 1990, 1994	21
Sulley Muntari (Ghana)	5	5	0	2006, 2010, 2014	9
Javier Mascherano (Argentina)	5	5	0	2006, 2010, 2014	16
Lothar Matthäus (Germany)	5	5	0	1982, 1986, 1990, 1994, 1998	25
André Kana-Biyik (Cameroon)	4	3	1	1990, 1994	4

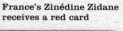

France's Zinédine Zidane receives a red card

Referee Roberto Rosetti of Italy shows the yellow card to Mexico's Rafael Márquez

FIFA PRIZE MONEY AT WORLD CUP FINALS

Stage	Team	Prize money – 2010	Prize money – 2014
Participation fee	32 teams	$1m each	$1.5m each
Group stage (eliminated)	16 teams	$8m each	$8m each
Round of 16 (losers)	8 teams	$9m each	$9m each
Quarter-finals (losers)	4 teams	$14m each	$14m each
Fourth place	1 team	$18m	$18m
Third place	1 team	$20m	$20m
Runners-up	1 team	$24m	$25m
Champions	1 team	$30m	$35m

Three countries showed an interest in hosting the 1994 World Cup Finals – Morocco, Brazil and the United States. Morocco and Brazil were established football-playing nations, but the United States was not, and when FIFA announced the tournament was theirs, some doubted it would be a success.

UNITED STATES 1994

With no footballing tradition in the United States, FIFA attached a condition to the awarding of the World Cup Finals – that the United States had to create a professional football league (a soccer league, as the game is known in the United States). The United States Soccer Federation was happy to oblige and promised to establish a league, which it did in 1993 (the first season of Major League Soccer began in 1996).

Concerns that the United States wasn't ready to host football's greatest show were soon put aside, and the tournament delivered record crowds, exciting play and a high goal count. Football's final frontier had been crossed.

Rule changes

FIFA brought in some significant changes for the 1994 competition. In the group stage, instead of two points for a win, there were three. The "three points for a win" system had been used in England since 1981, but had been slow to catch on elsewhere. The idea behind it was simple – that teams would not settle for a draw if there was the prospect of gaining two extra points for a win. FIFA hoped it would encourage attacking, open play, and reduce the number of dull and drawn games which had become a feature of the group stage of the Finals. It worked, and with the 1994 World Cup as the showcase, the system became widely adopted around the world.

Another change was the introduction of the back-pass rule, stopping a goalkeeper from handling the ball when a teammate had deliberately passed it back to him. It was a measure designed to stop time-wasting by goalkeepers.

Above: Roberto Baggio misses in the penalty shoot out, meaning Brazil win the 1994 World Cup Final. Opposite Top: Brazil's Jorginho holds the World Cup aloft. Bottom: Russian forward Oleg Salenko shoots past Cameroon's goalkeeper Jacques Songo'o, his record fifth goal of the game.

1994 WORLD CUP FINALS

Host country	United States
Dates	17 June – 17 July (31 days)
Teams	24
Venues	9 (in 9 host cities)
Matches played	52
Goals scored	141
Top scorer	Hristo Stoichkov, Bulgaria Oleg Salenko, Russia (6 each)
Attendance	3,587,538 (68,991 per match)
Champions	Brazil (4th title)
Runners-up	Italy
Third place	Sweden
Fourth place	Bulgaria

Official 1994 Poster

THE FINAL

0 (0) BRAZIL
BRAZIL WON 3–2 ON PENALTIES,
AFTER EXTRA TIME

COACH
CARLOS PARREIRA

0 (0) ITALY

COACH
ARRIGO SACCHI

Date: 17 July 1994
Attendance: 94,194
Venue: Rose Bowl, Pasadena, California

Brazil and Italy had each won the World Cup three times, and to reach the 1994 Final they had scored 19 goals between them and conceded eight. They had met in a Final once before, back in 1970 when Brazil had emerged 4–1 winners. With FIFA's new rules bringing in attacking play, there was every expectation of a high-scoring game, but the opposite was the case and the Final was a defensive disappointment with very few goal-scoring chances. It was 0–0 after 90 minutes, and still 0–0 after playing 30 minutes of extra time. For the first time, a World Cup Final was decided by a penalty shoot-out, and when Italy's Roberto Baggio stepped up to take the last of his side's five spot kicks, he had to score to keep Italy's hopes alive. He put the ball over the bar. It was the cruelest way to lose, and Baggio cut a forlorn figure as Brazil celebrated their fourth World Cup triumph.

Rose Bowl, Pasadena, California, opened 1922

More nations than ever before took part in the qualifiers for France 1998, competing for places in the bigger-than-ever World Cup Finals which FIFA had increased from 24 to 32.

France was awarded the Finals in preference to Morocco and, as hosts, did not need to go through the ordeal of qualifying. However, having failed to qualify for the previous two tournaments (Italy 1990 and United States 1994), some voiced doubts about whether France would be strong enough to progress beyond the group stage. The French team, playing at home, were under pressure to perform – and they did.

Playing in front of fiercely patriotic home crowds, France coasted through the first four matches, winning them all and scoring 10 goals and conceding just one. In the quarter-finals they faced Italy, beaten finalists four years previously in a penalty shoot-out. For Italy, history repeated itself, and after 120 minutes of dull, goalless football, they were knocked out, again on penalties.

Croatia, the surprise team

In the semi-final, France came up against Croatia, making their first appearance in the Finals. The Croatians were the tournament's surprise team and had crushed Germany 3–0 in the quarter-finals,

but they could not pass France, who beat them 2–1.

The hosts, France, were in the Final, where they were set to meet defending champions Brazil, who had not had an easy route to get there. Beaten 2–1 by Norway in the group stage, and forced to a penalty shoot-out against Holland in the semi-final, the South Americans seemed vulnerable.

1998 WORLD CUP FINALS

Host country	France
Dates	10 June – 12 July (33 days)
Teams	32
Venues	10 (in 10 host cities)
Matches played	64
Goals scored	171
Top scorer	Davor Šuker, Croatia (6)
Attendance	2,785,100 (43,517 per match)
Champions	France (1st title)
Runners-up	Brazil
Third place	Croatia
Fourth place	Holland

Official 1986 Poster

THE FINAL

3 (2) FRANCE
ZIDANE 27, 45
PETIT 90

COACH
AIMÉ JAQUET

0 (0) BRAZIL

COACH
MARIO ZAGALLO

Date: 12 July 1998
Attendance: 75,000
Venue: Stade de France, Paris

A dream Final – Hosts vs. Champions – began with the unexpected drama of Brazil's teamsheet. Their star player, Ronaldo, the reigning FIFA World Player of the Year, was not named. In reaching the Final, Ronaldo had scored four and helped with three of Brazil's goals. For him to miss the Final was unthinkable. Then, shortly before kick-off, the teamsheet was revised, and Ronaldo was back on it. The official explanation was he'd had a seizure earlier in the day and was deemed unfit to play, but he recovered and was given his place back. Whatever the truth, Brazil's talisman played the full 90 minutes, but it was clear he was not fully fit. Worse still, the rest of the Brazilian team seemed lethargic. France, on the other hand, played the game of their life, fired up by an inspirational Zinédine Zidane, whose two headed goals put the hosts in control by half-time. Emmanuel Petit rounded off the 3–0 win for France with a last-minute goal. The country where the World Cup idea had begun celebrated winning the trophy for the first time, made all the sweeter for claiming the victory on home soil.

Stade de France, Paris, opened 1998

A new century brought a new stage for the World Cup Finals – the first time they had been hosted by more than one nation, and the first time in Asia. Co-hosts South Korea and Japan promised a tournament to remember, and they duly delivered.

 # KOREA/JAPAN 2002

The 17th staging of the World Cup was something of a milestone. It was the first held in Asia, the first held on a continent other than Europe or the Americas, the last that included the Golden Goal rule, and the only World Cup to be jointly hosted by more than one country. Korea and Japan were awarded the tournament in 1998.

The countries had six years to prepare for the world's greatest footballing event, and between them they built 20 stadiums, the majority from scratch. Both hosts were awarded automatic places at the Finals, with South Korea hosting the opening match and Japan taking the Final.

For the first time, all seven previous winners of the World Cup reached the Finals – Argentina, Brazil, England, France, Germany, Italy and Uruguay.

Defending champions and reigning European Champions France had the honor of the opening match against World Cup newcomers Senegal. In a shock result, Senegal beat the holders 1–0, and with France not scoring in either of their next two games, they were out and on the plane back home, picking up the record of the worst World Cup performance by a defending champion. France was not the only early elimination – Russia, Poland and Portugal also fell at the group stage.

South Korean adventure

South Korea was the surprise team of the tournament, with wins against Poland, Portugal and then Italy, in a game that was decided three minutes from the end of extra time by a Golden Goal. It took them into a quarter-final contest with Spain, whom they dismissed in a penalty shoot-out. The South Korean journey ended in the semi-finals, in a 1–0 defeat to Germany, who went into the Final and a losing meeting with Brazil.

Above: Rivaldo lifts the trophy as Brazil celebrates after winning the World Cup with victory over Germany. Opposite Top: South Korea's Ahn Jung-hwan celebrates his Golden Goal against Italy. Bottom: Senegal players celebrate after defeating France 1-0 in the opening match of the World Cup Finals in Seoul.

2002 WORLD CUP FINALS

Host country	Korea and Japan
Dates	31 May – 30 June (31 days)
Teams	32
Venues	20 (in 20 host cities)
Matches played	64
Goals scored	161
Top scorer	Ronaldo, Brazil (8)
Attendance	2,705,197 (42,269 per match)
Champions	Brazil (5th title)
Runners-up	Germany
Third place	Turkey
Fourth place	South Korea

2002 FIFA WORLD CUP
KOREA/JAPAN
31 MAY – 30 JUNE

Official 2002 Poster

THE FINAL

2 (0) BRAZIL
RONALDO 67, 79

COACH
LUIZ FELIPE SCOLARI

0 (0) GERMANY

COACH
RUDI VÖLLER

Date: 30 June 2002
Attendance: 69,000
Venue: International Stadium, Yokohama, Japan

Brazil had made it to their third successive Final, and wanted to banish the memories of their lacklustre performance four years earlier in France. One Brazilian player in particular had more than most to prove – Ronaldo, whose poor form in the Final in France had contributed to his team's defeat.

Brazil vs. Germany was the World Cup Final many had longed for. With seven World Cup titles between them, it was the first time they had met in a Final. In reaching the last match, Germany had conceded just one goal and scored 14. They held out until mid-way through the second half, when Ronaldo shot Brazil ahead, followed by a second 12 minutes later. Brazil lifted the World Cup for a fifth time, and Ronaldo, with eight goals, finished as the tournament's top-scorer.

International Stadium, Yokohama, opened 1998

A change of rules meant that the previous tournament winners – in this case, Brazil – would not automatically qualify for the next Finals. Instead, they would have to earn their place on merit, alongside 30 other nations. The only automatic place from now on would be for the host nation.

GERMANY 2006

Germany was awarded the 2006 World Cup in a closely contested competition that left South Africa, considered by many to be the favorites, the underbidders. Allegations of bribery and corruption to swing the vote in Germany's favor cast a shadow over the whole process.

Eight nations qualified for the Finals for the first time: Angola, Czech Republic, Ghana, Ivory Coast, Togo, Trinidad and Tobago, Ukraine, and Serbia and Montenegro. European Champions Greece, along with Belgium, Turkey and Cameroon failed to qualify.

Exciting competition

The opening game revived a World Cup tradition that had lapsed after the 1970 tournament, with the home nation, not the defending champions, being given the honor of the first match. Germany's opponents were Costa Rica, and in a six-goal thriller the hosts claimed a 4–2 victory. It set the scene for an exciting competition.

Australia, the only qualifiers from Oceania, acquitted themselves well and qualified from a tough group. In the next round they faced Italy, who secured a narrow victory with a controversial penalty in the fifth minute of added time.

Germany made it to the semi-finals, but their dream of playing in the Final on home soil came undone in a 2–0 defeat by Italy. In the other semi-final, France, who had already knocked out Brazil, overcame Portugal, setting up a meeting with Italy.

2006 WORLD CUP FINALS

Host country	Germany
Dates	9 June – 9 July (31 days)
Teams	32
Venues	12 (in 12 host cities)
Matches played	64
Goals scored	147
Top scorer	Miroslav Klose, Germany (5)
Attendance	3,359,439 (52,491 per match)
Champions	Italy (4th title)
Runners-up	France
Third place	Germany
Fourth place	Portugal

Official 2006 Poster

THE FINAL

1 (1) ITALY
MATERAZZI 23
ITALY WON 5–3 ON PENALTIES,
AFTER EXTRA TIME

COACH
MARCELLO
LIPPI

0 (0) FRANCE
ZIDANE 7

COACH
RAYMOND
DOMENECH

Date: 9 July 2006
Attendance: 69,000
Venue: Olympic Stadium, Berlin

It was to be French star Zinédine Zidane's last match, and what bigger stage to bow out on but the Final of the World Cup. It was Zidane's penalty against Portugal in the semi-finals that had brought France to the Final, and in the seventh minute against Italy he did it again, scoring from the penalty spot. Zidane seemed to be writing himself into the record books, but history would show it was for a monumental mistake.

The sides went in level at half-time, and after 90 minutes it was still 1–1. But it's what happened in extra time that wrote the headlines when Zidane was sent off for head-butting an opponent in the chest. It was a moment of red mist stupidity with which Zidane is forever remembered, and a sad way to end a glittering career.

The game went to penalties, and the miss by David Trezeguet signed off a Final that France would want to forget, as the World Cup went to Italy for the fourth time.

Olympic Stadium, Berlin, opened 1936

Opposite: Italy's captain Fabio Cannavaro raises the World Cup as he celebrates with his teammates. Top: Germany's Miroslav Klose volleys the ball in a match against Ecuador, going on to be the tournament's top scorer. Center: Italy's Marco Materazzi reacts after being head-butted by France's Zinédine Zidane during the Final. Bottom: Wayne Rooney is stunned as he is given a red card in the game against Portugal.

In a short-lived policy to rotate the World Cup Finals around FIFA's six football confederations, only bids from African nations were invited for the 2010 tournament, guaranteeing it would travel to Africa for the first time. If South Africa had felt they'd missed out on hosting the 2006 Finals, 2010 was set to be their year.

SOUTH AFRICA 2010

From the start, South Africa 2010 was a noisy, colorful event. The hosts opened the tournament, playing against Mexico, to the deafening sound of vuvuzelas blown by the crowd. These horn-like instruments were largely unknown outside of South Africa before the tournament, but very soon their deep, monotone notes were drowning out football commentators, much to the frustration of the world's TV audiences. They are now banned at many sporting events. As for the opening match, South Africa celebrated a draw, and then went on to dismiss out-of-sorts France, sent home without a win. Defending champions Italy were also dumped out, finishing bottom of their opening stage group without a win to their name.

Tough for African nations

Despite South Africa's spirited performance, they lost out to Mexico on goal difference, setting the unwanted record as the first host nation not to make it through the group stage. There were similar disappointments for other African nations in the Finals, with Algeria, Cameroon, Ivory Coast and Nigeria all falling at the first stage. Only Ghana progressed through the tournament, eventually losing to Uruguay on penalties in the quarter-finals.

In the semi-finals, it was a familiar story of Europe vs. South America, with Holland overcoming Uruguay and Spain getting the better of Germany.

2010 WORLD CUP FINALS

Host country	South Africa
Dates	11 June – 11 July (31 days)
Teams	32
Venues	10 (in 9 host cities)
Matches played	64
Goals scored	145
Top scorer	Diego Forlán, Uruguay
	Thomas Müller, Germany
	Wesley Sneijder, Holland
	David Villa, Spain (5 each)
Attendance	3,359,439 (52,491 per match)
Champions	Spain
Runners-up	Holland
Third place	Germany
Fourth place	Uruguay

Official 2006 Poster

THE FINAL

1 (0) SPAIN
INIESTA 116

COACH
VICENTE DEL BOSQUE

0 (0) HOLLAND

COACH
BERT VAN MARWIJK

Date: 11 July 2010
Attendance: 84,490
Venue: Soccer City, Johannesburg

Spain's tournament started poorly with a 1–0 defeat by Switzerland (it turned out to be the first time the eventual winners had lost their opening match). But then Spain got into their stride with five low-scoring wins in which they conceded only one goal. Holland's journey had seen them dismiss all opposition, including Brazil, netting 12 on their way to the Final.

After 90 minutes the score was still 0–0, and the match went into extra time. It seemed to be heading for a penalty shoot-out, but in the 116th minute, Andrés Iniesta scored the winning goal for Spain, becoming the first European team to triumph outside Europe. They also claimed the record for the winning team scoring the fewest goals – a miserly eight in their seven matches.

Spain had played in their blue change strip, which they abandoned for their famous red shirts to receive the trophy.

Olympic Stadium, Berlin, opened 1936

Opposite: Spain players celebrate with the FIFA World Cup trophy after victory in the Final. Top: Holland's Arjen Robben (L) in action against Spain's Andrés Iniesta. Center: Ghana's Asamoah Gyan celebrates aftering scoring against the United States in extra time during a a second round match. Bottom: A fan blows the vuvuzela at the 2010 World Cup opening match between South Africa and Mexico.

Both Brazil and Colombia made bids to host the 2014 World Cup Finals, but when Colombia withdrew, the contest went straight to Brazil. The award was made in 2007, but despite having seven years to prepare, some of the venues were barely finished by the time the tournament began.

BRAZIL 2014

It was the football that soon started to make the headlines. On day two, a rematch of the 2010 Final was promised, with defending champions and reigning European Champions Spain drawn against Holland. In one of the most unforeseen results in World Cup history, Holland demolished Spain 5–1, and when Chile beat the Spaniards 2–0, the holders were eliminated in the group stage. England and Italy were also out at the group stage, in a group that saw Costa Rica finish top, undefeated, despite being considered underdogs and expected to finish last.

In the knock-out stage, Costa Rica met Greece. They had never met before, and for Greece it was the first time they reached the last-16. The match went to extra time and then to penalties, which Costa Rica won 5–3. Next up for Costa Rica was Holland, in the quarter-finals. It was another match that went to penalties: 4–3 in favor of the Dutch, who seemed to be on unstoppable form.

Sensational semis

The Finals were turning into a high-scoring tournament, but with the semis set at Brazil vs. Germany and Holland vs. Argentina, few would have put money on the goal glut continuing. History was about to be made.

Brazil and Germany had met only once before in the tournament's long history, in the 2002 Final (won by Brazil 2–0). Within the first 30 minutes Germany had put five into the back of the Brazilian net, and two more came in the second half. Brazil scored in the 90th minute, making the final score 7–1 to Germany. It was the worst ever defeat for a host nation, the biggest ever defeat in a World Cup semi-final, and it ended Brazil's 62-match unbeaten streak in competitive home matches. Germany pulled off arguably the most extraordinary World Cup victory of all time, and booked their place in the Final.

The other semi was characterised by a lack of goals, 0–0 after extra time leading to the agony of penalties, which went 4–2 to Argentina.

2014 WORLD CUP FINALS

Host country	Brazil
Dates	12 June – 13 July (32 days)
Teams	32
Venues	12 (in 12 host cities)
Matches played	64
Goals scored	171
Top scorer	James Rodríguez, Colombia (6)
Attendance	3,429,873 (53,592 per match)
Champions	Germany (4th title)
Runners-up	Argentina
Third place	Holland
Fourth place	Brazil

Official 2014 Poster

 FULL TIME

BRAZIL v GERMANY

1 - 7

90' OSCAR

11' MUËLLER
23' KLOSE
24' 26' KROOS
29' KHEDIRA
69' 79' SCHUERRLE

THE FINAL

1 (0) GERMANY
GÖTZE 113

COACH
JOACHIM LÖW

0 (0) ARGENTINA

COACH
LOUIS VAN GAAL

Date: 13 July 2014
Attendance: 74,738
Venue: Maracanã Stadium, Rio de Janeiro

In a tight, tense final, neither side gave much away. On 30 minutes, Argentina put the ball in the back of Germany's net, only to have the goal disallowed for offside. After 90 minutes, the game finished 0–0 and went into extra time — the third World Cup Final in a row to play an additional 30 minutes. In the second period of extra time the deadlock was finally broken by Germany, when substitute Mario Götze controlled the ball on his chest and volleyed into the Brazilian net.

Germany had won their fourth World Cup title, and their first title since German reunification. It was the first time a European team had won the tournament in the Americas.

Maracanã Stadium, Rio de Janeiro, opened 1950

Opposite Left: Germany celebrate victory with trophy. Right: Germany's Mario Goetze shoots to score during extra time. Above Top: Scoreboard shows the results at the end of the 2014 World Cup semi-finals between Brazil and Germany. Center: Argentina's Lionel Messi (L) in action with Germany's Bastian Schweinsteiger. Bottom: Costa Rica's Giancarlo Gonzalez celebrates victory over Italy.

WORLD CUP AWARDS

JULES RIMET CUP

For the first 16 years of its existence, from 1930 until 1946, the trophy awarded to the winners of the World Cup was officially known as the Victory trophy, as it represented a winged figure of Nike, the ancient Greek goddess of victory. It was more commonly known as the World Cup or Coupe du Monde. In 1946, it was renamed the Jules Rimet Cup, honoring FIFA's president who had initiated the tournament.

Made of gold-plated silver and mounted at first on a marble base and later on one of blue lapis lazuli, it stood 35cm high. In 1966, while on display in London, it was stolen, and recovered a few days later discarded under a bush. In 1970, Brazil won the Jules Rimet Cup for a third time, and were allowed to keep it, as had been stipulated by Jules Rimet in 1930. The cup went on display in Rio de Janeiro and was stolen in 1983, never to be recovered. It is widely believed to have been melted down.

The Jules Rimet Trophy

FIFA WORLD CUP

The present World Cup trophy, which depicts two human figures holding up the world, was first awarded in 1974. Made of 18-carat gold it weighs 6.175kg and stands 36.8cm high. The base has space for 17 inscriptions, which will cover tournaments up to and including the 2038 World Cup.

Germany was the first nation to win the new trophy for the third time in 2014, but unlike the original trophy, a three-time winner is no longer able to own it outright. Instead, the trophy remains in the permanent possession of FIFA, and is kept at their headquarters in Switzerland. The winning team is presented with a gold-plated replica, which they hold onto for four years, until the next tournament.

FIFA World Cup trophy

Brazilian soccer player Ronaldo holds up the FIFA World Cup Top Scorer trophy during the FIFA annual gala in Madrid December 17, 2002.

GOLDEN BOOT

The Golden Boot award goes to the top goalscorer of the World Cup Finals. First awarded in 1982, it was originally the Golden Shoe award, and was renamed the Golden Boot award in 2010.

Tournament	winner	Goals
1982 Spain	Paolo Rossi, Italy	6
1986 Mexico	Gary Lineker, England	6
1990 Italy	Salvatore Schillaci, Italy	6
1994 United States	Oleg Salenko, Russia	
	Hristo Stoichkov, Bulgaria	6
1998 France	Davor Šuker, Croatia	6
2002 Korea/Japan	Ronaldo, Brazil	8
2006 Germany	Miroslav Klose, Germany	5
2010 South Africa	Thomas Müller, Germany	5
2014 Brazil	James Rodríguez, Colombia	6

GOLDEN BALL

The Golden Ball award is presented to the best player at the World Cup Finals, with runners-up receiving the Silver Ball and Bronze Ball awards as the second and third most outstanding players in the tournament.

Tournament	Golden Ball winner
1962 Chile	Garrincha, Brazil
1966 England	Bobby Charlton, England
1970 Mexico	Pelé, Brazil
1974 Germany	Johan Cruyff, Holland
1978 Argentina	Mario Kempes, Argentina
1982 Spain	Paolo Rossi, Italy
1986 Mexico	Diego Maradona, Argentina
1990 Italy	Salvatore Schillaci, Italy
1994 United States	Romário, Brazil
1998 France	Ronaldo, Brazil
2002 South Korea / Japan	Oliver Kahn, Germany
2006 Germany	Zinédine Zidane, France
2010 South Africa	Diego Forlán, Uruguay
2014 Brazil	Lionel Messi, Argentina

German goalkeeper Oliver Kahn holds up the FIFA Best World Cup Player trophy during the FIFA annual gala in Madrid December 17, 2002. Kahn became the first goalkeeper to win FIFA's Golden Ball award which recognizes the best player in the World Cup.

FAIR PLAY TROPHY

The Fair Play trophy goes to the team with the best disciplinary record at the World Cup Finals. Only teams that reach the knockout phase are eligible.

Tournament	Fair Play trophy winners
1970 Mexico	Peru
1974 West Germany	West Germany
1978 Argentina	Argentina
1982 Spain	Brazil
1986 Mexico	Brazil
1990 Italy	England
1994 United States	Brazil
1998 France	England
	France
2002 South Korea / Japan	Belgium
2006 Germany	Brazil
	Spain
2010 South Africa	Spain
2014 Brazil	Colombia

GOLDEN GLOVE

The Golden Glove award goes to the best goalkeeper of the World Cup Finals. The award was introduced in 1994, and was originally known as the Lev Yashin award, in honor of the late Soviet goalkeeper considered by many to be the greatest goalkeeper in the history of the game. It was renamed the Golden Glove award in 2010.

Tournament	Golden Glove winner
1994 United States	Michel Preud'homme, Belgium
1998 France	Fabien Barthez, France
2002 South Korea / Japan	Oliver Kahn, Germany
2006 Germany	Gianluigi Buffon, Italy
2010 South Africa	Iker Casillas, Spain
2014 Brazil	Manuel Neuer, Germany

FIFA Fair Play Award trophy

1990 FIFA World Cup Third / Fourth Place play-off. The England and Italy teams on the podium after the match where England were presented with the FIFA Fair Play Award.

Real Madrid's goalkeeper Iker Casillas holds up his 2010 World Cup Golden Glove award.

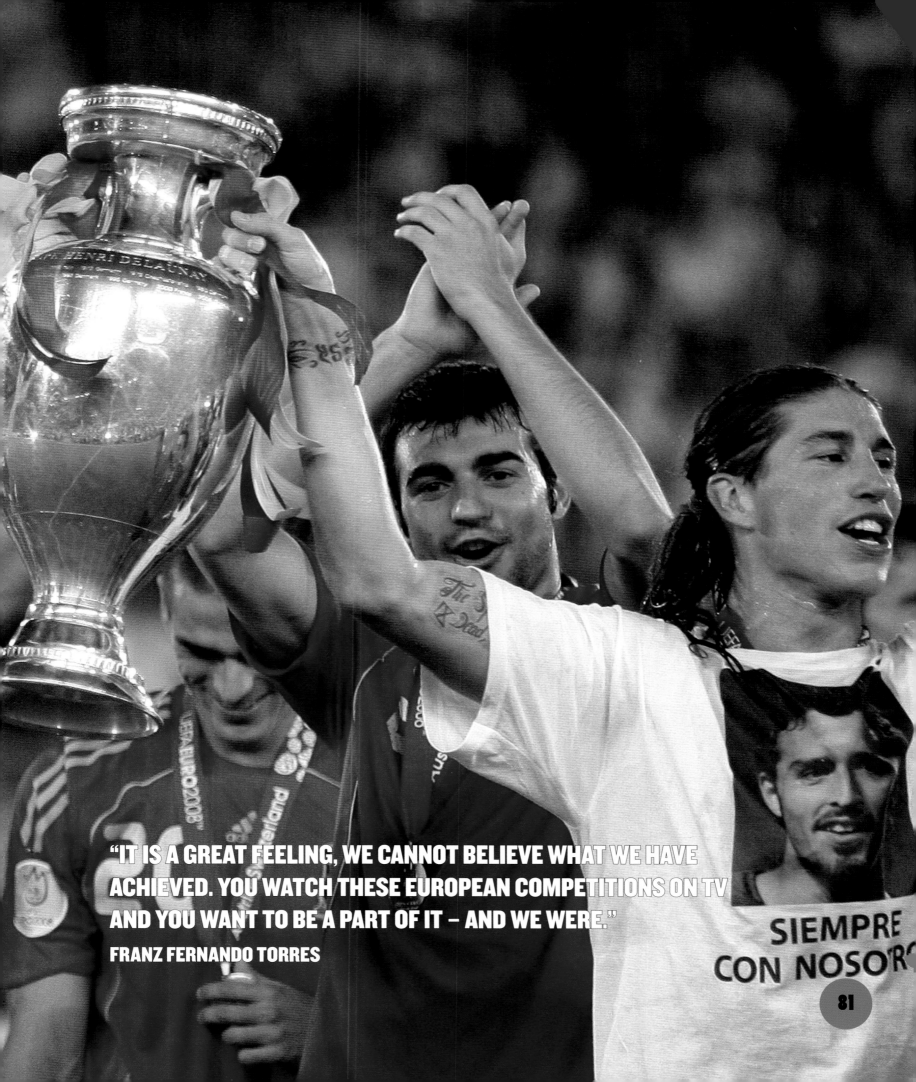

"IT IS A GREAT FEELING, WE CANNOT BELIEVE WHAT WE HAVE ACHIEVED. YOU WATCH THESE EUROPEAN COMPETITIONS ON TV AND YOU WANT TO BE A PART OF IT – AND WE WERE."

FRANZ FERNANDO TORRES

France 1960

Apart from regional tournaments such as the Home Internationals for the national teams of the United Kingdom or the Balkan Cup, Europe lacked a national team competition for some thirty years after the inauguration of the FIFA World Cup.

A European-Wide Competition

Henri Delaunay (1883-1955) was a former footballer who spent his youth playing for Parisian side Étoile des Deux Lacs. A refereeing career was cut short due to injury but Delaunay entered football administration, becoming chairman of his former club and chairing the 1929 meeting which led to the formation of FIFA. Two years earlier, Delaunay had first conceived the idea of a pan-European competition for national football teams but it wasn't until he became the first General Secretary of the Union of European Football Associations (UEFA) in 1954, that serious progress was made. Delaunay died the following year, but his son, Pierre, picked up the baton and flushed by the success of the European Champions' Club Cup for clubs, which had begun in 1955, a new tournament was agreed in 1957 at the UEFA executive congress in Cologne, Germany. The competition was named the European Nations' Cup (which later became known as the UEFA European Championships, and then later, EURO) with the winners' trophy organized by Pierre Delaunay, named after his father and designed by Arthus-Bertrand. The European Nations' Cup kicked off in style in front of 100,572 spectators at the Tsentralni Lenin Stadium in Moscow on 28 September 1958. Anatoli Ilyin became the competition's first scorer after four minutes as the Soviet Union ran out 3-1 winners over Hungary.

The Soviet team were one of 17 UEFA member nations that entered the inaugural tournament. West Germany, Italy, England and the Netherlands did not participate.

The first tournament was based around a qualifying format of pairs of home and away games with the winner progressing to the quarter-finals which would set up the four teams participating in the finals tournament. The first round saw France steamroller Greece 8-2 on aggregate although French defender Roger Marche became the first to score an own goal in the tournament. France would then go on to defeat Austria 5-2 and 4-2 in the quarter-finals to qualify for the tournament and were chosen as hosts for the finals.

There they faced Yugoslavia who had overcome Bulgaria and Portugal in qualifying, whilst the Soviet Union would play Czechoslovakia in Marseille. The latter game saw Valentin Ivanov score twice as the Soviets won 3-0, whilst the hosts were defeated in a thrilling match at the Parc des Princes stadium in Paris. After cruising into a 3-1 lead, the French were stunned by a Yugoslav comeback of two goals within a minute of each other by striker Dražan Jerković, taking the scoreline to Yugoslavia 5 France 4, still the highest-scoring EURO finals match.

Above: The Soviet Union winning team of the 1960 European Championships. Opposite Top: Action from the first ever EURO final between USSR and Yugoslavia. Bottom: The finals were be dominated by a Goalkeeper, as Lev Yashin led the Soviet Union to glory over Yugoslavia.

1960 EUROPEAN NATIONS CUP

Host country	France
Dates	6 July – 10 July
Teams	4
Venues	2 (in 2 host cities)
Matches played	4
Goals scored	17
Top scorer	Viktor Ponedelnik, Milan Galić, Dražan Jerković, Valentin Ivanov, François Heutte (2 goals)
Attendance	78,958 (19,740 per match)
Champions	Soviet Union
Runners-up	Yugoslavia
Third place	Czechoslovakia
Fourth place	France

THE FINAL

2 (0) SOVIET UNION
METREVELI 49
PONEDELNIK 113

1 (1) YUGOSLAVIA
GALIĆ 43

Date: 10 July 1960
Attendance: 17,966
Venue: Parc des Princes

The Yugoslavs met the reigning Olympic champions in the final, led by legendary goalkeeper Lev Yashin who reeled off a string of saves to deny the attack-minded Yugoslavian team. The Yugoslavs appeared to master the heavy pitch and rainy conditions better and went ahead after a cross from Dražan Jerković was bundled home by Milan Galić who equalled the record, at the time, of scoring in ten consecutive international matches.

The Soviets equalized shortly after half-time when goalkeeper Blagoje Vidinić failed to hold onto a long range shot from Valentin Bubukin and Slava Metreveli nipped in to score. The game went into added time and became an increasingly cagey affair before striker Viktor Pondelnik headed home from a Mikheil Meskhi cross. "That was the star moment of my life," Pondelnik would comment afterwards. The Soviets saw out the last seven minutes of the game to become the competition's first champions.

Yashin

Chokheli   Krutikov   Maslyonkin

Voinov   Netto

Metreveli   Bubukin
Ivanov   Ponedelnik   Meskhi

Kostić   Jerković   Matuš
Galić   Sekularac

Perušić   Žanetić

Jusufi   Miladinović   Durković

Vidinić

Parc des Princes, Paris

Spain 1964

Twenty nine teams entered qualifying for the second European Nations' Cup. England entered for the first time but were crushed 6-3 by France over their two games .

Denmark, on the other hand, crushed Malta 9-2 on aggregate and Northern Ireland defeated Poland 2-0 at home and 2-0 away. The real headline story of qualifying, however, involved European minnows, Luxembourg.

The tiny principality had a population of just 300,000 and faced a well-drilled Dutch side. A 1-1 draw was followed by a momentous 2-1 win courtesy of two goals from Camille Dimmer as the Netherlands were bundled out of the competition. Luxembourg nearly repeated the feat in the quarter-zfinals, drawing their two matches with Denmark, 3-3 and 2-2, but succumbing to a deciding play-off game 1-0. Denmark were joined in the finals, hosted in Spain, by the Soviet Union, Spain and a strong, if ageing Hungarian team, led by their dominant center forward, Florian Albert.

José Villalonga's Spanish side played out a tense semi-final match against Hungary which went into extra time after a 1-1 scoreline at full time. The game was settled in the 112th minute when Amancio Amaro Varela scored following a Carlos Lapetra corner. In the other semi-final, the Soviet Union defeated Denmark comfortably with the 1960 competition hero, Viktor Ponedelnik on the scoresheet in the Soviet's 3-0 victory at Barcelona's Camp Nou. The stage was therefore set for a final featuring two teams that should have played each other during qualifying for the 1960 competition before Spain's withdrawal from the competition.

Top: Spain celebrate their 2-1 victory in the 1964 final versus the Soviet Union
Above: Spain's Luis Suárez in 1962. Opposite Top: Jesús María Perada, center, in action in the final. Bottom: Lev Yashin concedes the opening goal in the final.

1964 EUROPEAN CHAMPIONSHIP

Host country	Spain
Dates	17 June – 21 June
Teams	4
Venues	2 (in 2 host cities)
Matches played	4
Goals scored	13
Top scorer	Jesús María Pereda, Ferenc Bene, Dezső Novák (2 goals)
Attendance	156,253 (39,063 per match)
Champions	Spain
Runners-up	Soviet Union
Third place	Hungary
Fourth place	Denmark

THE FINAL

 2 (1) SPAIN
PEREDA 6
MARCELINO 84

 1 (1) SOVIET UNION
KHUSAINOV 8

Date: 21 June 1964
Attendance: 79,115
Venue: Santiago Bernabeu, Madrid

Luis Suárez was widely considered the best playmaking midfielder in Europe at the time and he orchestrated the opening goal in the final with a cross from the right which eluded the Soviet defense and was hit home by Jesús María Pereda – a striker who had once played for Real Madrid in the Bernabeu but at the time of the final featured for Madrid's fierce rivals, Barcelona.

Spanish elation was short-lived, however, as Galimzyan Khusainov equalized just two minutes later. The game entered a long period of cagey, cat and mouse tactics, with few clear chances and both defenses prevailing until the 84th minute when Pereda turned from scorer to provider. His whipped cross was directed goalwards by Marcelino Martínez Cao via a diving header which sent the predominantly Spanish crowd into raptures. The Soviets pressed but could not find a second equalizer and Spain became the first hosts to become European champions. Incidentally, Marcelino would be in action in another final four days later when he scored the winner again, as his club Real Zaragoza defeated Valencia CF to win the Inter-Cities Fairs Cup.

Santiago Bernabeu, Madrid

Italy 1968

Italy were selected as hosts for the third edition of the tournament which still featured four teams in the finals but otherwise, underwent a number of changes.

Gone were the two-legged home and away knockout rounds in qualifying, replaced by seven groups of four and one group of three as the number of teams expanded to 31 with Scotland and West Germany making their competition debuts. The name of the competition was also changed to the European Football Championship.

Goals flowed and fortunes swung this way and that in some of the qualifying groups, most notably group 6 where Romania thrashed Cyprus 7-0 only to concede seven against Switzerland who themselves were beaten 5-0 by Italy. The Italians emerged group winners and narrowly prevailed over a talented Bulgarian side at the quarter final to become the first team to book a place at the finals. They were followed by Yugoslavia and England who knocked out defending champions Spain courtesy of a stirring 2-1 away win with goals from Martin Peters and Norman Hunter. The final berth was taken by the Soviet Union who managed an excellent quarter-finals comeback against Hungary, a team that would later in 1968 be crowned Olympic football champions.

The finals tournament was memorable often for statistical rather than footballing reasons with little free-flowing football on display. Italy prevailed over the Soviet Union team only via a coin toss after their game had finished goalless after extra time. The other semi-final was a tetchy, tackle-ridden affair between England and Yugoslavia which saw 49 free kicks awarded by referee, José María Ortiz who also showed a red card to Alan Mullery, the first Englishman sent off in a full international. The game burst into life in the 85th minute when the tournament's top scorer, Dragan Džajić hit an exquisite volley past Gordon Banks to propel Yugoslavia to their second European final.

Top Left: Italy line up before the Final replay. Above: Italian captain, Facchetti celebrating winning the coin toss vs the Soviet Union. Opposite Top: Bobby Charlton in action. Bottom: Italy in action as they dominate the Final replay.

1968 EUROPEAN CHAMPIONSHIP

Host country	Italy
Dates	5 June – 10 June
Teams	4
Venues	3 (in 3 host cities)
Matches played	5
Goals scored	7
Top scorer	Dragan Džajić (2 goals)
Attendance	260,916 (52,183 per match)
Champions	Italy
Runners-up	Yugoslavia
Third place	England
Fourth place	Soviet Union

THE FINAL

1 (0) ITALY
DOMENGHINI 80

1 (1) YUGOSLAVIA
DŽAJIĆ 39

Date: 10 June 1968
Attendance: 32,866
Venue: Olympic Stadium, Rome

A skilled Yugoslavian team caused a number of problems for an injury-hit Italian side shorn of standout midfielder, Gianni Rivera who had been injured in the semi-final. The Italians were thankful that their goalkeeper, Dino Zoff (who had made his national team debut in the quarter finals win over Bulgaria) was in prime form. Zoff was finally beaten in the 39th minute by Dragan Džajić but, otherwise kept the Yugoslavs at bay.

As the game progressed deep into the second half, it looked as if the Yugoslavs might prevail until Angelo Domenghini crashed in a free-kick on the 80th minute. With neither side able to press home any advantage, even during extra time, a replay of the final had to be hastily reorganized and held two days later. Italian coach Ferruccio Valcareggi made five changes to his starting eleven and Italy dominated the match, scoring twice in the first half via Luigi Riva and Pietro Anastasi, and looking relatively untroubled throughout to become the second hosts in a row to be crowned European champions.

Olympic Stadium, Rome

BELGIUM 1972

With matches held in Brussels, Antwerp and Liege, EURO 1972 would feature a West German side reaching the tournament for the first time.

England, Italy and Belgium all bid to host the 1972 tournament but with the hosts only decided after qualifying. Italy and England failed to make the final four from the 32 sides that entered qualifying, so Belgium were made hosts. West Germany had made significant progress in international football with their performances at the 1966 and 1970 FIFA World Cups. After cruising through their group and defeating England 3-1 away during qualifying quarter finals – their first win on English soil — they were widely considered the favorites. Coach Helmut Schön could call upon Europe's most dangerous striker in Gerd Müller who had just come off the back of a stellar season with his club, Bayern Munich, in which he had scored 50 goals in the Bundesliga and cup competitions combined.

The Germans entered the tournament in confident, ebullient form, none more so than Müller who scored both goals as West Germany eased past the hosts 2-1. The Soviet Union had topped their group in qualifying, defeated Yugoslavia in the quarter finals and then at the tournament, reached the final after knocking out Hungary 1-0. Their only goal came from central defender and future President of the Football Federation of Ukraine, Anatoliy Konkov.

Top: Soviet Union line up before the final. Above: Paul Van Himst on the ball for Belgium against West Germany. Opposite Top: Gerd Müller celebrates after scoring. Bottom: Müller lifts the trophy.

1972 EUROPEAN CHAMPIONSHIP

Host country	Belgium
Dates	14 June – 18 June
Teams	4
Venues	4 (in 3 host cities)
Matches played	4
Goals scored	10
Top scorer	Gerd Müller (4 goals)
Attendance	121,880 (30,470 per match)
Champions	West Germany
Runners-up	Soviet Union
Third place	Belgium
Fourth place	Hungary

THE FINAL

3 (1) GERMANY
MÜLLER 28, 58
WIMMER 52

0 (0) SOVIET UNION

Date: 18 June 1972
Attendance: 43,437
Venue: Heysel Stadium, Brussels

With a 4–1 mailing less than a month earlier in a friendly against West Germany, the Soviets knew they would need their strongest defense. All four German goals that day had come from Gerd Müller and now he was at it again, roaming the pitch as a lone center forward, ably assisted midfield by players like Günter Netzer and Uli Hoeneß. It was Netzer's volley onto the crossbar upon which Müller pounced, did the Soviets — score in the 28th minute.

Müller doubled his tally in the 58th minute, six minutes after Herbert Wimmer had played a one-two pass with Jupp Heynckes and slotted the ball to the left of Soviet keeper, Yevgeniy Rudakov. With Sepp Maier largely untroubled in the German goal and Franz Beckenbauer at his imperious best stepping out of defense to snuff out opposition attacks and link the German defense and midfield, the Germans were in control and ran out the comprehensive winners.

Heysel Stadium, Brussels

YUGOSLAVIA 1976

The last tournament to feature just four finalists, EURO 1976 will forever be remembered for the first penalty shootout in the competition's history.

It would also be remembered for the outrageous chipped penalty attempt by Antonin Panenka that gave Czechoslovakia their first major international trophy.

Qualifying followed the now typical format of eight groups of four teams with each group's winner contesting a two-legged quarter final tie to reach the finals of the competition. One of the surprise arrivals in the quarters were Wales, who had lost their first qualifying game 2-1 against Austria but had rallied to win their remaining five fixtures in a row to top their group at the expense of Austria and Hungary. The Welsh fell agonisingly at the quarter final stage to the eventual hosts, Yugoslavia, who would be joined by West Germany, the defending champions, the Netherlands, who qualified for the first time, and Czechoslovakia, who had bounced back following a 3-0 defeat to England in their first qualifying game.

The tournament proved an entertaining but close affair with both semi-finals, the final and the third place play-off games all going to extra time. There was controversy aplenty with the game between Czechoslovakia and the 1974 World Cup runners-up, the Netherlands, ending as 10 v 9 after Welsh referee Clive Thomas sent off Dutchmen Johan Neeskens and Wim van Hanegem after earlier dismissing Czech midfielder, Jaroslav Pollák. Meanwhile, in the other semi-final, a pulsating game saw the Yugoslavs race into a two goal lead in the first half only for West Germany to reply with four goals from their two substitutes, Dieter Müller and Heinz Flohe.

Top: The unfancied Czech line-up before the final. Above: Ivo Viktor after recieving his winners medal. Opposite Top: Dieter Müller heads for West Germany. Bottom: Czechs lift the cup after the penalty shoot-out.

1976 EUROPEAN CHAMPIONSHIP

Host country	Yugoslavia
Dates	16 June – 20 June
Teams	4
Venues	2 (in 2 host cities)
Matches played	4
Goals scored	19
Top scorer	Dieter Müller (4 goals)
Attendance	106,087 (26,522 per match)
Champions	Czechoslovakia
Runners-up	West Germany
Third place	Netherlands
Fourth place	Yugoslavia

THE FINAL

2 (2) CZECHOSLOVAKIA
ŠVEHLÍK 8
DOBIAŠ 25
CZECHOSLOVAKIA WON 5-3 ON PENALTIES

2 (1) WEST GERMANY
MÜLLER 28
HÖLZENBEIN 89

Date: 20 June 1976
Attendance: 30,790
Venue: Stadion FK Crvena Zvezda

Czechoslovakia roared out of the blocks at the start of the final. Ján Švehlík stunned the defending champions in the eighth minute by scoring the tournament's fastest goal. The Czechs doubled their lead seventeen minutes later after Marián Masný's free-kick was only partially cleared and Karol Dobiaš struck an angled shot that crept past Sepp Maier in the German goal.

Germany hit back quickly with a Dieter Müller strike before half time but found Czech goalkeeper, Ivo Viktor in commanding form. The Dukla Prague keeper reeled off a string of fine saves as Germany pressed for an equalizer but could do nothing about the header from Bernd Hölzenbein a minute from time. A goalless period of extra time led to the spectacle of a penalty shootout for the first time at a EUROs tournament. The first seven penalties all resulted in goals before Uli Hoeneß struck his attempt over the bar. It left Antonín Panenka to go down in history as he waited for Maier to dive to his left before chipping the ball softly and cheekily into the center of the goal.

Stadion FK Crvena Zvezda, Belgrade

Italy 1980

With interest in the EUROs booming and a clamor for more places at the tournament to be made available, UEFA expanded the competition so that eight teams would contest the finals.

Responding to a booming interest in the EUROs and a clamour for more places, UEFA expanded the competition to eight finalists. The hosts were chosen in advance and, for the first time, were exempt from qualification. The remaining seven places were awarded to the winners of seven qualifying groups with the qualifying knock out round, the quarter finals, scrapped.

Qualifying saw the Soviet Union and France fail, but Greece succeeded for the first time and were joined by five teams making their second EUROs appearance: England, for whom Kevin Keegan had scored seven goals, the most by any player in qualifying; Spain, Belgium, the Netherlands and Italy. The format of the finals changed as well with no semi-finals but with the winners of the two groups of four heading straight for the final.

Sadly, the new format resulted in some turgid football as teams vied not to lose rather than win at times. Eight of the 12 group games were low-scoring draws or 1-0 wins with Czechoslovakia's 3-1 win over Greece the only game won by more than a margin of one goal. West Germany's two wins and a draw against Greece saw them through to the final whilst the second group was tighter with both Italy and Belgium on four points and with a goal difference of plus one. Belgium went through to their first major international final, having scored three goals to Italy's one.

Top: Spain in action against England. Above: René Vandereycken of Belgium. Opposite Top: Germany's Horst Hrubesch celebrates after scoring the winning goal in the final. Bottom: Jupp Derwall, West Germany manager.

1980 UEFA EUROPEAN CHAMPIONSHIP

Host country	Italy
Dates	16 June – 20 June
Teams	4
Venues	4 (in 4 host cities)
Matches played	14
Goals scored	27
Top scorer	Klaus Allofs (3 goals)
Attendance	345,463 (24,676 per match)
Champions	West Germany
Runners-up	Belgium
Third place	Czechoslovakia
Fourth place	Italy

THE FINAL

2 (1) WEST GERMANY
HRUBESCH 10, 88

1 (0) BELGIUM
VANDEREYCKEN 75

Date: 22 June 1980
Attendance: 47,864
Venue: Stadio Olimpico, Rome

Czechoslovakia roared out of the blocks at the start of the final. Ján Švehlík stunned the defending champions in the eighth minute by scoring the tournament's fastest goal. The Czechs doubled their lead seventeen minutes later after Marián Masný's free-kick was only partially cleared and Karol Dobiaš struck an angled shot that crept past Sepp Maier in the German goal.

Germany hit back quickly with a Dieter Müller strike before half time but found Czech goalkeeper, Ivo Viktor in commanding form. The Dukla Prague keeper reeled off a string of fine saves as Germany pressed for an equalizer but could do nothing about the header from Bernd Hölzenbein a minute from time. A goalless period of extra time led to the spectacle of a penalty shootout for the first time at a EUROs tournament. The first seven penalties all resulted in goals before Uli Hoeneß struck his attempt over the bar. It left Antonin Panenka to go down in history as he waited for Maier to dive to his left before chipping the ball softly and cheekily into the center of the goal.

Stadio Olimpico, Rome

France 1984

Record crowds enjoyed fine weather and a joyful atmosphere, and savored record numbers of goals, nine of which came from homegrown hero, Michel Platini.

Whilst qualifying continued as before, with seven places available, there was one key adjustment to the finals format. The semi-finals stage was reinstated, meaning that the top two sides in each group still retained the chance of being champions. After a close 1-0 win for France over Denmark in the opening game, the goals started to come as a formidable French side, blessed with the midfield trio of Alain Giresse, Jean Tigana and Michel Platini hit full stride. Belgium were blown away 5-0 by France in Group A whilst Denmark inflicted a similar scoreline on Yugoslavia. Both victors would progress from Group A after recording 3-2 wins in their last group games over Yugoslavia and Belgium respectively.

In Group B, a major shock looked in store for the defending champions, West Germany, as they were held to a goalless draw by Portugal and conceded a penalty to Spain in their final group game. Lobo Carrasco's attempt was saved by Harald Schumacher in the German goal and, with a draw enough to take West Germany through, all looked serene until the 90th minute when Antonio Maceda rose to head the ball home and take Spain through at West Germany's expense. Maceda would provide a late equalizer again in the semi-final which saw Spain progress past Denmark following a penalty shootout where they met the hosts who had defeated Portugal 3-2 after extra time, courtesy of a goal in the 119h minute by Platini. France had served a feast of exciting football.

Top Left: France's Michel Platini shoots against Spain. Above: Joy and despair as Spain's Luis Arconada allows the ball to spill over the line. Opposite Top: Germany's Klaus Allofs tackles Spain's Victor Muñoz. Bottom: Platini with trophy.

1984 UEFA EUROPEAN CHAMPIONSHIP

Host country	France
Dates	12 June – 27 June
Teams	8
Venues	7 (in 7 host cities)
Matches played	15
Goals scored	41
Top scorer	Michel Platini (9 goals)
Attendance	599,669 (39,978 per match)
Champions	France
Runners-up	Spain
Third place	Denmark
Fourth place	Portugal

THE FINAL

 2 (0) FRANCE
PLATINI 57
BELLONE 90

 0 (0) SPAIN

Date: 27 June 1984
Attendance: 47,368
Venue: Parc des Princes, Paris

With the weight of expectation on French shoulders following their entertaining progress to the final, it was Spain who started the game more brightly, launching strongly into tackles and fashioning chances often from the crosses of Santiago Urquiaga or the goal threat of Carlos Santillana who shot wide and also had a header cleared off the line by Patrick Battiston.

Platini was relatively quiet but his free kick in the 57th minute was badly fumbled by the normally reliable Luis Arconada in the Spanish goal and France went ahead. The game turned on that moment and even the 85th minute sending off of Yvon Le Roux for a second bookable offence – the first red card in a UEFA European Championship final match – could not deny Les Bleus. As the game was coming to a close, the excellent Jean Tigana released Bruno Bellone whose deft finish, clipping the ball over the Spanish goalkeeper, secured the game and the Championship for France. It was the only one of the team's 14 goals at the tournament which was scored by a striker.

Parc des Princes, Paris

UEFA European Championship Records First Half

Germany's Bernd Schneider (R) scores a penalty past San Marino goalkeeper Aldo Simoncini during their Euro 2008 Group D qualifying soccer match in Serravalle, San Marino, September 6, 2006.

BIGGEST WINS

The biggest victory in qualifying was achieved by Germany in 2006 when they defeated San Marino by a record scoreline of 13-0. Lukas Podolski scored four times whilst six other German players also scored, the most in a single qualifying game. At the finals, the most goals in a game remains the nine scored by Yugoslavia and France in the semi-final that ended 5-4 in the Yugoslavs' favor. Yugoslavia was also on the receiving end of a 6-1 defeat at EURO 2000, the most goals scored by one team in a single finals game. France in 1984, Denmark in 1984 and Sweden in 2004, also won by a five goal margin, each recording 5-0 wins.

HAT-TRICK HEROES

Michel Platini holds many of the records for hat-tricks (three goals in a game) at UEFA European Championships including being the only person to have scored two consecutive hat-tricks at a single tournament (EURO 1984) and the scorer of the fastest hat trick, taking just 18 minutes to score three times against Yugoslavia. The only substitute to score a hat trick at the finals is Dieter Müller who came on for West Germany in the 79th minute of the 1976 semi-final versus Yugoslavia and scored in the 82nd, 115th and 119th minutes of the game to take the Germans to the final.

France's Michel Platini scores against Yugoslavia 1984.

FIRST AND LAST GOALS

The fastest goal scored at the European Championships tournament came in 2004 when Russian forward Dmitri Kirichenko struck after just 68 seconds for Russia against Greece.

In contrast, the latest goal after kick-off was scored by Turkish striker Semih Şentürk against Croatia in the second minute of added time after 120 minutes of play in the EURO 2008 quarter final. Şentürk's goal took the match into a penalty shootout which Turkey eventually won by three penalties to one.

Russia's Dmitry Kirichenko celebrates his goal as Greece's goalkeeper Antonis Nikopolidis looks on.

GOALKEEPER RECORDS

Two goalkeepers have kept the most clean sheets at EUROs tournaments. The Netherlands' Edwin van der Sar and Spanish keeper Iker Casillas have both kept nine clean sheets. At EURO 2012, Casillas only conceded a single goal throughout the tournament and went 508 minutes without conceding a goal. The record for the most consecutive minutes without conceding, including qualifying, is 784 minutes by Italian goalkeeper Dino Zoff between 1975 and 1980. At the other end of the scale, Peter Schmeichel has conceded 20 goals, the most conceded at UEFA European Championship finals. The most a goalkeeper has let in at a single tournament was 13 by Yugoslavia's keeper, Ivica Kralj, at EURO 2000.

Spain's goalkeeper Iker Casillas makes a save against Portugal's Joao Moutinho during penalty shoot-out of the Euro 2012 semi-final.

TEAM PROGRESSION RECORDS

Germany (or West Germany) have reached the semi-finals of the Euros a record eight times, progressing to the final on six occasions whilst Spain boast the longest gap between winning the tournament, on debut in 1964 and then 44 years later in 2008. The Soviet Union hold the record for the most consecutive top four finishes with four in a row between 1960 and 1972.

Portugal and the Czech Republic have finished third or fourth the most times (three) whilst England hold the record for reaching the top eight of the tournament the most times (eight) without ever reaching the final.

MOST EUROPEAN CHAMPIONSHIPS WON

Champions	Team	Tournaments
3	Germany	1972, 1980, 1996
3	Spain	1964, 2008, 2012
2	France	1984, 2000
1	Soviet Union	1960
1	Italy	1968
1	Czechoslovakia	1976
1	Netherlands	1988
1	Denmark	1992
1	Greece	2004

CONSECUTIVE FINALS APPEARANCES

Only one man so far has appeared in three final matches of consecutive EUROs tournaments, the defensive midfielder, Rainer Bonhof who was part of a West German side that reached the final in 1972, 1976 and 1980. With two champions and one runners-up medals, Bonhof also holds the record for most EUROs honors as a player.

TOP SCORING TEAMS PER TOURNAMENT

Year	Team/Teams	Goals
1960	Yugoslavia	6 goals
1964	Hungary, Soviet Union, Spain	4 goals
1968	Italy	3 goals
1972	West Germany	5 goals
1976	West Germany	6 goals
1980	West Germany	6 goals
1984	France	14 goals
1988	Netherlands	8 goals
1992	Germany	7 goals
1996	Germany	10 goals
2000	France, Netherlands	13 goals
2004	England, Czech Republic	10 goals
2008	Spain	12 goals
2012	Spain	12 goals

GOALS PER TOURNAMENT

Year	Matches	Goals	Goals Per Game
1960	4	17	4.25
1964	4	13	3.25
1968	5	7	1.40
1972	4	10	2.50
1976	4	19	4.75
1980	14	27	1.93
1984	15	41	2.73
1988	15	34	2.27
1992	15	32	2.13
1996	31	64	2.06
2000	31	85	2.74
2004	31	77	2.48
2008	31	77	2.48
2012	31	76	2.45

France's Michel Platini scores against Yugoslavia 1984.

MOST UEFA EUROPEAN CHAMPIONSHIP TOURNAMENT GOALS

Player (country)	Goals	Tournaments
Michel Platini (France)	9	1984
Alan Shearer (England)	7	1992, 1996, 2000
Ruud van Nistelrooy (Netherlands)	6	2004, 2008
Patrick Kluivert (Netherlands)	6	1996, 2000
Zlatan Ibrahimović (Sweden)	6	2004, 2008, 2012
Thierry Henry (France)	6	2000, 2004, 2008
Cristiano Ronaldo (Portugal)	6	2004, 2008, 2012
Nuno Gomes (Portugal)	6	2000, 2004, 2008

England's Alan Shearer celebrates scoring the winner against France, 1992.

WEST GERMANY 1988

EURO 1988 is recalled for the flair and enterprise shown by the Dutch team as well as Marco van Basten's wonderful volley in the final.

EURO 1988 should also be remembered as a well-organized, high quality competition enjoyed by nigh on 850,000 live spectators and millions more on TV.

Qualifying had resulted in two strong groups of teams. Group A was packed with talent with Italy, West Germany and Spain, all of whom treated the fourth side in their group, Denmark, as whipping boys. With Italy indebted to Gianluca Vialli's goal to overcome Spain and West Germany similarly reliant on Rudi Voller, who struck twice in their 2-0 win over the Spaniards progressed to the semi-finals.

In Group B, England had arrived in good spirits after an impressive qualifying campaign that saw them score 19 goals and concede only one, but were shocked in their opening game by a Republic of Ireland side coached by their former World Cup winner, Jack Charlton. Things went from bad to worse for England with two comprehensive 3-1 defeats at the hands of the two teams who qualified from Group B, the Soviet Union and the Netherlands.

The Dutch had been indebted to Marco van Basten for his clinical hat-trick in the England game and he duly obliged again in an epic semi-final against their West German rivals, which saw the initiative swing to and fro with a penalty scored by each

team. In the end, before van Basten slid into the penalty area and hooked the ball past German goalkeeper Eike Immel to score the winner just two minutes from time. In the other semi-final, a committed Soviet Union side managed to unpick Italy's defense to win 2-0 and reach their fourth EUROs final match.

Top Left: Paolo Maldini in action for Italy against Spain. Top Right: Ireland's Ray Houghton celebrates after scoring the only goal of the game against England. Above: Gullit and Van Basten hug in celebration during the final. Opposite Top: Holland's Marco Van Basten celebrates with Frank Rijkaard after scoring the second goal against USSR. Bottom: Holland's Ruud Gullit in action against England.

1988 UEFA EUROPEAN CHAMPIONSHIP

Host country	West Germany
Dates	10 June – 25 June
Teams	8
Venues	8 (in 8 host cities)
Matches played	15
Goals scored	34
Top scorer	Marco van Basten (5 goals)
Attendance	849,844 (56,656 per match)
Champions	Netherlands
Runners-up	Soviet Union
Semi-finalists	West Germany
	Italy

THE FINAL

2 (1) NETHERLANDS
GULLIT 32
VAN BASTEN 54

0 (0) SOVIET UNION

Date: 25 June 1988
Attendance: 72,308
Venue: Olympiastadion, Munich

Despite lining up without key defender Oleg Kuznetsov, due to suspension, the Soviet Union started the game the better of the two sides before the Dutch team began to gain control of key areas of the pitch. It was the second spell in charge for the architect of Total Football, Rinus Michels, who had masterminded the extravagantly gifted Dutch side of the 1970s that reached the final of two FIFA World Cups. Here, he utilised the passing accuracy of 37 year old veteran midfielder Arnold Mühren to release twin strikers Ruud Gullit and Marco van Basten into danger areas. Both scored, the latter with an incredible dipping volley from an acute angle off a hanging Arnold Muhren cross. It still ranks as one of the finest ever goals in UEFA history. The Soviets had a chance to get back into the game later in the second half when Sergey Gotsmanov was brought down in the penalty area by the Dutch goalkeeper Hans van Breukelen. But he immediately made amends by blocking Igor Belanov's low shot and the Netherlands ran out comfortable winners.

Olympiastadion, Munich

SWEDEN 1992

Whilst the tournament largely followed the same format as before, changes were afoot. The political landscape of Europe had changed dramatically following the fall of the Berlin Wall in 1989 and the break-up of the Soviet Union in 1991, which spun out many small republics. Eleven of these emerging nations would compete at EURO 1992 as the Commonwealth of Independent States (CIS).

West Germany and East Germany were originally drawn to play each other in the same qualifying group but had reunified into one nation and so qualifying Group 5 progressed with only four and not five teams. Further novelty was provided by San Marino and the Faroe Islands entering qualification for the first time, the latter recording an historic win over Austria whilst Scotland qualified for the first time by topping Group 2. They were expected to be joined by Yugoslavia who had qualified strongly with 14 out of 16 points but civil war struck the country and the resulting United Nations sanctions prevented Yugoslavia from taking part. Denmark were invited to take their place just 10 days before the tournament started.

With relatively little preparation and having failed to register a point in the previous UEFA European Championships, few were expecting much from Dane Richard Møller Nielsen's side. They had also lost their best player, Michael Laudrup to a disagreement with the coach. It took a narrow 2-1 victory over France to get Denmark through their group and into the semi-finals where they shocked the Netherlands by taking the game into a penalty shootout.

There, Peter Schmeichel saved Marco van Basten's attempt to win 2-2 (5-4 on penalties). In the other semi-final, the hosts proved strong opponents but could not deny the German team who crept past them 3-2 with Karl-Heinz Riedle scoring twice.

Top Left: Denmark's Peter Schmeichel pushes a shot round the post. Top Right: Germany's Karl-Heinz Riedle scores the winning goal against Sweden to put them into the final. Above: Denmark team celebrate victory in the Final over Germany. Opposite Top: Holland's Marco Van Basten celebrates with Frank Rijkaard after scoring the second goal against Russia. Bottom: Swedes celebrate as semi-finalists.

1992 UEFA EUROPEAN CHAMPIONSHIP

Host country	Sweden
Dates	10 June – 26 June
Teams	8
Venues	4 (in 4 host cities)
Matches played	15
Goals scored	32
Top scorer	Dennis Bergkamp, Tomas Brolin, Henrik Larsen, Karl-Heinz Riedle (3 goals)
Attendance	430,111 (28,674 per match)
Champions	Denmark
Runners-up	Germany
Semi-finalists	Sweden
	Netherlands

THE FINAL

 2 (1) DENMARK
JENSEN 18
VILFORT 78

 0 (0) GERMANY

Date: 26 June 1992
Attendance: 37,800
Venue: Ullevi, Gothenburg

With Denmark missing their influential midfielder, Henrik Andersen, Germany dominated the early stages of the final. The German team, with Jurgen Klinsmann prominent, called Peter Schmeichel into action early with a series of saves from Stefan Reuter, Guido Buchwald and Karl-Heinz Riedle. With 18 minutes on the clock, a chance fell to John Jensen who had only scored one goal in his previous 47 internationals. His powerful shot from the right-hand corner of the penalty area stunned Germany.

Denmark needed their defense to stay sharp and Schmeichel to be at his committed best as he dived, scrambled and parried away chance after chance created by Germany. Even when Schmeichel was beaten shortly into the second half, Kent Nielsen was on hand to clear off the line. As the game went deep into the second half, the Danes had a sting in their tale and it came when Kim Vilfort eluded the German defense and scored with his shot going in off the post. A frustrated German side still pressed and gathered five yellow cards during the game but could not make their pressure tell and Denmark became the unlikeliest champions so far.

Ullevi, Gothenburg, Sweden

ENGLAND 1996

The year 1996 was about change in the UEFA. To accommodate the expansion to 48 members, the finals would include 16 teams and a quarter-final knock out round was added.

Another change was that three points, rather than two, were awarded for a win, placing a premium on securing victories in the group stage.

For the first time in EUFA history, England won hosting duties. Tournament play saw there were few shocks overall in qualifying or in the group stages with France and Spain dominating Group B and Portugal and Croatia cruising through Group D. Italy and Russia lost out to Germany and the Czech Republic in Group C whilst the most eagerly anticipated fixture in the group stages was the "Battle of Britain" match between England and Scotland in Group A. It didn't disappoint, with end-to-end action, a penalty save by David Seaman and a stunning goal from Paul Gascoigne, who flicked the ball up and over Scottish skipper, Colin Hendry, and met the falling ball on the volley to rifle it home. England's 2-0 victory against the Scots was followed by a comprehensive 4-1 win over a Dutch side whose single goal by Patrick Kluivert ensured they sneaked into the quarter finals ahead of Scotland.

The knockout stages were close with four out of the six matches that formed the quarter and semi-finals going to penalty shootouts. The Czech Republic continued their tradition of excelling at penalties, not missing one, as they reached the final at France's expense after their match at Old Trafford had ended in a goalless draw. The other semi-final between England and Germany was widely regarded as the match of the tournament and started explosively with EURO 1996's fastest goal, headed in after three minutes by Alan Shearer before Stefan Kuntz equalized 13 minutes later. Despite numerous chances, with Darren Anderton hitting the post and Kuntz's headed goal disallowed, the game went to penalties where at 5-5, Gareth Southgate's attempt was saved by Andreas Köpke, Andreas Möller struck the winning penalty to send Germany into the final for a record fifth time.

Top Left: Czech Rep celebrate Miroslav Kadlec's winning penalty vs France.
Top Right: England's Paul Gascoigne fires home England's second goal against Scotland. Above: Alan Shearer celebrates his second goal with Teddy Sheringham.
Opposite Top: Italy's Pierluigi Casiraghi scores his and Italy's second goal vs Russia. Bottom: Germany captain Jürgen Klinsmann lifts the trophy while guest of honor HRH Queen Elizabeth II looks on.

1996 UEFA EUROPEAN CHAMPIONSHIP

Host country	England
Dates	8 June – 30 June
Teams	16
Venues	8 (in 8 host cities)
Matches played	31
Goals scored	64
Top scorer	Alan Shearer (5 goals)
Attendance	1,275,857 (41,157 per match)
Champions	Germany
Runners-up	Czech Republic
Semi-finalists	England
	France

THE FINAL

2 (0) GERMANY
BIERHOFF 73, 95

1 (0) CZECH REPUBLIC
BERGER 59

Date: 30 June 1996
Attendance: 73,611
Venue: Wembley Stadium, London

The final was to be the first major football tournament to be decided by a golden goal should the scores be level at full time. The first goal scored in extra time would see play stop and the scoring side declared the winner. Karel Poborský, who would be declared Man of the Match despite finishing on the losing side, was tripped in the 58th minute by Matthias Sammer. Despite German protests that the offence occurred outside the box, a penalty was awarded which was scored by Patrick Berger past German keeper, Andreas Köpke.

Facing a second runners-up spot in a row, Berti Vogts brought on Oliver Bierhoff in the 69th minute. It appeared a tactical masterstroke four minutes later when he rose high to head home Christian Ziege's crossed free kick to equalize. The game remained level at 90 minutes so entered extra time with the prospect of a golden goal. It arrived five minutes later when Biefhoff turned and struck a left foot shot which deflected off Michal Horňák and past Petr Kouba in the Czech goal to become the first three-time winners of the competition.

Wembley Stadium, London

BELGIUM AND THE NETHERLANDS 2000

The dawn of a new millennium brought the first UEFA European Championship to be co-hosted by two nations. The UEFA decided to award the tournament to a joint bid by the Netherlands and Belgium.

The tournament featured the most goals at a single EUROs competition with 85 scored and a number of against-the-odds performances.

Defending champions Germany finished bottom with just a single point, and the previous tournament semi-finalist, England, also failed to qualify, while Portugal and Romania got through. In Group B, despite starting brightly with a 3-1 win over Sweden, the co-hosts Belgium were knocked out whilst in Group C, Yugoslavia made one of the biggest comebacks in EUROs history by salvaging a 3-0 down to Slovenia with a 3-3 draw. The Yugoslavs then suffered an equally dramatic reverse in their last group game, losing to Spain 4-3 in a see-sawing contest that stood out as the most entertaining match of the tournament.

Spain, themselves, were tipped as potential finalists but could not find a way past a determined French team in the quarter-finals for whom Zinédine Zidane starred. The French were the FIFA World Cup holders but had to dig deep in their semi-final against Luis Figo, Nuno Gomes and the rest of the Portuguese team and required a penalty, despatched by Zidane in the 117th minute, to go through. The defensive Italians who had eased past Romania 2-0 in the quarters were forced to stage a rearguard action in their semi-final after Gianluca Zambrotta was sent off in the 34th minute

for a second bookable offence. Dutch profligacy in front of goal and two missed penalties in normal time saw the game go into a penalty shootout in which Italy prevailed.

Top Left: Zidane celebrates scoring the Golden Goal in the semi-final vs Portugal. Top Right: France's David Trezeguet scores the winning goal vs Italy. Above: Holland's Patrick Kluivert celebrates scoring his 4th goal vs Yugoslavia. Opposite Top: Holland's Frank De Boer has his penalty saved by Italy's keeper Francesco Toldo. Bottom: French team celebrate winning the European Championship Trophy.

2000 UEFA EUROPEAN CHAMPIONSHIP

Host country	Belgium, the Netherlands
Dates	10 June – 2 July
Teams	16
Venues	8 (in 8 host cities)
Matches played	31
Goals scored	85
Top scorer	Patrick Kluivert, Savo Milošević (5 goals)
Attendance	1,122,833 (36,220 per match)
Champions	France
Runners-up	Italy
Semi-finalists	Portugal
	Netherlands

THE FINAL

2 (0) FRANCE
WILTORD 90+3
TREZEGUET 103

1 (0) ITALY
DELVECCHIO 55

Date: 2 July 2000
Attendance: 48,200
Venue: De Kuip Stadium, Rotterdam

Billed as a classic game of French attack versus stout Italian defense, the Italians turned out to give as good as they got, creating chances which weren't converted until the second half when a Francesco Totti backheel released Gianluca Pessotto down the right whose cross was volleyed in from close range. France substituted the quiet Dugarry for Sylvain Wiltord and it was his last gasp equalizer in the third minute of added on time at the end of the match that sent the game into extra time. Francesco Toldo in the Italian goal had been resolute throughout and in extra time needed treatment after making a superb save from a close range effort by Robert Pires. It was Pires in the 103rd minute of the game who pulled back the ball to David Trezeguet who thundered a first time shot into the roof of the net. Trezeguet's golden goal meant that France had become the first reigning world champions to also hold the European crown.

De Kuip Stadium, Rotterdam

PORTUGAL 2004

Cristiano Ronaldo nails his first international goal, but it was not enough to beat Greece, even after their 24 year absence.

Portugal was awarded the right to host EURO 2004 in 1999 beating bids from Spain and a combined bid from Austria and Hungary.

Also fresh to the pitch were newcomers Latvia, who qualified after defeating Turkey in the play-offs and then caused an upset by showing great resilience to draw with Germany. A final group game between old foes Germany and the Czech Republic saw the former crash out of the tournament. They were not alone amongst the supposed favorites, however, as Italy and Spain also failed to get out of their group, whilst Greece sneaked through in second place ahead of Spain and Russia after Portugal had rallied and won their final two group games.

The Portuguese knocked out England via a penalty shootout with their goalkeeper, Ricardo, proving a double hero by saving Darius Vassell's attempt and then scoring the winning penalty. They were joined in the semi-finals by the Netherlands who won their first penalty shootout at a major competition, versus Sweden, and by Greece who shocked France with a display of defensive resilience to win 1-0. The same scoreline would see Otto Rehhagel's side reach the final, defeating a technically-gifted Czech Republic team who had beaten Denmark comfortably 3-0 in the quarter finals. There, they would be joined by the hosts for whom Cristiano Ronaldo opened the scoring in the first half followed by a screaming shot

from Maniche from the corner of the penalty area. With Ruud van Nistelrooy isolated in attack, the Netherlands' consolation goal came from an own goal by Jorge Andrade.

Top Left: Bulgaria's Zdravko Lazarov (R) is tackled by Italy's Gianluca Zambrotta.
Top Right: Portugal's Cristiano Ronaldo (R) reacts as teammate Luis Figo walks away during their match against Greece. Above: Greece's Antonios Nikopolidis in action with Pauleta (Portugal). Opposite Top: Angelos Charisteas heads in the winner for Greece in the final vs Portugal. Bottom: Theo Zagorakis of Greece lifts the trophy.

2004 UEFA EUROPEAN CHAMPIONSHIP

Host country	Portugal
Dates	12 June – 4 July
Teams	16
Venues	10 (in 8 host cities)
Matches played	31
Goals scored	77
Top scorer	Milan Baroš (5 goals)
Attendance	1,156,473 (37,306 per match)
Champions	Greece
Runners-up	Portugal
Semi-finalists	Netherlands
	Czech Republic

THE FINAL

1 (0) GREECE
CHARISTEAS 57

0 (0) PORTUGAL

Date: 4 July 2004
Attendance: 62,865
Venue: Estádio da Luz, Lisbon

The final marked the first time that the same two teams had contested the opening and closing fixture of the UEFA European Championships. Portugal, on home ground, were firm favorites against a team ranked at 120/1 to win the tournament at its outset. Luis Felipe Scolari left top scorer, Nuno Gomes, on the bench but still possessed in Luis Figo, Maniche, Deco and Ronaldo a formidable attacking force.

The Portuguese side had 17 shots on goal compared to Greece's four but were often wayward or brought out the best in the opposing goalkeeper, Antonis Nikopolidis, who made a number of solid saves. Greece didn't even gain a corner until the second half and it proved to be their only one throughout the game. They made it count, though, as the ball in from Angelis Basinas was headed firmly into the back of the net by Angelos Charisteas. Highly organized in defense, Greece had to weather a storm of attacking intent, but Luis Figo's missed chance in the 89th minute was their last scare, replaced with tears of joy and disbelief at the final whistle for a fairy-tale ending for a team that until the tournament's start had never won a match at a EUROs finals.

Estádio da Luz, Lisbon

AUSTRIA AND SWITZERLAND 2008

The 13th EUROs was the second to be co-hosted. Sixteen teams qualified, the hosts automatically. England was notably absent and Russia, newcomers in 2004, were in the game. The Cup winners would lift a new 8-kg Henri Delaunay trophy created by London jewelers Asprey.

With the group games often tight, surprises were in store. Unusually, three of the four group winners: Croatia, Spain and the Netherlands were victorious in all three of their games. At the other end of the spectrum, France endured a dismal tournament, thrashed 4-1 by the Netherlands as they finished bottom of Group C. Neither of the hosts progressed out of their groups although Switzerland did at least win a game, beating Group A winners, Portugal 2-0.

Turkey proved a surprise package and specialized in stirring, late finishes. Arda Turan scored in the second minute of extra time to defeat Switzerland, whilst against the Czech Republic Nihat Kahveci struck twice in two minutes (the 87th and 89th) to win a thriller, 3-2. Turkey continued to provide late entertainment in the knockout rounds, scoring in effectively the 122nd minute at the very end of extra time to force a shootout with Croatia which they won. They even equalized late in the semi-final in the 86th minute but could not stop Germany via a 90th minute goal from Philipp Lahm, from reaching the final. Their opponents there, Spain, save for a penalty shootout over Italy in the quarters, had made relatively serene progress through the tournament, winning every game and only conceding three goals whilst scoring 11 in return.

Top Left: Turkey's Nihat Kahveci shoots to score his second goal against Czech Republic. Top Right: Trix and Flix, Euro 2008 mascots. Above: Spain's Iker Casillas saves a shot during the penalty shoot-out against Italy. Opposite Top: Spain's Fernando Torres is swamped by teammates David Silva, Andrés Iniesta, Joan Capdevila, and Xavi after scoring during their EURO 2008 final soccer match against Germany. Bottom: Fernando Torres scores past Germany's goalkeeper Jens Lehmann during their EURO 2008 final.

2008 UEFA EUROPEAN CHAMPIONSHIP

Host country	Austria and Switzerland
Dates	7 June – 29 June
Teams	16
Venues	8 (in 8 host cities)
Matches played	31
Goals scored	77
Top scorer	David Villa (4 goals)
Attendance	1,140,902 (36,803 per match)
Champions	Spain
Runners-up	Germany
Semi-finalists	Russia
	Turkey

THE FINAL

1 (0) SPAIN
TORRES 33

0 (0) GERMANY

Date: 29 June 2008
Attendance: 51,428
Venue: Ernst Happel Stadion, Vienna

Turkey proved a surprise package and specialized in stirring, late finishes. Arda Turan scored in the second minute of extra time to defeat Switzerland, and then whilst against the Czech Republic, Nihat Kahveci struck twice in two minutes (the 87th and 89th) to win a thriller, 3-2. The Turks continued to provide late entertainment in the knockout rounds, scoring in effectively the 122nd minute at the very end of extra time to force a shootout with Croatia which they won. They even equalized late in the semi-final in the 86th minute but could not stop Germany via a 90th minute goal from Philipp Lahm, from reaching the final. Their opponents there, Spain, save for a penalty shootout over Italy in the quarters, had made relatively serene progress through the tournament, winning every game and only conceding three goals whilst scoring 11 in return.

Ernst Happel Stadion, Vienna

POLAND & UKRAINE 2012

EURO 2012 featured rousing football and mostly good player discipline. Only four penalties and four red cards were awarded throughout the entire tournament.

Poland and Ukraine built five new stadiums between them to co-host the last UEFA European Championships to feature 16 teams (24 teams will contest EURO 2016).

Co-hosts Poland and Ukraine had to update their infrastructure considerably, building five stadiums between them. Nevertheless they were eliminated at the group stage as were the surprise underperformers, the Netherlands who didn't muster a single point from their three Group B games. Russia were the unluckiest at the group stage possessing the same qualifying points as Greece and a superior goal difference, but losing out because of their head to head record which had seen Greece defeat them 1-0. Topping their group, Group A, was the Czech Republic who became the first group winners at a EUROs tournament to qualify with a negative goal difference.

The Czech Republic and another group winner, England, both fell at the quarter final stage whilst Germany gave one of the performances of the tournament in beating a spirited Greece side, 4-2. Joachim Low's team entered the semi-finals in good spirits but were undone by Italy for whom Andrea Pirlo gave a playmaking masterclass whilst Mario Balotelli showed his explosive class,

scoring both goals in their 2-1 victory. In the other semi-final, Spain and Portugal contested a hard-fought draw that resulted in a penalty shootout. Both teams missed their first penalty but Cesc Fàbregas would go on to score the winning penalty to take Spain into the final for the second time in a row.

Top Left: Juan Mata is mobbed by teammates after he scores the fourth goal for Spain. Top Right: Official UEFA Euro 2012 mascots Slavek (L) and Slavko before the Poland vs Greece game. Above: Mario Balotelli scores the second goal for Italy against Germany. Opposite Top: Poland's Wojciech Szczesny fouls on Greece's Dimitris Salpingidis for which the keeper is shown a red card. Bottom: Ukraine's Andriy Shevchenko scores his second goal during their Group D game against Sweden.

2012 UEFA EUROPEAN CHAMPIONSHIP

Host country	Poland and Ukraine
Dates	8 June – 1 July
Teams	16
Venues	8 (in 8 host cities)
Matches played	31
Goals scored	76
Top scorer	Mario Mandžukić, Mario Gómez, Cristiano Ronaldo, Mario Balotelli, Fernando Torres, Alan Yelizbarovich Dzagoev (3 goals)
Attendance	1,140,902 (36,803 per match)
Champions	Spain
Runners-up	Italy
Semi-finalists	Germany
	Portugal

THE FINAL

4 (2) SPAIN
SILVA 14, ALBA 41
TORRES 84, MATA 88

0 (0) ITALY

EURO 2012
POLAND-UKRAINE

Date: 1 July 2012
Attendance: 63,170
Venue: Olympic Stadium, Kiev

Spain entered the final with the experience gleaned from seven of their eleven starters seeing play in the previous final. A header from the unexpected source of diminutive midfielder, David Silva got Vicente del Bosque's team rolling in the 14th minute and a weary Italian side lost their tigerish defender, Giorgio Chiellini, to injury seven minutes later. Passing and pressure took their toll late in the half when Xavi's precise pass picked out Spanish full back Jordi Alba who struck an equally precise shot past Italian goalkeeper, Gianluigi Buffon.

The uphill battle got steeper for the Italians in the 62nd minute when Thiago Motta was injured and stretchered off. With all three substitutes already deployed by Cesare Prandelli, the Italians had to play on for over a quarter of the game with just ten men. In contrast, Spain were able to field three fresh, second half substitutes that could exploit Italian fatigue. Two of whom, Juan Mata and Fernando Torres scored, the latter becoming the first to score in two EURO final matches.

Olympic Stadium, Kiev

UEFA European Championship Records Second Half

Spain's soccer fans cheer during their EURO 2012 final soccer match against Italy.

RECORD CROWDS

The highest and lowest attendance at a European Championship match occurred at the same tournament in 1964. The Hungary v Denmark game attracted a mere 3,869 spectators who rattled around the mighty Camp Nou stadium, home to Barcelona. The final, held at Real Madrid's Bernabéu stadium, saw a record 79,115 fans watch Spain beat the Soviet Union.

EURO 2012 holds the record for the highest tournament attendance with 1,440,846 fans at games. Of these, England and Sweden's Group D game was the best attended, with 64,640 present.

YOUNGEST AND OLDEST

Dutch defender Jetro Willems became the youngest player in Euro Champs history when he played against Denmark at EURO 2012 aged 18 years, 71 days. It was his first ever game for the Netherlands. The youngest goalscorer in the championship's history was Switzerland's Johan Vonlanthen Benavídez who scored in 2004 versus France aged 18 years and 141 days.

The youngest player to play in a EURO final was Cristiano Ronaldo. He was just 19 years and 150 days old when he faced Greece in UEFA EURO 2004. In the previous tournament, Portugal faced the competition's oldest ever player when German legend, Lothar Matthäus lined up against them as a sweeper at the age of 39 years and 91 days. Matthäus also holds the record for the longest span of tournament appearances, 20 years and 6 days, after appearing at the 1980 UEFA European Championship and then the 1984, 1988 and 2000 competitions.

Jetro Willems, Holland (vs Portugal 2012)

PENALTY SHOOTOUTS

There have been 15 penalty shootouts at UEFA European Championships between 1976 and 2012. The most penalties taken in a shootout was 18 in Czechoslovakia's 9-8 win on penalties in the third place play-off game at EURO 1980. The most players to miss in a shootout occurred at EURO 2000 where three Dutch players (Frank de Boer, Japp Stam and Paul Bosvelt) and one Italian (Paolo Maldini) all missed during the semi-final.

DISCIPLINARY RECORDS

Greek defender Georgios Karagounis holds the record for the most cautions (yellow cards) received at UEFA European Championships with a total of eight collected at EURO 2004, 2008 and 2012. He wasn't alone at EURO 2004 where a record 154 yellow cards were brandished by referees, the most of any tournament whilst the previous competition, EURO 2000, saw the most red cards awarded in a tournament – a total of ten. These included the dismissal of Portugal's Nuno Gomes for pushing the referee after the semi-final versus France was decided by a golden goal in the 117th minute in favor of the French. A Frenchman at EURO 2008, Éric Abidal holds the record for the fastest red card received at the tournament when he was sent off after just 24 minutes.

Greece's Georgios Karagounis (C) talks to Ivory Coast's Didier Drogba after a foul on Andreas Samaris.

QUALIFYING RECORDS

The Republic of Ireland and Hungary have played more EURO qualifying matches than any other teams, 121 games in total. The most successful qualifiers have been the Soviet Union (and Russia) with 11 successes out of 15 attempts, followed by Spain with 10 appearances.

In terms of qualifying ratios, Croatia have only failed to qualify once in six attempts (in 2000). Four teams have played more than 100 qualifying matches and have yet to qualify for the tournament: Luxembourg (109 matches), Malta (102), Cyprus (104) and Finland (104), the latter team also holding the record of most qualifying wins (27) without reaching the finals.

QUALIFYING WINNERS AND LOSERS

Spain have scored the most goals (283) and won the most qualifying games – 81 in all – whilst three nations: Andorra, San Marino and Gibraltar have yet to win a single qualifying game. Unlike the other two minnows, San Marino have registered one draw, but have conceded 289 goals in their 66 qualifying games. The record, though, is held by Luxembourg who have let in 303 goals yet scored only 44 in their 109 matches.

Poland's Robert Lewandowski during the 2016 group D qualification game against Republic of Ireland

PENALTY SHOOTOUTS

There have been 15 penalty shootouts at UEFA European Championships between 1976 and 2012. The most penalties taken in a shootout was 18 in Czechoslovakia's 9-8 win on penalties in the third place play-off game at EURO 1980. The most players to miss in a shootout occurred at EURO 2000 where three Dutch players (Frank de Boer, Japp Stam and Paul Bosvelt) and one Italian (Paolo Maldini) all missed during the semi-final.

Team	Played	Win	Loss	% Win
Czech Republic	3	3	0	100%
Turkey	1	1	0	100%
Spain	4	3	1	75%
Italy	4	2	2	50%
Denmark	2	1	1	50%
France	2	1	1	50%
Portugal	2	1	1	50%
Germany	2	1	1	50%
England	4	1	3	25%
Netherlands	4	1	3	25%
Croatia	1	0	1	0%
Sweden	1	0	1	0%

Arkadiusz Milik, Poland

EURO 2016 QUALIFYING

Qualifying games for EURO 2016 resulted in 694 goals being scored. Poland's Robert Lewandowski notched the most with 13 goals whilst the most goals scored in any one game was 9 during Poland's 8-1 thrashing of Gibraltar.

Leading Goalscorers EURO 2016 Qualifying

13	Robert Lewandowski	Poland
11	Zlatan Ibrahimović	Sweden
9	Thomas Müller	Germany
8	Artem Dzyuba	Russia
8	Edin Džeko	Bosnia and Herzegovina
7	Wayne Rooney	England
7	Marc Janko	Austria
7	Kyle Lafferty	Northern Ireland

Leading Assist Makers EURO 2016 Qualifying

6	Vladimír Weiss	Slovakia
6	Arkadiusz Milik	Poland
6	Senad Lulić	Bosnia and Herzegovina
5	Xherdan Shaqiri	Switzerland
4	Breel Embolo	Switzerland
4	Niall McGinn	Northern Ireland
4	Mesut Özil	Germany
4	Shaun Maloney	Scotland

INTERNATIONAL COMPETITIONS

"THE MORE DIFFICULT THE VICTORY, THE GREATER THE HAPPINESS IN WINNING." - PELÉ

Copa América

South America was the first continent to have a competition between its national teams. A one-off tournament to celebrate an Argentinean national holiday had been held between Argentina, Uruguay and Chile in 1910. Six years later, a four team competition featuring the 1910 sides plus Brazil was organized and during the tournament, the South American Football Association — CONEMBOL — was formed.

The Campeonato Sudamericano de Fútbol (South American Football Championship) as it was originally called, has been held in a wide variety of formats and numbers of teams as other South American countries joined in the competition. At times, this led to an imbalance in team quality and lopsided results, the record being Argentina's 12-0 mauling of Ecuador in 1943 and their 11-0 thrashing of Venezuela in 1975. As professionalism increased, games have tended to get tighter and more competitive.

The competition was officially named the Copa América in 1975 and until 1987 did not feature a single tournament host as games were played home and away in the different countries. The competition has had to contend with plenty of disputes, low attendances when the host nation wasn't playing, financial problems, and issues with clubs releasing players, and the increasing draw of international club competitions. Yet its appeal has endured as witnessed by the 170,000 fans in Brazil's Maracanã stadium for the final of the 1989 edition and the more than a million spectators who came to watch games at the 2007 tournament.

Big Three Dominance

The competition has been dominated by the big three South American nations of Argentina, Brazil and Uruguay and it wasn't until the 16th competition that another country, Peru, won the competition. Argentina leads the way with 15 championships, closely followed by Uruguay with 14 victories and then, somewhat surprisingly, given their prowess on the international stage at the World Cup, Brazil with just six titles. Both of the Copa's leading goalscorers hail from the big three with Argentina's Norberto Méndez and Brazilian attacker, Zizinho tied on 17 goals with Teodoro Fernández of Peru and Severino Varela of Uruguay joint second with 15 goals each.

New Invitees

Pressure to attract greater sponsorship and television coverage saw CONMEBOL alter the format of the Copa in 1993. The tournament was expanded to twelve sides which involved inviting two national teams from CONCACAF (Confederation of North, Central America and Caribbean Association Football), which for the first edition,

were Mexico and the USA. Mexico have remained the most frequent invitees with nine shows, and the most successful with three third place finishes (1997, 1999 and 2007) and two appearances in the final, in 1993 and 2001. Other CONCACAF invitees include Costa Rica and Honduras who caused a massive shock at the 2001 Copa by knocking out Brazil 2-0 at the quarter final stage and then beating Uruguay to finish third. Japan were also invited to attend the tournament in 1999 whilst in 2015, Jamaica made their first appearance at the competition.

21st Century Copa

The first Copa of a new century saw shocks with Argentina withdrawing from the competition after security concerns and Colombia, propelled by the goals of Víctor Aristizábal, who became the tournament top scorer, a strong defense and Iván Córdoba's 65th minute goal, took the competition for the first time.

The 43rd Copa América of the competition in 2011 contained many shocks and surprises. In a tournament featuring world class strikers such as Lionel Messi, Luis Suárez, Sergio Agüero and Neymar, it was Peru's Paolo Guerrero who top scored as his side finished third, beating Venezuela 4-1 in a play-off game. Neither Argentina nor Brazil reached the semi-finals but unheralded Paraguay did, despite not winning a single game in regulation game time as all their victories came via penalty shootouts. Paraguay's run was ended by the form team of the tournament, Uruguay, and their dynamic strike partnership of Luis Suárez and Diego Forlán.

The 2015 Copa América in Chile attracted smaller crowds than recent tournaments but great public and media attention as Brazil were knocked out in the quarter finals by Paraguay whilst the hosts vanquished cup-holders Uruguay at the same stage, courtesy of a Mauricio Isla goal. After sneaking past Colombia via a shootout in the quarters, Argentina announced themselves as firm favorites by thrashing Paraguay 6-1, yet were undone in the final by Chile on penalties with Alexis Sánchez dispatching the winning attempt with a cheeky Panenka-styled soft chip down the middle. It was Chile's third final but the first time they won the competition, albeit slightly bittersweet for their head coach, Jorge Sampaoli, who is Argentinean.

An agreement between CONCACAF and CONMEBOL resulted in a special edition of the tournament, the Copa América Centenario, held to commemorate 100 years since the very first tournament. Held in June-July 2016 in the United States at 10 different stadiums, the tournament featured an expanded field of 16 national teams with all 10 members of CONMEBOL including defending champions, Chile, as well as six teams from the North, Central American and Caribbean region.

SOUTH AMERICAN CHAMPIONSHIP /COPA AMÉRICA FINALS

Year	Winner	Score	Runner-Up
1910	Argentina	4-1	Uruguay
1916	Uruguay	0-0	Argentina
1917	Uruguay	1-0	Argentina
1919	Brazil	1-0, 2-2	Uruguay
1920	Uruguay	1-1	Argentina
1921	Argentina	1-0	Brazil
1922	Brazil	3-0, 1-1	Paraguay
1923	Uruguay	2-0	Argentina
1924	Uruguay	0-0	Argentina
1925	Argentina	2-2, 4-1	Brazil
1926	Uruguay	2-0	Argentina
1927	Argentina	3-2	Uruguay
1929	Argentina	4-1	Paraguay
1935	Uruguay	3-0	Argentina
1937	Argentina	1-0, 2-0	Brazil
1939	Peru	2-1	Uruguay
1941	Argentina	2-1	Uruguay
1942	Uruguay	1-0	Argentina
1945	Argentina	3-1	Brazil
1947	Argentina	6-0	Paraguay
1949	Brazil	1-2, 7-0	Paraguay
1953	Paraguay	2-1, 3-2	Brazil
1955	Argentina	1-0	Chile
1956	Uruguay	2-1	Chile
1957	Argentina	3-0	Brazil
1958	Argentina	1-1	Brazil
1959	Uruguay	5-0	Argentina
1963	Bolivia	2-0	Paraguay
1967	Uruguay	1-0	Argentina
1975	Peru	2-1*	Colombia
1979	Paraguay	3-0, 0-1	Chile
1983	Uruguay	2-0, 1-1	Brazil
1987	Uruguay	1-0	Chile
1989	Brazil	1-0	Uruguay
1991	Argentina	3-2	Brazil
1993	Argentina	2-1	Mexico
1995	Uruguay	1-1 (5-3 pen)	Brazil
1997	Brazil	3-1	Bolivia
1999	Brazil	3-0	Uruguay
2001	Colombia	1-0	Mexico
2004	Brazil	2-2	Argentina
2007	Brazil	3-0	Argentina
2011	Uruguay	3-0	Paraguay
2015	Chile	0-0 (4-1 pen)	Argentina

* held over three games (0-1, 2-0, 0-0)

Opposite page: Alexis Sánchez holds the Copa América trophy as he celebrates with his teammates following their victory over Argentina. Left: Chile's Alexis Sánchez and Argentina's Marcos Rojo during the Copa América 2015 final.

African Nations Cup

It started small with just three teams – Egypt, Sudan and Ethiopia – competing in Sudan in 1957 in an explosive final when Egypt triumphed 4-0 over Ethiopia with all goals scored by Mohamed Diab Al-Attar – a standing record. The tournament has grown into Africa's premier international competition and one followed widely around the world due to the presence of many top-flight footballers playing for their countries.

Champions

Despite spells of dominance by teams like Ghana in the 1960s and Cameroon in the 1980s, only one nation has won three African Cup of Nations in a row – Egypt. Fourteen different countries in total have won the African Cup of Nations with champions drawn from all over the continent. Northern champions include Tunisia, Morocco, Algeria and seven times winners, Egypt. South Africa won in 1996, the first year they were re-admitted to the tournament after being barred for the country's policy of apartheid. In 2002, Cameroon became the first team in 37 years to defend and retain the title when they beat Senegal 3-2 on penalties after the game had ended 0-0. It is one of eight finals so far that have gone to a shootout, the latest in 2015. The 1992 final was especially notable as the first final of a major international competition in which all 11 players on the pitch, including goalkeepers, took penalties as Ivory Coast finally defeated Ghana 11-10 after 24 penalties had been taken.

Only one final has been decided by a replay – the 1974 tournament decider held in Egypt in which Zaire's Pierre Ndaye Mulamba scored two goals in the 2-2 draw versus Zambia and then, a further two goals two days later in the replay to see his country home 2-0. His record of nine goals in a single African Cup of Nations remains a competition record whilst Samuel Eto'o holds the record for goals overall with a total of 18.

Cup of Nations Qualifying

As the tournament has increased in importance and interest and the number of independent nations in Africa has risen, so the numbers of teams striving to gain a place at the tournament has grown; 51 teams, for example, entered qualifying for the 2015 tournament. Participation at the tournament was increased slowly – from three to four teams in 1962, up to six teams the following year and then boosted to eight places in 1968.

The eight team tournament format stayed in place until 1992 by which time 34 teams entered qualifying. Since 1996 though, Africa's premier tournament has offered places for 16 national teams. In 1982, the continent's football governing body, the Confederation of African Football (CAF) removed the two-player per team limit on foreign based players allowing countries to select the best footballers,

but issues sometimes remain over recalling foreign-based players, especially star performers from big clubs in the European leagues. Qualifying can remain tough and 2010 champions Egypt failed to make it to either the 2012 or 2013 edition of the tournament. In contrast, Botswana, Equatorial Guinea and Niger reached the tournament for the first time 2012 whilst Cape Verde debuted in 2013. Sixteen nations including Somalia, Chad, Gambia and Djibouti have never qualified for the competition. Their number also include South Sudan, the continent's newest nation, which took part in qualifying for the first time in 2015.

2012, 2013 and 2015 / Recent Tournaments

The latest editions of the tournament have featured some outstanding football as well as drama, tight games and shocks and surprises. There was an emotional triumph for Zambia, who had twice been

Above: Cameroon's Samuel Eto'o (C) is challenged by Tunisia's Issam Jemâa (L) and Hocine Ragued. Opposite Top: Yaya Touré (C) celebrates with teammates winning the 2015 African Nations Cup final against Ghana. Bottom Left: A Ghana fan cheers during their African Nations Cup semi-final game. Far Right: Egyptian soccer players celebrate with their trophy after defeating Ivory Coast in a penalty shoot out at the African Nations Cup final, 2006.

runners-up, in 2012, winning an 18 penalty shootout against the Ivory Coast in the final which was held in Libreville, the capital city of Gabon, and mere kilometres from where 18 members of the 1993 Zambian African Cup of Nations squad plus seven coaches and officials were killed in a plane crash.

The tournament was switched to odd years after 2012 to avoid clashes with the FIFA World Cup. The 2013 tournament, eventually held in South Africa, after original hosts, Libya could not stage the competition due to civil war, saw two highly touted sides in Tunisia and Ivory Coast exit early whilst highly unfancied Burkina Faso staged a stirring progression through the rounds, inspired by the player of the tournament, Jonathan Pitroipa. Burkina Faso

defeated Ethiopia, Togo and a strong Ghanaian side to reach the final against Nigeria who had overcome Mali 4-1 in the other semi-final. Sunday Mba's sumptuous volley in the 40th minute gave Nigeria their first championship in 19 years.

The 2015 tournament was to be held in Morocco but fears concerning the spread of the Ebola virus epidemic saw it eventually staged in Equatorial Guinea. Previous finalists Burkina Faso finished bottom of their group as did Cameroon and South Africa. Ghana overcame the hosts in the semi-final 3-0 with their second goal by Mubarak Wakaso notable as the African Cup of Nations' 1,500th goal. They could not, however, prevail over the Ivory Coast in the final and had to settle with their fifth runners-up placing – a tournament record.

AFRICAN CUP OF NATIONS WINNERS

Year	Champions
1957	Egypt
1959	Egypt
1962	Ethiopia
1963	Ghana
1965	Ghana
1968	Congo-Kinshasa
1970	Sudan
1972	Congo-Brazzaville
1974	Zaire
1976	Morocco
1978	Ghana
1980	Nigeria
1982	Ghana
1984	Cameroon
1986	Egypt
1988	Cameroon
1990	Algeria
1992	Ivory Coast
1994	Nigeria
1996	South Africa
1998	Egypt
2000	Cameroon
2002	Cameroon
2004	Tunisia
2006	Egypt
2008	Egypt
2010	Egypt
2012	Zambia
2013	Nigeria
2015	Ivory Coast

Asian Games and AFC Asian Cup

Asian football is represented by two international competitions since the 1950s when the Asian Cup was founded by the fledgling Asian Football Confederation (AFC). The first competition featured seven of the 12 founding AFC members in a tournament held in Hong Kong.

The AFC Asian Cup

The early competitions featured a finals tournament for just four teams which was expanded to six in 1972 when a semi-finals and final match were introduced. Iran won that competition as well as the 1968 Asian Cup and have been ever-present at the tournament between 1968 and 2015. Along with South Korea, they have played in the most Asian Cup finals games, 62 in total. The 1980s saw the Middle East region dominate with victories for Kuwait and Saudi Arabia before Japan embarked on a period of four victories in six tournaments. Japan's third title came at the 2004 tournament hosted in China which saw almost one million spectators attend matches.

In a continent where political rivalries have sometimes spilled over into much more, withdrawals and boycotts have occasionally blighted the competition. Former champions, Israel were expelled from the Asian Football Confederation in 1975 and would later join UEFA whilst political disputes before the 1992 Asian Cup saw 14 teams refuse to enter the tournament. The Iranians played a fractious 1992 tournament where three of their players had received one year bans behind them to emerge victorious at the following competition, also winning the fair play award and possessing the tournament's highest goalscorer in Ali Daei. As the tournament has grown in prestige, so the number of places available at the competition has risen, to 10 in 1980, 12 in 1996 and 16 in 2004. The 2019 tournament, hosted by the United Arab Emirates, will be expanded from 16 teams to 24 teams, with the qualifying process also acting as part of the qualification process for the 2018 FIFA World Cup.

Australian Impact

Australia left the Oceania Football Confederation (OFC) in 2006, citing a lack of competition, to join the AFC. They entered their first Asian Cup the following year in a tournament co-hosted by four nations: Thailand, Indonesia, Malaysia and Vietnam, the latter making their tournament debut like Australia. The Socceroos have since finished runners-up in the 2011 competition and hosted the 2015 tournament where over 705,000 spectators watched the 32 games at a tournament which saw Palestine make their Asian Cup debut.

Bouyed by five goals from tournament top scorer, Ali Mabkhout, the United Arab Emirates reached the semi-finals where they were defeated 2-0 by Australia for whom Trent Sainsbury and Jason Davidson scored within the first quarter of an hour. With a 2–0 victory over Uzbekistan in the quarter finals, South Korea set a

tournament record for appearing in ten semi-finals. The South Koreans, coached by German legend and EURO 1980 winner, Uli Stielike, eased past Iraq 2-0 to contest the final against Australia, a game watched by 76,385 spectators inside Sydney's Stadium Australia. The hosts scored twice to take their tally to 14 goals and become the tournament's leading scorers as they won their first AFC Asian Cup. One of their scorers in the final, Massimo Luongo who plays his club football for Queens Park Rangers in the English Championship, won the player of the tournament award.

Football At The Asian Games

The Asian Games is a multi-sport competition featuring a wide range of sports. The 2014 games, held in South Korea, featured typical Olympic sports such as athletics, cycling and gymnastics along with sports of an Asian origination including Kabaddi and the Chinese traditional martial art of Wushu. Football has been a part of the games since the inaugural Asian Games in 1951 where six teams: India (who played barefoot in the first competition), Burma, Iran, Indonesia, Afghanistan and Japan competed in matches which according to

Above: Iraq's Saad Abdulameer (L) fights for the ball against Iran's Sardar Azmoun. Opposite, clockwise from Top Left: Japan's Shinji Kagawa and Qatar's Mesaad Al-Hamad in action, 2011 Asian Cup quarter-final. Australia's captain Mile Jedinak holds the Asian Cup trophy as the team celebrate winning their 2015 Asian Cup final against South Korea. Iraq's soccer players pose for a team photo before their final match against Saudi Arabia in 2007. Uzbekistan's Vitaliy Denisov (L) is tackled by North Korea's Cha Jong-Hyok.

the football statistical organisation RSSSF, lasted just 60 minutes in duration. Games were extended to 80 minutes at the May, 1954 tournament the year that the Asian Football Confederation (AFC) was formed.

Early tournament successes by India, Burma and Taiwan left South Korea runners-up on three occasions and Iran on two. Both would go on to win the competition, Iran on three occasions and South Korea on four including the most recent edition in 2014 in which 29 national teams competed including East Timor for the first time. Since the 2002 Asian Games, the squad selection rules mirror the Olympics with the vast majority of each team under 23 years of age but with up to three over-23 players allowed. A women's tournament at the Asian Games kicked off in 1990 and has seen China and North Korea dominate winning three championships each with only Japan in 2010 breaking the monopoly.

ASIAN CUP WINNERS

Year	Winners	Runners-Up
1956	South Korea	Israel
1960	South Korea	Israel
1964	Israel	India
1968	Iran	Burma
1972	Iran	South Korea
1976	Iran	Kuwait
1980	Kuwait	South Korea
1984	Saudi Arabia	China
1988	Saudi Arabia	South Korea
1992	Japan	Saudi Arabia
1996	Saudi Arabia	UAE
2000	Japan	Saudi Arabia
2004	Japan	China
2007	Iraq	Saudi Arabia
2011	Japan	Australia
2015	Australia	South Korea

ASIAN GAMES WINNERS

Year	Champions
1951	India
1954	Taiwan
1958	Taiwan
1962	India
1966	Burma
1970	Burma & S. Korea (shared)
1974	Iran
1978	N. Korea, S. Korea (shared)
1982	Iraq
1986	South Korea
1990	Iran
1994	Uzbekistan
1998	Iran
2002	Iran
2006	Qatar
2010	Japan
2014	South Korea

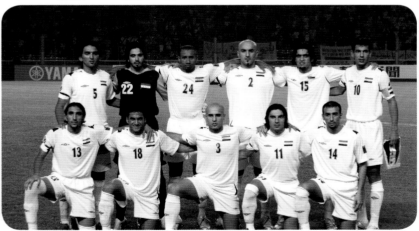

INTERNATIONAL COMPETITIONS

CONCACAF Gold Cup

The Caribbean nations along with those of North America and Central America compete in a mostly biannual tournament which since 1991 has been called the CONCACAF Gold Cup.

Tournament Beginnings

Two associations once governed the region. The North American Football Confederation (NAFC) contained the United States, Canada, Mexico and Cuba as members whilst most of the rest of the region was administered by the Confederación Centroamericana y del Caribe de Fútbol (CCCF) which was founded in 1938. Both organisations founded their own regional competition with Costa Rica dominant in the CCCF Championship winning seven of the ten championships held between 1941 and 1961.

The two organisations merged in 1961 to form The Confederation of North, Central America and Caribbean Association Football (CONCACAF). The first CONCACAF Championship was held in 1963 and featured a five team and a four team group with the top four sides entering a further round-robin mini-league from which Costa Rica emerged triumphant. The tournaments that followed mostly featured six teams whilst between 1973 and 1989, the competition acted as qualifying for the CONCACAF region's entries to the FIFA World Cup.

In 1991, the year after the election of Jack Warner as President of CONCACAF, the championships was revised and rebadged as the CONCACAF Gold Cup. Twenty-eight nations competed for the qualifying places available at the eight team tournament which was hosted in the United States, with the Gold Cup awarded in the Los Angeles Coliseum in front of around 39,000 spectators when the United States defeated Honduras on penalties.

Invited Guests

Six teams from outside the region have been invited to take part in the competition. The first, Brazil, sent an Under 23 team to the 1996 tournament under the tutelage of World Cup winning player and coach, Mário Zagallo. The Brazilians thrashed Honduras 5-0, defeated the United States in the semi-final but lost to Mexico 2-0 in the final. They returned in 1998 (where they finished third) and 2003 when they were again runners-up.

In 2000, the tournament numbers were expanded from 10 to 12 with invitations going out to three non-CONCACAF teams: South Korea from the Asian Football Confederation and CONMEBOL members, Colombia and Peru. South Korea failed to make it out of their group although this came down to a coin toss which they lost after the Asian side found themselves tied on points and goal difference with the eventual champions, Canada. The two South American teams fared better with Peru reaching the semi-finals where they were beaten by eventual runners-up Colombia who themselves, had defeated the United States in a low-scoring shootout by two penalties to one after their quarter final match was drawn 2-2. South Korea returned to the Gold Cup in 2002 along with Ecuador whilst at the 2005 edition, Colombia returned and reached the semi-finals whilst South Africa made it to the quarter-finals.

Mexico v USA

The overwhelming story of the CONCACAF Gold Cup era has been of a two way battle between North American rivals, Mexico and the United States. All 13 tournaments so far have been hosted in the USA or co-hosted by the USA and either Canada or Mexico, and save for Canada's triumph in 2000, have been won by Mexico (7 times) or the USA (5 times). Whilst Mexican fans recall several dominating wins over their rivals such as the comprehensive 5-0 victory in the 2011 Gold Cup final, the United States hold the record for most semi-final participations with 12. Mexico's Luis Roberto Alves holds the record for the most goals scored at a single Gold Cup (11) with seven of his strikes coming in a single game – Mexico's 9-0 mauling of Martinique. His total tally of Gold Cup goals was overtaken by the USA's Landon Donovan who has scored 18 goals in total.

The 2015 Gold Cup

Fourteen venues were used for the 2015 Gold Cup including BMO Field in Toronto, Canada – the first time that that country had hosted Gold Cup finals matches. A record 1,090,282 tickets were sold for the games in a tournament occasionally marred by poor refereeing decisions and off-field drama including threatened player strikes by a Jamaican team who would go on to shake up the tournament by knocking the United States out in a tense 2-1 victory. It was Jamaica's second ever win over the USA who included the tournament's top scorer in Clint Dempsey with seven goals, and the first time a Caribbean nation had made it to the Gold Cup final. The "Reggae Boyz" were beaten 3-1 in the final by Mexico for whom, Andrés Guardado was awarded the Golden Ball as the tournament's most outstanding player. Panama, who defeated the USA in the third place play-off game, qualified for the Copa América Centenario in 2016 as a result. So did, Haiti, Cuba and Trinidad and Tobago.

Opposite Top: Landon Donovan (U.S.) shoots and scores from a penalty shot against El Salvador. Bottom Left: Matt Besler of the U.S. leaps over Blas Pérez of Panama during the second half of the CONCACAF Gold Cup final. Far Right: Jamaica midfielder Garath McCleary and Mexico defender Oswaldo Alanís compete for a header during the second half of the CONCACAF Gold Cup final.

CONCACAF CHAMPIONSHIP / CONCACAF GOLD CUP CHAMPIONS AND RUNNERS UP

Year	Winner	Runner-Up
1963	Costa Rica	El Salvador
1965	Mexico	Guatemala
1967	Guatemala	Mexico
1969	Costa Rica	Guatemala
1971	Mexico	Haiti
1973	Haiti	Trinidad & Tobago
1977	Mexico	Haiti
1981	Honduras	El Salvador
1985	Canada	Honduras
1989	Costa Rica	USA
1991	USA	Honduras
1993	Mexico	USA
1996	Mexico	Brazil
1998	Mexico	USA
2000	Canada	Colombia
2002	USA	Costa Rica
2003	Mexico	Brazil
2005	USA	Panama
2007	USA	Mexico
2009	Mexico	USA
2011	Mexico	USA
2013	USA	Panama
2015	Mexico	Jamaica

FIFA Confederations Cup

Once every four years (and every two or three years in the past), the winners of each confederation's major international competition for national teams get to compete against each other and the FIFA World Cup holders in a tournament FIFA insists is important for football development and a competition they sometimes describe as, "the Champion of Champions."

The King Fahd Cup

The idea for the tournament came from Saudi Arabia's Prince Faisal ibn Fahd who wished to celebrate Saudi Arabia's Asian Cup winning success in 1988 with a series of games featuring the world's best national teams. The original competition, called the Intercontinental Championship for the King Fahd Cup, took place in Riyadh in October, 1992. It featured four teams: hosts Saudi Arabia, Ivory Coast (1992 African Cup of Nations winners), Argentina (1991 Copa América champions) and 1991 CONCACAF Gold Cup winners, the United States. A straightforward semi-final, final and third place play-off format saw the four games garner an average attendance of over 42,000. Locals cheered on the Saudi team as they defeated the United States 3-0 to reach the final where Argentina, coached by Alfio Basile triumphed 3-1 courtesy of goals from Diego Simeone, Leonardo Rodriguez and Claudio Caniggia. The second edition of the King Fahd Cup welcomed surprise UEFA EURO 1992 winners, Denmark (see pp102-103) along with Japan, Argentina, Mexico and Nigeria in a six team competition. The Danes would surprise again, beating Argentina 2-0 in the final.

FIFA In Charge

In 1997, the tournament was still held in Saudi Arabia but had been taken over by FIFA who renamed it the FIFA Confederations Cup. With the change of name came a new trophy, an expansion in competing teams to eight and a decision to host it every two years, which was switched to every four years in 2005. Twenty teams have reached the semi-final and 11 the final including a distraught Cameroon team in 2003, who had suffered the on-pitch collapse and death of Cameroon midfielder Marc-Vivien Foé during their semi-final contest with Colombia.

The 1997 Confederations Cup saw a Brazil team boasting Ronaldo and Romário in peak form. Romário would end up the tournament top scorer with seven goals, still a record, aided by Brazil's 6-0 demolition of Australia in the final where both he and Ronaldo netted a hat-trick. Brazil nearly repeated the feat in 1999 but succumbed to Mexico in the final. Their fans can content themselves with their recent run which has seen them win the last three Confederation Cups in a row; their 4-1 defeat of old foes Argentina in the 2005 final via goals from Adriano (two), Kaká and Ronaldinho, being a particularly fond memory. Not

so warmly recalled by Tahiti fans will be their side's appearance at the 2013 tournament as OFC Champions in which they were beaten 10-0 by Spain – the competition's biggest scoreline – as well as suffering a 6-1 defeat to Nigeria and an 8-0 thrashing by Uruguay.

Distraction Or Opportunity?

Seen by some as a sideshow or a distraction away from the very real business of qualifying and competing in other tournaments, the FIFA Confederations Cup has occasionally suffered from withdrawals by teams such as France in 1999 and Germany twice, in 1997 and 2003. However, for the country holding the tournament, the Confederation Cup provides a vital opportunity to rehearse, test and fine tune procedures, stadiums and infrastructure prior to the arrival of the world's biggest football tournament. Some coaches also see it as a valuable opportunity to recreate tournament conditions for their squad and support team as well as monitor up close the opposing players and the teams' tactics.

Above: Fernando Torres scores the ninth goal for Spain vs Tahiti. Opposite, clockwise from Top Left: FIFA Confederations Cup 2013 Logo. Neymar celebrates scoring Brazil's second goal vs Spain. Ronaldinho of Brazil scores a goal against Argentina. Bernard Parker and Iraq's Nashat Akram in action.

TOURNAMENT FINALS

Year	Winners	Runners-Up	Score
1992	Argentina	Saudi Arabia	3-1
1995	Denmark	Argentina	2-0
1997	Brazil	Australia	6-0
1999	Mexico	Brazil	4-3
2001	France	Japan	1-0
2003	France	Cameroon	1-0 (golden goal)
2005	Brazil	Argentina	4-1
2009	Brazil	United States	3-2
2013	Brazil	Spain	3-0

KING FAHD CUP/FIFA CONFEDERATION CUP ATTENDANCES

Year	Host	Total attendance	Matches	Avg attendance
1992	Saudi Arabia	169,500	4	42,375
1995	Saudi Arabia	165,000	8	20,625
1997	Saudi Arabia	333,500	16	20,844
1999	Mexico	970,000	16	60,625
2001	South Korea/Japan	557,191	16	34,824
2003	France 2003	491,700	16	30,731
2005	Germany	603,106	16	37,694
2009	South Africa	584,894	16	36,556
2013	Brazil	804,659	16	50,291

Olympic Games

Football wasn't selected as an Olympic sport when the modern games began in Athens in 1896 but soon found its way in. A two match, three-team tournament was held at the 1900 Olympics for which Belgium sent a group of students whilst England were represented by an amateur club, Upton Park FC from East London augmented by winger Arthur Turner who joined Upton Park from Crouch End Vampires for the Olympics.

Early Olympics

Football at the 1900 and 1904 Olympics was considered unofficial and not part of Olympic records and statistics, although a gold medal was awarded retrospectively for the Canadian winners of the three-team 1904 tournament (whose opponents, Christian Brothers College and St Rose Parish both hailed from the United States). The 1908 games was different as football became a part of the full program but only five nations entered teams (although France entered two: an A and B team). After defeating Sweden 12-1, Netherlands 4-0 and Denmark 2-0, the Great Britain team, captained by Vivian Woodward, became the first official gold medalists. The team repeated the feat in 1912 in Stockholm for which 11 countries had sent competing teams. With the exception of the 1932 Olympics held in Los Angeles, football has appeared as a medal sport ever since.

Only For Amateurs

From the outset, Olympic football was for amateurs only. As such, the Olympics could lay claim to being the sport's world championship. Uruguay, who were Olympic champions in 1924 and 1928, were the logical choice by FIFA to stage the very first FIFA World Cup in 1930. As professional football took greater hold around the world's leading leagues in the 1920s onwards, many of football's best players turned professional and were therefore exempt from Olympic selection. After World War II, this led to the rise of dominance by the Soviet Union and its Eastern European Communist bloc allies whose teams were full of players who were nominally amateur with state-paid jobs but who actually played football full-time. Between 1952 and 1988, every Olympic gold medal-winning team came from this region of the world with the exception of the 1984 games where France defeated Brazil in the final at a games which were boycotted by the Soviet Union and its allies.

Professional And Development

Change was in the air in the 1980s and the IOC debated with FIFA how to embrace professionalism without damaging the status of the

FIFA World Cup as the pre-eminent competition in world football. The initial compromise in place for the 1984 and 1988 games was to bar professional players from the two strongest regions – Europe and South America – but to let all others send paid-to-play footballers. This was altered in 1992 to professional players in all teams providing they were under 23 as the focus shifted to encouraging young player development. The 1996 Olympics saw a slight tweak to the rule with three over-23 year old players allowed in each nation's squad, allowing Chilean striker Iván Zamorano to top score at the 2000 Olympics at the age of 30. A number of young, promising players have blossomed at the Olympics including 2004 top scorer Carlos Tevez and at the 2008 games, Sergio Agüero and Lionel Messi who also became gold medalists with Argentina. Excellence as an amateur Olympian has long been a springboard to a professional career. From the gold medal-winning Hungarian team of 1952, Zoltan Czibor would transfer to Barcelona, AS Roma, and teams in Austria. Sandor Kocsis, who spent eight years in Barcelona, and the legendary Ferenc Puskás left to star for Real Madrid.

Above: Great Britain vs South Korea London 2012 Men's Olympic Football Tournament Quarter Final. Aaron Ramsey (C) celebrates scoring the first goal for Great Britain with Craig Bellamy and Tom Cleverley. Opposite Top: Brazil's Sandro (L) and Thiago Silva tackle Mexico's Jorge Enríquez during their men's soccer final gold medal match, 2012. Bottom left: 1996, Nigeria celebrate beating Argentina in the final for the gold medal. Right: The women's USA side poses before the semi final soccer match against Canada at the London 2012 Olympic Games.

Women's Olympic Football

Following a long period of concerted lobbying for inclusion, women's football became a medal sport at the Atlanta Olympics in 1996. In this initial competition, the top eight finishers at the Women's World Cup the previous year were invited to the tournament. Today, the tournament admits 12 teams who are selected on the basis of continental or regional qualifying tournaments or from the winners of established competitions. For example, the winner of the 2014 Copa América Femenina – Colombia – took South America's berth at the 2016 Rio Olympics. The United States has dominated the women's tournament with one silver and four gold medals, the latest secured in London despite a resolute performance from Canada in the semi-final which ended 4-3 in the US team's favor.

OLYMPIC MEDALLISTS (MEN'S)

Year	Gold	Silver	Bronze
1908	Great Britain	Denmark	Netherlands
1912	Great Britain	Denmark	Netherlands
1920	Belgium	Spain	Netherlands
1924	Uruguay	Switzerland	Sweden
1928	Uruguay	Argentina	Italy
1936	Italy	Austria	Norway
1948	Sweden	Yugoslavia	Denmark
1952	Hungary	Yugoslavia	Sweden
1956	USSR	Yugoslavia	Bulgaria
1960	Yugoslavia	Denmark	Hungary
1964	Hungary	Czechoslovakia	East Germany
1968	Hungary	Bulgaria	Japan
1972	Poland	Hungary	Soviet Union, E. Germany
1976	East Germany	Poland	Soviet Union
1980	Czechoslovakia	East Germany	Soviet Union
1984	France	Brazil	Yugoslavia
1988	USSR	Brazil	West Germany
1992	Spain	Poland	Ghana
1996	Nigeria	Argentina	Brazil
2000	Cameroon	Spain	Chile
2004	Argentina	Paraguay	Italy
2008	Argentina	Nigeria	Brazil
2012	Mexico	Brazil	South Korea

OLYMPIC MEDALLISTS (WOMEN'S)

Year	Gold	Silver	Bronze
1996	USA	China	Norway
2000	Norway	USA	Germany
2004	USA	Brazil	Germany
2008	USA	Brazil	Germany
2012	USA	Japan	Canada

FOOTBALL'S FAMILY OF NATIONS

"SPORT HAS THE POWER TO INSPIRE AND UNITE PEOPLE. IN AFRICA, SOCCER ENJOYS GREAT POPULARITY AND HAS A PARTICULAR PLACE IN THE HEARTS OF PEOPLE." – NELSON MANDELA

129

The Global Game

From its origins in Europe and spread to South America and other parts of the world, football has blossomed into a truly global sport. In 2012, a year after becoming an independent nation, South Sudan sent a football team to its first international match, where it drew 2-2 with Uganda. Defender Richard Justin scored the new country's first goal. That same year, South Sudan became the 209th national team in football's world governing body, FIFA. The members of the six associations shown here operate within their own national, regional and continental confederations.

UEFA

Union des Associations Européennes de Football
Founded: 1954
Members: 53
Headquarters: Nyon, Switzerland
Website: www.uefa.com

CONMEBOL

Confederación Sudamericana de Fútbol
Founded: 1916
Members: 10
Headquarters: Luque, Grand Asunción, Paraguay
Website: www.conmebol.com

FIFA

Fédération Internationale de Football Association
Founded: 1904
Members: 209
Headquarters: Zurich, Switzerland
Website: www.fifa.com

AFC
Asian Football Confederation
Founded: 1954
Members: 46
Headquarters: Kuala Lumpur, Malaysia
Website: www.the-afc.com

CONCACAF
Confederation of North, Central American and Caribbean Association Football
Founded: 1961
Members: 35
Headquarters: Miami, USA
Website: http://www.concacaf.com

OFC
Oceania Football Confederation
Founded: 1966
Members: 11
Headquarters: Auckland, New Zealand
Website: www.oceaniafootball.com

CAF
Confédération Africaine de Football
Founded: 1957
Members: 54
Headquarters: 8th of October City, Egypt
Website: www.cafonline.com

UEFA Nations I

Albania

Founded: 1930
Affiliated to FIFA: 1932
FIFA World Ranking: 36
Major honors: Balkan Cup champions, 1946, Qualified for Euro 2016

A founder member of UEFA in 1954, Albania has mostly occupied the lower places in qualifying groups for major tournaments. That all changed during the qualifying campaign for Euro 2016 where defensive stalwart, Lorik Cana (also the country's record appearance holder with 89 caps) and wily former Torino and Udinese coach, Giovanni De Biasi (in charge since 2011), led the Albanians to sensational victories over Portugal and two draws against Denmark to qualify for their first major competition.

Andorra

Founded: 1994
Affiliated to FIFA: 1996
FIFA World Ranking: 201

This tiny principality has recorded only one competitive international victory, a 1-0 win against Macedonia in 2004 in their 2006 World Cup qualifying group. Two other wins in friendlies have also occurred, versus Belarus and Albania.

Armenia

Founded: 1992
Affiliated to FIFA: 1992
FIFA World Ranking: 123

As part of the Soviet Union until 1991, Armenian club football's biggest achievement was FC Ararat Yerevan winning the Soviet Higher League and cup in 1973. The national team narrowly failed to qualify for EURO 2012, finishing third in their group after defeating Slovakia twice and drawing with Russia. Full back Sargis Hovsepyan has made a record 131 appearances for the national side.

Austria

Founded: 1930
Affiliated to FIFA: 1932
FIFA World Ranking: 36
Major honors: FIFA World Cup semi-finals, 1934, 1954

Despite appearing at multiple World Cups and possessing, at times, strong professional clubs including Rapid Vienna and FC Red Bull Salzburg, the Austrians have struggled to reach the EUROs, with EURO 2008 their first appearance. The same year they switched from their traditional black and white strip graced by

legendary Austrian players including Hans Krankl, Matthias Sindelar and Andreas Herzog, to red and white. The current national team possesses standout talents in experienced defender Christian Fuchs, midfield schemer Marko Arnautović and striker Marc Janko who has scored 25 goals for the national team.

Azerbaijan

Founded: 1992
Affiliated to FIFA: 1994
FIFA World Ranking: 116

Azerbaijan entered international competition with attempts to qualify for EURO 1996 but has so far failed to make its mark at a major tournament despite a passionate support at its National Stadium in Baku. Under German coach Berti Vogts. Between 2008 and 2014, there was some improvement and several notable wins, arguably the biggest a 1-0 victory over Turkey in qualifying for EURO 2012.

Belarus

Founded: 1989
Affiliated to FIFA: 1992
FIFA World Ranking: 67

Belarus supplied a number of footballers to the Soviet national team before becoming independent. Amongst the country's most famous players are six time Belarussian Player of the Year, Arsenal and Barcelona midfielder, Alexander Hleb and former BATE Borisov midfielder, Sergey Krivets. BATE Borisov have dominated the Belarussian Premier League winning every league title from 2006 to 2015.

Belgium

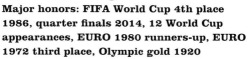

Founded: 1895
Affiliated to FIFA: 1904
FIFA World Ranking: 1
Major honors: FIFA World Cup 4th place 1986, quarter finals 2014, 12 World Cup appearances, EURO 1980 runners-up, EURO 1972 third place, Olympic gold 1920

Founder members of FIFA and with a

national league since 1896, Belgium football was one of just four European sides to play in the first FIFA World Cup. A long-running production line of quality Belgian players from Jan Ceulemans to Enzo Scifo have lit up club football in Europe even if the talent did not always translate to national team success. Belgian clubs such as Anderlecht have won the UEFA Cup and Cup Winners' Cup whilst Brugge reached the final of the European Cup. The country's

current crop of star players – from Kevin De Bruyne and Thibault Courtois to Eden Hazard, Vincent Kompany and Romelu Lukaku – are rated their most talented and exciting yet and has seen manager Marc Wilmots' side soar from 66th in the world in 2009 to the top position in the FIFA World Rankings in November 2015.

Bosnia and Herzegovina

Founded: 1992
Affiliated to FIFA: 1996
FIFA World Ranking: 21

This Balkan country was part of Yugoslavia until 1992 and provided many players for the Yugoslav team including Mirsad Fazlagić and Ivica Osim who were both selected for UEFA's team of the tournament after EURO 1968. Reaching a FIFA World Ranking high of 13 in 2013, and led by Eden Džeko, the record goalscorer with 45 goals, the national team's fortunes have been mixed. They appeared at their first World Cup in 2014, finishing third in Group F but failed to reach EURO 2016 after losing a play-off to the Republic of Ireland.

Bulgaria

Founded: 1923
Affiliated to FIFA: 1924
FIFA World Ranking: 75
Major honors: FIFA World Cup fourth place 1994, seven World Cup appearances, Olympic silver 1968, bronze 1956.

Bulgarian club football was dominated by Sofia-based clubs such as CSKA Sofia until strong teams such as Ludogorets Razgrad and Litex Lovech emerged from other parts of the country. These two teams have won the Bulgarian league from 2010 to 2015. The national team's peak came at the 1994 World Cup when with temperamental but gifted midfielder Hristo Stoichkov running the show, they stunned defending champions Germany to reach the semi-finals where they were narrowly beaten by Italy. There has since been a decline in the national team's fortunes with EURO 2004, the last major tournament qualified for.

Croatia

Founded: 1992
Affiliated to FIFA: 1932
FIFA World Ranking: 18
Major honors: FIFA World Cup third place 1998, EURO 1996 quarter finals, EURO 2008 quarter finals

Croatia supplied the Yugoslavia national team with many players before becoming independent in 1991. They have qualified for five out of six UEFA European Championships and four out of five FIFA World Cups. Known for producing skilful, technical players, their finest hour came when beating Germany 3-0 and knocking them out of the 1998 World Cup as they progressed to a third place finish. Davor Šuker was that tournament's leading goalscorer whilst the current crop of Croation players, including high-class midfield playmakers such as Ivan Rakitić and Luka Modrić, play for Europe's leading clubs.

Cyprus

Founded: 1934
Affiliated to FIFA: 1948
FIFA World Ranking: 79

Football was brought to the island by the British in the 1870s and 1880s. Although making little impact in internationals, clubs from Cyprus have progressed in European competition, contesting a number of UEFA Champions League and Europa League group stages. In 2012, APOEL FC made history by becoming the first Cypriot team to reach the quarter finals of the UEFA Champions League.

Opposite page: Austria's Marko Arnautović (R) and Liechtenstein's Martin Rechsteiner fight for the ball during their Euro 2016 qualifier.
Above: Belgium's Kevin De Bruyne (C) celebrates his goal with teammates Romelu Lukaku and Kevin Mirallas during their 2014 World Cup qualifier against Wales.

UEFA Nations II

Czech Republic

Founded: 1901
Affiliated to FIFA: 1907
FIFA World Ranking: 25
Major honors: Euro 1996 runners-up, Euro 2004 third place.

As part of Czechoslovakia, famous Czech sides like Sparta Prague and Viktoria Plzeň provided players who were instrumental in the national team's successes overseas which included two runners-up places in the 1934 and 1962 FIFA World Cup as well as winning EURO 1976. Since the country split with Slovakia, the Czechs have appeared in just one World Cup but have lit up the European stage, qualifying for every UEFA European Championship including EURO 2016 and romping through the rounds at EURO 1996 before losing a tight final to a golden goal scored by Germany.

Denmark

Founded: 1889
Affiliated to FIFA: 1904
FIFA World Ranking: 40
Major honors: EURO 1992 champions, EURO 1988 third place, EURO 1964 fourth place, FIFA World Cup quarter finalists 1998, Confederations Cup champions 1995.

Denmark's first clubs were formed in Copenhagen with competitions starting in 1889. As a small nation whose clubs were strictly amateur until 1978, it struggled to compete at the top level. That situation changed in the 1980s when a clutch of gifted players including brothers Michael and Brian Laudrup, Jesper Olsen and Soren Lerby emerged to take Denmark to their first FIFA World Cup in 1986. Six years later came the high water mark of Danish football with the side, now containing the formidable Peter Schmeichel in goal, winning EURO 1992. The Danes would also defeat Argentina in 1995 to win the Confederations Cup. At club level, FC Copenhagen have led the way in the Danish Superliga winning nine of the last 15 championships.

England

Founded: 1863
Affiliated to FIFA: 1905
FIFA World Ranking: 9
Major honors: FIFA World Cup champions 1966, fourth place 1990, 14 World Cup appearances, Euro 1968 third place, Euro 1996 third place

The birthplace of football, England retains an allure of the game for many global fans millions of whom follow English Premier League teams from afar. The EPL lays claim to being the most exciting and most watched league in the world, even if the technical quality is not always of the very highest. What isn't in doubt is that English clubs have had a major impact in Europe, winning the European Cup or Champions League 12 times and the UEFA Cup Winners' Cup or UEFA Cup 15 times. In addition, English clubs finished as runners-up 21 times in major European competitions. At national team level, the myth of English superiority was dented by the shock USA defeat at the 1950 World Cup – the first England entered – and footballing lessons handed out by a magnificent Hungarian team in 1953 and 1954 friendlies. England rallied under Alf Ramsey's tutelage and Bobby Moore's captaincy and triumphed at the 1966 World Cup. Despite producing highly talented players ever since – from Kevin Keegan, Bryan Robson and Gary Linker to Alan Shearer, Steven Gerrard and Wayne Rooney – England have yet to hit those heights again. Spirited 1990 World Cup and EURO 1996 campaigns gave fans hope before both were cruelly dashed by lost penalty shootouts to German teams.

Estonia

Founded: 1921
Affiliated to FIFA: 1923
FIFA World Ranking: 88

Following its independence from the former Soviet Union, a top flight national league, the Meistriliiga, came into existence with ten semi-professional teams in a March to November league season. In international football, Estonia have mostly been on the receiving end of defeats but they possess one of the most capped players in football history, midfielder Martin Reim who has made 157 appearances.

Faroe Islands

Founded: 1979
Affiliated to FIFA: 1988
FIFA World Ranking: 94

The fourth smallest UEFA member by population, with just 5,600 FIFA-registered football players, the Faroe Islands national team produced their first official victory in 1989, a 1-0 win over Canada. During EURO 2016 qualifying, they locked a shock away victory over Greece, a team ranked 169 places above them. Then they repeated the feat at their home Tórsvøllur stadium in front of a rapt 4,600 crowd.

Finland

Founded: 1907
Affiliated to FIFA: 1908
FIFA World Ranking: 47
Major honors: Olympic Games fourth place, 1912

Finland has produced some outstanding players, from record goalscorer Jari Litmanen to former Liverpool central defender Sami Hyypiä, but rarely enough of them in one era to trouble bigger teams or to qualify for major tournaments. Most of its current national team play for clubs at home or in the leagues of its Scandinavian neighbors. One exception is Niklas Moisander, frequent captain of the current side and Finnish Footballer of the Year in 2012 and 2013 who plays for Sampdoria in Serie A.

France

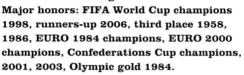

Founded: 1919
Affiliated to FIFA: 1904
FIFA World Ranking: 24
Major honors: FIFA World Cup champions 1998, runners-up 2006, third place 1958, 1986, EURO 1984 champions, EURO 2000 champions, Confederations Cup champions, 2001, 2003, Olympic gold 1984.

If England is the birthplace of football, then France is the home of international competition. French pioneers like Jules

Rimet, Gabriel Hanot and Henri Delaunay were inspirations behind the FIFA World Cup, European Cup and the European Championship. The French were in the thick of the action from the start, even though, they sometimes struggled to convert the undoubted talent into results in the crucial late stages of competitions. Astonishingly, Les Bleus didn't reach a UEFA European Championships finals for 24 years, after finishing fourth the in the very first competition. The free-playing "Blue Brazil" side of the 1980s, featuring an exciting, mobile midfield spearheaded by Michel Platini, swept all before them at EURO 1984, and a similarly talented team emerged in the mid-1990s with the world's best player at the helm in Zinédine Zidane. France would be champions of Europe and the world in 2000 only to be dumped out of the next World Cup two years later. They bounced back to

contest the 2006 World Cup Final versus Italy. As hosts of EURO 2016, they have high hopes of rediscovering the formula for footballing success.

FYR Macedonia

Founded: 1948
Affiliated to FIFA: 1994
FIFA World Ranking: 138

Whilst football in Macedonia celebrated its centenary in 2009, the young country played its first international match in 1993, a 4–1 win against Slovenia. The team has enjoyed occasional victories over other starred opponents, most notably during qualifying for EURO 2008, when they defeated eventual group winners Croatia 2-0 but they have yet to reach a major tournament.

Georgia

Founded: 1990
Affiliated to FIFA: 1992
FIFA World Ranking: 120

Georgia played its first official international match in 1990 whilst still part of the Soviet Union. Its top flight league, called the Umaglesi Liga and containing 16 teams has been won most often by Dinamo Tblisi who in the past were a force in Soviet soccer, winning the Soviet Supreme League in 1964 and 1978 and securing the UEFA Cup Winners' Cup in 1981.

Gibraltar

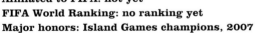

Founded: 1895
Affiliated to FIFA: not yet
FIFA World Ranking: no ranking yet
Major honors: Island Games champions, 2007

One of the oldest football associations, yet still not a full member of FIFA, Gibraltar was finally accepted as UEFA's newest and smallest (population approximately 30,000) member in 2013. The team features mostly amateur players including three Casciario brothers, Kyle, Ryan and Lee, and were humbled repeatedly in EURO 2016 qualifying, but at least Lee Casciaro scored Gibraltar's first goal in top flight competition, versus Scotland.

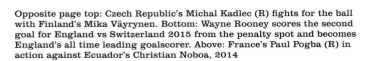

Opposite page top: Czech Republic's Michal Kadlec (R) fights for the ball with Finland's Mika Väyrynen. Bottom: Wayne Rooney scores the second goal for England vs Switzerland 2015 from the penalty spot and becomes England's all time leading goalscorer. Above: France's Paul Pogba (R) in action against Ecuador's Christian Noboa, 2014

UEFA Nations III

no team has finished in the top three at more World Cups (12) or notched the 16 consecutive top eight or better finishes at the tournament (1954-2014) that Germany have achieved.

The run began when West Germany toppled the favorites, Hungary, in the 1954 Final but peaked with a EURO 1972 and 1974 World Cup double by a side blessed with the elegant sweeper, Franz Beckenbauer, tigerish midfielder Günter Netzer and goal machine, Gerd Müller upfront. Reunified with East Germany in 1992, Germany has more than six million players registered with the German Football Association, the DFB, with the top league, Bundesliga, thriving and attracting 13.32 million fans in the 2014-15 season.

Germany

Founded: 1900
Affiliated to FIFA: 1904
FIFA World Ranking: 4
Major honors: FIFA World Cup champions 1954, 1974, 1990, 2014, runners-up 1966, 1982, 1986, 2002, EURO 1972 champions, EURO 1980 champions, EURO 1996 champions,

Germany remain Europe's most consistent performers at the international level. They are leading matchwinners (23) and goalscorers (65) at the UEFA European Championships, a tournament they first qualified for in 1972 and have appeared at every finals since. They are also the only European country to win the FIFA World Cup in South America when a series of strong team performances from Joachim's Lüw's side secured the 2014 trophy whilst

Greece

Founded: 1926
Affiliated to FIFA: 1927
FIFA World Ranking: 39
Major honors: EURO 2004 champions, EURO 2012 quarter finals.

When Panathinaikos reached the final of the European Cup in 1971, versus Ajax, it represented an extraordinary achievement for a team of predominantly amateur players. Top flight football in Greece didn't turn professional until 1979 with Olympiakos, AEK Athens and Panathinaikos dominating the league. Greece has only reached three out of 20 FIFA World Cups, their first coming in 1994, and only two of the first 12 UEFA European Championships - in 1980 and 2004. The latter, though, ended in triumph with Greece the most unexpected of EURO champions. A hero of that team, Giorgos Karagounis, is the record Greek cap holder with 139 appearances.

Hungary

Founded: 1901
Affiliated to FIFA: 1907
FIFA World Ranking: 19
Major honors: FIFA World Cup runners-up 1938, 1954, quarter finals 1934, 1962, 1966, Olympic gold 1952, 1964, 1968, EURO 1964 third place.

Hungary possessed the best team in Europe in the 1950s packed with attacking prowess from the likes of Zoltán Czibor, Sándor Kocsis, Nándor Hidegkuti and the incomparable Ferenc Puskás. From June 1950 to November 1955, Hungary lost just one out of 50 international games, winning 42 and scoring more than 200 goals in the process. Seven of these came in a 7-1 thrashing of England in 1954. The same year, Hungary entered the World Cup as favorites, reached the final but squandered a two goal lead to lose 3-2 to West Germany. Recently however, Hungary failed to qualify for 10 UEFA European Championships in a row before a team containing Zoltán Gera and Balázs Dzsudzsák reached EURO 2016 via a play-off win over Norway.

Iceland

Founded: 1947
Affiliated to FIFA: 1947
FIFA World Ranking: 38

A remarkable rise has seen Iceland leap from 131st in the FIFA World Rankings to a high of 28th in 2014 after the twin head coaches, Lars Lagerbäck and Heimir Hallgrímsson, sparked a remarkable EURO 2016 qualifying campaign. With Gylfi Sigurðsson and Kolbeinn Sigþórsson adding significant goal threat to a well-drilled team ethic, Iceland sensationally defeated the Netherlands, Czech Republic and Turkey on the way to reaching the EURO 2016 finals.

Israel

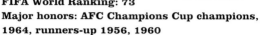

Founded: 1928
Affiliated to FIFA: 1929
FIFA World Ranking: 73
Major honors: AFC Champions Cup champions, 1964, runners-up 1956, 1960

The only nation to have played World Cup qualifying games on every continent, Israel was a member of the Asian Football Confederation between 1954 and 1974 a period in which they made their only World Cup appearance, in 1970. Forced out from the AFC, Israel spent a long spell in the wilderness, even grouped by FIFA in the Oceania group for World Cup qualifying before joining UEFA in 1994, three years after its leading clubs such as Maccabi Tel Aviv were admitted into Champions League qualifying.

Italy

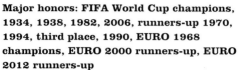

Founded: 1898
Affiliated to FIFA: 1905
FIFA World Ranking: 15
Major honors: FIFA World Cup champions, 1934, 1938, 1982, 2006, runners-up 1970, 1994, third place, 1990, EURO 1968 champions, EURO 2000 runners-up, EURO 2012 runners-up

The first Italian football clubs emerged in Turin and Genoa in the 1880s and a regionally-grouped Italian Football Championship began in 1898. This was superceded by Serie A in 1929, a league which has spent lavishly to attract many of the world's greatest players over the decades. World-famous Italian clubs such as Internazionale, AC Milan and Juventus have appeared in the European Cup/Champions League finals (27) and UEFA Cup/Europa League finals (15) more times than any other nation and in total have won 44 major competitions including nine Intercontinental Cups. The country's national team, known as The Azzurri (The Blues) are always considered tough opponents despite a meager return of just one UEFA European Championships crown. Italy has fared far better at the World Cup, winning two consecutive FIFA World Cups under the guidance of Vittorio Pozzo in the 1930s and reaching the semi-finals or better seven times from 1970 onwards.

Kazakhstan

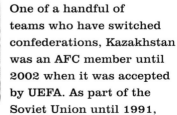

Founded: 1914
Affiliated to FIFA: 1994
FIFA World Ranking: 131

One of a handful of teams who have switched confederations, Kazakhstan was an AFC member until 2002 when it was accepted by UEFA. As part of the Soviet Union until 1991, no Kazakh side competed in the Soviet Top League until FC Kairat Almaty in 1960. The Kazakhstan Professional League began in 1992, features 12 teams and has been won by nine clubs so far.

Latvia

Founded: 1921
Affiliated to FIFA: 1923
FIFA World Ranking: 100

Traditionally, the strongest of the Baltic nations, Latvia missed out on a place at the 1938 World Cup by a whisker, losing a play-off to Austria 2-1. Sixty-five years later and Latvia celebrated as their team defeated Turkey in a play-off to qualify for EURO 2004. Skonto FC were champions in the first 13 years of the Latvian Higher League (formed 1992) but have only won one title since as competition has intensified.

Liechtenstein

Founded: 1934
Affiliated to FIFA: 1976
FIFA World Ranking: 165

One of Europe's minnows, Liechtenstein are frequently fodder in qualifying competitions although the 2006 World Cup campaign saw two wins (against Luxembourg) and a draw against Portugal. The principality does not possess their own football league. Instead, teams play in the Swiss leagues with FC Vaduz their highest ranked side, currently playing in the Swiss Super League.

Lithuania

Founded: 1922
Affiliated to FIFA: 1923
FIFA World Ranking: 128

Football plays second fiddle to basketball as the country's national sport and fans of the national team have to be content with the occasional shock win or brave draw over bigger opposition, most notably, a 1-1 draw against Italy in EURO 2008 qualifying and a 3-0 win over Romania in qualifying for the 2010 FIFA World Cup.

Opposite page: Germany's Thomas Müeller (R) fights for the ball with Georgia's Kakhi Makharadze during their EURO 2016 qualifier.
Above: Italy's Gianluigi Buffon clears the ball next to Italy's Gianluca Zambrotta and France's Zinédine Zidane during the World Cup 2006 final.

UEFA Nations IV

Luxembourg

Founded: 1908
Affiliated to FIFA: 1910
FIFA World Ranking: 142

Luxembourg's first international victory came against France all the way back in 1914. By summer 2015, though, the national team had become regular whipping boys, recording just 25 wins in 353 games and shipping 1,004 goals. Later in 2015 came some cause for cheer with 1-0 wins over both Macedonia and, somewhat surprisingly, Greece.

Malta

Founded: 1900
Affiliated to FIFA: 1960
FIFA World Ranking: 161

Malta's first international was a 3-2 loss to Austria in 1957 and fans had to get used to regular defeats in competitive fixtures with occasional victories against more lowly ranked teams. In 2013, Malta claimed their first World Cup qualifying win in twenty years against Armenia with the winning goal struck by their all-time leading scorer, Michael Mifsud (40 goals).

Moldova

Founded: 1990
Affiliated to FIFA: 1994
FIFA World Ranking: 155

The Moldovan National League was formed in 1992, the year that the country gained independence from the former Soviet Union. The ten team league is mostly battled for by two clubs: FC Sheriff Tiraspol and FC Zimbru Chișinău who between them have won 21 of the league's first 24 seasons.

Montenegro

Founded: 1931
Affiliated to FIFA: 2007
FIFA World Ranking: 84

A combined Serbia and Montenegro team competed at the 2006 FIFA World Cup tournament before the two nations went their separate ways and the country played its first international in 2007, versus Hungary. An early record of only seven losses in their first 23 matches saw them rise up the rankings and saw them finish third in their 2014 World Cup qualifying group and fourth in their EURO 2016 qualifying group.

Netherlands

Founded: 1889
Affiliated to FIFA: 1904
FIFA World Ranking: 14
Major honors: EURO 1988 champions, FIFA World Cup runners-up 1974, 1978, 2010, third place 2014

It's not just their brilliant orange home strip which has lit up international football. After a fallow period in the 1940s and 1950s, Dutch football ignited in the 1960s with Ajax's triumphs at club level and the emergence of a creative Dutch side coached by Rinus Michels and featuring Johan Cruyff as its brightest star as the Dutch proved many neutrals' favorites in the 1974 and 1978 World Cups. The leading Eredivisie clubs such as Ajax, Feyenoord and PSV Eindhoven (who have won 69 league titles between them) have continued to produce

technically-gifted players from Ruud Gullit and Marco van Basten to Arjen Robben, Dennis Bergkamp and more recently Wesley Sneijder and Memphis Depay. Yet given the output of footballing talent, it is surprising that the Dutch have missed out on qualifying on occasion, missing out on ten World Cups in the past and most recently, failing to reach EURO 2016.

Northern Ireland

Founded: 1880
Affiliated to FIFA: 1911
FIFA World Ranking: 29
Major honors: FIFA World Cup quarter-finals 1958, 1982, Home Championships champions 8 times.

Northern Ireland won the very last Home International Championship (competed for by Northern Ireland, England, Scotland and Wales) in 1984. Two years earlier, they had defeated Spain 1-0 at the World Cup to reach the quarter finals for the second time in their history. Martin O'Neill, a player in the team that qualified for the 1982 and 1986 World Cups, became head coach in 2011 and masterminded the team's EURO 2016 campaign qualifying for their first EUROs comfortably. With football in the country mostly amateur or semi-pro, almost all of the national team players play for clubs in England and Scotland.

Norway

Founded: 1902
Affiliated to FIFA: 1908
FIFA World Ranking: 50
Major honors: Olympic bronze medal 1936, Women's FIFA World Cup champions 1995, runners-up 1991.

Football has been played in

Norway since the 1890s with the country's first official match ending in an 11-3 loss to Sweden in 1908. The country has not made the strides forward experienced by its neighbors Sweden and Denmark, qualifying for just one UEFA European Championships and three World Cups (1938, 1994 and 1998). In the latter competition, they recorded their most famous victory, over Brazil. In contrast, the Norwegian women's national team triumphed in the 1995 Women's World Cup, have reached the final of the Women's European Championship and won Olympic gold in 2000.

Poland
Founded: 1919
Affiliated to FIFA: 1923
FIFA World Ranking: 34
Major honors: FIFA World Cup third place 1974, 1982. Olympic gold, 1972

Almost 80 clubs have competed in the Polish top league, known as the Ekstraklasa, since its formation in 1927 including sides like Legia Warsaw and Lech Poznan that have enjoyed some success in European competition without winning major trophies. Despite producing a number of standout players including Zbigniew Boniek, Grzegorz Lato and Kazimierz Deyna, EURO 2008 was Poland's first UEFA European Championships. They have fared better at World Cups, attending seven and twice reaching the semi-finals. The current side spearheaded by the prolific Bayern Munich striker, Robert Lewandowski, qualified for EURO 2016.

Portugal
Founded: 1914
Affiliated to FIFA: 1923
FIFA World Ranking: 7
Major honors: FIFA World Cup third place, 1966, fourth place, 2006, EURO 2004 runners up, EURO semi-finals 1984, 2000, 2012

From Eusébio and Luis Figo to their all-time leading goalscorer, Cristiano Ronaldo, Portugal have produced some stunning attacking players over the decades. Whilst their World Cup record, away from two semi-final appearances, has been relatively modest, they have excited and entertained at a number of UEFA European Championships despite being the only EURO hosts to lose the final, in 2004 after defeating Denmark, the Netherlands and the Czech Republic along the way. Domestic club football in Portugal has been dominated by Benfica, Sporting CP and Porto, who between them have won 79 of the 81 league championships held so far. The 18-team Primeira League attracted 3,091,276 fans in the 2014-15 season, whilst further afield, Portuguese clubs have won four European Cups and two UEFA Cups.

Republic of Ireland
Founded: 1921
Affiliated to FIFA: 1923
FIFA World Ranking: 30
Major honors: FIFA World Cup quarter-finals, 1990

The Republic were the first team outside of the UK to defeat England in England winning 2-0 in 1949. However, World Cup participation wouldn't occur for another 41 years when the Jack Charlton-managed side progressed out of their group undefeated and then defeated to reach the quarter finals. The country's domestic league, won most often by Shamrock Rovers, sees its best players transferred primarily to the English and Scottish clubs.

Romania
Founded: 1909
Affiliated to FIFA: 1923
FIFA World Ranking: 16
Major honors: FIFA World Cup quarter-final, 1994, EURO 2000 quarter-finals

Professional football arrived in Romania in 1909 with the arrival of the Divizia A league which later became Liga 1. Steaua Bucureşti emerged as the country's most successful club, winning 26 league titles and storming Europe in the mid-1980s winning European Cup (1984-85) and European Cup Winners' Cup (1986) trophies. The national team have only sporadically managed to qualify for major competitions, though, including just four World Cups since 1938.

Russia
Founded: 1912
Affiliated to FIFA: 1912
FIFA World Ranking: 23
Major honors: EURO 2008 semi-final

In 2010, Russia was awarded the rights to host the 2018 FIFA World Cup. The country has a long footballing history including being a major part of the former Soviet Union which won EURO 1960 and made three other finals (1964, 1972, 1988) as well as the 1966 FIFA World Cup semi-final. Competing as Russia since 1992, the national team has qualified for five out of six UEFA European Championships with the squad almost exclusively drawn from players now playing their club football domestically. Russian clubs have competed well in European competition with CSKA Moscow winning the 2004/05 UEFA Cup and Zenit St. Petersburg winning the 2007/08 UEFA Cup and UEFA Super Cup. Clubs below Russia's top two divisions, the National Football League and the Second Division are divided into five regional zones to ease the burden of travel across the world's largest country.

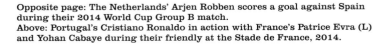

Opposite page: The Netherlands' Arjen Robben scores a goal against Spain during their 2014 World Cup Group B match.
Above: Portugal's Cristiano Ronaldo in action with France's Patrice Evra (L) and Yohan Cabaye during their friendly at the Stade de France, 2014.

UEFA Nations V

San Marino

Founded: 1931
Affiliated to FIFA: 1988
FIFA World Ranking: 198

True minnows who have yet to win a World Cup or EUROs qualifying match, the amateur players of San Marino did at least in 2015 record their first away goal in 12 years when losing 2-1 to Lithuania. Andy Selva with eight goals remains the only Sammarinese player to have scored more than one international goal.

Scotland

Founded: 1873
Affiliated to FIFA: 1910
FIFA World Ranking: 46
Major honors: FIFA World Cup 8 appearances, Home International Championships champions 41 times.

Participants in the first international match versus England, Scotland played the, "auld enemy" annually in the Home Internationals until 1989 but only a handful of occasions since, the most recent being their contests in qualifying Group F for the 2018 FIFA World Cup. Scotland's last international tournament appearances were in the 1990s and a struggling domestic game which sees most of the national team play their club football over the border in England, has resulted in a drop in their ranking and tougher qualifying group draws as a result.

Serbia

Founded: 1919
Affiliated to FIFA: 1923
FIFA World Ranking: 51

Football first came to Serbia in the 1890s and its leading clubs such as Red Star and Partizan developed in and around Belgrade. The country was part of Yugoslavia for much of the twentieth century and then played as Serbia and Montenegro until

2006. By appearing at the 2010 World Cup with Serbia, star midfielder Dejan Stanković became the first footballer to play for three different nations at World Cups. His international retirement in 2013 leaves experienced players like captain, Branislav Ivanović and Aleksandr Kolarov to help bring through a new wave of talented youngsters.

Slovakia

Founded: 1938
Affiliated to FIFA: 1994
FIFA World Ranking: 25

Eight of the starting eleven for Czechoslovakia in the EURO 1976 final match hailed from Slovakia but since the splitting of the nation in two in 1993, the country has struggled to qualify for major competitions. That changed with a successful EURO 2016 qualifying campaign in which players like Marek Hamšík and Martin Škrtel contributed to victories over Spain, Ukraine and Belarus as they made it to France for the finals.

Slovenia

Founded: 1920
Affiliated to FIFA: 1992
FIFA World Ranking: 59

Slovenia gained its independence from Yugoslavia in 1991 and played its first match versus Estonia the following year. The side gained a place at EURO 2000 with a shock play-off win over Ukraine and also made it to the 2002 and 2010 FIFA World Cups. Recent campaigns have seen the side fall agonizingly just short of qualifying for EURO 2012 and 2016 as well as the 2014 FIFA World Cup.

Spain

Founded: 1913
Affiliated to FIFA: 1904
FIFA World Ranking: 3
Major honors: FIFA World Cup champions, 2010, fourth place 1950, EURO 1964 champions, EURO 2008 champions, EURO 2012 champions, Olympic gold 1992

For decades, Spain's tale was one of unfulfilled promise. Its powerhouse La Liga clubs, Barcelona and Real Madrid,

Above: Spain's Cesc Fàbregas (L) and César Azpilicueta chase Ukraine's Andriy Yarmolenko during the EURO 2016 Group C qualifier, 2015.
Opposite page: Hal Robson-Kanu scores the second goal for Wales, playing Scotland in the 2014 World Cup qualifiers.

frequently overcame European opponents yet the national team remained unable to build on its sole success, winning EURO 1964 as hosts. Spain's long wait for glory came in 2008 when a team built upon the close-passing possession style of football favored by Barcelona and featuring metronomic midfield pairing Xavi Hernandez and Andrés Iniesta swept all before them, defeating Italy, Russia and Germany amongst others to win the tournament. They defended their title four years later, this time as World Champions after their 2010 triumph in South Africa. Spain were awarded FIFA Team of the Year for six successive seasons (2008-13) and despite a 2014 World Cup flop, are still rated highly with veterans Iniesta, Iker Casillas and Sergio Ramos part of a side seeking to defend a proud unbeaten record of 51 World Cup qualifying games stretching back to 1993.

Sweden

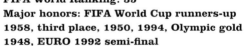

Founded: 1904
Affiliated to FIFA: 1904
FIFA World Ranking: 35
Major honors: FIFA World Cup runners-up 1958, third place, 1950, 1994, Olympic gold 1948, EURO 1992 semi-final

Despite losing the great Gunnar Nordahl when he moved to Milan as the national team only selected amateurs at the time, Sweden possessed one of the best international teams of the 1950s, finishing in the top three in three consecutive World Cups. The Swedes have appeared at 11 World Cups in total and the last five UEFA European Championships, assisted by star players including Henrik Larsson and their current talisman, the maverick Paris St Germain forward and all-time leading goalscorer, Zlatan Ibrahimović.

Switzerland

Founded: 1895
Affiliated to FIFA: 1904
FIFA World Ranking: 12
Major honors: FIFA World Cup quarter finals 1934, 1938, 1954

World Cup hosts in 1954, Switzerland made their first UEFA European Championship appearance at EURO 1996 and have qualified for three EURO finals since

including EURO 2016. Their appearance at the 2006 World Cup brought the freak record of being the first team to be eliminated from the second round despite not conceding a single goal after they lost a penalty shootout to Ukraine. Recent incarnations of the national team have been renowned for being well-organized and difficult to beat as witnessed by the Swiss maintaining a top 20 spot in the FIFA World Rankings since 2011.

Turkey

Founded: 1923
Affiliated to FIFA: 1923
FIFA World Ranking: 20
Major honors: FIFA World Cup third place 2002, EURO 2008 semi-final, Confederations Cup semi-final, 2003,

The Turkish Superleage was launched in 1959, nine years after Turkey qualified for but were unable to attend the 1950 FIFA World Cup due to financial issues. They made it to the 1954 tournament after winning a coin toss with Spain in a play-off for the final European place at the competiton. That was their last World Cup until the team's superb third place finish at the 2002 World Cup. Replacing talismanic striker Hakan Şükür who scored a record 51 goals in 112 appearances between 1992 and 2007 has proven difficult but Turkey qualified for EURO 2008 where they recorded wins over the Netherlands and Czech Republic and EURO 2016.

Ukraine

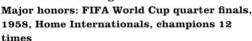

Founded: 1991
Affiliated to FIFA: 1992
FIFA World Ranking: 27
Major honors: FIFA World Cup quarter finals, 2006

Ukraine played its first match as an independent nation against Hungary in 1992. They reached their first World Cup in 2006 and the following year peaked at 11th in the FIFA World Rankings. With leading clubs Shakhtar Donetsk and Dynamo Kiev

providing the majority of the national team, Ukraine have endured heartbreak by losing four qualifying play-offs in a row to miss out on EURO and World Cup tournaments since 2006. It was a case of fifth time lucky, though, as the side coached by Mykhaylo Fomenko, managed to reach EURO 2016.

Wales

Founded: 1876
Affiliated to FIFA: 1910
FIFA World Ranking: 17
Major honors: FIFA World Cup quarter finals, 1958, Home Internationals, champions 12 times

Wales became the third team to contest an international fixture when they faced Scotland in 1876. Despite producing some outstanding individual talents such as John Charles, Ryan Giggs and Ian Rush, Welsh fans have had relatively little to cheer until their side, marshalled by coach, Chris Coleman and starring Aaron Ramsey, Ashley Williams and Gareth Bale qualified for the EURO 2016 – their first major championship since the 1958 FIFA World Cup. Top Welsh clubs such as Swansea City and Cardiff City compete in the English league system including the EPL whilst lower tier sides play in the Welsh Premier League or in divisions split into north and south Wales.

CONMEBOL Nations

when Mario Kempes' tournament-leading six goals helped the side to become world champions on home soil. A young Maradona had not been selected by coach Menotti controversially, but he got his chance to inspire Argentina to repeat success again in 1986. Maradona's heir as the focal point of the national team, Lionel Messi, has not been able to prompt his side to similar glories although he was awarded player of the tournament at the 2014 FIFA World Cup.

Brazil

Founded: 1914
Affiliated to FIFA: 1923
FIFA World Ranking: 6
Major honors: FIFA World Cup champions, 1958, 1962, 1970, 1994, 2002, runners-up 1950, 1998, third place 1938, 1978, Copa América eight times, Confederations Cup champions 1997, 2005, 2009, 2013

The most successful and, arguably, influential footballing nation of all, legend has it that football in Brazil began in 1894 when a 20 year old Brazilian, Charles Miller, returned from his schooling in

Argentina

Founded: 1893
Affiliated to FIFA: 1912
FIFA World Ranking: 2
Major honors: FIFA World Cup champions 1978, 1986, runners-up 1930, 1990, 2014, Copa América champions 14 times, Confederations Cup champions, 1992, runners-up 1995, 2005, Olympic gold 1988, 1996, 2008, 2012

English and Italian immigrants popularised football in Argentina in the 1870s onwards with the first national league forming in 1891. By 1930, the league had expanded to an outrageously large 36 teams, all of whom played each other once. The following year saw the introduction of professionalism and a breakaway 18-team league competition won by Boca Juniors who remain one of Argentina's leading teams who together have won the Copa Libertadores 22 times.

On the national stage and after the first tournament, Argentina were mostly also-rans at World Cups until the 1970s

Top: Argentina's Lionel Messi walks with his silver medal past the Copa América trophy after defeat to Chile in the 2015 final.
Above: Brazil's Neymar falls after a tackle by Argentina's Leandro Gonazles, as Nicolas Tagliafico and Rodrigo Battaglia look on during their Conmebol U20 championship game, 2011.

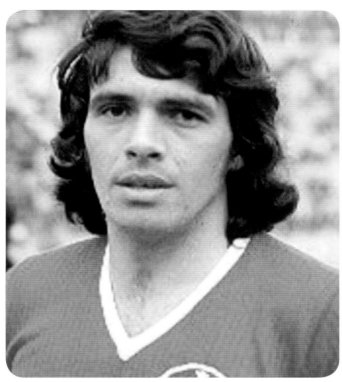

since their third place finish in 1938, Brazil have only once exited the tournament at the group stage (1966) and have offered a consistently high threat to opponents as witnessed by their 11 top four and 17 top eight finishes. The Brazilian team that graced the 1970 World Cup featuring Pele, Rivelino, Tostão and Jairzinho is considered by many to be the finest ever whilst the Zico-inspired team of the early 1980s and the turn of the century side containing Ronaldo and Romario also impressed. Continentally, eight Copa América titles and 11 runners-up placings appears rather scant reflection on the long periods in which Brazilian teams have lit up the international scene.

England with two footballs and rule book intent on promoting the game. Football caught on although the world-famous gold shirts and blue shorts only arrived for the 1954 World Cup. The only team to win World Cups on four different continents,

Bolivia

Founded: 1925
Affiliated to FIFA: 1926
FIFA World Ranking: 72
Major honors: Copa América champions 1963, runners-up 1997

The year 1963 is etched in Bolivia's collective football memory as the team won their one and only Copa América, defeating Brazil in the final in an epic match that ended 5-4. The national team has reached just three World Cups (1930, 1950 and 1994), the latter assisted by Bolivia's first victory over Brazil in World Cup qualifying. Marco Etcheverry remains Bolivia's greatest player fondly remembered in the MLS for his many seasons with DC United.

Chile

Founded: 1895
Affiliated to FIFA: 1916
FIFA World Ranking: 5
Major honors: FIFA World Cup third place 1962, Copa América champions 2015, runners-up 1955, 1956, 1979, 1986

Chile was home of the second oldest football federation in South America and on the international stage have been consistently competitive. The country's leading club, Colo Colo won the Copa Liberatadores in 1991 whilst the national team has appeared at nine World Cups. Recent progress was made under two Argentinean head coaches, Marco Bielsa and Jorge Sampioli, the latter blessed with major world talents including Alexis Sanchez, Arturo Vidal and acrobatic goalkeeper and most capped Chilean, Claudio Bravo. Chile have reached two successive Round of 16 stages at the 2010 and 2014 World Cups but in 2015 eclipsed previous achievements with their first Copa América crown, going unbeaten through the tournament and soaring into the top five of the FIFA World Rankings as a result.

Colombia

Founded: 1924
Affiliated to FIFA: 1932
FIFA World Ranking: 8
Major honors: FIFA World Cup quarter final 2014, Copa América champions 2001, runners up 1975

With a domestic league ranked third strongest in South America, Colombia has a reputation for producing highly skilled and explosive players such as Colombian legend Carlos Valderrama, Faustino

Top: Elias Figueroa, the only Chilean player to have played at three FIFA World Cups - in 1966, 1974 and 1982. Above: Colombia's James Rodríguez (L) fights for the ball Argentina's Marcos Rojo during their 2018 World Cup qualifying soccer match in Barranquilla, Colombia, 2015

CONMEBOL Nations contd.

Asprilla and one of the undoubted stars of the 2014 FIFA World Cup, James Rodríquez. It was Colombia's first appearance at the tournament since a run of three participations in the 1990s when the world embraced the skill and vision of the afro-haired Valderrama but were appalled at the tragedy of Andrés Escobar who was shot dead shortly after the 1994 World Cup for his own goal against the United States. Colombia have taken part in every Copa América since 1975, the year in which they finished runners-up but in 2001, they set a record by not conceding a single goal throughout the competition.

Ecuador

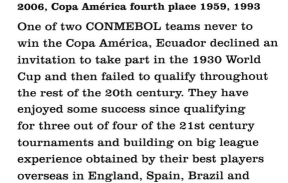

Founded: 1925
Affiliated to FIFA: 1927
FIFA World Ranking: 13
Major honors: FIFA World Cup Round of 16, 2006, Copa América fourth place 1959, 1993

One of two CONMEBOL teams never to win the Copa América, Ecuador declined an invitation to take part in the 1930 World Cup and then failed to qualify throughout the rest of the 20th century. They have enjoyed some success since qualifying for three out of four of the 21st century tournaments and building on big league experience obtained by their best players overseas in England, Spain, Brazil and Mexico amongst others.

Paraguay

Founded: 1906
Affiliated to FIFA: 1925
FIFA World Ranking: 42
Major honors: FIFA World Cup quarter finals 2010, Copa América champions, 1959, 1973, runners-up 1922, 1929, 1947, 1949, 1963, 2011

Despite being one of the smaller CONMEBOL nations, Paraguay have a proud footballing history with eight appearances at World Cups including the 2010 edition where they helped knock out Italy and beat Japan in the Round of 16, only to lose 1-0 to eventual champions,

Spain in the quarter finals. Skippered by their veteran striker and leading scorer with 32 goals, Roque Santa Cruz, Paraguay enjoyed strong 2011 and 2015 Copa Américas. In the latter, they finished fourth with the knocking out of Brazil at the quarter finals stage an undoubted highlight.

Peru

Founded: 1922
Affiliated to FIFA: 1924
FIFA World Ranking: 43
Major honors: Copa América champions 1939, 1975, third place 1927, 1935, 1949, 1955, 2011

Peru have run through 24 different national team coaches since 1982 as they seek the right blend of selection and tactics to see them recapture the heights of their earlier World Cup and Copa América-challenging teams. Although they failed to qualify for the 2014 FIFA World Cup, highly creditable third place finishes in back-to-back Copa América tournaments in 2011 and 2015 hinted at brighter things to come. In both tournaments, the leading scorer was Peruvian striker, Paolo Guerrero, the only member of recent Peru squads to play his club football in Brazil (for Flamengo).

Uruguay

Founded: 1900
Affiliated to FIFA: 1923
FIFA World Ranking: 11
Major honors: FIFA World Cup champions 1930, 1950, fourth place 1954, 1970, 2010, Copa América champions 15 occasions including 2011, runners-up 6 times, Olympic gold 1924, 1928

The first World Cup hosts and World Champions, Uruguay was also the first South American entrant into Olympic football and won back-to-back golds in the 1920s. Traditionally strong in the Copa América

tournament, the national team holds the record for the most titles ahead of Argentina and Brazil whilst their two leading clubs, Peñarol and Nacional, have won eight Copa Libertadores between them. With Óscar Tabárez in charge since 2006, an unusually long period in international management (and his second following his 1988-1990 tenure), continuity has enabled the side to deal with retirements of former stars such as Diego Forlán. Luis Suárez and Edinson Cavani now provide an, at times, razor-sharp spearhead. Their Copa América triumph in 2011 showing how a nation of less than four million people are still punching above their weight in footballing terms.

Venezuela

Founded: 1926
Affiliated to FIFA: 1952
FIFA World Ranking: 81
Major honors: Copa América fourth place, 2011

The only South American side to neither win the Copa América nor reach the FIFA World Cup, Venezuela have won just 23 of their 122 World Cup qualifying matches before the 2018 campaign begins. There is some cause for cautious optimism due to their best placed finish of sixth occurring in the 2014 campaign and the emergence of exciting youngsters including Yohandry Orozco and Salomón Rondón.

Above: The 1950 World Cup winners, Uruguay, team line-up. Opposite Top: Garrincha in action in 1962, one of the greatest Brazilian footballers of all time. Bottom: 1962 World Cup Final in Chile: The Brazilian team with captain Mauro Ramos de Oliveira holding the trophy.

CAF Nations 1

Algeria

Founded: 1962
Affiliated to FIFA: 1964
FIFA World Ranking: 36
Major honors: Africa Cup of Nations champions 2000, FIFA World Cup Round of 16 2014, four World Cup appearances, 1982, 1986, 2010, 2014

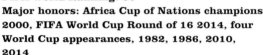

Algeria's first clubs formed in 1897 in the coastal city of Oran. The country first qualified for the FIFA World Cup in 1982, stunning West Germany 2-1 with the winner struck by Algerian record caps holder, Lakhdar Belloumi and also defeating Chile, but a controversial draw between Austria and Germany enabled both European sides to go through at Algeria's expense. In 2014, the side finally made it out of their World Cup group for the first time with the highlight being an entertaining 4-2 victory over South Korea. A clutch of highly talented players in their early or mid-twenties including Yacine Brahimi, Nabil Bentaleb, Riyad Mahrez and Islam Sliman give Algeria's passionate fans hope for much more to come from their team as witnessed from their 7-0 thrashing of Tanzania at the end of 2015.

Angola

Founded: 1979
Affiliated to FIFA: 1980
FIFA World Ranking: 111
Major honors: FIFA World Cup appearance 2006, Africa Cup of Nations quarter finals 2008, 2010

In 2006, Flavio Amado made Angolan football history when he scored the country's first ever goal at a World Cup finals, versus Mexico. The "Sable Antelopes" drew this game and their second with Iran only to lose 1-0 to Portugal, but have failed since to fully capitalize on this success although they did host and reach the quarter finals of the 2010 Africa Cup of Nations.

Benin

Founded: 1962
Affiliated to FIFA: 1964
FIFA World Ranking: 77

Benin was known as Dahomey when it made its World Cup qualifying debut for the 1974 World Cup. It has failed to reach the World Cup but has qualified three times for the Africa Cup of Nations. The "Squirrels" current squad is captained by English Premier League footballer, Stéphane Sessègnon.

Botswana

Founded: 1970
Affiliated to FIFA: 1978
FIFA World Ranking: 92

Despite a lowly ranking, the Zebras reached the Africa Cup of Nations tournament in 2012 for the first time in their history. An excellent campaign saw Stanley Tshoshane's team defeat Togo, Chad and qualifying Group K favorites, Tunisia both home and away to top their group. So far, Botswana has been unable to build on this success and have failed to qualify for subsequent tournament yet still keep a FIFA World Ranking in the top 100.

Burkina Faso

Founded: 1960
Affiliated to FIFA: 1964
FIFA World Ranking: 85
Major honors: Africa Cup of Nations runners-up 2013, fourth place 1998

Playing as Upper Volta until 1984, Burkina Faso have more recently emerged as rising stars. After just one African Cup of Nations appearance up to 1994, they have participated in nine out of 11 tournaments. In 2013, the national team progressed to the final of the Africa Cup of Nations, defeating Ethiopia, Togo and tournament heavyweights, Ghana, before narrowly losing to Nigeria. The "Stallions" would endure more heartbreak the same year when leading 3-2 from the first leg in their final qualifier, needed nothing more than a draw in Algeria to reach their first FIFA World Cup, only for Algerian captain, Madjid Bougherra, to score and end Burkina Faso's 2014 World Cup dream.

Burundi

Founded: 1948
Affiliated to FIFA: 1972
FIFA World Ranking: 119

The Burundi Premier League, formed in 1972 contained 16 teams until 2009 when it was reduced to 12 clubs. Its most successful side, Vital'O FC, have won 19 league titles since the 1980s including the 2014-15 title. The league's clubs supply around half of the national team squad with the remainder playing for clubs strewn all over the African continent.

Cameroon

Founded: 1959
Affiliated to FIFA: 1962
FIFA World Ranking: 62
Major honors: Africa Cup of Nations champions 1984, 1988, 2000, 2002, runners-up 1986, 2008, FIFA World Cup quarter final 1990, Olympic gold 2000, Confederation Cup runners-up 2002

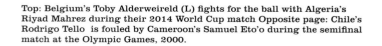

Top: Belgium's Toby Alderweireld (L) fights for the ball with Algeria's Riyad Mahrez during their 2014 World Cup match Opposite page: Chile's Rodrigo Tello is fouled by Cameroon's Samuel Eto'o during the semifinal match at the Olympic Games, 2000.

The Indomitable Lions have made an impact on the World Cup ever since their debut in 1982 in which they managed to hold the tournament winners, Italy and third placed Poland to draws in their group. At the 1990 tournament, veteran striker Roger Milla captivated a global audience with his goal celebrations as Cameroon topped their group ahead of Romania, the Soviet Union and defending champions, Argentina. By virtue of beating Colombia in the Round of 16, they became the first African side to reach a World Cup quarter finals. In total, they have appeared at seven World Cups but their greatest year involved triumphs in two other competitions and featured new young starlets such as 16 year old goalkeeper Idriss Kameni and predatory striker Samuel Eto'o. In 2000, they won the Africa Cup of Nations for a third time and won gold at the Olympics, knocking out Brazil in the quarter finals, Chile in the semis and Spain in the final.

Cape Verde Islands

Founded: 1982
Affiliated to FIFA: 1986
FIFA World Ranking: 33
Major honors: Africa Cup of Nations quarter finals 2013

The Federação Caboverdiana de Futebol (FCF) was formed in 1982, seven years after Cape Verde became independent of Portugal. After decades of near misses, the Blue Sharks find themselves riding high in the FIFA rankings as a reflection of a sharp improvement in form which saw them knock out continental heavyweights, Cameroon, to qualify for their first Africa Cup of Nations in 2013. There, they powered through their group to reach the quarter finals on debut – a stunning achievement. This was backed up by qualification for the next AFCON tournament in 2015 and only one defeat throughout the year which also included a surprise away victory over Portugal in a friendly.

Central African Republic

Founded: 1961
Affiliated to FIFA: 1964
FIFA World Ranking: 112
Major honors: CEMAC Cup champions, 2009

Traditional underdogs, Les Fauves (The Wild Beasts) exhibited an upturn in more recent performances which saw them win the CEMAC Cup – a tournament for Central African nations – in 2009 and record their first World Cup qualifying win in 2012 when they defeated Botswana 2-0. Many older fans in the country still hark back to the team's famous 2-0 win over the Ivory Coast as the country's finest performance.

Chad

Founded: 1962
Affiliated to FIFA: 1964
FIFA World Ranking: 113
Major honors: CEMAC Cup champions 2014

Chad kept apart from most international competition until the 1990s but now play their home games in the 20,000-capacity Stade Omnisports Idriss Mahamat and in 2015 appointed former Cameroon player Rigobert Song as its head coach. The year before "Les Sao" triumphed at the CEMAC Cup, their first major regional trophy but have yet to reach the finals of the Africa Cup of Nations.

Comoros

Founded: 1979
Affiliated to FIFA: 2005
FIFA World Ranking: 174

New on the international stage, Comoros first qualifying attempt, for the 2010 World Cup, ended in a 10-2 on aggregate defeat by Madagascar. An improving side has since managed to hold Ghana to a draw and defeat Lesotho. The majority of Comoros national team squad play their club football in France, often in Ligue 2 or the Championnat National.

Congo

Founded: 1962
Affiliated to FIFA: 1964
FIFA World Ranking: 54
Major honors: Africa Cup of Nations champions, 1972, fourth place 1974

The Diables Rouges (Red Devils) have never qualified for the FIFA World Cup and only sporadically for the African Cup of Nations but did win the competition in 1972 when they defeated Mali 3-2 in the final with two goals from Jean Michel M'Bono who in 2010 became president of the Fédération Congolaise de Football.

Congo DR

Founded: 1919
Affiliated to FIFA: 1964
FIFA World Ranking: 57
Major honors: Africa Cup of Nations champions 1968, 1974, third place 1998, 2015, African Nations Championship champions 2009, 2016, FIFA World Cup appearance 1974

Playing its first international in 1948 as Belgian Congo and from 1971 to 1997 known as Zaire, the Democratic Republic of Congo became the first sub-Saharan team to reach the World Cup in 1974. In the 1990s, the Leopards reached three consecutive Africa Cup of Nations quarter finals and have made 15 appearances at the competition in total. Its powerhouse club TP Mazembe is one of the strongest in Africa and won back-to-back CAF Champions League titles in 2009 and 2010 as well as a further triumph in the 2015 season.

Djibouti

Founded: 1979
Affiliated to FIFA: 1994
FIFA World Ranking: 204

Lying at the bottom of the FIFA World Rankings, Djibouti, played their first international in 1947 as the French colony, French Somaliland. Mostly at the receiving end of defeats, the team suffered their second worst defeat (9-0 v Rwanda) in 2007 but in the same year, did manage to secure their first ever win in a FIFA sanctioned international game when defeating Somalia in a qualifier for the 2010 World Cup.

CAF Nations 2

into international competition since independence in 1993. Financial issues and other difficulties in the country have caused a number of player defections at overseas matches and tournaments such as the 2012 CECAFA Cup which saw 17 players apply for asylum in the host country, Uganda. Creative recruitment of players overseas such as Swedish-born striker Henok Goitom have helped make the team more competitive, at the lower levels of competition.

Egypt

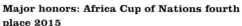

Founded: 1921
Affiliated to FIFA: 1923
FIFA World Ranking: 55
Major honors: Africa Cup of Nations champions 1957, 1959, 1986, 1998, 2006, 2008, 2010, runners-up 1962, third place 1963, 1970, 1974

Egypt was the first African nation to appear at a FIFA World Cup (1934) so it is a surprise, given their strength in continental competition where they have won a record seven African Cup of Nations crowns, that "the Pharoahs" have only been able to qualify for one further World Cup (in 1990). Much of Egypt's success in the past 25 years was underpinned by the sterling performances of two brothers, Hossam and Ahmed Hassan, the latter the country's record caps holder with 184 appearances between 1995 and 2012. The domestic club scene, particularly revolving around fierce Cairo rivals, Zamalek and El Ahly, remains strong and has provided 14 CAF Champions League winners and five runners-up.

Equatorial Guinea

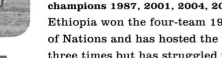

Founded: 1957
Affiliated to FIFA: 1986
FIFA World Ranking: 64
Major honors: Africa Cup of Nations fourth place 2015

A ten year gap occurred between this country's first and second international matches against China in 1975 and Congo in 1985. For many years the national team did not enter African Cup of Nations qualifying but in 2006 won the right, along with Gabon, to co-host the 2012 tournament where they reached the quarter finals, defeating Senegal and Libya. The country stood in as hosts again three years later and went a stage further, reaching the semi-finals and gaining the significant scalp of Tunisia in the process.

Eritrea

Founded: 1996
Affiliated to FIFA: 1998
FIFA World Ranking: 204

Eritrea has not enjoyed an easy path

Ethiopia

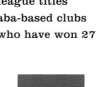

Founded: 1943
Affiliated to FIFA: 1952
FIFA World Ranking: 124
Major honors: Africa Cup of Nations champions 1962, runners-up 1957, CECAFA Cup champions 1987, 2001, 2004, 2005

Ethiopia won the four-team 1962 Africa Cup of Nations and has hosted the tournament three times but has struggled to make a major impact since the 1960s. A league competition which began in the 1940s was rebadged as the National League in 1998 and since then, all bar two league titles have been won by Addis Ababa-based clubs particularly St George FC, who have won 27 titles in total.

Gabon

Founded: 1962
Affiliated to FIFA: 1966
FIFA World Ranking: 83
Major honors: Africa Cup of Nations quarter finals 1996, 2012

Gabon's first international was a 5-4 defeat to Upper Volta in 1960 but the national team either didn't enter or qualify for an Africa Cup of Nations until 1994. Recent national squads have relied heavily on European-based players including their standout forward and Borussia Dortmund player, Pierre-Emerick Aubameyang who in 2015 became Gabon's first African Footballer of the Year.

Above: Emad Motaeb (L), Hossam Hassan (C) and Ahmed Hassan (R) of Egypt celebrate, 2006 African Cup of Nations. Opposite: Ivory Coast's Souleyman Bamba (L) and Arthur Boka (R) challenge Nigeria's Brown Ideye during their African Nations Cup (AFCON 2013) quarter final game.

Gambia

Founded: 1952
Affiliated to FIFA: 1968
FIFA World Ranking: 165

Gambia's national league, now called the GFA League First Division, has operated since 1965. But it no longer supplies the footballers who make up recent national team squads who are invariably selected from clubs overseas such as Abdou Jammeh who has played in Russia and Finland and Abdoulie Mansally who plays for Real Salt Lake in the MLS. In 2014, the country was banned by FIFA for two years for fielding over-age players at an U-20 football tournament.

Ghana

Founded: 1957
Affiliated to FIFA: 1958
FIFA World Ranking: 41

Major honors: Africa Cup of Nations champions 1963, 1965, 1978, 1982, runners-up 1968, 1970, 1992, 2010, 2015, FIFA World Cup quarter finals 2010, Olympic bronze 1992

The Black Stars have long been a major force in African football making 20 Africa Cup of Nations appearances and winning 50 games at the tournament. A recent level of consistency aided by top class players including Jordan and André Ayew, Christian Atsu and record caps holder Asamoah Gyan who has also scored 48 goals, has seen Ghana reach five semi-finals in a row at the tournament between 2008 and 2015 as well as participating at the last three FIFA World Cups.

Guinea

Founded: 1960
Affiliated to FIFA: 1962
FIFA World Ranking: 61

Major honors: Africa Cup of Nations runners-up 1976

Since their international debut in 1962, Guinea have qualified for 11 Africa Cup of Nations. In 2001, FIFA issued a two year ban for government interference in the country's football association. The national team bounced back, qualifying for the 2004, 2006 and 2008 African Cup of Nations and reaching the quarter finals in each instance. They made it a fourth quarter final in 2015 whilst in 2012, they exited at the group stage but not without beating Botswana 6-1.

Guinea-Bissau

Founded: 1974
Affiliated to FIFA: 1986
FIFA World Ranking: 147

Yet to qualify for the Africa Cup of Nations, this West African nation's senior team mostly follow the example of their country's leading player of the 1990s and 2000s, Titi Camara who played for Lens, Marseille and Liverpool, and play their club football in Europe, predominantly in Portugal.

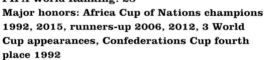

Ivory Coast

Founded: 1960
Affiliated to FIFA: 1964
FIFA World Ranking: 28

Major honors: Africa Cup of Nations champions 1992, 2015, runners-up 2006, 2012, 3 World Cup appearances, Confederations Cup fourth place 1992

The Elephants have had periods of success in the past but the last decade has seen them emerge as one of Africa's strongest teams. In 2014, the team was hit by the retirements of two legends, record caps holder Didier Zokora in midfield and record goalscorer Didier Drogba upfront. Defensive stalwart Kolo Touré retired the following year but his brother and four time African Footballer of the Year, Yaya Touré along with Saloman Kalou, Wilfried Bony and Gervinho still offer much threat to opponents.

Kenya

Founded: 1960
Affiliated to FIFA: 1960
FIFA World Ranking: 99

Major honors: CECAFA Cup champions 1975, 1981, 1982, 1983, 2002, 2013

Kenya reached the Africa Cup of Nations for the first time in 1972 and have made five appearances in total, the last in 2004. Victor Wanyama was appointed captain in 2013, the same year as Kenya won their fifth CECAFA Cup, sweeping aside Sudan 2-0 in the final.

Lesotho

Founded: 1932
Affiliated to FIFA: 1964
FIFA World Ranking: 152

The Crocodiles have made little impact in continental competitions, failing to qualify for the Africa Cup of Nations on multiple occasions. Its top flight competition, the Lesotho Premier League, is competed for by clubs whose players possess amateur or semi-professional status.

Liberia

Founded: 1936
Affiliated to FIFA: 1964
FIFA World Ranking: 101

Liberia's greatest player, George Weah became the first African to be made FIFA World Player of the Year in 1995. The explosive striker helped his country reach the 1996 and 2002 Africa Cup of Nations and narrowly miss out on heading to the 2002 FIFA World Cup by just a single point. In 2015, Weah's son George Weah Jr was called up to the national team for the first time.

Libya

Founded: 1962
Affiliated to FIFA: 1964
FIFA World Ranking: 105

Major honors: Africa Cup of Nations runners-up 1982, African Nations Championship champions 2014

The "Mediterranean Knights" first entered international competition at the 1953 Pan Arab Games but didn't appear at an Africa Cup of Nations until 1982 which they hosted. They have since made it to the 2006 and 2012 tournaments but secured their first major tournament victory two years later, beating Ghana on a penalty shootout at the 2014 African Nations Championship.

CAF Nations 3

Madagascar

Founded: 1961
Affiliated to FIFA: 1964
FIFA World Ranking: 129

Football is organized in this Indian Ocean island by the Fédération Malagasy de Football (FMF). It administers the national team who have twice won the Indian Ocean Island Games but have never reached the Africa Cup of Nations. Madagascar's top flight competition is the THB Champions League which is held between 24 clubs that, unusually, qualify each year from the country's 22 regional leagues.

Malawi

Founded: 1966
Affiliated to FIFA: 1968
FIFA World Ranking: 104
Major honors: All-Africa Games bronze 1987

Football was brought to the region by European colonists, a number of whom played in the first international in 1957 before independence when Malawi was known as Nyasaland. In 1975, the national team known as The Flames, took part in the CECAFA Challenge Cup, reaching the final where they lost to Kenya. They have since twice reached the finals of the Africa Cup of Nations, in 1984 and 2010 but not progressed beyond the first round.

Mali

Founded: 1960
Affiliated to FIFA: 1964
FIFA World Ranking: 68
Major honors: Africa Cup of Nations runners-up 1972, third place 2012, 2013, fourth place 1994, 2002, 2004

Mali have contested seven out of eight African Cup of Nations tournaments (2002-15) without winning the competition but finishing in the top four six times. The current squad possesses plenty of experience and talent and includes Bakary Sako, AJ Auxerre striker Fantamady Diarra and the former Barcelona and current Roma midfielder, Seydou Keita who has amassed a Malian record of 102 caps and 25 goals. He is the nephew of the most famous Malian footballer, Salif Keita who became the first to play overseas in France and the first Malian to win African Footballer of the Year, in 1970.

Mauritania

Founded: 1961
Affiliated to FIFA: 1970
FIFA World Ranking: 107

The former French colony has never made it to the Africa Cup of Nations although it did reach the finals of the African Nations Championship in 2014. The majority of the national team are selected from clubs who play in Ligue 1 Mauritania which was formed in 1976 and won in the 2014-15 season by FC Tevragh-Zeina.

Mauritius

Founded: 1952
Affiliated to FIFA: 1964
FIFA World Ranking: 172

For the first 20 years of their international history, Mauritius only played the neighboring islands of Madagascar and Réunion. Since that time, the national team has only won one World Cup qualifying match (versus Uganda in 2003) but did make it to the finals of the 1974 Africa Cup of Nations. The current side relies on the expertise brought by the Bru brothers, Kévin and Jonathan, both of whom play for clubs in Europe.

Morocco

Founded: 1955
Affiliated to FIFA: 1960
FIFA World Ranking: 80
Major honors: Africa Cup of Nations champions 1976, runners-up 2004, third place 1980, FIFA World Cup Round of 16 1986, Arab Nations Cup champions 2012

Above: Morocco's Mehdi Namli (No. 23, left) celebrates his goal with teammates during their African Nations Cup Group A match against South Africa

The second African nation, after Egypt, to appear at a FIFA World Cup in 1970, Morocco's first international was a 3-3 thriller with Iraq back in 1957. The "Lions of the Atlas" have since appeared at three further World Cups. At the 1986 tournament, they drew with England and Poland and defeated Portugal 3-1 to become the first African team to progress from their group. At the 1998 World Cup, a 3-0 win over Scotland wasn't quite enough and they failed to progress out of their group by a single point. The current national side, captained by Bayern Munich defender, Medhi Benatia, are striving to recapture past glories but have qualified for seven of the past 10 Africa Cup of Nations finals whilst Moroccan clubs have won five CAF Champions League titles.

Mozambique

Founded: 1976
Affiliated to FIFA: 1980
FIFA World Ranking: 102

The national team reached a high in the FIFA World Rankings of 67 in 1997 after appearing at the 1996 Africa Cup of Nations tournament where they drew with Tunisia but lost to Ghana and the Ivory Coast. It has since qualified for two further Africa Cup of Nations competitions and in 2011 opened a new national stadium, Estádio do Zimpeto, in the capital city of Maputo.

Namibia

Founded: 1990
Affiliated to FIFA: 1992
FIFA World Ranking: 134

Playing its first international in 1989 as South-West Africa against Angola, Namibia has reached two African Cup of Nations tournaments, in 1998 and 2008. The vast majority of its current national team play for clubs at home such as the nine times league champions Black Africa S.C, or in neighboring South Africa.

Niger

Founded: 1961
Affiliated to FIFA: 1964
FIFA World Ranking: 109

The national team has only attempted qualifying for tournaments sporadically but has achieved some notable results including defeating eventual 2010 Africa Cup of Nations champions Egypt 1-0 in 2010 and reaching the 2012 and 2013 editions of the competition. Their first match against European opposition occurred in 2014, a narrow 2-1 defeat to Ukraine.

Nigeria

Founded: 1945
Affiliated to FIFA: 1960
FIFA World Ranking: 63

Major honors: Africa Cup of Nations champions 1980, 1994, 2013, runners-up 1984, 1988, 1990, 2000, Olympic gold 1996, silver 2008, FIFA World Cup Round of 16 1994, 1998, 2014, Confederations Cup fourth place 1995

The Super Eagles have become an almost ever-present at FIFA World Cups and the only African team to have qualified for five of the last six tournaments. At the 1994 World Cup, they defeated Bulgaria 3-0 whilst in 1998, they beat both Bulgaria and Spain. In between, the team became the first African nation to win the Olympic football tournament. Nigeria's Africa Cup of Nations record is extraordinary. In the 20 tournaments held between 1976 and 2013, the Super Eagles qualified for 16 and on only two occasions failed to finish outside the top three teams. The current side led by Ahmed Musa, who scored two goals against Argentina in the 2014 World Cup, includes seasoned internationals like John Obi Mikel, and Lazio midfielder, Ogenyi Onazi but has lost the services of its most capped player, goalkeeper Vincent Enyeama who announced his international retirement in 2015 after 101 matches.

Rwanda

Founded: 1972
Affiliated to FIFA: 1978
FIFA World Ranking: 85

The national team, nicknamed Amavubi (The Wasps), has frequently struggled against continental opposition but did qualify for the African Cup of Nations for the first time in 2004 where they won one and drew one of their three games. Their 2015 qualifying campaign ended in disaster when after defeating Congo in a penalty shootout, Rwanda was disqualified from the competition for fielding an ineligible player, Daddy Birori.

São Tomé e Principe

Founded: 1975
Affiliated to FIFA: 1986
FIFA World Ranking: 159

After a long period of inactivity, beginning in 2003, São Tomé e Principe returned to the international fray, entering qualifying for the 2014 FIFA World Cup with a 5-0 loss to Congo followed by a creditable 1-1 draw four days later against the same opponents. They began qualifying for the 2018 World Cup with a victory, over Ethiopia, 1-0.

Senegal

Founded: 1960
Affiliated to FIFA: 1964
FIFA World Ranking: 45

Major honors: FIFA World Cup quarter final 2002, Africa Cup of Nations runners-up 2002, fourth place 19656, 1990,

Senegal's finest year came in 2002 when they finished second to Cameroon at the Africa Cup of Nations and appeared in their first FIFA World Cup finals. Facing the defending champions, France, in the opening game of the tournament, the "Lions of Terenga" sprang an almighty shock with Pape "Papa" Bouba Diop scoring the winner. Top Senegalese footballers eschew their own country's Premier League in favor of playing for clubs abroad. Twenty-three of the 25-man squad picked to play their 2018 World Cup qualifier against Madagascar, for example, played their club football in Europe.

Seychelles

Founded: 1979
Affiliated to FIFA: 1986
FIFA World Ranking: 191

The least populous full member of CAF with a population under 100,000, the Seychelles play their home games at the 10,000 capacity Stade Linité. They have not reached an Africa Cup of Nations tournament so far but in 2011 did win the Indian Ocean Island Games – a seven team tournament – beating Mauritius in the final.

CAF Nations 4

Sierra Leone

Founded: 1960
Affiliated to FIFA: 1960
FIFA World Ranking: 117

Civil war in the past and the Ebola epidemic more recently has disrupted the country's footballing activities. A number of national team players traditionally played for domestic clubs including FC Johansen and Mighty Blackpool, whilst current players abroad include Mohamed Bangura (Dalian Yifang, China), Umaru Bangura (Dinamo Minsk, Russia) and national team captain, Kei Kamara (Columbus Crew, USA).

Somalia

Founded: 1951
Affiliated to FIFA: 1962
FIFA World Ranking: 204

Little funding, poor facilities and a background of political unrest has seen Somalia barely enter competition over the years. They have only entered qualifying for the Africa Cup of Nations once, in 1974, but with a national stadium under construction, the intent is to compete to reach the 2019 competition.

South Africa

Founded: 1991
Affiliated to FIFA: 1992
FIFA World Ranking: 73
Major honors: Africa Cup of Nations champions 1996, runners-up 1998, third place 2000, Confederation Cup fourth place 2009, World Cup three appearances

South Africa was expelled from CAF in 1958 and FIFA in 1961 for the government's segregationist policy. It wasn't until apartheid was dismantled and a new, multi-racial football association formed in 1991 that the country was readmitted into international competition. Possessing standout players such as Mark Fish and Lucas Radebe in defense and from 1997, record goalscorer, Benni McCarthy in attack, "Bafana Bafana" reached three Africa Cup of Nations semi-finals in a row as well as the 1998 and 2002 FIFA World Cups. A third appearance was assured in 2004 when the country was selected to become Africa's first World Cup hosts for the 2010 edition.

South Sudan

Founded: 2011
Affiliated to FIFA: 2012
FIFA World Ranking: 140

CAF's newest member, South Sudan played its first recognized international match against Uganda in 2012 in the new nation's capital, Juba. Three years later, it won its first game, versus Equatorial Guinea in qualifying for the 2017 Africa Cup of Nations. The South Sudan Football Championship was set up in 2011 with its first winners in 2012. So far, Atlabara Football Club have emerged twice as league champions.

Sudan

Founded: 1936
Affiliated to FIFA: 1948
FIFA World Ranking: 136
Major honors: Africa Cup of Nations champions 1970, runners-up 1959, 1963. African Nations Championship third place, 2011

Sudan hosted the first Africa Cup of Nations in 1957 and has qualified for eight tournaments overall. Most of its highest finishes and best performances came within the first 20 years of the competition after which it did not qualify for some 32 years. The country's top flight club competition, the Sudan Premier League, started in 1965 and with two short hiatuses (1975-1976 and 1978-80) has been run annually ever since. Teams from Sudan's largest city, Omdurman, have dominated the competition, winning 43 of the 45 first league titles.

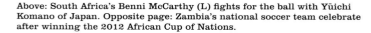

Above: South Africa's Benni McCarthy (L) fights for the ball with Yūichi Komano of Japan. Opposite page: Zambia's national soccer team celebrate after winning the 2012 African Cup of Nations.

Swaziland

Founded: 1968
Affiliated to FIFA: 1978
FIFA World Ranking: 127

Swaziland are one of the continent's more lowly sides, rarely capable of troubling Africa's top teams. Fans had to wait 16 years in between celebrating victories in World Cup qualifying games, with the side finally defeating Togo 2-1 in 2008. A recent run in 2015 and 2016 of four unbeaten games including a 0-0 draw with Nigeria ranks amongst the best the side has achieved.

Tanzania

Founded: 1930
Affiliated to FIFA: 1964
FIFA World Ranking: 125

Tanzania attended their one and only Africa Cup of Nations in 1980, six years after German ex-goalkeeper, Bert Trautmann, had spent two years in the country forming coaching associations and helping to organize and improve the game there. The country's two biggest clubs Simba Sports Club and Young Africans both hail from Dar-es-Salaam and have won 14 of the last 15 Tanzanian Premier League titles between them.

Togo

Founded: 1960
Affiliated to FIFA: 1964
FIFA World Ranking: 103

Togo made their FIFA World Cup debut in 2006 and have made it to seven Africa Cup of Nations finals. It should have been eight but as the team traveled through Angola heading to the 2010 tournament, their team bus was attacked by terrorists leaving three dead and a number of players and officials wounded. The team withdrew from the competition and were initially barred from entering the next two tournaments until FIFA intervened. The team, led by captain and record goalscorer, Emmanuel Adebayor, achieved their first quarter final placing at the Africa Cup of Nations in 2013.

Tunisia

Founded: 1957
Affiliated to FIFA: 1960
FIFA World Ranking: 48
Major honors: Africa Cup of Nations champions 2004

Tunisia's appearance at the 1978 FIFA World Cup made Abdelmajid Chetali the first African coach at a World Cup and saw his side become the first African nation to win a finals match when they defeated Mexico 3-1. It was one of four World Cup appearances for the "Eagles of Carthage" who have also hosted the Africa Cup of Nations three times, becoming champions on the third occasion by overcoming Morocco in an all-North Africa final. A strong domestic league has also enabled Tunisian clubs to prosper at continental level, reaching the final of the CAF Champions League on 11 separate occasions.

Uganda

Founded: 1924
Affiliated to FIFA: 1960
FIFA World Ranking: 70
Major honors: Africa Cup of Nations runners-up 1978, CECAFA Cup champions 14 times

Football was brought to Uganda at the turn of the 20th century and the Kabaka's Cup, established in 1925, remained its top club competition until 1971 when it became the Uganda Cup. Two of the country's leading clubs, Simba FC in 1972 and SC Villa in 1991, have reached the final of the CAF Champions League. Internationally, Uganda can match stronger opponents on the day but have not been able to qualify for the Africa Cup of Nations since finishing as runners-up in 1978. The national team did, however, go on a 14 game unbeaten run lasting almost two years from May 2014.

Zambia

Founded: 1929
Affiliated to FIFA: 1964
FIFA World Ranking: 76
Major honors: Africa Cup of Nations champions 2012, runners-up 1974, 1994, CECAFA Cup champions 1984, 1991

Tragedy struck Zambian football in 1993 after a plane ferrying the 18 players of the national team plus officials to Senegal for a FIFA World Cup qualifier crashed, killing all onboard. Astonishingly, Zambia regrouped and made it to the final of the Africa Cup of Nations the following year, but lost to Nigeria 2-0. Eighteen years later, Zambia finally won the competition, a testament to the series of excellent players the country has produced over the decades. Most highly rated of all remains legendary striker Godfrey Chitalu who scored a record 79 goals in 111 games between 1968 and 1980.

Zimbabwe

Founded: 1965
Affiliated to FIFA: 1965
FIFA World Ranking: 131

Two appearances at Africa Cup of Nations (2004, 2006) is scant return for a series of Zimbabwean sides which have possessed talented players and were ranked as high as 40 in the FIFA World Rankings back in 1995. In June 2015, Zimbabwe played Malawi for a 53rd time, far and away their most frequent opponents, but were then suspended from competition by FIFA for internal wranglings and unpaid debts.

AFC Nations 1

Afghanistan
Founded: 1922
Affiliated to FIFA: 1948
FIFA World Ranking: 154
Major honors: SAFF Championships champions 2013

A founder member of the AFC but one that has made only a slight impact, Afghanistan have never qualified for the Asian Cup or World Cup. In 2013, after years of rebuilding following conflict in the country, they stunned world football by winning the SAFF Championship defeating India in the final.

Australia
Founded: 1961
Affiliated to FIFA: 1963
FIFA World Ranking: 68
Major honors: Asian Cup champions 2015, runners-up 2011, OFC Nations Cup champions 1980, 1996, 2000, 2004, Confederations Cup runners up 1997, third place 2001

Football in Australia extends all the way back to 1880 when a game between Wanderers and King's School of Parramatta was played. In a sports-mad country where soccer ranked cricket and rugby, football was helped kept alive by the enthusiasm of European immigrants. The national team, dubbed the Socceroos, had only fitful success until they qualified for the 1974 World Cup, lost two play-offs for a World Cup place in 1998 (v Iran) and 2002

(v Uruguay) but have qualified for every tournament since. A switch to the AFC gave both the Socceroos and the country's best clubs the chance to test themselves regularly against Asian opposition with success as Australia won the 2015 prestigious AFC Asian Cup. At club level, the A League replaced the National Soccer League in 2005. The now ten-team league is standalone without relegation and attracted 1,826,776 spectators in the 2014-15 season.

Bahrain
Founded: 1957
Affiliated to FIFA: 1968
FIFA World Ranking: 130
Major honors: Asian Cup fourth place 2004, Arab Cup runners-up 1985, 2002

Bahrain have risen up the rankings on the way to become a middleweight in the AFC. They have twice reached the intercontinental play-offs for World Cup qualifying, just two matches away from reaching football's biggest stage. In 2005, they were defeated by Trinidad and Tobago and four years later, suffered defeat to New Zealand. In both play-offs, the Bahrainis drew one game and lost the other by a single goal margin.

Bangladesh
Founded: 1972
Affiliated to FIFA: 1976
FIFA World Ranking: 177

Bangladesh have only reached one Asian Cup tournament, back in 1980. The current squad consists of home-based footballers who play for clubs in the Bangladesh Premier League (the successor to the National Football Championship which, itself, began in 2000). Sheikh Jamal Dhanmondi SC with three titles and Abahani Dakar with four titles are its most successful teams.

Bhutan
Founded: 1983
Affiliated to FIFA: 2000
FIFA World Ranking: 193

A footballing minnow in Asia, Bhutan only competed against neighboring nations in south Asia until it entered the qualifying rounds for the 2000 Asian Cup. Many of the current national team are under 23 years of age and drawn from Bhutan's biggest club - Thimphu City.

Brunei Darussalam
Founded: 1959
Affiliated to FIFA: 1969
FIFA World Ranking: 184

With just 20 FIFA-registered clubs and under 1,500 players, the Brunei national team has a small pool to select from. The country has often eschewed entering international tournaments in favor of sending a representative team to play in Malaysia's domestic competitions. FIFA banned Brunei from competing between 2009 and 2011 for government interference in the country's football association.

Cambodia
Founded: 1933
Affiliated to FIFA: 1954
FIFA World Ranking: 183
Major honors: Asian Cup fourth place 1972

One of Asia's weakest sides over the decades, their only success came with a fourth place at the 1972 Asian Cup when the team was known as the Khmer Republic national football team (1970-75). After a bright start with a win and a draw in their first two 2018 FIFA World Cup qualifying games, Cambodia endured a torrid remainder of 2015, losing their next seven qualifiers.

China PR
Founded: 1924
Affiliated to FIFA: 1931
FIFA World Ranking: 93

Above: Australia's Massimo Luongo (21) on his way to collect the Most Valuable Player award of the Asian Cup, 2015. Opposite page: Iraq's Marwan Hussein Al-Ajeeli challenges Iran's goalkeeper Alireza Haghighi during their Asian Cup quarter-final

Major honors: Asian Cup runners-up 1984, 2004, third place 1976, 1992

The booming Chinese Super League has attracted increasing interest with over 5.3 million spectators in 2015, the fifth season in a row that Guangzhou Evergrande Taobao FC have won the title. The club have twice won the AFC Champions League and were the first Chinese side to take part in the FIFA Club World Cup in 2013. Internationally, the men's team has been unable to build upon its FIFA World Cup debut in 2002 whilst China's women's team, the "Steel Roses," has made bigger strides with eight Women's Asian Cup titles and a runners-up spot at both the Olympics (1996) and the FIFA Women's World Cup (1999).

Chinese Taipei

Founded: 1936
Affiliated to FIFA: 1954
FIFA World Ranking: 181
Major honors: Asian Games gold 1954, 1958, Asian Cup third place 1960, fourth place 1968

After some notable successes in the 1950s and 1960s, Chinese Taipei (formerly known as Taiwan) has struggled to make an impact. Hopes are rising for the future, though, based largely on increasing numbers of Chinese Taipei footballers playing in China's professional leagues, amongst them Chen Po-Liang, regarded as the country's best player.

Guam

Founded: 1975
Affiliated to FIFA: 1996
FIFA World Ranking: 156

Any joy at Guam finally playing their first international game in 1972 versus Fiji was quickly tempered by a 12-0 defeat. The island has only entered World Cup qualifying campaigns twice, the latter, for the 2018 tournament saw the team managed by former Seattle Sounders coach, Gary White, win their first ever qualifying match, beating Turkmenistan 1-0, followed a month later by a second victory, this time over India.

Hong Kong

Founded: 1914
Affiliated to FIFA: 1954
FIFA World Ranking: 137
Major honors: Asian Cup third place, 1956, East Asian Games champions 2009

Hong Kong's first FIFA-recognized match was a 3-3 thriller versus South Korea in 1954 and two years later they hosted the AFC Asian Cup. Attempts to qualify for every World Cup since 1974 have ended early but in 2009, they defeated North Korea in the semi-final of the East Asian Games and surprised favorites Japan in the final, winning both games by penalty shootouts to win their first international competition.

India

Founded: 1937
Affiliated to FIFA: 1948
FIFA World Ranking: 162
Major honors: Asian Games champions 1951, 1962, Asian Cup runners-up 1964, South Asian Football Federation Cup champions 7 times.

India qualified for the 1950 FIFA World Cup but withdrew and didn't play another World Cup qualifying game until 1985. Back in the 1950s and early 1960s, they possessed one of the strongest national teams in Asia. Cricket still obsesses the majority of the Indian nation, but the development of a professional club I-League from 2007 and the Indian Super League in 2013 is designed to stimulate interest as is the staging of the FIFA U-17 World Cup India in 2017.

Indonesia

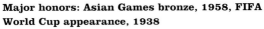

Founded: 1930
Affiliated to FIFA: 1952
FIFA World Ranking: 180
Major honors: Asian Games bronze, 1958, FIFA World Cup appearance, 1938

Football is popular amongst Indonesians but a limited infrastructure and much in-fighting between those that run the game there has limited development. In November 2015, Indonesia was suspended by FIFA for government interference in the country's football association. As a result, Indonesia were barred from attempting qualify for either the 2018 FIFA World Cup or the 2019 AFC Asian Cup.

Iran

Founded: 1920
Affiliated to FIFA: 1948
FIFA World Ranking: 44
Major honors: Asian Cup champions 1968, 1972, 1976, third place 1980, 1988, 1996, 2004, Asian Games gold 1949, 1990, 1998, 2002

Currently, the highest-rated Asian in the FIFA World Rankings, Iran has a strong footballing past with three consecutive Asian Cup triumphs and four appearances at FIFA World Cups. As of 2015, the team had won 209 and only lost 58 of its 343 international matches, their first official game being a 0-0 draw with Afghanistan in 1941. Iran possesses one of the strongest-ranked club leagues in Asia. Iran's Persian Gulf Pro League is the only league in West Asia which is allocated two places for clubs each year in the AFC Champions League.

Iraq

Founded: 1948
Affiliated to FIFA: 1950
FIFA World Ranking: 89
Major honors: Asian Cup champions 2007, fourth place 1976, 2015, Asian Games gold medal 1982, FIFA World Cup appearance, 1986

Iraq's national team brought some sporting pride to the war-torn country with a magnificent display at the 2007 AFC Asian Cup, defeating favorites, South Korea in the semi-final and Saudi Arabia in the final to win the competition for the first time. Whilst Ali Adnan plays for Serie A side, Udinese and Ahmed Yasin Ghani for Swedish team AIK, most of the national team also play at home for one of the Iraqi Premier League's 20 clubs. The league has seen 11 different champions since its formation in 1974. Two Iraqi clubs, Al Shorta SC in 1971 and Al-Karkh SC in 1989 have been runners-up in the AFC Champions League.

AFC Nations 2

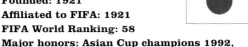

Japan

Founded: 1921
Affiliated to FIFA: 1921
FIFA World Ranking: 58
Major honors: Asian Cup champions 1992, 2000, 2004, 2011, FIFA World Cup Round of 16 2002, 2010, Confederations Cup runners-up 2001, Olympic bronze 1968

Although now regarded as one of the continent's heavyweights, it has not always been the case. Before the 1990s, Japan's high water mark had been their bronze medal at the Mexico Olympics and they did not reach the finals of the Asian Cup until 1988. The establishment of a fully professional league, the J-League in 1993 saw an upturn in public interest and player development. Five years later, the team made their first appearance at the FIFA World Cup. Japan's first high profile footballer to play overseas, Hidetoshi Nakata, became a major celebrity in Japan and a number of Japanese footballers have followed, now playing in the strongest leagues in Europe from Keisuke Honda at AC Milan to Shinji Kagawa at Borussia Dortmund. To emphasize their globetrotting status, Japan are the only nation from outside of the Americas to take part in the Copa América, in 1999.

Jordan

Founded: 1949
Affiliated to FIFA: 1956
FIFA World Ranking: 82
Major honors: Asian Cup quarter finals 2004, 2011

Jordan's most frequent international opponents have been Iraq who they have beaten 11 times and drawn 11 times in 47 internationals. The national team scored 30 goals in a strong run in qualifying for the 2014 World Cup to reach the intercontinental play-off, losing to Uruguay at the last hurdle. Undeterred, "Al-Nashāmā" (the Chivalrous) began qualifying for the 2018 competition with a bang, defeating Tajikistan twice and recording notable victories over both Iraq and Asian Cup-holders, Australia.

Korea DPR (North Korea)

Founded: 1945
Affiliated to FIFA: 1958
FIFA World Ranking: 95
Major honors: FIFA World Cup quarter final 1966, Asian Cup fourth place 1983, AFC Challenge Cup champions 2010, 2012, Olympic quarter finals 1976

Under former player, Kim Jong-hun, North Korea reached their second FIFA World Cup in 2010. Whilst a narrow defeat to Brazil earned praise, two further losses meant the side did not make the impact of their predecessors in 1966 who became the first team from Asia to reach a World Cup quarter finals. This was achieved with one of the all-time greatest World Cup shocks, a 1-0 win over Italy courtesy of a goal by Pak Doo-Ik, a corporal in the North Korean Army. The country's DPR Korea League operates a closed doors policy with no foreign transfers and its clubs cannot participate in AFC club competitions.

Korea Republic (South Korea)

Founded: 1933
Affiliated to FIFA: 1948
FIFA World Ranking: 53
Major honors: FIFA World Cup fourth place 2002, Asian Cup champions 1956, 1960, runners-up 1972, 1980, 1988, 2015, Asian Games champions 1970, 1978, 1986, Olympic bronze 2012

In 1954, South Korea became the second team from Asia after Dutch East Indies (Indonesia) to enter the FIFA World Cup. Since their debut, the "Taeguk Warriors" have made it to a further eight World Cups with the undoubted high point, their semi-final appearance before adoring home fans in 2002, achieved by an incredible run involving wins over Poland, Portugal, Italy and Spain. They have been a fixture at every World Cup since, partly due to the benefits of a strong domestic club scene centered on the K-League whose clubs have won ten AFC Champions League titles, and due to experience of top players playing in top leagues overseas. The 2000s saw South Korea notch three semi-final and one final appearances in five Asian Cups as well as an Olympic bronze medal at the 2012 tournament.

Above: Referee Ali Al Badwawi tries to stop a scuffle amongst players during the 2007 AFC Asian Cup game between Japan and South Korea

Kuwait

Founded: 1952
Affiliated to FIFA: 1964
FIFA World Ranking: 133
Major honors: Asian Cup champions 1980, runners-up 1976, third place 1984, FIFA World Cup appearance 1982

The one-time holders of the biggest win achieved in international football when they defeated Bhutan 20-0 in 2000, Kuwait's most successful side including lively striker Faisal Al-Dakhil, emerged in the late 1970s. The team won the 1980 Asian Cup defeating South Korea 3-0 in the final and made it to the quarter finals of the 1980 Olympics. Two years later, the team made its one and only appearance at the FIFA World Cup gaining a draw with Czechoslovakia and losing narrowly to England 1-0.

Kyrgyzstan

Founded: 1992
Affiliated to FIFA: 1994
FIFA World Ranking: 105

Following the break-up of the Soviet Union, Kyrgyzstan played its first match against Uzbekistan in 1993. The current side includes foreign-based players such as Spartak Semey midfielder, Anatoliy Vlasichev and captain, Azamat Baymatov who plays in Bahrain for Sitra. Their most experienced player with 54 caps, Vadim Kharchenko, however plays at home for FC Dordoi, the country's leading club.

Laos

Founded: 1951
Affiliated to FIFA: 1952
FIFA World Ranking: 178

With a mostly amateur league system, the Laos national team's first appearance in an Asian-wide tournament was at the 2014 AFC Challenge Cup for Asia's emerging footballing nations where they finished bottom of their group. The following year provided little cheer with just one victory (over local rivals, Cambodia) from ten matches.

Lebanon

Founded: 1933
Affiliated to FIFA: 1936
FIFA World Ranking: 140

Lebanon has appeared at one Asian Cup, in 2000, but got desperately close for the 2015 edition when a pair of 5-2 victories over Thailand and two draws with Kuwait left them just one point short of qualifying. The two dominant clubs in the country are both based in Beirut: Nejmeh SC and Al-Ansar Sporting Club.

Macau

Founded: 1939
Affiliated to FIFA: 1978
FIFA World Ranking: 195

This Chinese-administered territory began attempts to qualify for FIFA World Cups only in the early 1990s and have come up short, rarely getting through more than one or two rounds of qualifying. Domestically, the Liga de Elite has struggled with club withdrawals from the league and is now a ten team competition.

Malaysia

Founded: 1933
Affiliated to FIFA: 1954
FIFA World Ranking: 171
Major honors: Asian Games bronze 1962, 1974, AFF Championships champions 2010

Before Malaysia's founding as a nation in 1963, the separate states of North Borneo, Sarawak and Malaya competed independently with Malaya winning a bronze medal at the Asian Games. The team has reached three Asian Cup tournaments and won the AFF Championships for southeast Asian countries in 2010.

Maldives

Founded: 1982
Affiliated to FIFA: 1986
FIFA World Ranking: 157
Major honors: South Asian Football Federation Cup champions 2008

The Maldives have yet to face the top level of Asian-wide competition having never qualified for the Asian Cup but they did host the SAFF Cup in 2008. Home advantage proved valuable as the team mostly drawn from the 8-team Dhivehi League defeated Pakistan, Nepal and India in the final to win a major trophy for the first time in their footballing history.

Mongolia

Founded: 1959
Affiliated to FIFA: 1998
FIFA World Ranking: 201

Mongolia was inactive in international football between 1960 and 1998 and has not fared well since returning to competition with a humbling 15-0 defeat to Uzbekistan their record loss. The national team has only won nine games in total, four of those against Guam.

Myanmar

Founded: 1947
Affiliated to FIFA: 1948
FIFA World Ranking: 153
Major honors: Asian Cup runners-up 1958, Asian Games gold 1966, 1970

The "White Angels" were one of Asia's leading football forces in the 1960s but have fallen down the rankings in more recent times as witnessed by their first World Cup qualifying matches, against China in 2007, which ended in 4-0 and 7-0 defeats.

Nepal

Founded: 1951
Affiliated to FIFA: 1972
FIFA World Ranking: 188
Major honors: SAFF Championship semi-finals, 1993, 2011, 2013

Nepal first entered qualifying for the FIFA World Cup in the 1980s and although they rarely get close to obtaining a place at the tournament have had some notable victories. Some promising young players under development, do give Nepal hope for the future. In 2012, striker, Bimal Gharti Magar made his national team debut against Bangladesh at the tender age of 14, becoming the youngest player to represent his country at full senior level.

Oman

Founded: 1978
Affiliated to FIFA: 1980
FIFA World Ranking: 97

Oman's rise in the early 21st century was based around a golden generation of players who took the country on an incredible journey at the 1995 FIFA U-17 World Cup, reaching the semi-final after victories over Germany, Canada and Nigeria. The senior team has not yet reached a FIFA World Cup but has qualified for Asian Cups in 2004, 2007 and 2015, the latter via players almost exclusively selected from the 14-team Oman Professional League.

AFC Nations 3

Pakistan

Founded: 1948
Affiliated to FIFA: 1948
FIFA World Ranking: 185
Major honors: SAFF Championship semi-final 1997, 2005

Pakistan have rarely risen above 150 in the FIFA World Rankings nor have they qualified for the Asian Cup. They have had some limited success at more regional competitions, reaching the semi-finals of the SAFF Championship twice but were knocked out of 2018 World Cup qualifying by Yemen at an early stage.

Palestine

Founded: 1928
Affiliated to FIFA: 1988
FIFA World Ranking: 110
Major honors: AFC Challenge Cup champions 2014

With its first organized football clubs dating back to the 1920s, Palestine entered qualifying for the 1934 World Cup but the political conflicts in the region prevented it from competing for over six decades. Despite ongoing issues with Israel which has seen players detained or refused entry, the national team brought some cheer with a stunning AFC Challenge Cup victory in 2014 which took them into the top 100 of the FIFA World Rankings and gained them a place at their first Asian Cup in 2015.

Philippines

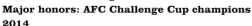

Founded: 1907
Affiliated to FIFA: 1930
FIFA World Ranking: 134
Major honors: AFC Challenge Cup runners-up, 2014

The Philippines recorded their biggest win in 1917 when they mauled Japan 15-2 at the Far Eastern Championship Games. Fifty years later, Japan gained revenge winning 15-0 in qualifiers for the 1968 Olympics. Philippine football has mostly stayed in the doldrums and it was only in 2011 that the national team gained their first victory in World Cup qualifying games when the side managed to defeat Sri Lanka 4-0.

Qatar

Founded: 1960
Affiliated to FIFA: 1972
FIFA World Ranking: 78
Major honors: Asian Games gold 2006, Gulf Cup of Nations champions 1992, 2004, 2014

The surprise winners of the bid process to host the 2022 FIFA World Cup, Qatar has a modest record in the Asian Football Confederation. Its highest placed finish at the Asian Cup is fifth but it did win the Asian Games football tournament as host in 2006. The country's top clubs compete in the Qatar Stars League and four cup competitions. One of its former stars, Mansour Muftah, remains the national team's record goalscorer with 53 goals.

Saudi Arabia

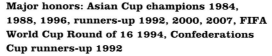

Founded: 1956
Affiliated to FIFA: 1956
FIFA World Ranking: 55
Major honors: Asian Cup champions 1984, 1988, 1996, runners-up 1992, 2000, 2007, FIFA World Cup Round of 16 1994, Confederations Cup runners-up 1992

Large scale investment in Saudi Arabian football began in the 1970s with foreign coaches imported, facilities constructed and resources allowing leading clubs such as Al Ahli, Al Nasr and Al Hillal to develop. Al Hillal have won the most Saudi league titles (12) whilst Al-Ittihad triumphed in the AFC Champions League twice, in 2004 and 2005. In addition, Saudi clubs have been Champions League runners-up eight times, the most recent in 2014. Internationally, the national team has proved strong competitors in the AFC and enjoyed a spectacular run at their first of four FIFA World Cup finals. The 1994 team beat Morocco and Belgium, the latter with a goal from Saeed Owairan – the goal of the tournament.

Singapore

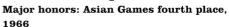

Founded: 1892
Affiliated to FIFA: 1952
FIFA World Ranking: 148
Major honors: Asian Games fourth place, 1966

The oldest football association in Asia has struggled to embed a high level club competition with the S.League struggling and player development reliant on overseas competition. Foreign clubs have been invited to compete in the S.League in an attempt to revive its fortunes, one of whom, Brunei DPMM FC, won the title in 2015.

Sri Lanka

Founded: 1939
Affiliated to FIFA: 1952
FIFA World Ranking: 189
Major honors: SAFF Championship champions 1995

Football was introduced to Sri Lanka by British military forces in the 1890s and 1900s. From a high of 126th in the world in 1996, Sri Lanka's ranking has slid downwards as results declined and football increasingly was eclipsed by the nation's number one sport, cricket. The Sri Lanka Premier League has a distinctly military air with leading clubs by the name of Navy, Air Force and Army SC.

Syria

Founded: 1936
Affiliated to FIFA: 1937
FIFA World Ranking: 125

Syria have competed in five Asian Cups but their qualification attempts for the 2010 World Cup saw them disqualified for fielding an ineligible player against Tajikistan. Despite significant disruption in their war-torn country which means all home games are played outside of its borders, the national team only lost two games and won 10 out of 13 from the middle of 2014 to the end of 2015.

Opposite page: Thailand's Kiatisuk Senamuang (13) is fouled by Iraq's Ali Rehema during their AFC Asian Cup Group A match

Tajikistan

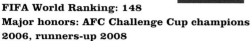

Founded: 1936
Affiliated to FIFA: 1994
FIFA World Ranking: 148
Major honors: AFC Challenge Cup champions 2006, runners-up 2008

Football is Tajikistan's most popular sport with a national league established in 1937 with Dinamo Stalinabad (now Dynamo Dushanbe) its first champion. The current national team is mostly filled with players from leading club, Istiklol winners of the 2014 and 2015 Tajik League title.

Thailand

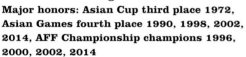

Founded: 1916
Affiliated to FIFA: 1925
FIFA World Ranking: 120
Major honors: Asian Cup third place 1972, Asian Games fourth place 1990, 1998, 2002, 2014, AFF Championship champions 1996, 2000, 2002, 2014

First playing in the early 20th Century as Siam before renamed Thailand in 1949, the Thai national team first entered World Cup qualifying for the 1974 tournament and appeared at a number of Olympic football tournaments. A strong contender for regional championships in south-east Asia, Thailand's latest triumph came when winning the AFF Championship (known as the Suzuki Cup) in 2014 under their head coach and celebrated former player, Kiatisuk Senamuang who as a striker for the national team scored a record 71 goals in 134 appearances.

Timor-Leste

Founded: 2002
Affiliated to FIFA: 2005
FIFA World Ranking: 170

Football was popularised here by Portuguese colonists but the country's footballers have relatively few good quality pitches and facilities and consequently are one of the minnows and newest teams in the Asian Football Confederation. Nine years after their first international match, Timor-Leste finally won a fixture and in spectacular style beating Cambodia 5-1.

Turkmenistan

Founded: 1992
Affiliated to FIFA: 1994
FIFA World Ranking: 114

The national team has made the quarter finals of the Asian Games twice but only qualified for the Asian Cups final once, in 2004. The majority of its leading footballers play for the ten clubs who contest the Ýokary Liga each season which runs from April to November. FK Köpetdag Aşgabat with six league titles are the most successful Ýokary Liga club.

United Arab Emirates

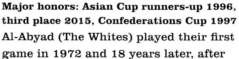

Founded: 1971
Affiliated to FIFA: 1974
FIFA World Ranking: 65
Major honors: Asian Cup runners-up 1996, third place 2015, Confederations Cup 1997

Al-Abyad (The Whites) played their first game in 1972 and 18 years later, after being coached by two former Brazilian World Cup winners in Mário Zagallo and Carlos Alberto Parreira, found themselves making their first appearance at a FIFA World Cup. The 12 team UAE Arabian Gulf League (formerly the Pro League) is the peak of club competition and has been won most often by Al Ain who in 2003 became the first UAE club to win the AFC Champions League.

Uzbekistan

Founded: 1946
Affiliated to FIFA: 1994
FIFA World Ranking: 71
Major honors: Asian Cup fourth place 2011, quarter finals 2004, Asian Games champions 1994

A rather turbulent management scene has seen some 20 head coaches come and go in the first 21 years since independence but Uzbekistan are the strongest of the Central Asian nations. Their breakthrough tournament performance occurred at the 2004 Asian Cup where they topped a tough group containing Saudi Arabia, Iraq and Turkmenistan and went on to the quarter finals where they were beaten in a penalty shootout by Bahrain. At every Asian Cup since, they have reached the quarter finals stage or, in 2011, the semi-finals.

Vietnam

Founded: 1962
Affiliated to FIFA: 1964
FIFA World Ranking: 146
Major honors: Asian Cup fourth place 1956, 1960, quarter finals 2007

Whilst split into two countries, South Vietnam finished fourth at the Asian Cup twice. Today, the Vietnamese national team play their home games at the 40,000-capacity Mỹ Đình National Stadium which opened in 2003, three years after Vietnam's top club competition, the V League turned fully professional. The V League now has two divisions, V1 which contained 14 clubs in 2016 and V2 which featured 10 teams.

Yemen

Founded: 1962
Affiliated to FIFA: 1980
FIFA World Ranking: 175

Yemen was formed in 1990 when North and South Yemen reunited. With a small playing base of under 10,000 registered footballers, the national team has endured some tough years including going winless throughout 2013 for example. It did, however, get close to qualifying for the 2002 World Cup when finishing just one point and one place behind the United Arab Emirates.

CONCACAF Nations 1

Anguilla

Founded: 1990
Affiliated to FIFA: 1996
FIFA World Ranking: 204

With a population of barely 15,000, being merely competitive is this tiny Caribbean nation's goal. Its first official international was played in 1991 – a 1-1 draw against Montserrat – only one of three draws and four wins the team has achieved since.

Antigua and Barbuda

Founded: 1928
Affiliated to FIFA: 1972
FIFA World Ranking: 90

This island nation's first official international match in 1972 ended in a sobering 11-1 thrashing at the hands of Trinidad and Tobago and remains their worst ever defeat. The team has improved as is seen from a FIFA World Ranking that places them above Latvia, Guatemala and China. Peter Byers holds both the record for most caps (69) and most goals (38).

Aruba

Founded:
Affiliated to FIFA:
FIFA World Ranking: 115

Formerly part of the Netherlands Antilles, Aruba had their hopes dashed during qualifying for the 2014 World Cup when they were knocked out on penalties after their two legged tie with St. Lucia had ended 6-6 on aggregate.

Bahamas

Founded: 1967
Affiliated to FIFA: 1968
FIFA World Ranking: 204

Lodged at the bottom of the FIFA World Rankings, the Bahamas only sporadically competes in international competitions with its last CONCACAF Gold Cup campaign, a failed attempt at qualifying for the 2007 edition. Their sole 2015 fixture resulted in a 5-0 defeat at the hands of Bermuda.

Barbados

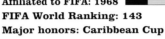

Founded: 1910
Affiliated to FIFA: 1968
FIFA World Ranking: 143
Major honors: Caribbean Cup fourth place 2005

Barbados have never reached a major tournament and with the exception of several players including captain, Emmerson Boyce who has played for Wigan and Blackpool in the English leagues, the team comprises amateurs or semi-pro players. The team was disqualified from continuing their 2018 World Cup qualifying campaign after fielding an ineligible player.

Belize

Founded: 1980
Affiliated to FIFA: 1986
FIFA World Ranking: 120

The weakest of the Central American sides in the region, Belize have yet to win a game against their neighbors, Guatemala in 10 attempts, their most played opponent. After beating the Cayman Islands and Dominican Republic, Belize exited qualifying for the 2018 FIFA World Cup, losing to Canada. The Premier League of Belize was set up in 2011, with Belmopan Bandits its most successful side with four league titles.

Bermuda

Founded: 1928
Affiliated to FIFA: 1962
FIFA World Ranking: 158
Major honors: Pan American Games runners-up 1967

Bermuda's current squad is drawn from

semi-professional clubs in the United States sprinkled with players from professional England clubs such as Huddersfield striker, Nahki Wells and Mansfield Town's Reggie Lambe. Fans with long memories warmly recall the 1967 Pan-American Games where Bermuda reached the final where they were defeated by Mexico.

British Virgin Islands

Founded: 1974
Affiliated to FIFA: 1996
FIFA World Ranking: 199

A single draw and nine defeats in their ten matches during 2014 and 2015 tells a tale of a team always found at the bottom of the FIFA World Rankings in line with their registered player base of just 435 footballers. In 2000 to 2001, their technical director was André Villas-Boas who would go on to become head coach of Tottenham Hotspur, Chelsea, Porto and since 2014, Zenit St Petersburg.

Above: Brazil's Fabio (L) and Canada's Nick Dasovic tussle during a FIFA Confederations Cup match in 2001. Opposite page Top: El Salvador midfielder Pablo Punyed is fouled by Costa Rica defender Giancarolo González. Bottom: Mexico lifts the CONCACAF Gold Cup after beating Jamaica 3-1.

Canada

Founded: 1912
Affiliated to FIFA: 1913
FIFA World Ranking: 85
Major honors: CONCACAF Gold Cup
champions, 1985, 2000, third place 2002, 2007,
World Cup appearance 1986, Olympic gold 1904
Football has played second fiddle to ice
hockey and other sports in the past but
is on the rise. Canada has had three
professional teams in the MLS since 2012
along with FC Edmonton and Ottawa
Fury in the second tier competition, the
North American Soccer League. Under
Spanish coach Benito Floro, the national
team only lost one game out of the 14
they played during 2015, whilst the same
year saw the staging of the FIFA Women's
World Cup finals attended by over 1.35
million spectators. Canada's previous high
point had been a spell at the turn of the
millennium where they defeated CONCACAF
giants, Mexico, along with Haiti, Trinidad
and Tobago and Colombia in the final to win
the 2000 Gold Cup.

Cayman Islands

Founded: 1966
Affiliated to FIFA: 1992
FIFA World Ranking: 196
Major honors: Caribbean Cup fourth place 1995
With limited competitive success, an
attempt was made in 2000 to draft in
eight players from England, including
Barry Hayles and Wayne Allison to play
for the national team in a World Cup
qualifier which was quashed by FIFA. The
Islands' limited football infrastructure was
devastated by Hurricane Ivan in
2004 but rebuilt with stadiums
hosting games of the eight-team
Cayman Islands Premier League,
won in 2014/15 by Scholars
International for the eighth time
since 2000.

Costa Rica

Founded: 1921
Affiliated to FIFA: 1927
FIFA World Ranking: 31
Major honors: FIFA World Cup
quarter final, 2014, CONCACAF Gold
Cup champions 1963, 1969, 1989,
Copa América quarter final, 2001
Boasting the best international
record of the Central American nations,
Costa Rica's national team has given its
fans a fair amount to shout about over the
decades, none more so than their epic 2-1
victory over Mexico in 2001 in a game
played at Mexico City's Estadio Azteca
where Mexico had never previously lost a
World Cup qualifier. Costa Rica have made
it to four FIFA World Cups, most notably in
2014 when they sensationally defeated both
Uruguay and Italy to top Group D before
also beating Greece to reach the quarter
finals. The country's national Primera
División consists of 12 clubs that play two
competitions a year with Deportivo Saprissa
its most successful side. Some of the
national team are drawn from the domestic
leagues but many play overseas including
Keylor Navas (Real Madrid), Bryan Oveido
(Everton), Álvaro Saborío (D.C. United) and
veteran, Míchael Umaña (Persepolis in Iran).

Cuba

Founded: 1924
Affiliated to FIFA: 1929
FIFA World Ranking: 139
Major honors: World Cup quarter final 1938,
Caribbean Cup champions 2012, runners-up
1996, 1999, 2005
Cuba were the first Caribbean nation to
reach a FIFA World Cup, traveling to France
in 1938 where they beat Romania after a
replay but succumbed 8-0 to Sweden in
their quarter final. They have taken part
in 10 qualifying campaigns since but have
yet to reach the finals again. A fourth place
finish at the CONCACAF Championship
in 1971 was a high point within their
continental championship but a recent
slump from a FIFA World Rankings high
of 46 in 2006 reflects the national team's
problems, not helped by a number of player
defections to the United States, amongst the
most recent of which being four members of
Cuba's CONCACAF Gold Cup 2015 squad.

CONCACAF Nations 2

Curaçao

Founded: 1921
Affiliated to FIFA: 1932
FIFA World Ranking: 150
Major honors: CONCACAF Gold Cup third place 1963, 1969 (as Netherlands Antilles)

Curaçao played an international match versus Aruba all the way back in 1924. After a long period as part of the Netherlands Antilles until 2010, Curaçao was named in FIFA's members lists a year later, inheriting the Netherlands Antilles status and statistical records. UEFA Champions League winner and Dutch striker, Patrick Kluivert was appointed manager of the national team in March 2015.

Dominica

Founded: 1970
Affiliated to FIFA: 1994
FIFA World Ranking: 176

An island nation of around 79,000 people, Dominica's national team has only won three World Cup qualifying games so far, versus Antigua and Barbuda in 1996, the Bahamas in 2004 and then an 11 year wait until they defeated the British Virgin Islands in 2015.

Dominican Republic

Founded: 1953
Affiliated to FIFA: 1958
FIFA World Ranking: 160

Despite joining FIFA more than half a century ago, the Dominican Republic has only sporadically competed in competitions. Its first official international was a two-legged tie versus Haiti as part of qualifiers for the 1968 Olympics, a pair of games that Haiti won 14-0 on aggregate. In spite of victories over Puerto Rico, Aruba and the British Virgin Islands, the team has never qualified for the CONCACAF Gold Cup.

El Salvador

Founded: 1935
Affiliated to FIFA: 1938
FIFA World Ranking: 98
Major honors: CONCACAF Gold Cup runners-up 1963, 1981, World Cup appearances 1974, 1982, CCCF Championship champions 1943, runners-up 1941, 1961

El Salvador has struggled in recent years with a match-fixing scandal in 2013 resulting in 14 players receiving life bans. The top level league, the Primera División, remains popular with its most successful club, FAS, having won the league championship 17 times as well as winning the CONCACAF Champions Cup back in 1979. The national team plays its home games at the 53,400-capacity monumental Stadium Cuscatlán – the biggest football stadium in Central America.

Grenada

Founded: 1924
Affiliated to FIFA: 1978
FIFA World Ranking: 162
Major honors: Caribbean Cup runners-up 1989, 2008

Grenada shocked Trinidad and Tobago and also defeated Barbados before knocking out Cuba on penalties to reach the final of the Caribbean Cup in 2008. This gave the "Spice Boys" a precious berth at the 2009 CONCACAF Gold Cup for the first time, a feat the team repeated two years later. Grenada's Kithson Bain was the 2008 Caribbean Cup's joint top scorer whilst Ricky Charles remains the team's all-time goalscorer with more than 30 up until his retirement in 2011.

Guatemala

Founded: 1919
Affiliated to FIFA: 1946
FIFA World Ranking: 96
Major honors: CONCACAF Championship champions 1967, runners-up 1965, 1969

Guatemala have been around the fringes of major tournaments, qualifying for three Olympic games (1968, 1976, 1988) and multiple CONCACAF Gold Cups but never the World Cup. Two CONCACAF Gold Cup quarter final places in 2007 and 2011 hinted at better things to come but failures to qualify have dented optimism, most notably the 2014 FIFA World Cup where the side notched up an impressive nine wins in CONCACAF region qualifying, second only to the United States, yet just fell short. The team is still captained by Guatemala's long-serving striker Carlos Ruiz who holds the Guatemalan records for appearances (125) and goals (59) and was voted MLS Most Valuable Player of the season all the way back in 2002.

Guyana

Founded: 1902
Affiliated to FIFA: 1970
FIFA World Ranking: 162

Nicknamed the Golden Jaguars, Guyana went on an impressive 14 match unbeaten run between 2005 and 2007 which saw them soar 90 places in the FIFA World Rankings. An equally impressive qualifying run for the 2014 FIFA World Cup saw them play their first match at Mexico's Estadia Azteca in 2012, but later that year a player strike over payments saw the national team not play an international match for 22 months.

Left: Jamaica's Garath McCleary (22) and Mexico's Oswaldo Alanis compete during the CONCACAF Gold Cup final.
Opposite Page Top: Mexico's Claudio Suárez (R) and Ecuador's Agustin Delgado tussle during their Copa América match 2004. Bottom: Mexico's Gibran Lajud makes a save against Honduras.

Haiti

Founded: 1904
Affiliated to FIFA: 1934
FIFA World Ranking: 65
Major honors: CONCACAF Gold Cup champions 1973, runners-up 1971, 1977, Caribbean Cup champions 2007

Haiti's national team peaked in the 1970s when it performed well in CONCACAF championships and reached the World Cup in 1974 after defeating Mexico, Trinidad and Tobago and Honduras in qualifying. Haiti's 2016 squad is built on players from clubs all over the world, including Jean-Eudes Maurice in Vietnam, Alex Junior Christian in Portugal and Frantz Bertin at Mumbai City in India.

Honduras

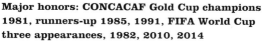

Founded: 1935
Affiliated to FIFA: 1946
FIFA World Ranking: 91
Major honors: CONCACAF Gold Cup champions 1981, runners-up 1985, 1991, FIFA World Cup three appearances, 1982, 2010, 2014

A middleweight team in the CONCACAF region, Honduras have managed to qualify for three FIFA World Cups, the first in 1982 a year after their greatest regional triumph - winning the 1981 CONCACAF Championship. Their consistency in this competition in recent years is shown by their four third-place finishes in five Gold Cups between 2005 and 2013. At their first World Cup, they drew with hosts Spain as well as Northern Ireland whilst the 2010 tournament featured the retirement of their talismanic striker, Carlos Alberto Pavón – Honduras' record goalscorer with 57 goals in 101 appearances between 1993 and 2010.

Jamaica

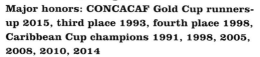

Founded: 1910
Affiliated to FIFA: 1962
FIFA World Ranking: 51
Major honors: CONCACAF Gold Cup runners-up 2015, third place 1993, fourth place 1998, Caribbean Cup champions 1991, 1998, 2005, 2008, 2010, 2014

The Reggae Boyz have enjoyed a number of high points since the national team played its first official match back in 1925. They reached their first FIFA World Cup in 1998 where they notched a victory over Japan, 2-1. The scorer of both goals, Theodore Whitmore would go on to manage the Jamaican team which captured Caribbean Cup titles in 2008 and 2010. Under coach Winfried Schafer, the team consisting of local players mixed with professionals playing for clubs in England and the United States, progressed to the final of the 2015 CONCACAF Gold Cup, knocking the United States out at the semi-finals stage.

Mexico

Founded: 1927
Affiliated to FIFA: 1929
FIFA World Ranking: 22
Major honors: FIFA World Cup quarter finals 1970, 1986, CONCACAF Gold Cup champions 1965, 1971, 1977, 1993, 1996, 1998, 2003, 2009, 2011, 2015, Copa América runners-up 1993, 2001, Olympic gold 2012

The first nation to host two FIFA World Cup tournaments, Mexico have been World Cup regulars with 15 appearances at the finals and have managed to progress out of their group and into the Round of 16 for the last six consecutive tournaments, a record only matched by Brazil and Germany. Continentally, Mexico have been the dominant force in the region, overpowering the USA and all-comers on multiple occasions, best seen by their 1993 Gold Cup performance where they thrashed Canada 8-0 and Jamaica 6-1 before humbling the USA 4-0 in the final. They defeated invitees Brazil in the final at the next Gold Cup and defeated the USA team in 1998 to become the only three-in-a-row winners of the competition. Central to these and other strong performances was Mexico's most capped player, Claudio Suárez. "El Emperador" (The Emperor), who played a record 177 times for his country between 1992 and 2006 anchoring the defense. Mexico have always possessed flair and an eye for the unexpected in attack, be it the tricks of goalscoring legend, Hugo Sánchez or the blistering pace of Javier Hernández. Olympic champions in 2012, Mexico played a grueling 23 match schedule between March and November 2015, losing just two, as they won the CONCACAF Gold Cup for a record tenth time.

Montserrat

Founded: 1994
Affiliated to FIFA: 1996
FIFA World Ranking: 187

A fitful series of appearances on the international scene resulted in Montserrat's first official international victory not coming until 2012, versus the British Virgin Islands. The current squad is mostly drawn from British-based players playing for non-league or lower league clubs. The handful of home games the team does play are usually held at Blakes Estate Stadium which has a capacity of around 1,000.

CONCACAF Nations 3

Nicaragua

Founded: 1931
Affiliated to FIFA: 1950
FIFA World Ranking: 108

Football plays second fiddle to baseball in Nicaragua and the national team has struggled to make an impact. Almost all of its players are drawn from clubs in the country's top league – the 10-team Primera División de Nicaragua – which has been dominated a record 25 times by one of Central America's oldest clubs, Diriangén FC, who were formed in 1917.

Panama

Founded: 1937
Affiliated to FIFA: 1938
FIFA World Ranking: 60
Major honors: CONCACAF Gold Cup runners-up 2005, 2013, semi-finals 2011, 2015

It's been a rapid rise in recent seasons for a pacy and highly competitive Panamanian national team that have finished in the top four of the last three CONCACAF Gold Cups. They also came desperately close to reaching the 2014 World Cup, leading USA 2-1 with less than two minutes to go – a result that would have left them facing New Zealand in a play-off for a World Cup berth – before the US scored twice in stoppage time. A number of the team play in the Liga Panameña de Fútbol whilst veteran leading scorer (41 goals) Luis Tejada plays his club football in Peru.

Puerto Rico

Founded: 1940
Affiliated to FIFA: 1960
FIFA World Ranking: 172

It took 30 years and 40 games after their first international versus Cuba (a 1-1 draw in 1940) before the Puerto Rican national team won a game – 3-0 versus the Bahamas. The Juan Ramón Loubriel Stadium is the national team's home, seating 22,000, and where, in 2012, they entertained a full-strength Spain in a friendly in which the home side performed admirably before losing 2-1. For a long time there was no unified league structure for clubs and the Puerto Rico Islanders club (formed in 2004) played in US leagues including NASL before suspending operations in 2012, by which time the Puerto Rico Soccer League had begun.

St. Kitts and Nevis

Founded: 1932
Affiliated to FIFA: 1992
FIFA World Ranking: 118
Major honors: Caribbean Cup runners-up 1997

The "Sugar Boyz" have only had enjoyed occasional success in their confederation with several strong showings in the Caribbean Cup their high points. In November 2015, the national team traveled to play their first ever matches in Europe against Andorra and Estonia. Devaughn Elliot became the first St. Kitts and Nevis player to score against European opposition as the team recorded the first away victory (1-0 v Andorra) by a team from the Caribbean Football Union on an opponent's home soil.

St. Lucia

Founded: 1979
Affiliated to FIFA: 1988
FIFA World Ranking: 145

St Lucia's first international match was a highly creditable 1-1 draw with Jamaica in 1989. They have hit rare heights such as when defeating US Virgin Islands 14-1 in 2001. Yet, with a population of less than 190,000 people in total, have mostly succumbed to more powerful footballing nations, although a 3-1 away win over Antigua and Barbuda in 2015 was a bright spot.

Above: Kenwyne Jones , Stern John and Brent Sancho of Trinidad and Tobago pressure Paraguay goalkeeper Aldo Bobadilla. Opposite page: Michael Bradley of the U.S. celebrates after scoring in the CONCACAF Gold Cup Final against Mexico.

St. Vincent and the Grenadines

Founded: 1979
Affiliated to FIFA: 1988
FIFA World Ranking: 144
Major honors: Caribbean Cup runners-up 1995

The "Vincy Heat" as the national team is nicknamed reached a CONCACAF Gold Cup in 1996 after progressing to the final of the Caribbean Cup the previous year. They are part of the highly competitive NLA Premier League formed in 2009 for domestic clubs in the region. Hope International FC won the league's ribbon in 2014-15.

Suriname

Founded: 1920
Affiliated to FIFA: 1929
FIFA World Ranking: 190
Major honors: Caribbean Cup champions 1978, runners-up 1979, CONCACAF Gold Cup sixth place 1977

Although geographically located on the South American continent, Suriname competes as a CONCACAF side and amongst its best performances were narrow failures to qualify for the 1964 and 1980 Olympic football tournaments. Many famous Dutch footballers – from Ruud Gullit to Edgar Davids – were of Suriname descent and attempts are ongoing to enable Dutch players to compete for Suriname.

Trinidad and Tobago

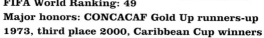

Founded: 1908
Affiliated to FIFA: 1964
FIFA World Ranking: 49
Major honors: CONCACAF Gold Up runners-up 1973, third place 2000, Caribbean Cup winners 1989, 1992, 1994, 1995, 1996, 1997, 1999, 2001

In 2005, Trinidad and Tobago defeated Bahrain in a two-game intercontinental play-off to book their first participation at the FIFA World Cup the following year where they managed a draw against Sweden. Traditionally one of the strongest of all Caribbean nations, they have also qualified for more CONCACAF Gold Cups than any other team in their region. As of 2016, this small Caribbean nation remains ranked above South Korea, Japan and Australia and drew with the United States in 2016 in a qualifying game for the 2018 FIFA World Cup.

Turks and Caicos Islands

Founded: 1996
Affiliated to FIFA: 1998
FIFA World Ranking: 197

These tiny islands are one of the region's smallest and least successful sides and tend to exit qualifying for tournaments in the earliest stages, as recent qualifying

for the 2018 FIFA World Cup showed. There, they were beaten by St. Kitts and Nevis 6-2 at home and 6-2 away as they crashed out.

US Virgin Islands

Founded: 1992
Affiliated to FIFA: 1998
FIFA World Ranking: 178

These CONCACAF minnows have only won four matches throughout their international history. The first three victories were all against the British Virgin Islands but in March 2015, they managed to secure a 1-0 win over a different opponent, Barbados.

USA

Founded: 1913
Affiliated to FIFA: 1914
FIFA World Ranking: 32
Major honors: Fifa World Cup third place, 1930, CONCACAF Gold Cup champions 1991, 2002, 2005, 2007, 2013, runners-up 1989, 1993, 1998, 2009, 2011, Confederations Cup runners-up 2009, Copa América fourth place, 1995

Whilst record books show the US national team's first official match as a 3-2 win over Sweden in 1916, they had played Canada in two fixtures as far back as 1885. After appearing at the 1930, 1934 and 1950 World Cups, the latter involving a seismic shock with their defeat of England, there would be a 40 year gap before USA graced the tournament again. Since Italy 1990, though, the US have been ever-present hosting a widely-praised World Cup in 1994 and reaching the quarter finals in 2002. A number of attempts at bringing club football to a wider audience have come and gone but Major League Soccer (MLS) kicked off in 1996 and is now thriving. MLS expansion continues with New York City FC and Orlando City Soccer Club competing since 2015 and longer term plans to expand to 28 teams. In addition, the US team has dominated international women's football. They have won three FIFA Women's World Cups.

OFC Nations

American Samoa

Founded: 1984
Affiliated to FIFA: 1998
FIFA World Ranking: 167

One of the region's traditionally weakest teams, American Samoa holds the unenviable record of suffering the biggest defeat in World Cup qualifying, a 31-0 mauling at the hands of Australia in 2001 and did not record a win in 29 international matches. Performances are on the up in more recent times as witnessed by their first World Cup qualifying win, over Tonga in 2011 and further victories came in the qualifying campaign for the 2018 FIFA World Cup.

Cook Islands

Founded: 1971
Affiliated to FIFA: 1994
FIFA World Ranking: 167
Major honors: Polynesia Cup runners-up 1998, 2000

Enormous geographical challenges face the Cook Islands Football Association with under 25,000 inhabitants of a set of islands spread over an area the size of Western Europe. A football headquarters at Matavera has given the islanders a modern base and facilities to play and train at and the national team started qualification for the 2018 World Cup well with two victories out of three in their first round group.

Fiji

Founded: 1938
Affiliated to FIFA: 1963
FIFA World Ranking: 186
Major honors: OFC Nations Cup third place, 1998, 2008, South Pacific Games winners, 1991, 2003

The 2016 OFC Nations Cup will mark Fiji's eighth appearance in this tournament. In a nation more captivated by rugby, football struggles to compete at times. Star player, Roy Krishna who plays as a striker for Wellington Phoenix in the A-League captains a national side drawn almost entirely from domestic teams such as Suva FC, Nadi FC and Ba FC.

New Caledonia

Founded: 1928
Affiliated to FIFA: 2004
FIFA World Ranking: 181
Major honors: OFC Nations Cup runners-up 2008, 2012, Pacific Games gold medal, 2007, 2011, 2015

This French territory of some 270,000 people became FIFA's 205th member in 2004 and has finished in the top three at the OFC Nations Cup four times. Its most famous footballing family are the Gope-Fenepej brothers Georges and John who have both played professional football in France. Georges scored the team's second goal in their famous OFC Nations Cup 2012 semi-final win over New Zealand.

New Zealand

Founded: 1891
Affiliated FIFA: 1948
FIFA World Ranking: 150
Major honors: Oceania Nations Cup champions 1973, 1998, 2002, World Cup group stage, 1982, 2010

The All Whites are now the premier team in the OFC after Australia moved to the Asian Football Confederation. Many of its leading players ply their trade overseas or are part of the Wellington Phoenix who compete in the A-League. The New Zealand team have appeared at three Confederations Cups, 1999, 2003 and 2009. At the 2010 World Cup, New Zealand failed to progress out of the group stage but were the only team eliminated who did not lose a game. Pick of their matches was an excellent 1-1 draw with then defending world champions, Italy. The All Whites failed at the final hurdle during qualifying for the 2014 World Cup, losing narrowly to a strong

Mexican side in a play-off match for a final World Cup place.

Papua New Guinea

Founded: 1962
Affiliated to FIFA: 1963
FIFA World Ranking: 203
Major honors: Pacific Games bronze medal, 2015

The year 2016 will see the country host the OFC Nations Cup for the first time, a decade after its national league for domestic

Top: New Zealand's players take part in a training session at Azteca stadium in Mexico City, 2013. Above: Australia's Tim Cahill (L) is tackled by Axel Tematua of Tahiti in OFC Nations Cup match.

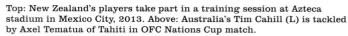

clubs was established. One of its clubs, PRK Hekari United managed to win the OFC Champions League in 2009/10, defeating Waitakere United from New Zealand in the final. The national team had a strong 2015 Pacific Games defeating Fiji in their final match to take third place.

Samoa

Founded: 1968
Affiliated to FIFA: 1986
FIFA World Ranking: 167

A rise up the lower reachings of the FIFA World Rankings reflects Samoa's recent form which saw them defeat both their local rivals, American Samoa and Tonga in their 2018 World Cup qualification campaign. Desmond Fa'aiuaso holds the appearances (14) and goals scored (7) records for the national team.

Solomon Islands

Founded: 1978
Affiliated to FIFA: 1988
FIFA World Ranking: 200
Major honors: OFC Nations Cup runners-up 2004, third place 1996, 2000.

A 17-0 victory over Wallis and Futuna in 1991 remains a highlight, but the Solomon Islands' greatest achievement came at the 2004 OFC Nations Cup. There, victories over Fiji, Vanuatu and a 4-0 win over Tahiti was followed by an impressive 2-2 draw against Australia. Both of the goals in that game were scored by Commins Menapi who remains the nation's leading scorer with a superb strike rate of 34 goals in 37 appearances.

Tahiti

Founded: 1989
Affiliated to FIFA: 1990
FIFA World Ranking: 191
Major honors: OFC Nations Cup champions, 2012, runners-up 1973, 1980, 1996, Polynesia Cup champions 1994, 1998, 2000

Tahiti's 12,000 or so registered football players provided the bedrock of the under-20 team that became U-20 champions of Oceania in 2008. Four years later came the islands' greatest footballing hour when Eddy Etaeta's team won all five of their games to become OFC Nations Cup champions, an astonishing achievement. The following year, Tahitians welcomed home their most famous player, Marama Vahirua, who played over 120 games for French Ligue 1 team, Nantes as well as enjoying a spell with Monaco

Tonga

Founded: 1965
Affiliated to FIFA: 2004
FIFA World Ranking: 204
Major honors: Polynesian Cup runners-up, 1994

Propping up the bottom of the FIFA World Rankings alongside Somalia, Eritrea and the Bahamas is a tough place to be but there are small causes for some optimism with Tongan club, Lotoha'apai United narrowly missing out on a place on the OFC Champions League, losing out on goal difference. Many of the national team squad, who only contest matches sporadically, consists of players unattached to clubs.

Vanuatu

Founded: 1934
Affiliated to FIFA: 1988
FIFA World Ranking: 194
Major honors: OFC Nations Cup fourth place 1973, 2000, 2002, 2008

Vanuatu are consistent performers at the OFC Nations Cup and winners of the 1990 Melanesian Cup on its first staging. At the 2004 OFC Nations Cup, they recorded their most notable victory — a historic 4–2 win over New Zealand.

OFC Nations
Tuvalu, Kiribati, Niue Islands

Top: Tahiti players celebrate winning the 2012 OFC Nations cup. Bottom: Vanuatu goalkeeper and captain David Chilia celebrates the win against New Zealand with teammate Lexa Bule Bibi in the OFC Nations Cup in Adelaide, 2004. Vanuatu won 4-2.

CLUB
COMPETITIONS

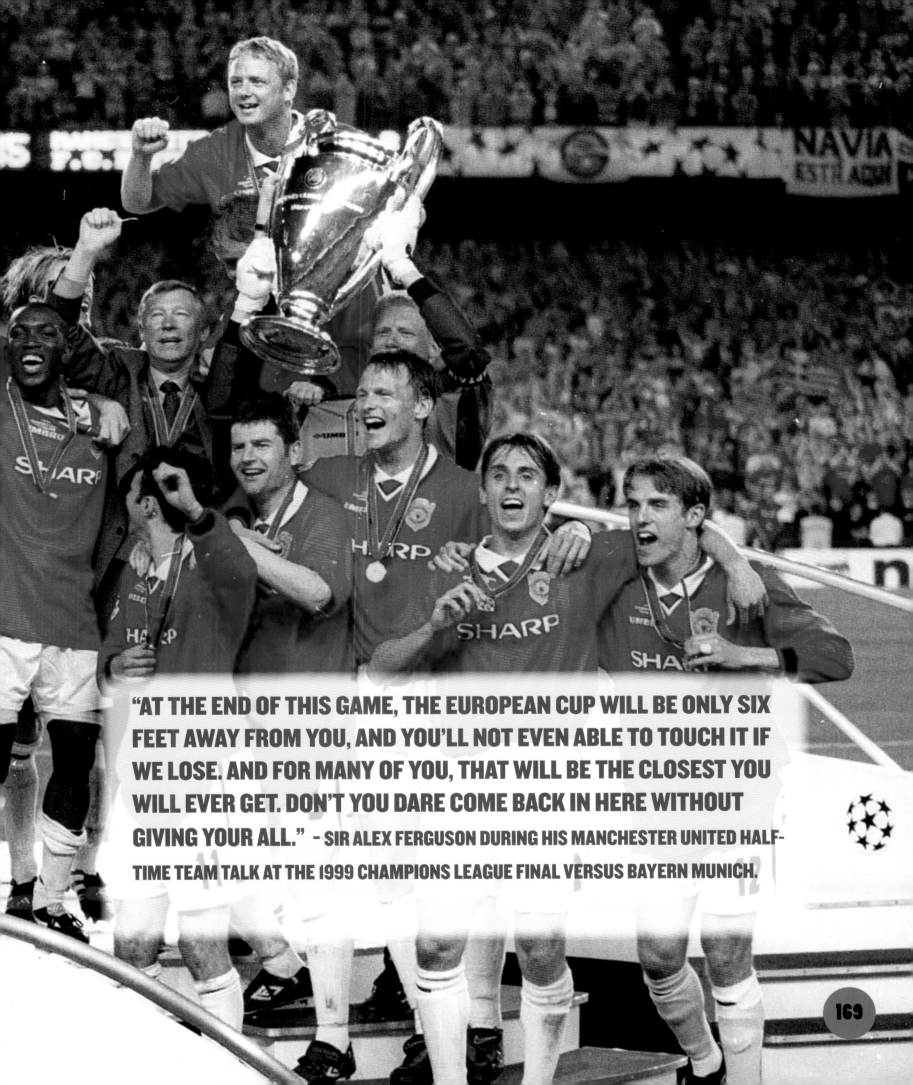

"AT THE END OF THIS GAME, THE EUROPEAN CUP WILL BE ONLY SIX FEET AWAY FROM YOU, AND YOU'LL NOT EVEN ABLE TO TOUCH IT IF WE LOSE. AND FOR MANY OF YOU, THAT WILL BE THE CLOSEST YOU WILL EVER GET. DON'T YOU DARE COME BACK IN HERE WITHOUT GIVING YOUR ALL." - SIR ALEX FERGUSON DURING HIS MANCHESTER UNITED HALF-TIME TEAM TALK AT THE 1999 CHAMPIONS LEAGUE FINAL VERSUS BAYERN MUNICH.

The European Cup and Champions League

The glittering prize of European club football, the UEFA Champions League is the wealthiest, most prestigious and most watched club competition in the world. An estimated TV audience of over 180 million viewed the 2015 final between Barcelona and Juventus and hundreds of millions more tune in to the competition's 125 group and knockout games.

Early Days

European club competitions began with the Mitropa Cup, pioneered by Austrian Hugo Meisl, which featured contests between central European nations including Czechoslovakia, Yugoslavia, Austria, Hungary and Italy. The Latin Cup was a similar regional competition, starting in 1949 and contested by Spanish, French, Italian and Portuguese clubs. Other tests of a particular club's prowess in the 1940s and 1950s came in friendlies against foreign teams which often drew large crowds to matches, curious to see these exotic opponents in the flesh especially at a time when there was little footage or live televised broadcast of matches. Amongst these friendlies, Wolverhampton Wanderers inspired claims to be champions of Europe in 1954 after defeating both Spartak Moscow of the Soviet Union and top Hungarian side, Honvéd. This brought a withering response from some quarters, especially the editor of French newspaper, *L'Équipe*, Gabriel Hanot, a former French national team player. He helped organize meetings and drummed up support for his plan of a European competition played on a home and away basis each season to determine which club was, indeed, pre-eminent in Europe.

FIFA approved the plan in May 1955 and UEFA were charged with organizing the competition which began later that year. Teams for the first European Champions Cup were selected by *L'Équipe* but four refused the invitation. Chelsea were replaced by Polish side, Gwardia Warsaw whilst Holland Sport, Honvéd and BK Copenhagen's places were taken by PSV Eindhoven, Vörös Lobogó and Aarhus respectively. The competition kicked off on the 4th September 1955 in Lisbon as Sporting Lisbon entertained Yugoslavia's Partizan Belgrade in an exciting 3-3 draw. The competition's first goal was scored by Sporting's João Baptista Martins and plenty more followed with entertaining scorelines such as Vörös Lobogó 6-3 win over Anderlecht and AC Milan's 7-2 demolition of Rapid Wien. It was fitting then that the first European

Cup culminated in an exciting and dramatic final in which Real Madrid defeated Stade Reims 4-3.

Champion Clubs Of the Sixties

Real went on to totally dominate the competition in its founding years, with its stellar players to the fore including the great Alfredo Di Stéfano who managed an incredible record of scoring in five consecutive finals, including a hat-trick in the 1960 final. Before a crowd of over 127,000 spectators crammed into Hampden Park, Real's performance against an enterprising and skilled Eintracht Frankfurt team remains one of the finest spectacles ever witnessed in European football.

Real's great Spanish rivals, Barcelona would topple the Madrid side, knocking them out of the 1960/61 competition only to lose to Benfica in the final. Real Madrid were not done, though, and contested the 1962 and 1964 finals, losing to Benfica and Internazionale

respectively before winning their sixth title in 1966, a result that set several records yet to be broken. These include the oldest winner of a final, the magical Hungarian forward Ferenc Puskás (39 years, 39 days) and the most frequent winner of the European Cup – Real's silky winger, Francisco Gento with six titles to his name.

English clubs had entered the European Cup from its second season onwards but the likes of Manchester United, Burnley and Tottenham Hotspur had failed to progress all the way. It took a Scottish team made up of players all born within 50km of their club's ground to become the first British winners of the European Cup when Celtic overcame favorites Internazionale in 1967. Manchester United followed with England's first title the following season.

The 1970s and 1980s

The 1970s saw only four winners of the competition as the total footballing Ajax side, sparked by Johan Cruyff won a hat-trick of European Cups, immediately followed by Bayern Munich becoming the first German champions and embarking themselves on a three year dominance of the competition. Their talismanic striker, Gerd Müller, would distinguish himself during this period by becoming in 1977, the first and only player to top the goalscoring charts in four European Cup seasons in a row.

The 1970s also saw the first penalty shootout used to decide a drawn game in the competition in 1970 when Everton and Borussia Mönchengladbach drew their second round pair of matches with Everton prevailing 4-3. Shootouts would be required to settle ten European Cup or Champions League finals, the most recent being Chelsea's 4-3 shootout win over Bayern Munich in 2012 to win their first European title.

In the 1980s, a range of new winners emerged including Steaua Bucureşti, Hamburg, PSV Eindhoven and Red Star Belgrade as English influence in the competition was halted after the tragic events at the Liverpool v Juventus European Cup Final in 1985 where rioting fans caused a wall to collapse resulting in the deaths of 39 spectators. English clubs were banned from European competition as a result and it would be six years before they took part. AC Milan won their first European Cup for twenty years in 1989 beginning a period of impressive Italian participation in which only the 1991 final from 1989 to 1998 failed to include an Italian team.

The Champions League Era

In 1992/93, UEFA unveiled a much-altered competition which they renamed the UEFA Champions League. It now featured two four-team mini leagues known as the group stages, filled by winners of several rounds of knockout matches with the two group winners meeting each other in the final. This was expanded for the 1994/95 season to create four groups of four with eight of the places awarded to seven seeded teams plus the defending champions with the other places filled by clubs playing preliminary rounds of matches. Louis Van Gaal's young Ajax team where crowned 1994-95 champions assisted by an especially youthful strike squad including two of the youngest Champions League winners in Nwankwo Kanu and Patrick Kluivert, both 18 years old.

Further changes have occurred as UEFA and the top clubs realized the scale of the money that the competition was capable of generating with the number of groups, and thus, games increasing to six groups in 1997 and eight groups in time for the 1999/2000 season, the same year as entry requirements were altered so the three highest-ranked leagues according to UEFA (at the time, Spain, Italy and Germany) could enter four clubs in the competition.

Opposite: Alfredo di Stefano in the 1956 European Cup final. Top: Manchester United's George Best parades the 1968 EURO Cup trophy. Left: Liverpool's Vladimir Smicer scores during 2005 UEFA Champions League Final shoot-out. Previous: Spain's Fernando Torres (L) and Sergio Ramos (R) after ousting Germany for the 2008 EUFA Championship. Torres' suit is a tribute to Antonio Puerta.

The European Cup and Champions League contd.

In the 2015-16 Champions League, 78 clubs from 53 nations took part in qualifying. These ranged from big beasts of European football such as Lazio, Ajax, Sporting CP and Manchester United to minnows such as Andorra's FC Santa Coloma and Lincoln Red Imps, Gibraltar's first ever side in the competition. After the qualifying and play-off rounds are completed the group stage games take place, between September and December, with the top two sides from each group advancing to the knockout stages of the competition where they play two-legged fixtures home and away. At the group stage, only Real Madrid have won all six of their games in two Champions League seasons, the last in 2014/15. The previous season, Real managed to win five and draw one of their group games before unusually playing the three knockout rounds prior to the final (Round of 16, quarter final and semi-final) all against German opponents. Defeating city rivals Atlético Madrid in the final 4-1 not only gave Real their first Champions League crown since 2002, it also gave the side and their delirious fans the fabled, "la Décima" (the tenth) European Cup or Champions League title in their 13th final, both records for the competition.

Major Money Spinner

Fuelled by booming sales of lucrative television and other media rights to broadcast Champions League games in more than 200 territories around the world, UEFA was able to furnish clubs taking part in the 2014/15 Champions League with payments totalling £752.9 million. These were calculated on the basis of number of wins, draws and progression through the competition as well as a percentage of the TV rights accorded each country. Each Champions League club was awarded 8.6 million Euros for participating in the group state and an additional one million Euros for a win and half a million Euros for a draw. Progression bonuses included 3.5 million Euros for reaching the quarter final stage and 10.5 million Euros for winning the final. Barcelona, as champions, took home a combined total of 61,027,000 Euros for their 2014/15 Champions League campaign.

TOP OF THE LEAGUE: MOST FREQUENT CHAMPIONS

9 Real Madrid	1956, 1957, 1958, 1959, 1960, 1966, 1998, 2000, 2002, 2014
7 AC Milan	1963, 1969, 1989, 1990, 1994, 2003, 2007
5 Liverpool	1977, 1978, 1981, 1984, 2005
5 Bayern Munich	1974, 1975, 1976, 2001, 2013
5 Barcelona	1992, 2006, 2009, 2011, 2015
4 Ajax	1971, 1972, 1973, 1995
3 Inter Milan	1964, 1965, 2010
3 Manchester United	1968, 1999, 2008

Opposite Top: AC Milan coach Ancelotti, VP Adriano Galliani and captain Paolo Maldini. Left: Barcelona's Lionel Messi in action, 2015 UEFA Champions League Final. Top: Basta is challenged by Bayer Leverkusen's Wendell. Center: Real Madrid celebrate with their 2014 UEFA Champions League win. Above: Shakhtar Donetsk's Luiz Adriano celebrates scoring on BATE Borisov.

EUROPEAN CUP / CHAMPIONS LEAGUE FINALS

Year	Champions	Score	Runners Up
1955-56	Real Madrid	4-3	Stade de Reims
1956-57	Real Madrid	2-0	Fiorentina
1957-58	Real Madrid	3-2	Milan
1958-59	Real Madrid	2-0	Stade de Reims
1959-60	Real Madrid	7-3	Eintracht Frankfurt
1960-61	Benfica	3-2	Barcelona
1961-62	Benfica	5-3	Real Madrid
1962-63	AC Milan	2-1	Benfica
1963-64	Internazionale	3-1	Real Madrid
1964-65	Internazionale	1-0	Benfica
1965-66	Real Madrid	2-1	Partizan Belgrade
1966-67	Celtic	2-1	Internazionale
1967-68	Manchester United	4-1	Benfica
1968-69	AC Milan	4-1	Ajax
1969-70	Feyenoord	2-1	Celtic
1970-71	Ajax	2-0	Panathinaikos
1971-72	Ajax	2-0	Internazionale
1972-73	Ajax	1-0	Juventus
1973-74	Bayern Munich	4-0	Atlético Madrid
1974-75	Bayern Munich	2-0	Leeds United
1975-76	Bayern Munich	1-0	Saint-Étienne
1976-77	Liverpool	3-1	Borussia Mönchengladbach
1977-78	Liverpool	1-0	Club Brugge
1978-79	Nottingham Forest	1-0	Malmo FF
1979-80	Nottingham Forest	1-0	Hamburg
1980-81	Liverpool	1-0	Real Madrid
1981-82	Aston Villa	1-0	Bayern Munich
1982-83	SV Hamburg	1-0	Juventus
1983-84	Liverpool	1-1 (4-2)	Roma
1984-85	Juventus	1-0	Liverpool
1985-86	Steaua Bucureşti	0-0 (2-0)	Barcelona
1986-87	Porto	2-1	Bayern Munich
1987-88	PSV Eindhoven	0-0 (6-5)	Benfica
1988-89	AC Milan	4-0	Steaua Bucureşti
1989-90	AC Milan	1-0	Benfica
1990-91	Red Star Belgrade	0-0 (5-3)	Marseille
1991-92	Barcelona	1-0	Sampdoria
1992-93	Marseille	1-0	AC Milan
1993-94	AC Milan	4-0	Barcelona
1994-95	Ajax	1-0	AC Milan
1995-96	Juventus	1-1 (4-2)	Ajax
1996-97	Borussia Dortmund	3-1	Juventus
1997-98	Real Madrid	1-0	Juventus
1998-99	Manchester United	2-1	Bayern Munich
1999-00	Real Madrid	3-0	Valencia
2000-01	Bayern Munich	1-1 (5-4)	Valencia
2001-02	Real Madrid	2-1	Bayer Leverkusen
2002-03	AC Milan	0-0 (3-2)	Juventus
2003-04	Porto	3-0	Monaco
2004-05	Liverpool	3-3 (3-2)	AC Milan
2005-06	Barcelona	2-1	Arsenal
2006-07	AC Milan	2-1	Liverpool
2007-08	Manchester United	1-1 (6-5)	Chelsea
2008-09	Barcelona	2-0	Manchester United
2009-10	Internazionale	2-0	Bayern Munich
2010-11	Barcelona	3-1	Manchester United
2011-12	Chelsea	1-1 (4-3)	Bayern Munich
2012-13	Bayern Munich	2-1	Borussia Dortmund
2013-14	Real Madrid	4-1	Atlético Madrid
2014-15	Barcelona	3-1	Juventus

European Club Competitions

A desire to increase the amount of contact and competition between clubs in the burgeoning leagues of Europe led to the founding and running of a number of cups, not all initially under the control of UEFA.

The Inter Cities Fairs Cup

Three European football officials including England's Stanley Rous and Otto Barassi – the Italian who had protected the original FIFA World Cup trophy from looting by hiding it under his bed in a shoebox throughout World War II – came up with the idea of a trophy for a series of friendly matches played between clubs in cities which regularly held trade fairs.

The Fairs Cup was initially hampered by a convoluted schedule. The first competition featuring 10 teams (after Cologne and Vienna withdrew) began in 1955 and didn't finish until 1958. It also saw a number of select XIs taking part with players culled from a range of different clubs. The competition settled down at the start of the 1960s, becoming an annual affair, attracting larger number of entrants and producing some engaging games and performances including Dinamo Zagreb winning the competition in 1967 and Valencia's back-to-back victories in 1962 and 1963, propelled by the free-scoring talents of Waldo Machado da Silva who became the competition's all-time leading scorer with 31 goals.

The UEFA Cup & Europa League

The Inter-Cities Fairs Cup was wound down in 1971 as UEFA introduced a new competition and new silver trophy on a marble base weighing 15kg, both called the UEFA Cup. The competition was traditionally for runners-up in European countries' leagues but was

expanded to include other higher-ranking teams who had not qualified for the European Cup.

Twenty-seven clubs have won the competition from 11 different nations including success for Sweden in 1982 and 1987 with IFK Göteborg's triumphs and a first for Turkey in 2000 with Galatasary's victory over Arsenal. Ukraine gained its first UEFA Cup winner with Shakhtar Donetsk in 2009 after which the competition was revamped as the Europa League.

This competition features a complex qualification system based on UEFA coefficients – rankings of a country's leagues and performance - with three preliminary rounds and a play-off phase which fill some of the 48 group stage places available. The top 12 ranked league's domestic cup winners enter the group stage directly as do the 10 defeated teams from the UEFA Champions League play-off round. Later in the competition, a further eight Champions League teams (all the third place finishers in their groups) enter the Europa League as well.

In an attempt to make the competition more attractive to entrants, every team reaching the group stage in the seasons between 2015 and 2018 received 2.4 million Euros with over 6 million for the Europa League winners who also receive a UEFA Champions League place the following season. Only two clubs have ever defended the UEFA Cup or Europa League successfully and both are from Spain. Real Madrid won

it in both 1984/85 and 1985/86, and Sevilla won back-to-back UEFA Cups in 2005/06 and 2006/07. Sevilla managed to repeat the feat in 2013/14 and 2014/15 defeating Benfica and Dnipro Dnipropetrovsk to become the competition's most frequent champions.

The European Cup Winners Cup

The winners of national cup competitions in Europe were invited to play in the Cup Winners Cup from 1960/61 until 1998/99. The first winners were Fiorentina who defeated Glasgow Rangers in a two-legged final. All European Cup Winners Cup finals after this point were decided over a single game or on three occasions (1962, 1964, 1971) went to a replay after the first game was drawn. Tottenham

Hotspur became the first English club to win a major European trophy when they defeated Atlético Madrid 5-1 in the 1963 final – a scoreline that remained the tournament's biggest winning margin in a final, whilst the following season came the tournament's biggest thrashing as a rampant Sporting CP put 16 goals past Cypriot club, APOEL, only conceding one in return on the way to winning their first and, so far, only European trophy. Barcelona would prove the competition's most successful side winning the cup on four occasions.

In the 1990s, as UEFA came under pressure to reduce fixture congestion and with the UEFA Cup and Champions League the two paramount European competitions, the competition was scrapped. Lazio, who defeated Mallorca in the final, would be the last champions with their attacking midfielder, Pavel Nedvěd the competition's last goalscorer. Since its abandonment, cup winners in Europe's strongest footballing nations including FA Cup winners in England, Coupe de France victors and Copa del Rey champions in Spain gain direct entry into the UEFA Cup.

Intertoto Cup

Considered something of a sideshow by the European footballing elite, but competed passionately for by many clubs, the Intertoto Cup started life as a summer competition for football pools companies to have games for customers to bet on. Ajax were the first winners in 1961 and after the knockout stages leading to a single winner were abandoned in 1967, the competition yielded no single winner.

UEFA took over control of the competition in 1995 and awarded three places (two in the first season) in the UEFA Cup to the best performing teams. With an increase in purpose, interest in the Intertoto increased; amongst those qualifying for the UEFA Cup through this route were European heavyweights: Juventus (1999), Paris Saint-Germain (2001) and Marseille (2005). The competition changed again in 2005 for three seasons with 11 UEFA Cup places awarded each year before 2008 became its last staging as part of its function was absorbed into the Europa League.

Opposite Top: Leeds United captain Billy Bremner at Manchester Airport with the Fairs Cup. Opposite Bottom: Liverpool players celebrate after winning the 2001 UEFA Cup. Above Top: Radamel Falcao became the record goalscorer in a single UEFA Cup or Europa League season with 17 goals in the competition. Above: Sevilla's José Antonio Reyes is challenged by Benfica's Luisão during the 2014 Europa League final. Left: Giovanni Trapattoni (R), the only manager, so far, to win the UEFA Cup three times.

South American Club Competitions

Frequently eclipsing South America's national team tournament, the Copa América, for passionate support and drama, the Copa Libertadores is the continent's pre-eminent club competition. Matches are broadcast in over 120 nations whilst the 2009 competition gained a total TV audience of over one billion for the first time.

Pre-Copa Competitions

The Copa Rio de La Plata was first staged in 1913 although official records cite the 1916 match between Uruguay champions, Nacional and Argentina's Racing Club de Avellaneda as the first official final. A competition between the champions of Uruguay and Argentina only, it was left to Chilean club, Colo-Colo, to organize a more representative competition which was only staged once, in 1948, and was called the South American Championship of Champions. Hosted in Santiago, the tournament featured a league of seven teams all of whom played each other with the winner the team topping the league, Vasco da Gama from Brazil. A journalist covering the tournament for French newspaper, *L'Équipe*, Jacques Ferran, and his editor, Gabriel Hanot, would prove instrumental in the formation of a similar tournament in Europe – the European Cup (see pp170-171).

Copa Libertadores

Agreed by a continental meeting in 1959, the Copa Libertadores kicked off the following year. Ecuador, Peru and Venezuela declined to send teams so the inaugural competition featured the league champions of seven South American nations including Uruguay's Peñarol who would dominate the early competitions. Unknown in Europe but a legend to many South Americans, Ecuadorian striker Alberto Spencer would record the competition's first hat-trick, in

Peñarol's first game in the competition, a 7-1 victory over Bolivian club, Jorge Wilstermann. Spencer would go on to become the record scorer in the competition with 54 goals for three clubs between 1960 and 1972. The tournament top scorer today is awarded the Alberto Spencer trophy for their feats.

Peñarol won the first two competitions but were defeated in the final of the third by Santos courtesy of two goals from Pelé. The Brazilian side were one of a number of teams who enjoyed consecutive championship victories in the 1960s and 1970s, most notably Independiente whose record of four Copa Libertadores championships in a row and 100% success rate in the final (seven out of seven) are unlikely to be matched in the near future. Reflecting that the tournament was not just a competition between the big three, Independiente had to face and beat two Chilean teams, one Brazilian and one Peruvian side in their historic four final run.

As the competition has risen in competitiveness, it has become increasingly difficult for champions to make their mark the following season. Since 1978, for example, only two clubs have defended the trophy: São Paulo (1992, 1993) and Boca Juniors (2000, 2001) as the roster of semi-finalists and finalists has grown. Ten of the semi-finalists since 2001 have reached that stage of the competition for the first time whilst the 21st century has seen new names on the trophy including LDU Quito from Ecuador, Argentina's San Lorenzo (in their

14th Copa Libertadores campaign) and Once Caldas from Colombia whose fairytale Copa 2004 saw them beat Brazilian giants Santos and São Paulo as well as defending champions and favorites, Boca Juniors on the way to glory.

The Copa Libertadores has been played in a bewildering variety of qualification and competition formats. The current format consists of six rounds with the first usually starting in February from which six teams join 26 more in eight four-team groups. The top two teams from each group enter knockout rounds with the finals in the South American winter. Mexican clubs have been competing regularly in the tournament since 2000 and have provided eight semi-finalists since that time. These included Tigres UANL who reached the final in 2015 only to be defeated by River Plate, who themselves, had beaten one of only three teams in the competition's history to record a perfect record in the group stage - Boca Juniors.

Copa Sudamericana

A competition for teams which performed well in their domestic leagues but failed to qualify for the Copa Libertadores was instituted in 1992 - the Copa CONMEBOL. It ran until 1999 when two tournaments: the Copa Mercosur (for clubs from Brazil, Argentina, Paraguay, Chile and Uruguay) and Copa Merconorte (for the remaining South American nations) stepped into its place. Bolivian club, The Strongest, were the only club to become champions twice in

either competition. These tournaments, designed to generate money from TV rights, were short-lived and replaced in 2002, by a new, single competition, the Copa Sudamericana.

The Copa Sudamericana is held in the second half of the year to avoid clashes with the Copa Libertadores, enabling clubs to potentially enter both competitions. This new competition received an early boost with the sensational surprise victory by Peruvian club, Cienciano, in the 2003 Sudamericana as they defeated Santos in the quarter-finals and River Plate in the final. Since that time, though, Argentinean clubs have exerted a grip on the competition with eight victories overall although a ninth, for Club Atlético Huracán in 2015 was thwarted after a penalty shootout in the final that gave Santa Fe from Colombia their first intercontinental title.

The champions each season get to play in the Recopa Sudamerican against the winner of the Copa Libertadores as well as to play in a one-off match held in Japan against Japan's J-League Cup winners. In 2015, River Plate managed to reverse a spell of five straight wins for Japanese teams, with a 3-0 win over Gamba Osaka.

COPA SUDAMERICANA CHAMPIONS

2002	San Lorenzo	Argentina
2003	Cienciano	Peru
2004	Boca Juniors	Argentina
2005	Boca Juniors	Argentina
2006	Pachua	Mexico
2007	Arsenal	Argentina
2008	Internacional	Argentina
2009	LDU Quito	Ecuador
2010	Independiente	Argentina
2011	Universidad de Chile	Chile
2012	São Paulo	Brazil
2013	Lanús	Argentina
2014	River Plate	Argentina
2015	Santa Fe	Colombia

Opposite Top: Argentine soccer club Boca Juniors team celebrate victory after defeating Brazil's Santos FC. Opposite Bottom: Olimpia players celebrate Isasi's goal against Argentine Boca Juniors. This page clockwise from top: The Copa Libertadores trophy. Colombia's Independiente Santa Fe players pose with the trophy after winning the Copa Sudamericana. Tabaré Viúdez of Argentina's River Plate holds off Israel Jiménez of Mexico's Tigres during the first leg of their Copa Libertadores final game, Mexico, 2015

Domestic Cup Competitions

Every member nation of FIFA runs some form of domestic league for its top football clubs to take part in and most have one or more knockout cup competitions. The oldest knockout cup competition of all is the Football Association (FA) Cup which first kicked off in 1871.

The FA Cup

The Kennington Oval in London hosted the first ever FA Cup Final in 1872 with Wanderers beating Royal Engineers 1-0. The competition final was initially held at different venues around London including Stamford Bridge and Crystal Palace before settling on Wembley Stadium from 1923. The Millennium Stadium in Cardiff, home of the only non-English club to win the FA Cup when Cardiff City defeated Arsenal in the 1927 final, hosted the competition's climax for six years (2001-2006) whilst Wembley was redeveloped.

Just 15 teams entered the inaugural FA Cup and three of these withdrew without playing a game. In contrast, 736 clubs entered the 2015/16 FA Cup with non-league teams having to progress through preliminary rounds before they get their crack at one of England's 92 professional league clubs. Some of the FA Cup's glamour and romance stems from the performances of lower league or non-league clubs and their giant-killing exploits, especially in the competition's third round where top Premier League and Championship clubs enter the fray. Whilst many non-league sides force draws and a lucrative replay with bigger opponents, non-league defeats of top teams are now extremely rare. When Premier League club Norwich City lost at their Carrow

Road home ground to non-league Luton Town in the 2012-13 FA Cup, it was the first such defeat since Sutton United defeated Coventry in 1989. Giant-killing at the hands of lower league opponents from League One and League Two does still occur as is well illustrated by Bradford City's comeback from 2-0 to deal a memorable defeat to that season's Premier League champions, Chelsea 4-2 in the fourth round of the 2014/15 FA Cup.

The FA Cup Final has tended in recent decades to be contested by Premier League teams. Only two finalists in the 21st century have come from outside the top flight whilst the last non top division FA Cup winners were West Ham United in 1979/80. Manchester United held the record for most FA Cup victories with 11 until Arsenal won both the 2013-14 and 2014-15 competitions, to record 12 FA Cup triumphs. Arsenal were also involved in the last FA Cup Final replay when the initial game in 1993 ended in a 1-1 draw versus Sheffield Wednesday. At the semi-final and final stages since 2000, drawn semi-finals and finals after extra time are played to a conclusion on the day via a penalty shootout. Only two finals so far, in 2005 and 2006 have been decided via penalties.

Cup Before League

Some cup competitions were founded before a country's league system and even performed the role as the pinnacle of that country's footballing competition. This was the case with the Emperor's Cup in Japan which was first held in 1921, long before the establishment of national football leagues - the amateur Japan Soccer League in 1965 and the professional J-League in 1992. A similar instance was found in Spain where the Copa del Rey was first played for in 1903, a quarter of a century before La Liga began. The winners of the first Copa del Rey, Athletic Bilbao are the second most successful team in the competition with 24 cups won and 14 runners-up finishes, the latest in 2015 when they were defeated 3-1 in the final by the Copa del Rey's most successful side, Barcelona with 27 victories.

Closed Or Open

Some club cup competitions are restricted to teams only operating in specific divisions of a country's league system such as the Coppa Italia Lega Pro for all 69 teams that play in Italy's third tier of football

and Mexico's Copa MX in its current format since 2012. Many cups, though, are "open" competitions in which, theoretically, any football club affiliated to the association, can enter via a preliminary round or local or regional cup competition with the possibility of entering the latter stages of the cup if they win through.

The Lamar Hunt U.S. Open Cup is North America's oldest cup competition, held since 1913/14 (when it was known as the National Challenge Cup). It features all the top Major League Soccer (MLS) teams but also teams from lower NASL and USL leagues. In 1999, USL league club, Rochester Rhinos became the only team from outside the MLS since it formed to win the cup, defeating the Colorado Rapids 2-0 in the final held in Columbus, Ohio.

The Coupe de France has one of the biggest entries in world football with amateur as well as professional teams allowed to enter. In 2013/14, a record 7,656 clubs entered the competition, a vast number which had to be whittled down by a lengthy series of qualifying rounds. It has, on occasion, seen some remarkable feats from smaller clubs such as in 2012 when Quevilly from the French third division knocked out both Marseille and Rennes on the way to the 2012 Coupe de France final against Lyons. Twelve years before that was the fairy-tale story of RUFC Calais. An amateur club whose players worked in offices, at the local docks or as teachers were guided expertly by Spanish coach, Ladislas Lozano, to beat French Ligue 1 clubs, Racing Strasbourg and Bordeaux to reach the final of the Coupe de France – the first time an amateur team had managed the feat since the cup began in 1917.

Opposite Top Left: Bolton's Billy Butler, Jimmy Seddon and Jimmy McClelland celebrate at the end of the 1929 FA Cup Final against Portsmouth.
Opposite Top Right: Arsenal celebrate with the trophy after winning the FA Cup 2015 Final. Top: Real Madrid's Pepe (L) and Sergio Ramos lifts up the King's Cup trophy (Copa Del Rey) after defeating Barcelona, 2016. Left: Paris Saint-Germain's captain Pedro Miguel Pauleta with the trophy as he celebrates with teammates in the French Cup final soccer match against Olympique Marseille in 2006. Above: Real Salt Lake forward Devon Sandoval attempts a bicycle kick shot on goal against D.C. United during their U.S. Open Cup final game

International Club Competitions Around The World

Every confederation today runs some form of competition for leading clubs of rival nations in their region to compete in. These competitions have often changed names and formats over the decade with many today now modeled on and named after the UEFA Champions League.

CONCACAF Champions League

A regional club competition for teams in the CONCACAF region began in 1962 as the Champions Cup. Whilst Mexico in particular, as well as some of the stronger Central American countries have provided the majority of the winning clubs, there have been notable exceptions amongst the champions, such as Transvaal from Suriname and Defence Force, a club from Trinidad and Tobago who were one of the last three teams in the competition when the final was cancelled in 1978 but managed to win outright in 1985. Only two MLS teams have won the competition, DC United in 1998 and the LA Galaxy in 2000.

Revamped as the Champions League for the 2008/09 season, the competition features 24 teams taking part in eight three-team groups. Central America nations receive 12 berths with all bar Belize and Nicaragua allotted two places per nation, whilst the Caribbean region hosts a separate qualifying competition to determine the three teams it sends to the Champions League. North America is allotted nine of the 24 places with Mexico and the US receiving four places each and Canada just one. Canada's entry in the 2014/15 competition, the Montreal Impact, became the first Canadian team to reach the two-match final where they lost 5-3 on aggregate to Club América, along with fellow Mexican club Cruz Azul, the most frequent winners of the competition.

CAF Champions League

The African Champions Cup was first held in 1964/65 when Oryx Douala from Cameroon became the first winners defeating Stade Malien from Mali 2-1 in a single game final. Subsequent editions of the tournament feature a two game final. The competition received a makeover in 1997 with the formation of a mini-league group stage for the remaining 32 clubs. The competition starts with 64 sides including the champions in each affiliated nation's league plus the second placed finisher in the 12 leagues ranked the strongest in Africa. Egypt's Al Ahly is the most successful club in African Champions Cup/CAF Champions League history having won the competition eight times. Egyptian rivals, Zamalek are next on five titles alongside the 2015

champions, TP Mazembe, who secured their fifth win after defeating USM Alger in the 2015 final by an aggregate score of 4-1.

Asian Champions League

The Asian Football Confederation had organized a series of different cup competitions for its leading clubs beginning with the Asian Champion Club Tournament in 1967 with three of the first four tournaments won by Israeli clubs, and the Asian Club Championship held from 1985 to 2002. In addition, the AFC also ran the Asian Cup Winners Cup from 1990 to 2002 which was won by Saudi Arabian teams six times. These latter two competitions were merged in 2002 to form the AFC Champions League - the continent's premier club competition and one that started with 28 clubs competing from 12 countries. It now features 32 clubs at the group stages, mostly drawn from the strongest leagues in Asia. Since 2009, the defending champions do not qualify automatically for the competition the following year.

After a flurry of winning performances from Middle Eastern and West Asian clubs, the pendulum in recent seasons has mostly swung eastwards to the traditional strongholds of Asian football like Japan and South Korea with Chinese and Australian clubs also performing well. Overall, it is two West Asian teams who hold the record for most semi-final appearances: Al-Hilal from Saudi Arabia with eight and Iranian club, Esteghlal with seven.

Above: Club America celebrate CONCACAF Champions League victory. Opposite clockwise from top left: Club America goalkeeper Muñoz makes a save against Montreal Impact. Western Sydney Wanderers celebrate netting the Asian Champions League 2014 trophy. Zamelak's Eied (L) fights for the ball with Al Ahly's El Saeid. China's Guangzhou Evergrande celebrate winning 2013 AFC Champions' League final.

Rest of the World Club Competitions

Competitions or one-off matches that pit the winners of various continental championships against each other have been run in differing formats for over half a century, beginning with the Intercontinental Cup between the world's two footballing powerhouses – South America and Europe.

The Intercontinental Cup

Discussed by UEFA and CONMEBOL for some time before its introduction in 1960, the Intercontinental Cup pitted the winners of the UEFA European Cup against the Copa Libertadores champions in a two-game competition, one match home and the other away. At the start, a third, a play-off match, was contested if neither team had won both matches or won and drawn the two games. Aggregate goals were not used to decide the result, so despite Peñarol losing 1-0 to Benfica in the 1961 competition but then thrashing their opponents 5-0 in the return fixture, the contest went to a play-off game which Peñarol won 2-1. From 1968 onwards, if the contest was tied, penalties were used to determine the winner.

After a bright start, a series of ill-disciplined matches in the late 1960s blighted the competition's reputation. Celtic's goalkeeper, Ronnie Simpson was injured by missiles thrown from the crowd during the warm-up for the second game of the 1967 Intercontinental Cup against Racing Club of Argentina. This proved to be a precursor to an outrageously chaotic third, play-off, match between the two teams dubbed "The Battle of Montevideo" by the press. Paraguayan referee Rodolfo Pérez Osorio was unable to control the match which descended into a series of cynical fouls and brawls. Osorio sent off two Racing Club players and in addition showed red cards to four of the Celtic team. The last player to receive his marching orders, Celtic's Bertie Auld, refused to leave the pitch and continued to play the match which Celtic lost 1-0 to a Juan Carlos Cárdenas goal in the 55th minute.

With other moments of violent behavior marring the competition and doubts over its value amongst European teams, some sides chose not to compete in the 1970s. Ajax refused to travel to enter the competition in 1971 and 1973 whilst Bayern Munich chose not to compete against Argentinean side, Independiente in 1974. In Bayern's place, traveled the European Cup runners-up, Atlético Madrid who would win the competition overturning a 1-0 away deficit by winning 2-0 in their home leg. The following year saw both Bayern, the European Cup champions and Leeds United, the runners-up, decline a place in the competition which was not held as a result.

A major change to the competition occurred in 1980 when Japanese automotive company, Toyota sponsored the competition on the proviso that its matches were held in Japan. The matches were held in Tokyo or neighboring Yokohama and were now one-off games with play continuing into extra time and finally, a penalty shootout should the scores remain level.

Uruguay's Nacional became the first Toyota Cup winners after defeating Nottingham Forest in front of 62,000 fans inside Tokyo's National Stadium. The change of format and neutral location helped revive the tournament which continued until 2004, after FIFA had introduced its replacement. In total, 25 clubs from 11 different countries won the Intercontinental or Toyota Cup with the continental balance just shaded by South America's 22 victories to Europe's 21.

FIFA Club World Cup

FIFA sanctioned a new competition to replace the Toyota Cup and one which guaranteed representation for all continental champions, not just those from South America and Europe. This new tournament got off to a lurching start with just the 2000 competition played before a four year hiatus in part due to the collapse of FIFA's marketing partner, ISL. Originally named the FIFA Club World Championship, the first edition offered US$28 million of prize money for the eight teams that entered the event held in Brazil and competed in two groups of four. When it was next hosted, this time in Japan, the format had changed to six teams all of whom were the champions of their respective confederation's top club competition.

In 2006, the competition's name was changed to the Club World Cup and the following year, the format was altered to seven teams to include one place allotted to the country hosting the competition. This is traditionally given to the league champions of the host country who then compete in a play-off game against the champion club from the weakest confederation, the OFC, to determine which team enters the unusual four team quarter final round. The two winners from the quarter finals are then drawn against the UEFA Champions League and Copa Libertadores champions who receive a passage straight through to this semi-final stage.

Before the 2016 tournament, Auckland City from the OFC hold the record for the most games played at the Club World Cup with 13 in seven different tournaments whilst Barcelona with three titles are the competition's most successful club.

Opposite Top Left: Manchester United's George Best beats the Estudiantes defense in the 1968 World Club Championship. Top Right: Bayern Munich celebrate their World Club Cup victory over Argentina's Boca Juniors at Tokyo's National Stadium, 2001. Bottom Left: Neymar of Brazil's Santos celebrates scoring against Japan's Kashiwa Reysol during their FIFA Club World Cup semi-final game, 2011. Bottom Right: Barcelona celebrate winning the FIFA Club World Cup Final against River Plate

WORLD'S TOP CLUBS

"TO BE THE ULTIMATE TEAM, YOU MUST USE YOUR BODY AND YOUR MIND. DRAW UP ON THE RESOURCES OF YOUR TEAMMATES. CHOOSE YOUR STEPS WISELY AND YOU WILL WIN. REMEMBER, ONLY TEAMS SUCCEED." - JOSÉ MOURINHO

A CLUB'S MANY PARTS

A football club is much, much more than just the starting XI plus the substitutes fielded on match day. Behind the scenes, hundreds of other staff are at work whilst the stadium, the club's colors, traditions and its place in the local community all contribute to making a professional football club much more than just a team of players. Managers, chairmen, players and support staff may all come and go, but fans remain a passionate, devoted and sometimes vociferous constant in the fabric of the club. The bond many fans feel goes beyond attending games and buying merchandise. It can extend, in the case of 2,300 fans of Bundesliga 2 club, FC Union, to volunteering to renovate for free the club's Alte Försterei stadium in 2008.

The Team Behind The Team

A large football club can be a significant employer. In 2015, the investor relations information for Manchester United, for example, listed its full-time employees as numbering 837. Many more are temporarily employed as turnstyle operators and matchday stewards in and outside the ground or as catering and hospitality staff. Only a proportion of the permanent employees will be tasked directly with footballing matters; modern clubs run large commercial departments and fully engage in press, media and outreach who help connect the club with both the local community and with the broader outside world. They also produce content for a club's in-house TV channel or web and other digital and social media. Real Madrid have over 19.7 million followers on Twitter whilst Barcelona top the league on Facebook with over 91.1 million fans.

On the footballing side, a modern manager or head coach tends to work as part of an increasingly large team answerable to him and consisting of specialist skills and fitness coaches, dietitians, physiotherapists, club doctors and experts in recovery and rehabilitation. Sports psychologists, a network of scouts both for opposition teams and potential signings, and a series of coaches and development officers for different age bands of youth teams are all typical roles whilst the increase in data analysis of player movements and fitness levels, has led to new roles as performance monitors and analysts.

In Reserve

Even with squad numbers limited in some competitions, there are still players on the periphery of the head coach's plans and who must brace themselves for a long period playing reserve football until injuries or opportunities come for them to shine or they can make a move away from the club. Reserve teams vary enormously, but often consist of promising footballers from a club's youth set-up mixed with players returning from injury as well as those members of the playing staff currently out of favor.

In some countries, such as Spain, the reserve team operates as a largely separate club entity and competes in the lower divisions of the country's league pyramid. In Germany, reserve clubs compete in the league pyramid but cannot rise and be promoted above the German third division (3. Liga). They were also once able to compete in the DFB-Pokal Cup up until 2008, which led in the 1992-93 season to Hertha Berlin reaching the quarter finals but their reserve team, Hertha BSC II, progressing to the final. Reserve teams of J League sides in Japan can enter the Emperor's Cup whilst in North America, MLS reserve teams from 2014 such as the Portland Timbers 2 and the New York Red Bulls II mix with famous old US clubs like Bethlehem Steel FC in the United Soccer League.

Club Colors

Every football club has their own, distinctive playing strip with usually two or more further strips to avoid color clashes with opponents. A change in a club's colors today provokes uproar amongst fans, especially given the rise in social media. In 2012, new Cardiff City owner Vincent Tan insisted the Welsh club change their colors to red after having played for some 114 years in blue. After repeated fan pressure, Tan eventually relented and the "Bluebirds" were back in blue during the 2014-15 season.

Many teams in the past, though, changed colors in a sometimes rather ad hoc fashion. Juventus used to play in pink shirts before switching to black and white stripes, inspired by English club, Notts County's strip whilst Leeds United had played in various combinations of blue and yellow until new manager, Don Revie insisted they switch to all-white in the hope of emulating Real Madrid. Boca Juniors left their change of colors to complete chance. According to legend, in 1906, the club which in its first two years of existence had already played in three different strips decided to play, from then on, in the colors of the flag displayed by the next ship that sailed into the port of La Boca. A Swedish vessel duly arrived and the club strip has stayed a mixture of blue and yellow ever since.

Shirts For Sale

Shirts, have of course, become a major money-spinner for clubs through sponsorship and through lucrative sales of replica strips to fans. In 2014 Bayern Munich sold 945,000 club shirts whilst in the 2013-14 season, 1,580,000 Real Madrid replica shirts were purchased by fans online or from the club's superstores. Although Uruguayan team, Peñarol pioneered shirt sponsorship in the 1950s, it was not prevalent in Europe until 1973 when German team Eintracht Braunschweig brokered a deal with local drinks producer Jägermeister to display its glowing cross and stag logo on the front of their shirts, debuting them in their Bundesliga encounter with FC Schalke 04. Jägermeister continued to sponsor the club until 1987, but four years before that, attempts to rename the team Eintracht Jägermeister were rebuffed by the German Football Association. Shirt sponsorship started to spread and in 1976, Kettering Town became the first British team to feature sponsored shirts in a deal worth less than £10,000. Manchester

United's 2014-2021 deal with US automotive maker, Chevrolet in contrast is worth a reported £53 million per season to the club.

Shirt sales and sponsorship and matchday revenue from tickets and other sales are just some of the revenue streams afforded modern football clubs. The range of merchandise available from club's superstores can be bewildering from toasters in the colors of Borussia Dortmund to MLS club San Jose Earthquakes' clay heads fashioned with the likeness of club striker, Steven Lenhart in which fans can grow plants to mimic the striker's former long hairstyle. Rights to broadcast live games via TV and other media comprise an increasingly large proportion of many clubs' income. Barcelona's 2014-15 revenue from broadcasting rights (€199.8 million), for example, eclipsed its matchday revenues (€116.9 million) - a state of affairs mirrored by many clubs fortunate enough to play their domestic football in one of the leagues, such as La Liga or the English Premier League, most in demand with global TV audiences.

Mascots

For some fans, particularly young ones, the sight of their friendly club mascot is very much a part of their matchday tradition. Before cuddly mascots like Flix and Trix became part of matchday, mascots were live animals such as Hennes the goat who took part in team photographs with the Cologne side in the 1950s. In Benfica's case the mascot remains live-one of several bald eagles kept by the club is released and soars round the ground before kick-off.

Opposite Top Left: Manchester's manager Sir Alex Ferguson and his coaching staff during a training session 2011. Above: Flix and Trix, the official 2008 World Cup mascots. Left: A typical shot of Barcelona's superstore

ENGLAND

Manchester United

Founded: 1878
Stadium: Old Trafford (75,653)

Formed by railway workers as Newton Heath LYR in 1878, the club took their current name in 1902 and moved from their Bank Street ground to Old Trafford in 1910, winning the league title in their first season at a ground later dubbed, "the Theater of Dreams." United's postwar history is mostly the tales of two long-serving and supremely successful managers who oversaw the club. Matt Busby managed the club from 1945 to 1969 during which time they won five league titles, two FA Cups and overcame the 1958 Munich Air Crash which saw the tragic loss of 23 players, officials and journalists, to become the first English team to win the European Cup. Busby's team, featuring legends of the game including Bobby Charlton, Denis Law and the incomparable George Best, thrilled neutrals and hardcore Red Devils fans alike. Alex Ferguson took charge of the club in 1986 until 2013 and after a shaky start, led United to a period of dominance unparalleled in English football. Bringing through a number of talented homegrown players such as Ryan Giggs, Paul Scholes and David Beckham, Ferguson showed flair in the transfer market to capture cheaply the likes of Peter Schmeichel, Roy Keane, Eric Cantona and Cristiano Ronaldo. He managed the club as it won 13 out of the first 21 English Premier League titles (from 1992-93) to boost their tally to a record 20 overall. In addition came two epic UEFA Champions League titles in 1998-99 (part of a unique treble including Premier League and FA Cup) and 2007-08 as well as a World Club Cup in 2008.

Manchester City

Founded: 1887
Stadium: City of Manchester Stadium (55,097)

Manchester City won the first of their five FA Cups back in 1904 when a Billy Meredith goal secured the win over Bolton Wanderers. Nineteen years later they moved to Maine Road where in 1934, an English record 84,569 fans attended a sixth round FA Cup tie versus Stoke. Under Joe Mercer and Malcolm Allison, the club enjoyed a successful period in the late 1960s winning the league and clinching the 1970 European Cup Winners' Cup. The club bounced between divisions for much of the 1980s and 1990s, dropping down to the second division, two below the Premier League, as recently as 1998-99, but since 2002 have remained in the top flight and the following year moved into their new stadium which had just hosted the 2002 Commonwealth Games. In 2008, the club was bought by the Abu Dhabi United Group who poured in investment. Waves of signings occurred in 2008, 2009 and 2010 with players such as Robinho, Vincent Kompany and David Silva joining the club and the arrival of Sergio Agüero for a fee of over £35 million in 2011. It was Agüero that scored the winning goal versus QPR in the 2011-12 season that clinched City's first league championship since 1967-68 with the club securing their fourth league title in 2013-14.

Arsenal

Founded: 1886
Stadium: Emirates Stadium (60,260)

Formed by a group of workers from the Woolwich Arsenal Armament Factory, the club started out with the name Dial Square before changing to Woolwich Arsenal in 1893. The "Woolwich" was dropped shortly after the club moved in to their famous Highbury Ground in North London in 1913. The team constructed by innovative manager, Herbert Chapman went on to win five of Arsenal's 13 league titles in the 1930s whilst a team featuring Arsenal favorites Charlie George, Bob Wilson and John Radford won both the 1970 Inter-Cities Fairs Cup and achieved a 1971 league and FA Cup double. Success was only occasional after this point until the arrival of former Monaco coach, Arsène Wenger in 1996 who has since taken the side through more than 1,100 matches. His "Invincibles" team featuring stars of the caliber of Dennis Bergkamp and Thierry Henry, went unbeaten through the 2003-04 Premier League season and recorded a total of 49 games without defeat. Since that time, the club has moved into their Emirates Stadium, approximately 500m from their old ground and have added three further FA Cups to their tally, now standing at a record 12.

Liverpool
Founded: 1892
Stadium: Anfield (44,742)

Liverpool had won five English league championships before Bill Shankly arrived in 1959, but these were a distant memory for a team struggling in the English second division at the time. Shankly shrewdly assembled a team that won three league titles and the 1973 UEFA Cup in his record 783 matches in charge. Shankly's assistant, Bob Paisley took over in 1974 establishing a tradition of appointing managers from within the club (most often from its fabled "Boot Room" – its coaching team) that would only end with the arrival of the club's first non-British coach, Gérard Houllier in 1998. Under Paisley, Liverpool enjoyed a glorious period in their history, winning 19 trophies in nine years (1974-83) including six of the club's total of 18 league titles and three of its five European Cups or Champions League crowns. Whilst success has been limited since, a Luis Suárez-inspired Liverpool nearly won the 2013-14 Premier League, scoring 101 goals but finishing runners-up and leaving the 1989-90 league title as the club's last – a situation that Jürgen Klopp, appointed in 2015, is keen to address.

Chelsea
Founded: 1905
Stadium: Stamford Bridge (41,798)

It took Chelsea 50 years from its founding by businessman Gus Mears to win their first English league title (1954-55) and precisely another 50 years for their second to come in José Mourinho's first season in charge. The club set a points record (95) for the Premier League yet to be beaten in 2004-05 as Mourinho signings including Didier Drogba, Petr Čech and, a season later, Michael Essien, made their mark. Three more Premier League titles followed as did four of the club's seven FA Cups and the prize, owner Roman Abramovich most desired, the UEFA Champions League in 2010-11, with the club defeating Barcelona in the semi-finals and Bayern Munich in the final. Despite John Terry's longevity (1998-2016) at the club, it is another formidable defender - Ron Harris – who holds the Chelsea's appearance record with 795 in all competitions between 1961 and 1980 whilst Frank Lampard is its record goalscorer with 211 between 2001 and his 2014 move to Manchester City.

Tottenham Hotspur
Founded: 1882
Stadium: White Hart Lane (36,284)

Spurs were the only non-league club since the league began in 1888 to win the FA Cup, a feat they achieved in 1901 whilst playing in the regional Southern League. They joined the English league in 1908 but it would not be until 1950-51 that they won the league championship with a side containing Alf Ramsey and Bill Nicholson; the latter would go on to manage Spurs from 1958 to 1974. Under Nicholson, the club won an English League and FA Cup double in 1960-61 (the first team to achieve the feat since Aston Villa in 1896-97) as well as becoming the first British side to win a significant European trophy – the 1963 Cup Winners' Cup. Further cup successes came to give the club eight FA Cups, four League Cups and two UEFA Cups. Since the advent of the Premier League, Spurs have struggled to break into the elite and fans have had to contend with a string of above mid-table finishes which gains them access to the Europa League but, so far, only one UEFA Champions League (2010-11) where they reached the quarter finals.

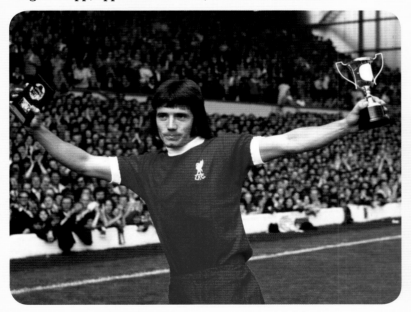

Opposite Top: Manchester City captain Vincent Kompany raises the League Cup trophy after his team's victory over Liverpool. Bottom: Manchester United celebrate winning the Champions League Final held at Luzhniki Stadium Moscow 21 May 2008 against Chelsea. Above: Liverpool's Kevin Keegan and his Young Player of the Year award, 1972. Right: Tottenham Hotspur's striker Harry Kane shoots

FRANCE

Paris Saint-Germain

Founded: (1970)
Stadium: Parc Des Princes (48,712)

New boys at French football's top table, Paris Saint-Germain was formed out of a desire amongst fans and businessmen for an elite football club in Paris. Their first major silverware was the Coupe De France in 1982, one of nine occasions on which they have won the cup. It was followed four years later by the club's first Ligue 1 championship as they finished three points ahead of Nantes. With new owners from Qatar buying a controlling stake in the club in 2011 and owning the club outright the following year, the club started bankrolling some eye-catchingly expensive signings. In 2011, PSG broke the French transfer record for Javier Pastore (€42 million) a figure equalled to sign Thiago Silva the following season, with David Luiz, Angel Di María and Edinson Cavani all arriving at PSG since at a cost of €60 million or more each. However, a slightly more affordable signing, Zlatan Ibrahimović (around €20 million) has become the club's top scorer with 136 goals. PSG's expensively-assembled side has dominated French football in recent seasons winning four league titles in a row from 2012-13 and recording a memorable French quadruple in 2014-15 winning Ligue 1, Coupe de France, Coupe de la Ligue and Trophée des Champions. In 2016, a record 9-0 thrashing of Troyes confirmed their status as Ligue 1 champions again with eight games still to be played.

Olympique Marseille

Founded: 1899
Stadium: Stade Velodrome (65,960)

The biggest and best known French club until the recent rise of Paris Saint-Germain, Marseille was originally formed as a

multi-sports club and enjoyed their first league championship in the amateur area before the professional competition now known as Ligue 1 was founded. They have since won nine Ligue 1 titles including five in a row in an astonishingly powerful run between 1989 and 1993. Bernard Tapie had arrived as chairman in 1986 and significant sums were spent to secure star players like Didier Deschamps, Enzo Francescoli and Jean-Pierre Papin who rampaged through Ligue 1, becoming the league's leading goalscorer in five consecutive seasons. In Europe, the club reached the European Cup semi-final in 1990, the final in 1991 and in the 1992-93 season defeated AC Milan to win the European Cup and making Fabien Barthez the then youngest goalkeeper to win the title. It all turned sour when the club was found guilty of match-fixing a league game in 1993 and were stripped of their league title, relegated but kept the European Cup, making them the only French winners of the trophy. The club's record has been more modest since but does include three Coupe de la Ligue victories in a row (2010, 2011, 2012), two Trophée des Champions, in 2010 and 2011, and four runners-up league finishes in nine seasons (2007-2015).

Olympique Lyonnais

Founded: 1899

Stadium: Parc Olympique Lyonnais (59,186)

Lyon were a middling French club who enjoyed moderate success such as winning the Coupe de France in 1964, 1967 and 1973 until it was bought by French businessmen Jean-Michel Aulas in 1987 who later developed an aggressive business model that saw players bought and sold on, often at a large profit. The turn of the century marked a transformation in the club's status as they embarked on a record-breaking run. In successive sides packed with talent including Michael Essien, Juninho Pernambucano, Florent Malouda and Karim Benzema, Lyons won seven consecutive Ligue 1 championships (2001-02 to 2007-08), the first under Jacques Santini, the last under Alain Perrin. The club went on to reach the semi-final of the 2009-10 UEFA Champions League in the same year that they finished Ligue 1 runners-up. Propelled by Ligue 1 top scorer Alexandre Lacazette's 27 goals, the club finished runners-up again in 2014-15.

AS Saint-Étienne

Founded: 1919

Stadium: Stade Geoffroy-Guichard (42,000)

AS Saint-Étienne were the team to beat in the 1960s and 1970s when they secured eight of their record ten French league titles and also won six Coupe de France during the period. The club set a still unbeaten record of 19 home wins in a season (1974-75) and the following year made it to the final of the European Cup for the first and only time, losing 1-0 to Bayern Munich. Saint-Étienne bounced back from three seasons in Ligue 2 to compete again in Ligue 1 from the 2004-05 season onwards and boast a proud record of 63 seasons in the top flight, second only to Marseille.

The club's ability to find and develop young players, from Michel Platini and Blaise Matuidi to Dimitri Payet and Kurt Zouma continued into the 21st century as the club reached the 2006-07 UEFA Cup for the first time in three decades and won their first Coupe de la Ligue in 2012-13.

AS Monaco

Founded: 1919

Stadium: Stade Louis II (18,523)

Monaco was formed from the merger of five local clubs in the principality, creating a team that would play its domestic football in France. The club won its first of seven league championships in the 1960-61 season and endured highs and lows in the 1970s with both relegation and a further league title in 1978 ably assisted by the the golden boot of Ligue 1 record goalscorer, Delio Onnis, who scored 223 goals for the club in just 280 games – an astonishing strike rate. Under Arsène Wenger's reign (1987-1995), Monaco added their fifth and last Coupe de France and developed future World Cup winners in Lilian Thuram, Thierry Henry and Emmanuel Petit as well as signing George Weah and Jürgen Klinsmann. The club has always been the bridesmaid in European competition, reaching the semi-final of the Champions League in 1994 and 1998, the final of the Cup Winners' Cup in 1992, where they were defeated by Werder Bremen and the 2003-04 UEFA Champions League final where they lost to Porto. A change of ownership following their surprise relagation to Ligue 2 in 2011, sees the club now owned by an investment group headed by Russian billionaire, Dmitry Rybolovlev. Major team rebuilding funds have enabled Monaco to bounce back to Ligue 1 and make high-profile signings including Radamel Falcao and James Rodríguez in recent seasons.

Opposite Top: Paris Saint-Germain's Thiago Silva and teammates celebrate winning the French Ligue 1 title, 2014. Bottom: Olympique Lyon's Alexandre Lacazette heads the ball past KAA Gent's goalkeeper Matz Sels during a Champions League game. Above: Moustapha Bayal Sall (L) of Saint-Étienne in action with Benjamin Mendy of Olympique Marseille in the "Le Classique." Above Right: Monaco's Anthony Martial (9) challenges Paris Saint-Germain's Thiago Da Silva and David Luiz.

ITALY

Internazionale (Inter Milan)

Founded: 1908

Stadium: Stadio Giuseppe Meazza (San Siro) (80,018)

In 1908, a group of players broke away from the Milan Cricket and Football Club to form their own side and two years later won the league championship, defeating Pro Vercelli in a final play-off game. Inter have featured in the Italian top division ever since and are the only Italian club never to suffer relegation from Serie A. The club has seen success in almost every decade since, winning the scudetto (championship) a total of 18 times including five in a row between 2006 and 2010 and finishing as runners-up on a further 13 occasions. They have also secured the Coppa Italia seven times and are five-time winners of the Supercoppa Italiana. The 1960s saw the club secure two Intercontinental Cups and two European Cups with a third European triumph coming in the UEFA Champions League in 2009-10. They have also notched three UEFA Cup victories, all occurring in the 1990s. The club plays its home games at the San Siro which was renamed in 1980 the Stadio Giuseppe Meazza, after the celebrated attacker who played over 400 matches for the club.

AC Milan

Founded: 1899

Stadium: Stadio Giuseppe Meazza (San Siro) (80,018)

Associazione Calcio Milan was formed by a collection of early football fans with a former British vice-consul, to Milan, Alfred Edwards, the club's first president. Playing in red and black from the start and from which their nickname "I Rossoneri" derives, the team won their first league title in 1901, and like their Milanese rivals, Inter, have won 18 league titles in total. Matches between the two clubs. Known as the Derby della Madonnina, after the Madonna statue on top of the Duomo nearby, often features. With both teams in the same city, fans are quick to remind players of previous defeats, like Milan's 6-0 hit on Inter in 2001. Milan has won five Coppa Italia and six Supercoppa Italiana trophies but abroad are Italy's most successful club with seven European Cup or UEFA Champions League crowns, three Intercontinental Cups, two Cup Winners' Cups and the FIFA Club World Cup title in 2007. The club has been associated with some of Europe's finest players from lethal Swede Gunnar Nordahl, the club's record goalscorer with 221 to silky defender, Paolo Maldini who made over 900 appearances for the club and whose number 3 shirt has been retired permanently by the club in his honor, as has the number 6 shirt for Franco Baresi.

AS Roma

Founded: 1927

Stadium: Stadio Olimpico (70,634)

Rome lagged behind the footballing cities of Milan and Turin (the latter home of Juventus and Torino) so in 1927, a number of Rome-based clubs merged with the aim of creating a club that could challenge at the highest level. The club has been a consistent contender for honors suffering relegation just once (1950-51) and have finished Serie A runners-up on 13 occasions including the

2013-14 and 2014-15 seasons. The club have also appeared in more Coppa Italia finals than any other team (17), triumphing on nine occasions, the last in 2008. They have also won the Supercoppa Italiana twice (2001, 2007) but their only European trophy remains the 1960-61 Intercontinental Cup. Roma began the new millennium in extravagant style, setting a club transfer record of £22.5 million for Gabriel Batistua, adding Hidetoshi Nakata and Walter Samuel and winning their third Serie A title in 2001, the same year as Daniele De Rossi also joined the squad and has since made over 500 appearances. He is eclipsed, however, by veteran Francesco Totti who first played for Roma in 1992 and in 2015, whilst playing against Serie A opponents, Sassuolo, scored his 300th goal in his 745th appearance for the club.

S.S. Lazio

Founded: 1900
Stadium: Stadio Olimpico (70,634)

Lazio share the Stadio Olimpico ground and a strong rivalry with AS Roma. The club was the home of Serie A's all-time leading goalscorer, Silvio Piola (274 Serie A goals) for much of his career (1934-43). A takeover in 1992 by Sergio Cragnotti changed the club's fortunes as the club began investing heavily in expensive new players including English maverick, Paul Gascoigne, Argentinean Juan Sebastián Verón, Italian striker Christian Vieri and, in 2000, breaking the world record transfer fee with the £35 million purchase of Hernán Crespo from Parma. The club won a treble of Coppa Italia, Supercoppa Italiana and their second Serie A title in 2000, the same year they produced their record highest UEFA Champions League wins, two 5-1 victories over Marseille and Shakhtar Donetsk. The club suffered financial difficulties and were excluded in 2006 from European competition for a match-fixing scandal but have since recovered, winning their fifth and in the 2012-13 season, their sixth Coppa Italia trophies.

Juventus FC

Founded: 1897
Stadium: Juventus Stadium (41,475)

Known as, "the Girlfriend of Italy" for its countrywide fanbase, and also, "La Vecchia Signora" (The Old Lady), Turin's most successful club didn't play their first match until 1900 whilst their memorable black and white-striped shirts were first worn in 1903. The owners of the Fiat automotive company, the Angelli family, took control of the club in 1923 and have financed the building of a large number of competition-winning teams. The club has won a record 31 Italian league titles. It would have been 33 except Juventus finished champions in both the 2004-05 and 2005-6 seasons. Those two Series A titles were revoked however and the club relegated to Serie B after it was found to be one of five clubs involved in the "Calciopoli" match-fixing scandal in 2006. Juventus bounced back as Serie B champions the following season and have since won four titles in a row beginning in 2011-12 season – their first in their new stadium. The club can also count 10 Coppa Italia and 7 Supercoppa Italiana in their domestic trophy cabinet. Despite becoming the first club to win all major European trophies including two UEFA Champions League titles (1985, 1996), it has since been a case of "what might have been" as the club has been losing finalists in the Champions League six times, including the 2014-15 final. Juventus' record signing remains Gianluigi Buffon - the world's most expensive goalkeeper when purchased from Parma for £32.5 million in 2001 - but the fee now looks outstanding value as the veteran stopper has made over 570 appearances for the club and in 2016 kept his eighth consecutive Serie A clean sheet in a 2-0 victory over Inter Milan.

Opposite Top: PAC Milan's Carlos Bacca (R) and Inter Milan's Jeison Murillo in action. Bottom: AS Roma's Francesco Totti celebrates with teammate Radja Nainggolan after scoring against Juventus. Above: Lazio's Stefano Mauri and President Claudio Lotito kiss the Italian Cup trophy as they celebrate beating AS Roma, 2013. Above Right: Juventus' Paul Pogba jumps to control the ball.

GERMANY

Bayern Munich
Founded: 1900
Stadium: Allianz Arena (75,000)

Although they did win the 1931-32 German National Championship, it is as a Bundesliga side that Bayern emerged as the most successful German club. Not admitted into the Bundesliga until the 1965-66 season, they have since progressed to secure a record 25 league titles so far, their first coming in 1968-69 as the backbone of an immensely strong and successful side was put in place with Sepp Maier in goal, the great Franz Beckenbauer linking defense and attack and upfront, goal machine Gerd Müller. "Der Bomber" was the Bundesliga's top scorer in seven seasons between 1967 and 1978 as Bayern swept all before them to win three European Cups in a row (1974-76), the 1976 World Club Cup and five Bundesliga titles up until 1981. The club has been champions on a regular and consistent basis ever since and have only finished outside the top three in three seasons since 1984-85. In 2001, the club both won the UEFA Champions League and decided to move grounds from the old Olympiastadion to the new Allianz Arena from 2005-6 season onwards. "FC Hollywood" as they are sometimes nicknamed captured their fifth European Cup/Champions League title in 2013 as part of a treble including the Bundesliga (won with a record 91 points) and DFB-Pokal, a competition they have won 17 times, also a record.

Hamburger SV
Founded: 1887
Stadium: Volksparkstadion (57,000)

This club lays claim to being the oldest surviving Bundesliga side in existence after it was formed in 1919 from the merger of three clubs, one of whom SC Germania, can trace its history back to 1887. It is also the only club to have played every season of the Bundesliga and can trace its participation in the top flight to long before that time, having won the 1923 German Football Championship. Club legend Uwe Seeler played a record 476 matches for Hamburg, scoring 404 goals in a career spanning three decades and winning the club's first of three DFB-Pokal cups in 1963, when he scored all three goals in Hamburg's 3-0 win over Borussia Dortmund. Seeler and the team endured disappointment in European competition as the side were beaten finalists in the 1967-68 European Cup Winners' Cup but the club did win the competition in 1977. Hamburg enjoyed its most successful spell under Austrian coach, Ernst Happel from 1981 to 1987. During that period, the "Red Shorts" won two Bundesliga titles, were twice runners-up and won their first and only European Cup, in 1983, defeating Juventus in the final.

Borussia Dortmund
Founded: 1908
Stadium: Signal Iduna Park (81,359)

Ballspielverein Borussia 09 e.V. Dortmund or BVB for short have won the Bundesliga eight times and finished runners-up on six further occasions. The "Black and Yellows" were long in the shadow of rivals, FC Schalke 04, but now proudly possess the largest average attendance for club football in the world as in excess of 80,000 attend every home Bundesliga match at the Westfalenstadion

(currently branded Signal Iduna Park due to sponsorship reasons) which replaced their former ground, Stadion Rote Erde, in 1974. Under inspirational captain, Matthias Sammer, the club were highly successful in the mid-1990s winning the UEFA Champions League courtesy of two goals in the final from Karl-Heinz Riedle. After suffering financial problems, they entered the doldrums, but with charismatic coach, Jürgen Klopp at the helm from 2008 to 2015, Dortmund enjoyed 179 wins and just 70 losses as they romped to two Bundesliga titles (2010-11, 2011-12), the 2011-12 DFB-Pokal and two DFL Supercups (2013, 2014). Former FSV Mainz 05 coach, Thomas Tuchel took BVB to second place in the 2015-16 season with a squad that contains German stars including Mats Hummels and Marco Reus augmented by foreign talent such as Japan's Shinji Kagawa, Serbian defender, Neven Subotić and Turkish midfielder, Nuri Şahin who in 2005 became the Bundesliga's youngest ever player at age 16 when he made his league debut for BVB.

FC Schalke 04
Founded: 1904
Stadium: Veltins-Arena (62,271)

Formed by a group of high school students, FC Schalke adopted their blue and white strip in 1924. A powerhouse in the 1930s when they played in the Gauliga Westfalen regional league, Schalke won 11 regional championships in a row (1934-44) and six national championships during the period. The 1970s saw them win the 1970-71 DFB-Pokal and narrowly miss out on two Bundesliga titles, the second in 1976-77 when they finished a single point behind Borussia Mönchengladbach. Throughout the 1970s, they were propelled by the goals of the prolific Klaus Fischer, the club's record goalscorer with 182 goals in the Bundesliga and 223 overall. In total the club has finished Bundesliga runners-up six times but, at least, leads the Revierderby or Ruhr Derby against rivals, Borussia Dortmund, with Schalke ahead by 58 wins to 48 in early 2016. Frequently selling-out their imposing Veltins-Arena stadium, the club is now one of the wealthiest in German football, boosted by a growth in membership from around 10,000 at the start of the 1990s to over 140,000 by 2016.

SV Werder Bremen
Founded: 1899
Stadium: Weserstadion (42,100)

Jostling for supremacy with their northern German rivals, Hamburger SV, Werder Bremen have enjoyed domestic success with six DFB-Pokal trophies as well as a continental triumph in the form of winning the 1991-1992 Cup Winners' Cup. The 2003-04 season was a standout one for the club and its coach, Thomas Schaaf (who would manage the side for 14 years from 1999 to 2013) as they became only the fourth side to achieve a Bundesliga and DFB-Pokal Cup double, assisted by Brazilian striker Ailton's 28 league goals during the campaign. They have been unable to repeat the feat since but came close with two further runners-up finishes (2005-06, 2007-08) in the Bundesliga as well as another DFB-Pokal triumph, this time in 2009 when a Mesut Özil goal saw them defeat Bayer Leverkusen. Their tally of league titles remains on four but with seven runners-up finishes and a runners-up placing in the 2008-09 UEFA Cup. Peruvian striker Claudio Pizarro was instrumental in getting Bremen to this final, scoring against rivals Hamburg in the semi-final during his second spell at the club. In 2015, he returned for a third spell and in 2016 broke Marco Bode's club record of 101 goals scored. With his tally augmented by over 80 goals for Bayern, Pizarro has now scored more Bundesliga goals than any other foreign player.

Borussia Mönchengladbach
Founded: 1900
Stadium: Borussia Park (54,057)

Founded as FC Borussia, the club secured their first major national honors in 1960 when they won the DFB-Pokal. By the 1970s, Die Fohlen (The Foals) possessed an excellent side captained by Berti Vogts and containing for large parts of the decade players like Uli Stielike, Rainer Bonhof, Jupp Heynckes and the Danish maestro, Allan Simonsen. Competing for honors at the same time as an excellent Bayern Munich side, it was an astonishing achievement to win five Bundesliga titles between 1970 and 1977 and take part in five European finals during the decade, winning two UEFA Cups (1975, 1979) but losing to Liverpool in the 1977 European Cup Final. Unlike Bayern, the club did not have the finances to keep hold of star players or rebuild with major signings and slipped out of contention, although since 2011-12, they have recorded high enough league finishes to qualify each year for European competition.

Opposite Top: Bayern Munich's Thomas Müller (C) celebrates with Robert Lewandowski. Bottom: Borussia Dortmund's Lukasz Piszczek celebrates with the German soccer championship trophy 2012. Above: Schalke 04's Raúl (L) and José Manuel Jurado celebrate. Above Right: Borussia Mönchengladbach captain Berti Vogts clears the ball away from Liverpool striker Kevin Keegan

SPAIN

Real Madrid

Founded: 1902

Stadium: Santiago Bernabéu Stadium (85,454)

Ranked by the Deloitte Football Money League as the world's wealthiest football club worth in excess of €2.5 billion and with revenues of €549.5 million in the 2013-14 season alone, Real Madrid have long been an elite club packed with talent, often recruited at great expense. Foreign signings first came in vogue under the presidency of Santiago Bernabéu de Yeste in the 1940s and 1950s who secured the services of legendary footballers including Ferenc Puskás, Paco Gento, Héctor Rial and Alfredo di Stéfano who went on an unparalleled run of five European Cup triumphs in a row. Between 1957 and 1965, Real were untouchable in the Bernabéu (which opened in 1947) and remained unbeaten for 121 home league matches, winning five of their record 32 La Liga titles consecutively. Real's first player-manager, Arthur Johnson (1910-1920) introduced their now world famous all-white playing strip which has since been worn by successive waves of star players including the galacticos of the early 2000s such as Luís Figo, Ronaldo and Zinédine Zidane. The latter was appointed head coach in 2016 and presides over an incredible array of talent including Gareth Bale, Iker Casillas (the club's second most appearances holder with 725, behind Raúl's 741) and Real's all-time leading goalscorer, Cristiano Ronaldo (352 goals). In 2013-14, Ronaldo blasted a record 17 goals in the UEFA Champions League to take Real Madrid to the fabled, "La Décima" – their tenth European Cup or UEFA Champions League crown, the most of any club.

Barcelona

Founded: 1899

Stadium: Camp Nou (99,354)

Formed by Swiss émigré Joan Gamper, after he placed an advertisement in a Catalan magazine, Barcelona's first major national trophy came in 1910 when the club won the first of its record 27 Copas del Rey. It has been a Spanish heavyweight ever since and from the start of La Liga in 1929, the club have finished twelfth once (1941-42) and ninth three times. In every other season, they have finished in the top six, securing 23 league championships in the process. These include seven in the 21st century including the 2014-15 title when the club finished with an astonishing +89 goal difference (scoring 110 and only conceding 21). Whilst they have not won as many La Liga titles as their fierce rivals, Real Madrid, they do boast the proud record

of being the only club to take part in European competition every season since the European Cup kicked off in 1955. This participation has netted them a record three Inter Cities Fairs Cups, four European Cup Winners' Cups and five European Super Cups. It took a surprisingly long time, given their stature, to win their first European Cup, in 1991-92. Four more have followed in 2005–06, 2008–09, 2010–11 and 2014–15. The club is one of the best supported in Europe and domestic fans are proud of their recent record of producing players for the Spanish national team. At the EURO 2012 final, for example, eight of the Spanish starting XI were Barça players. It is Argentina's Lionel Messi, though, that remains the glittering jewel in an all-South American front trio that comprises Neymar and Luiz Suárez. Messi is the

club's leading goalscorer with 448 goals for the senior team.

Atlético Madrid

Founded: 1903
Stadium: Vicente Calderón Stadium (54,907)

In the shadow of the two big beasts of Spanish football, the Colchoneros (mattress-makers for their red and white shirts) have nonetheless enjoyed considerable success over the decades. Whilst a UEFA Champions League crown has so far eluded them, they have won the UEFA Cup Winners' Cup, UEFA Super Cup, the 1974 Intercontinental Cup and two recent Europa League titles (2009-10, 2011-12), the latter under long-serving coach, Diego Simeone's shrewd eye. The club contests the Madrid derby with their crosstown rivals Real Madrid and suffered a 14 year run without a victory in the derby until 2013 when they defeated Real 2-1 to win their tenth Copa del Rey. The following year, the club broke the Barcelona-Real Madrid dominance of La Liga, becoming the first club since Valencia in 2003-04 to take the title away from the big two. Thirteen assists from Koke and 27 goals from Diego Costa gave Atlético Madrid its first title since 1995-96 and its tenth overall. The club plans a move to the Estadio Olímpico de Madrid with around a 70,000 capacity for the 2017-18 season.

Valencia CF

Founded: 1919
Stadium: Mestalla Stadium (55,000)

The club enjoyed great success in the 1940s, spurred on by their all-time record goalscorer, Edmundo Suárez whose tally of 269 goals included 186 in 210 La Liga games. Valencia won three of their six La Liga titles during this decade as well as two Copa del Rey trophies. Abroad, the club has won two Inter Cities Fairs Cups in 1962 and 1963 but had to wait 41 years to win its successor competition, the UEFA Cup, defeating Marseille in the 2004 final.

They also won the UEFA Cup Winners' Cup in 1979-80 and came desperately close to winning the UEFA Champions League, reaching the final in consecutive years (2000 and 2001) but losing to Real Madrid in the first and Bayern Munich in the second. Valencia fans have always enjoyed a prolific, whole-hearted striker leading their line from Waldo Machado in the 1960s to Argentinean Mario Kempes in the 1980s and David Villa in a five season spell during the 2000s. Fans' fervent hopes are pinned on 2015 club record signing, Rodrigo, bought for approximately €30 million from Benfica, one of a number of major signings made since 2014 when Singapore businessman, Peter Lim, secured a controlling stake in the club.

Athletic Bilbao

Founded: 1898
Stadium: San Mamés (53,289)

Formed in the Basque region of northern Spain, Athletic Bilbao's concentration on bringing through talented young Basque players has both its admirers and critics. It has certainly proven successful for spells including the 1930s and early 1940s when the club won five of its total of eight La Liga titles and the Javier Clemente era (1981-1986) where he coached the club to two La Liga titles, one Copa del Rey and the 1985 Supercopa de España. Los Leones (The Lions) have never been relegated from the top flight but have never won a major European trophy although they have gone close on several occasions, finishing as losing finalists in the 1976-77 UEFA Cup and the 2011-12 Europa League. In total, the club has won a total of 23 Copa del Rey trophies, second only to Barcelona. They have also reached the final a further 14 times, the latest in 2015 when the Lions couldn't repel Messi and Neymar in a 3-1 defeat. They were able to exact revenge later that year as they defeated Barcelona 4-0 in the first leg of the Supercopa de España and drew the second leg 1-1 to win their second Supercopa.

Sevilla

Founded: 1890
Stadium: Ramón Sánchez Pizjuán Stadium

Formed by a group of Scottish and Spanish football enthusiasts, the Red and Whites have spent 66 seasons in La Liga but have only one league championship for their troubles, won back in the 1945-6 season, five seasons after their biggest ever La Liga victory, an 11-1 thrashing of Barcelona. They have been more successful in cup competitions, most notably the Copa del Rey which they have won on five occasions, the latest in 2009-10, and in the UEFA Cup and Europa League where Sevilla's 2014-15 triumph was their fourth and a record. The club's reserve team, named Sevilla Atlético, was formed in 1958 and currently plays in the Segunda División B. Amongst the talent that has progressed from this team to Sevilla's first side have been Jesús Navas, Sergio Ramos and José Antonio Reyes who returned to Sevilla in 2012 and is currently the club's captain.

Opposite Top: Luís Figo (2L) is congratulated by teammates (L-R) David Beckham, Zinédine Zidane, Raúl and Ronaldo after scoring a penalty against AS Roma, 2004. Bottom: Barcelona's Neymar celebrates scoring goal with teammates Luis Suarez and Lionel Messi. Above: Athletic Bilbao's Aritz Aduriz is fouled by Barcelona's Sergio Busquets.

GREAT STADIUMS

History of the Stadia

Football was first played in open parks and pitches but as spectator numbers increased, dedicated football grounds were constructed. The first were built in England in the 1860s and 1870s. Some, such as Bramall Lane in Sheffield, home of Sheffield United, and Deepdale, home of Preston North End, still survive, albeit with major modifications over the years. As football blossomed in popularity, great stadiums have sprung up all over the world. Some have become mighty fortresses intimidating away teams who must play there whilst others have become a club or country's national teams' spiritual home.

Clubs were once largely standing room only. As a result, record attendances for most long-serving grounds were set before safety concerns led to many stadia becoming all-seater. In 1935, for example, Stamford Bridge was crammed with 82,905 spectators to watch their London derby with Arsenal. Today, the same ground has a listed maximum capacity of 41,798. Stadia in some countries, notably, Germany, do have standing terraces and areas. Borussia Dortmund's Signal Iduna Park is home to the fabled and colorful Die gelbe Wand (The Yellow Wall) formed by nigh-on 25,000 standing Dortmund fans dressed in the club's predominantly yellow colors.

Amsterdam Arena

With their former De Meer stadium seating just 19,000 a new ground for Ajax was a priority. It opened in 1996 and was the first in Europe to feature a sliding roof, enabling the stadium to host indoor events away from football. The roof weighs around 520 tonnes and takes approximately 20 minutes to open or close.

Camp Nou

Europe's largest club stadium with a capacity, as of 2015, of up to 99,354, Camp Nou is a sweeping concrete bowl in the heart of Barcelona. The club moved here from Camp de Les Corts in 1957 and celebrated in style, thrashing Jaén 6-1. In 2014, the club celebrated its 1000th league game at the Camp Nou with a 3-0 win over Celta Vigo.

Allianz Arena

Home to Bayern Munich and fellow ground-sharers, TSV 1860 München, the Allianz Arena opened in 2002 with a capacity of 69,000 which has been uprated to 75,000 following modifications. The exterior is covered in 2,874 inflated ETFE plastic panels which can be illuminated in different colors reflecting the home team. Visitors make use of the 9,800 space underground car park, considered the largest in Europe.

Old Trafford

In 1902 Newton Heath football club changed its name to Manchester United and sought to build a new stadium on the west side of Manchester. Old Trafford cost £60,000 to construct and was designed by noted Scottish architect, Archibald Leitch who was involved in the design of more

than 20 other grounds including Anfield (Liverpool), White Hart Lane (Tottenham Hotspur) and Stamford Bridge (Chelsea). After a series of redevelopments, Old Trafford is now England's largest club ground with a capacity of 75,731.

San Siro

Home of both Inter Milan (Internazionale) and AC Milan, the Giuseppe Meazza Stadium held just 35,000 on its opening in 1926, but has been repeatedly expanded to now hold 80,018 spectators. The ground's 11 distinctive towers, added during modernization for the 1990 FIFA World Cup, support the giant roof and provide spiral walkways up to the top tiers of the stands. This famous old ground has hosted four UEFA Champions League finals including the 2016 edition.

Estádio da Luz

Opened in 2003 and used for EURO 2004 matches, Benfica's home ground boasts an innovative design featuring 43m high steel arches from which a clear roof is suspended to admit light through to the pitch and the majority of the seats. The ground features a maximum capacity of 65,647 and hosted the 2014 UEFA Champions League final.

New Wembley Stadium

The original Wembley Stadium, complete with its iconic twin towers opened in 1923, cost £750,000 to build and hosted 82,000 seats. The new Wembley Stadium opened in 2007, cost approximately £757 million and holds 90,000. Its striking 133m tall arch spans 315m and at the time of construction was the longest single span roof structure in the world.

Estadia Azteca

The largest dedicated football stadium in the Americas, the Azteca was opened in 1966 and has hosted both the 1970 and 1986 World Cup Finals and thus Diego Maradona's infamous "hand of God" goal versus England. The pitch is 9.5m below ground level and surrounded by three giant rings of continuous tiers to form an imposing structure capable of holding 105,000 originally, but now 95,500.

Estadio Alberto J. Armando (La Bombanera)

The home of Boca Juniors opened in 1940 as a three-sided ground with deep stands. With the construction of a fourth, flat stand, the ground got its distinctive "D" shape – looking like a chocolate bonbon hence the 49,000 capacity stadia's most commonly-used name, La Bombanera.

FNB Stadium

Opened in 1989 and then expanded in 2009 for the 2010 FIFA World Cup when it was called Soccer City, the FNB's exterior clad in earthenware colors is designed to make it look like a traditional gourd pot, giving it its nickname of "the Calabash." With a maximum capacity of 94,736, it is the largest football stadium in Africa.

Maracanã

South America's most iconic ground, the Estádio Jornalista Mário Filho, better known as the Maracanã, was opened just in time for the 1950 FIFA World Cup. The monumental concrete structure has an official record attendance of 183,513 spectators for the 1954 international between Brazil and Paraquay although those present for the 1950 World Cup Final, including eventual President of FIFA, João Havelange, estimate that some 220,000 fans were present that day. What isn't in doubt is that two Brazilian legends remember the ground fondly. Zico scored 333 goals at the Maracanã throughout his club and national career whilst Pelé scored his 1000th professional goal there in 1969.

Opposite Top: Camp Nou. Bottom left: San Siro. Bottom Right: Allianz Arena
Above: Old Trafford. Above Right: La Bombonera.

REST OF EUROPE 1

Ajax

Founded: 1900

Stadium: Amsterdam Arena (53,500)

When Rinus Michels arrived as coach in 1965, Ajax had slipped from their earlier heights to facing relegation dogfights. He rapidly transformed the club with his brand of "Total Football," winning the Eredivisie the following season and reaching their first European Cup final in 1969. Ajax, possessing such stellar talents as Johan Cruyff and Ruud Krol, would win the competition three times in a row (1971, 1972, 1973) during a spell of six Dutch league titles in eight seasons. In total, the club has won 33 Eredivisie and 18 KNVB Cups, two Cup Winners' Cups and one UEFA Cup in 1992. Three years later, a young side coached by Louis Van Gaal won the UEFA Champions League whilst under former player Frank de Boer (head coach since 2010), Ajax have won four out of five league titles. The club's youth academy has long blazed a trail of innovative, creative coaching with the result being a seemingly endless production line of gifted and highly-skilled players from Dennis Bergkamp and Marco van Basten to Patrick Kluivert, Wesley Sneijder and Toby Alderweireld. Even those who had played their youth football and early career elsewhere, such as Luis Suárez and Zlatan Ibrahimović, appeared to benefit from a spell at the Netherlands' most famous and successful club.

PSV Eindhoven

Founded: 1913

Stadium: Philips Stadion (35,000)

Founded by technology company Philips on the site of the company's sports ground, PSV became the first Dutch club to enter the European Cup in 1955. The following season saw their striker Coen Dillen score 43 goals – still a Dutch league record – but sustained success didn't come until the 1970s with the club winning three of its 22 league titles that decade as well as the 1977-78 UEFA Cup. Willy van de Kerkhof was one of a handful of players to play in the UEFA Cup final and 10 years later, the European Cup Final in which PSV defeated Benfica whilst in the middle of a run of six league titles in seven seasons (ending in 1991-92). In total, the club has played 278 games in European competition including 149 in the European Cup or UEFA Champions League. PSV has since seen such talented players as Ronaldo, Ruud Gullit, Arjen Robben and in more recent times, Jeremain Lens, Georginio Wijnaldum and Memphis Depay don its red and white home strip before being sold at a profit to foreign clubs. Lens scored the last goal in the club's most celebrated game of recent times, a 10-0 thrashing of traditional rivals, Feyenoord in the 2010-11 league season.

Anderlecht

Founded: 1908

Stadium: Constant Vanden Stock (28,063)

Formed by a dozen football enthusiasts who met at the Café Concordia in 1908, Anderlecht reached Belgium's top division for the first time in the 1921-22 season where they finished twelfth, one place above relegation. Their first league title came in the 1946-47 season and 32 more have followed since, along with a further 20 runners-up finishes, often to either of their great rivals, Brugge or Standard Liège. From 1964-65 onwards, the club and its famous purple and white strip became a permanent fixture in European competition. The club has managed to qualify to compete in either the Champions League/European Cup, the UEFA Cup/Europa League or the Cup Winners' Cup for a staggering 52 consecutive seasons, second only to Barcelona. Whilst the UEFA Champions League title has eluded them, the team have won two European Cup Winners' Cups (in 1976 and 1978) and the UEFA Cup in 1983.

Benfica

Founded: 1904
Stadium: Estadio Da Luz (65,647)

Benfica's first major golden era began in the 1960s under the vastly experienced Hungarian coach, Béla Guttmann who assembled a team that blended pace and power to perfection with the marvelous Eusébio as its spearhead. They became the first team in Europe to overturn Real Madrid's dominance in the European Cup, winning back-to-back trophies in 1961 and 1962 and reached the final a further four times during the 1960s. The club has won the Primeira Liga 34 times including consecutive titles in the 2013-14 and 2014-15 seasons, the first of those two seasons including a notable Portuguese treble of league, Taça de Portugal (Portugal's main knockout cup) and the Taça da Liga (league cup) for the first time. They have won the Taça de Portugal 25 times – more than any other club and in the league are the only side to go unbeaten throughout a season, a feat achieved twice in 1972-73 and 1977-78. In addition, they hold the European record for most consecutive wins in a domestic league with 29 during 1971 and 1972.

Porto

Founded: 1893
Stadium: Estádio do Dragão (50,035)

The "Dragons" are one of Portugal's oldest clubs, formed by a port wine merchant enthused by football after he had visited England. They enjoyed sporadic success in their early decades with only five of their 27 Portuguese league titles and three of their 16 Taça de Portugal successes coming before the mid-1970s. The 1980s saw Porto jostle with Europe's leading clubs for supremacy in cup competitions with the high point, their defeat of Bayern Munich to win the 1986-87 European Cup. Porto's next major spell of success came with the appointment of José Mourinho in 2002. Signing Maniche, Nuno Valente, Benni McCarthy and others,

Mourinho forged a winning side that won the treble of 2002-03 league title, Portuguese Cup and the UEFA Cup, defeating Celtic in the final. The following season, they triumphed in the UEFA Champions League and in 2010-11, repeated their 2002-03 feats with a second treble including taking the Europa League crown by beating fellow Portuguese side, SC Braga in the final. In both their European Cup/Champions League winning seasons (1986-87, and 2003-04), Porto went on to win the Intercontinental Cup against South American opposition to boost their total collection of major trophies to 74.

Sparta Prague

Founded: 1893
Stadium: Generali Arena, formerly known as Stadion Letná (19,416)

This Czech Republic club has a long tradition of competing outside of its borders with its first great side entering the Mitropa Cup in the 1920s and winning the competition three times (1927, 1935, 1964). It has been known by a variety of names throughout its existence, beginning with Královské Vinohrady (King's Vineyard) when founded in 1893, it has always remained at the top of domestic club competition, collecting, according to UEFA, a record 36 league titles as as well as 20 domestic cups. Further European success has eluded the side that has contested 24 European Cup or UEFA Champions League seasons but the club has produced a large number of notable players over the years from top scorer at the 1934 FIFA World Cup, Oldřich Nejedlý to Karel Poborský, Petr Čech and Tomáš Rosický.

Opposite Left: Ajax celebrate winning the European Cup in 1972. Bottom: Guillaume Gillet celebrates scoring the first goal for Anderlecht against Tottenham. Above: Porto's Falcao scores against Braga's Paulão during their Europa League final, 2011. Above Right: Benfica's Miralem Sulejmani in action at the Estádio da Luz.

REST OF EUROPE 2

Celtic

Founded: 1888
Stadium: Celtic Park (60,411)

St. Mary's Church Hall in Glasgow's Calton district was the location of an 1887 meeting which resulted in the formation of the club, sparking a rivalry with its "Old Firm" rivals, the Rangers, which would last more than a century. Their first match was a year later. Celtic won 5-2. They moved to their famous Celtic Park ground four years later, where they remain still. Celtic's finest hour in Europe came during the 1966-67 season when they reached their first European Cup final against Italian thoroughbreds Inter Milan and won 2-1 with goals from Tommy Gemmell and Steve Chalmers to become the first British winner of the competition. The club also contested the final of the 1969-70 European Cup but had to wait until 2003 to reach the climax of another European competition, the final of the 2002-03 UEFA Cup where they lost to Porto. Celtic have won the Scottish League Championship on 46 occasions, most recently in the 2014–15 season whilst in the previous season, Celtic goalkeeper Fraser Forster set a league record of 1,256 minutes without conceding a goal. In addition, the club have secured the Scottish Cup 36 times and the Scottish League Cup 15 times.

Galatasaray

Founded: 1905
Stadium: Türk Telekom Arena (52,652)

The highest ranked (by UEFA) of Turkey's big three clubs, Galatasaray maintain fierce rivalries with fellow Istanbul heavyweights, Fenerbahçe and Beşiktaş. After enjoying an outstanding treble-winning season in 2014-15, they lead their

rivals in terms of league titles with 20, most Turkish Cup wins with 16 and most TFF Süper Kupa (Turkish Super Cup) triumphs with 14. Known for an intimidating home atmosphere, especially when foreign clubs came to play, the club went unbeaten at home in European football from 1984 to 1994. During this time, they recorded their best European Cup performance, reaching the semi-finals in 1988-89 to go with their four quarter-final appearances in the competition overall.

In 2000, the club finally made its breakthrough in European competition, defeating Arsenal to win the UEFA Cup and then, stunning Real Madrid to secure the European Super Cup. Their leading scorer in Europe that year remains one of their most feted players – Hakan Şükür, who played three spells for the club and is the Turkish Süper Lig all-time top scorer with 249 goals.

Olympiacos

Founded: 1925
Stadium: Georgios Karaiskakis Stadium (33,296)

With a record 43 Greek League championships won as well as 27 Greek Cups, Olympiacos can lay claim to being Greece's most successful club. Its 98,000 registered members would undoubtedly agree especially as all other Greek clubs combined, have won six league titles less. Although they have not secured a major European trophy, Olympiacos often provide stern opposition in Europa League and Champions League encounters and in 2013-14 notched wins over Benfica, Anderlecht and Manchester United in the Champions League as well as claiming the scalps of Juventus and Atlético Madrid the following season. In 2015-16, a runaway start with 17 consecutive league victories saw them wrap up the Greek Superleague title with six of their 30 matches still to play.

FC Basel

Founded: 1893

Stadium: St Jakob Park (38,512)

The strongest Swiss side in European competition, Basel won their first domestic league title in the 1952-53 season. In 2001, the club moved into their new purpose-built stadium, St Jakob Park which soon turned into a fortress. Between February 2003 and May 2006, FC Basel went 59 home games unbeaten on their way to becoming the dominant club in modern Swiss football. Ten of their total of 18 Swiss Super League titles have come in the 21st century whilst they also reached the UEFA Champions League Round of 16 in 2011-12 and 2014-15 and the UEFA Cup semi-finals in 2012-13. In total, the club has appeared in the Champions League in 17 seasons with Marco Streller its leading scorer in UEFA competitions with 24 goals. The club is known for a strong youth set-up which has helped produce not just Swiss national team talents such as Alexander Frei and Xherdan Shaqiri but also Croatia's Ivan Rakitić.

Spartak Moscow

Founded: 1922

Stadium: Otkrytiye Arena (44,929)

Formed as the Moscow Sport Circle, the club took the name Spartak in 1935, a year before they secured their first Soviet

Top League title. They would vie with Dynamo Kiev (now in the Ukraine) and Dynamo Moscow for status as the Soviet Union's most successful club. Spartak secured 12 Top League titles and finished runners-up 11 times with an especially strong spell in the 1950s and early 1960s when their midfield was graced by the long-serving Soviet national team captain, Igor Netto, but went into decline in the 1970s and were relegated for their first time in 1976. The club rebounded to dominate the first decade of the Russian League, winning eight out of the first nine league titles (1992-2001) and reaching the semi-finals of the 1990-91 European Cup, the UEFA Cup in 1997-98 and the quarter finals of the Europa League in 2010-11. In 2014, the club began playing its home matches at the Otkrytiye Arena which will also host 2018 FIFA World Cup games.

Dynamo Kiev

Founded: 1927

Stadium: National Sport Komplex Olimpiyskyi (70,050)

One of the most successful clubs in the Soviet Union with 13 Top League titles and nine Soviet Cups, Dynamo Kiev was the first team outside of Moscow to win the league title and the first Soviet club to win a European competition – the 1974-75 Cup Winners' Cup, a trophy they won for a second time in 1985-86. In addition, their legendary striker, Oleg Blokhin, the Soviet league's all-time top scorer, scored the only goal of the game to defeat Bayern Munich to win the European Super Cup in 1975. Following the break-up of the Soviet Union, the club embarked on a highly successful run in the newly formed Ukrainian Premier League, winning 14 titles since 1992 and, along with rivals, Shakhtar Donetsk, have dominated the competition, including a league and Ukrainian Cup double in the 2014-15 season under their former player-turned-coach Serhiy Rebrov.

Opposite Top: Billy McNeill is swamped by fans after Celtic's European Cup win 1967. Bottom: Galatasaray fans with flares. Above: Philipp Degen of FC Basel during the Swiss Super League soccer match against BSC Young Boys. Above Right: Dynamo Kiev's coach Serhiy Rebrov and players during training.

SOUTH AMERICAN CLUBS

River Plate

Founded: 1901
Stadium: El Monumental (61,68)

Resulting from the merger of La Rosales and the Santa Rosa Football Club, River Plate were promoted to Argentina's top division in 1908, finishing runners-up in its first year in the top flight. In 1923, the club moved to Recoleta, a wealthier district of Buenos Aires than their original home of La Boca, and saw the arrival of a series of expensive players, earning the squad the nickname "Millionaires." The club produced a series of powerful sides including the "La Maquina" (the Machine) team of the 1940s and won 12 national titles between 1936 and 1957, some with the assistance of Argentinean legend, Alfredo di Stéfano. With success in subsequent decades, especially in the 1990s, River Plate have won a record 36 league championships as well as eight domestic cups, the 1986 Intercontinental Cup and the Copa Libertadores in 1986 and 1996. In 2011, they were relegated for the first time in their history but bounced back strongly the following season to rejoin the Primera División in 2012-13, winning a league title in 2014 and the Copa Libertadores for a third time in 2015.

Boca Juniors

Founded: 1905
Stadium: Estadio Alberto J. Armando "La Bombonara" (49,000)

Formed in a poor docklands area of Buenos Aires, Boca Juniors' first Argentinean league title came in 1919 and they have since won 31 championships along with 23 runners-up finishes. Their latest title, in 2015, saw them finish 15 points and eight places above their fiercest rivals, River Plate. Superclásico derbies between these sides are always highly contested and passion can sometimes spill over into ill-discipline as witnessed by the January 2016 "friendly" that resulted in nine bookings and five red cards. One of the players in the game, Carlos Tévez, was the latest in a long line of former Boca players who return to the club later in their career including Fernando Gago, Juan Román Riquelme and the club's most famous player, Diego Maradona. It is the less-heralded Martín Palermo who holds Boca's all-time goalscoring record with 236 goals in all competitions. Boca have also thrived in continental competition, winning six Copa Libertadores and three Intercontinental Cups.

Santos

Founded: 1912
Stadium: Vila Belmiro (16,798)

Few clubs are so linked with one player but Santos is synonymous with Pelé, who made his debut for the club at the age of 15 in 1956 and played more than 1,000 matches for the side until 1974, scoring a record 541 goals in Brazilian league games alone. Santos had won the regional Campeonato Paulista twice before his arrival but the 1960s side of which he was a part enjoyed enormous success. The club won the competition eight times during the 1960s (and 21 times in total) as well as five Campeonato Brasileiro Série A national league championships in a row (1961-65). Their first two of three Copa Libertadores crowns came, too, in 1962 and 1963. The former year marked an unprecedented quadruple with the Paulista title, the Brazil Cup, Copa Libertadores and the Intercontinental Cup, the latter aided by a Pelé hat-trick in a 5-2

away victory over European champions Benfica. Santos added a third Copa Libertadores in 2011 to their eight Série A titles, a record co-held with Palmeiras.

São Paulo

Founded: 1930
Stadium: Estádio Cícero Pompeu de Toledo (67,052)

São Paulo has won 21 Campeonato Paulista and six Campeonato Brasileiro titles, three of which came in a row (2006-2008). They have also enjoyed spells in the international limelight, particularly in the early 1990s when coach Telê Santana, guided the side to consecutive Copa Libertadores crowns (1992, 1993) and in the same years defeated Barcelona and AC Milan to win the Intercontinental Cup twice. A succession of world-class players including Gerson, Careca, Falcao, Cafu and Kaká played for the Tricolors over the decades as they added a third Copa Libertadores and the FIFA World Club Cup in 2005 as well as a Copa Sudamericana title in 2012. The longest-serving player and the club's record appearance holder, goalkeeper Rogério Ceni, made more than 1,200 appearances before retiring in 2015 and unusually scored 131 goals as a free kick specialist and penalty taker.

Colo Colo

Founded: 1925
Stadium: Estádio Monumental (47,347)

Named after a Mapuche native South American leader, Colo Colo are the biggest and most successful club in Chile. They were founded by David Alfonso Arellano, who popularized the bicycle kick in Chile and is commemorated by the club after his untimely death in 1927 on a football tour to Spain, by a black line running above the club crest. Their first national league title (now called the Campeonato Nacional) came in 1937 and has been followed by a further 30

championships including the 2015 Apertura which saw the club go undefeated through the 15-match competition. Colo Colo have also won the Copa Chile 10 times, appeared in five semi-finals of the Copa Libertadores and in 1991, became the first Chilean club to win the Copa Libertadores with a 3-0 victory over Olimpia of Paraguay. Further continental success has not come, save for an appearance in the final of the 2006 Copa Sudamericana, but the club has enjoyed a strong start to the new century aided by goalscorers such as Humberto Suazo and Lucas Barrios (known as "the Panther") who struck 37 times in 2008 to match the season record set by club legend Luis Hernán Álvarez in 1963.

Peñarol

Founded: 1891
Stadium: Estadio Campeón del Siglo (43,000)

Formed by British railway workers as the Central Uruguay Railway Cricket Club to play cricket and football, the team won the inaugural Urugayan Championship in 1900 and in 1914 changed its name to Club Atlético Peñarol to reflect its location in the Peñarol district of Montevideo. The club has spent much of its domestic life locked in a tussle with city rivals Nacional for supremacy, easing ahead with a record 47 Uruguayan Primera División titles as well as a superior record in derby games between the two sides. The club also holds the record undefeated run in the Uruguayan league of 56 games, from 1966 to 1968. Continentally, the club is also Uruguay's most successful, becoming the first to go undefeated throughout a Copa Libertadores competition in 1960, making a record number of appearances in the competition (40) and becoming champions five times. After 80 years of playing at the city-owned Estadio Centenario, the club moved to their own stadium, the Campeón del Siglo, in 2016.

Opposite Top: Fernando Cavenaghi of Argentina's River Plate celebrates winning the second leg of the Copa Libertadores final against Mexico's Tigres. Bottom: Boca Juniors' Carlos Tevez in action against River Plate's Gonzalo Martinez. Above: São Paulo goalkeeper Rogério Ceni saves a penalty against Fluminense. Above Right: Mario Rizotto (L) of Independiente fights for the ball with Jaime Valdez of Colo Colo.

NORTH AND CENTRAL AMERICAN CLUBS

D.C. United
Founded: 1995
Stadium: Robert F. Kennedy Memorial Stadium (19,647)

One of the ten founder members of Major League Soccer (MLS), the Washington D.C.-based club hit the ground running by winning the inaugural season and turning it into an MLS Cup and U.S. Open Cup double by defeating the Rochester Raging Rhinos in the latter competition's final. Further MLS Cups came in 1997, 1999 and 2004, all assisted by the efforts of the club's leading goalscorer, Jaime Moreno from Bolivia. By the time he retired in 2010 Moreno held the club records for goals (131), assists (102) and appearances (329). The "Black and Red" secured their one and only CONCACAF Champions Cup title in 1998, defeating Toluca in the final. The club bounced back from a terrible 2013 MLS season where they set a record for fewest wins (three) yet, curiously, were able to secure their third U.S. Open Cup. The following season, their league form they rebounded as the side finished top of the Eastern Conference.

LA Galaxy
Founded: 1995
Stadium: StubHub Center (27,000)

The LA Galaxy's first squad included US stars such as Cobi Jones mixed with foreign imports including flamboyant goalkeeper, Jorge Campos. These propelled the side to the final of the inaugural MLS Cup but it wasn't until 2002 that the team won the competition. In total, LA Galaxy have topped the Western Conference eight times and have won five MLS Cups (2002, 2005, 2011, 2012, 2014) as well as two U.S. Open Cups (2001, 2005). The year after their first MLS title, the team moved from the Rose Bowl (their home for seven seasons) into a new stadium, the Home Depot Center (now named the StubHub Center). The club made worldwide news with their signing of David Beckham in 2007 and has made further eye-catching designated player signings from Europe, most notably Steven Gerrard and Mexican attacker Giovanni Dos Santos in 2015 and club captain Robbie Keane in 2011 who was the club's top scorer in four successive seasons (2012-15).

Deportivo Saprissa
Founded: 1935
Stadium: Estadio Ricardo Saprissa Aymá (23,112)

Costa Rica's Primera División is the strongest-rated league in the CONCACAF region outside of Mexico and the MLS, and Deportivo Saprissa is its leading club. Following a successful 2014-15 season, the club nicknamed "La S" (The S) or El Glorioso, could count 32 league championships and 15 runner-up finishes and has been an ever-present top league side since their promotion in 1949. In

addition, the side has won eight Costa Rican Cups, the most recent in 2013. Abroad, Saprissa have been a major force in continental competitions, recording a third place finish at the 2005 FIFA World Club Cup and 24 participations in the CONCACAF Champions League (or the former Champions Cup). In 2005, they defeated Mexican club, UNAM Pumas to win the competition for the third time. Their first two Champions Cup wins in 1993 and 1995 were aided by their most famous player and record appearance holder, striker Evaristo Coronado who scored 148 goals in 537 games.

Club América

Founded: 1916

Stadium: Estadio Azteca (95,500)

The year 2016 marks the 93rd consecutive season in the top flight for "The Eagles," one of only two teams to be an ever present force in Liga MX and its forerunners. The club has won 16 league titles, four of which came in the amateur era, and have been runners-up 11 times. The addition of six Copa MX (including one in the amateur era) also helps make them Mexico's most successful club domestically in the professional era. Abroad, Club América has attended seven Copa Libertadores and has reached the semi-finals on three occasions. They also finished fourth at the 2006 FIFA World Club Cup but it is in the CONCACAF Champions League where the Eagles have had their greatest impact, winning the competition on six occasions, the latest being in 2015 when they defeated Montreal Impact in the final.

C.D. Guadalajara

Founded: 1906

Stadium: Estadio Chivas (46,232)

Club Deportivo Guadalajara were founder members of the Mexican league and like their fierce rivals, Club América, with whom they contest Mexico's biggest derby match, El Súper Clásico, have never

been relegated in 93 seasons. The side, known colloquially as "las Chivas" (the Goats) were a dominant force in the amateur era when they won 13 Liga Occidental titles and in the professional era, have been league champions 11 times. They have also contested Copa Libertadores semi-finals on three occasions and in 2010 reached the final versus Santos. In stark contrast to Club América's foreign player-orientated transfer policy, CD Guadalajara have only signed and played Mexican players, a policy that has earned them both admiration amongst some fans and criticism from some sports

officials. Striker Omar Bravo, in his third spell with the club, is their leading league goalscorer with 131 goals and helped the club win their third Copa MX in 2015.

Deportivo Toluca

Founded: 1917

Stadium: Estadio Nemesio Díez (27,000)

Reaching the top flight in 1953 after being crowned Segunda División de México champions for the 1952–53 season, Toluca remained an ever present force in the top league for the next 82 seasons, winning the league title on ten occasions and finishing as runners-up six times. The first decade of the 21st century was a high water mark with five league titles as well as a second coveted CONCACAF Champions League title, in 2003 (the first was in 1968). Fans mourned the departure of club legend and record appearances holder, Antônio Naelson Matias, better known as Sinha, after the 2014 season but were buoyed by news of ground redevelopment which by 2017 is expected to increase capacity to 30,000.

Opposite Left: LA Galaxy's forward Robbie Keane in actionl against FC Dallas. Right:Deportivo Saprissa's players hold up the trophy after they won Costa Rica's first division championship title. Above: Club America players celebrate with the Concacaf trophy 2015. Left: Guadalajara Chivas striker Javier Hernandez (L) tussles with Jaguares defender Oscar Razo.

AFRICAN CLUBS

Tout Puissant Mazembe

Founded: 1939
Stadium: Stade TP Mazembe (18,500)

Formed by Benedictine missionaries in Lubumbashi (then, Elisabethville) as FC Saint-Georges, the club underwent a number of name changes including St Paul FC and FC Engelbert (from a tyre company that sponsored the club). TP Mazembe has a creditable claim to be the DR Congo's most successful club. It has won five Coupe du Congo competitions and 14 DR Congo national league titles, including four in a row (2011, 2012, 2013, 2014). This figure places it one ahead of AS Vita, but TP Mazembe has enjoyed far more success than its rival outside of the country's borders. In a golden period between 1967 and 1970, the club reached the final of the African Cup of Champions four times in a row, winning twice. They have also won consecutive CAF Champions League titles, in 2009 and 2010. In the latter year, they defeated Pachua of Mexico and Brazilian club Internacional to become the first African club to make it to the final of the FIFA World Club Cup whilst in 2015 the side defeated UN Algers to become CAF Champions League winners for a third time.

Espérance Sportive de Tunis

Founded: 1919
Stadium: El Menzah (39,858)

Esperance won their first Tunisian League title in the only season played during World War II (1940-41) some 14 years before Tunisia became independent. Nicknamed the "blood and golds" for their unusual playing colors, the club has won 14 Tunisian Cups and the African Cup Winners Cup in 1998 as well as two CAF Champions League titles, the first in 1994 against defending champions Zamalek and the second in 2011 against Moroccan club, Wydad Casablanca. At the end of the 20th Century, the club embarked on an unstoppable run of form, taking seven consecutive league titles (1997-98 to 2003-04) including not losing a single game in the 1999-2000 season. During this record-breaking period, the club supplied many of the players including Riadhi Jaidi and Khaled Badra that took the Tunisian national team to glory at the 2004 Africa Cup of Nations. Further league success has come including the 2013-14 title which brought the club up to 26 Tunisian league championships, exactly double that of their nearest rival, Club Africain with whom they share the El Menzah stadium.

Kaizer Chiefs

Founded: 1970
Stadium: FNB Stadium (94,796)

Returning home after a spell in the North American Soccer League, Kaizer Motaung and a group of his former Orlando Pirates teammates formed a new club in Soweto which they named after him and his NASL club, the Atlanta Chiefs. The club won the Life Cup in 1971 and three years later, their first South African league championship, the National Premier Soccer League, a feat they repeated in 1976, 1977, 1979 and 1981. They also enjoyed success in the National Soccer League in 1989, 1991 and 1992, the 1991 season propelled by 28 goals from the league's highest goalscorer, Fani Madida. Collins Mbesuma struck 35 goals in the

2004-05 season to help gain the Chiefs one of four South African Premier Division championships they have earned so far along with a record 15 MT8 Cups and the African Cup Winners' Cup in 2001 to make them South Africa's most successful club.

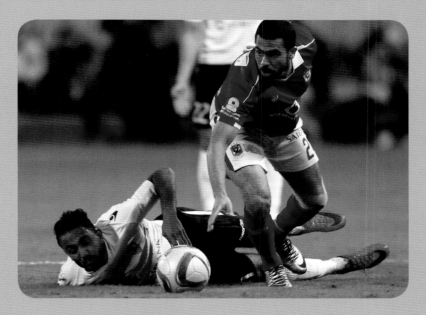

Al Ahly

Founded: 1907
Stadium: Mukhtar El-Tetsh

Though supporters of fierce rivals Zamalek might vehemently disagree, outside observers consider Al-Ahly as Egypt's, and Africa's leading club – a case made by their record eight CAF Champions League wins. With Egypt lacking a national league until 1949, the club competed in regional competitions and the Sultan's Cup, winning it seven times between 1923 and 1938. When a national league did begin, Al-Ahly swooped and dominated the competition, winning nine championships in a row until their run was stopped by Zamalek. The two sides contest the Cairo Derby – matches which can spill over into violence on the terraces and for which a foreign referee is often flown in to officiate as was the case in February 2016 when Hungary's Viktor Kassai took charge. Al-Ahly leads their Cairo rivals by 37 league titles to 12 and 35 Egypt Cups to 24. The intense level of success has not been a result of managerial continuity, though. The club has had over 20 coaches in charge in the 21st century alone, the latest appointment being Martin Jol in 2016.

Stade Malien Bamako

Founded: 1960
Stadium: Stade du 26 Mars (50,000)

In 1960, the year of Mali's independence from colonial rule, the Jeanne d'Arc du Soudan football club merged with Espérance de Bamako to form Stade Malien Bamako. The club performed well from its inception, winning the first of 18 Malian Cups in 1961 and their first national league title in 1970. A trio of Malian Première

Division titles in 2013, 2014 and 2015 brought their league championship haul to 20, just two behind rivals, Djoliba Athletic Club. Since 2001, the club has played at the Stade du 26 Mars in Bamako, which doubles as Mali's national stadium. It was there in the second leg of the 2009 CAF Confederations Cup Final versus Entente Sportive de Sétif that the club finally won their first major continental trophy, erasing the Algerian side's two goal advantage and winning the resulting penalty shootout.

Enyimba International FC

Founded: 1976
Stadium: Enyimba International Stadium (25,000)

Formed in the city of Aba and owned by the Nigerian state of Abia (formerly part of Imo state), Enyimba initially struggled to make any impact against Nigeria's leading clubs such as Shooting Stars and Rangers International, before heavy investment in the squad and coaching led to a spectacular turn-of-the-century turnaround in fortunes. Entering the 21st century, Enyimba won seven Nigerian Premier League titles between 2001 and 2015 as well as four Nigerian FA Cups during the period. Forays into continental competitions culminated in a 2003 CAF Champions League triumph, the first time Africa's most prestigious club competition was won by a team hailing from the continent's most populous country. Enyimba managed to repeat the feat the following year.

Opposite Top: Patient Mwepu of TP Mazembe (L) tussles with Andrés Andrade of Mexico's Club America. Bottom: Kaizer Chiefs' Jimmy Jambo in action in a pre-season friendly with Tottenham. Above Left: Al-Ahly's Ahmed Fathie (R) fights for the ball with El Zamalek's Mahmoud Kahraba during their Egyptian Premier League derby. Above: Enyimba forward Ekene Ezenwa (L) is challenged by Étoile Sahel defender Hachemi Bargui.

ASIAN CLUBS

Al-Hilal

Founded: 1957
Stadium: King Fahd Stadium (68,752)

Saudi Arabia's most successful club won the first season of the Saudi Premier League in 1976-77, finishing two points ahead of Al-Nasr. They had already won two of their seven King's Cup trophies, in 1961 and 1964, the latter via a penalty shootout against their great rivals, Al-Ittihad. In the late 1970s, they recruited notable Brazilian coaches and players including the World Cup winner, Roberto Rivelino in 1979. A string of league championships have followed, a record 13 in total, with a further 12 runner-up finishes are a testament to the club's consistency. Abroad, Al-Hilal has won each of the Asian Club Championship, the Asian Super Cup and the Asian Super Cup on two occasions. In 2014, assisted by the efforts of Asian Footballer of the Year, Nasser Al-Shamrani, Al-Hilal reached the final of the AFC Champions League after victories over UAE, Qatar and Uzbekistan but lost 1-0 to Western Sydney Wanderers.

Buriram United FC

Founded: 1970
Stadium: I-mobile Stadium (32,600)

Founded as the Provincial Electricity Authority FC, in Aytthaya in central Thailand, the club competed in the second and third divisions for a long period before their promotion led to a second place finish in the Thai League in the 2004-5 season. A first league championship came in 2008 before the club moved to Buriram

and took their current name in 2010. The following year was a memorable one for fans with a Thai Treble for the club of Thai League, Thai FA Cup and Thai League Cup and they have since won three further league titles in 2013, 2014 and 2015, the latter assisted by the goalscoring touch of the club's Brazilian striker, Diogo. The former Olympiacos and Palmeiras player scored 46 goals in 52 appearances for the club as it secured a notable five trophies, adding the Kor Royal Cup and the Mekong Cup (for clubs from southeast Asia) to their league, FA Cup and League Cup successes.

Sanfrecce Hiroshima

Founded: 1938
Stadium: Hiroshima Big Arch (50,000)

Starting out as Toyo Kogyo Syukyu Club - the works team of Toyo Industries – the club entered the inaugural season of the Japan Soccer League in 1965. Fifteen goals from Mutsuhiko Nomura that season helped propel the club to win the title and be the first to perform the double of league and the Emperor's Cup, defeating Yawata Steel in the final, 3-2. The team repeated the double two seasons later and in 1992, changed to their current name when they became a founder member of the fully professional J League. Despite employing a series of foreign coaches from Scotland, the Netherlands and Russia, the club failed to make much impact and in 2002, were the first former champions to be relegated. They would also face a second relegation from J1 League in 2007 but since their return to the top flight have emerged as a major force

with three J League championships in 2012, 2013 and 2015, 3 Japanese Super Cups and in 2015, a third place finish at the FIFA Club World Cup.

Guangzhou Evergrande Taobao
Founded: 1954
Stadium: Tianhe Stadium (58,500)
Founded as the Central and Southern China Sports Institute Football Team, the club bounced between the top and second division in China as evidenced by their five second tier championship titles, the last in 2010. In the same year, massive investment started to roll in from new shareholders, the Evergrande Real Estate Group, allowing the club to make major signings including Chinese national team captain, Zheng Zhi. The club has romped to five consecutive Chinese Super League titles (2011-2015), adding the Chinese FA Cup in 2012 and Chinese Super Cup in 2012 and 2016. It is also the first Chinese side to win the AFC Champions League twice (in 2013 and 2015). The club's current squad, managed by Luis Felipe Scolari since 2015, contains predominantly Chinese players with a smattering of foreign signings including ex-Spurs and Corinthians midfielder, Paulinho and former Porto and Atlético Madrid striker, Jackson Martínez whose 2016 transfer for approximately £31 million is a club record.

Seongnam FC
Founded: 1989
Stadium: Tancheon Sports Complex (16,250)
Initially named the Ilhwa Chunma Football Club, this Korean club has twice swapped locations in its relatively short life. As part of the K League's decentralization policy, they were forced to move out of Seoul to Cheonan in 1996 where they took the name Cheonan Ilhwa Chunma. By this time, they had already won a trio of K League titles in 1993, 1994 and 1995 as well as their first AFC Champions

League title in 1995. The club upped sticks again in 1999, moving to Seongnam, a satellite city of Seoul, and embarked on a second trio of K League titles (2001-2003) with a seventh coming in 2006. In 2009, fans welcomed the return of their legendary player, Shin Tae-Yong, as new coach. The former attacking midfielder played more than 270 matches for the club, and led the side to their second AFC Champions League title in 2010. Four years later, yet another name change occurred as the city government of Seongnam bought the club, renamed it Seongnam FC and changed its crest to feature a magpie – the symbol of the city and the nickname by which the club is now known.

Al-Ain
Founded: 1968
Stadium: Mohammed Bin Zayed Stadium (25,965)
The United Arab Emirates' most successful club, Al-Ain has undergone two changes of colors, starting in green and white, switching to red for the 1974-75 season and then making a further change to purple, after playing a friendly tournament in Morocco and admiring Anderlecht's purple strip. Al-Ain has won a record 12 UAE Pro League titles including the 2014-15 championship and finished runners-up on seven occasions. They have also contested 12 President's Cup finals, winning half of them as well as five UAE Super Cups. In 2003, the club went on a run in the AFC Champions League, defeating Al-Hilal, Qatari side Al Sadd, Esteghal of Iran and China's Dalian Shide to reach the final for the first time. Their victory there over Thai club, BEC Tero Sasana made them the first UAE club to win the competition. They have reached both the final (2005) and semi-finals (2014) since.

Opposite Top: Al Hilal's Yasser Al Qahtani (R) fights for the ball with Al Nasr's Ahmed Al Bahri during their Saudi King Cup qualifier. Bottom: Douglas (9) of Japan's Sanfrecce Hiroshima heads the ball to score against China's Guangzhou Evergrande. Above Left: Paulinho (L) of China's Guangzhou Evergrande celebrates with Zou Zheng after scoring against Mexico's Club America. Above: Fares Juma of UAE's Al Ain in action during the AFC Champions League semi-final soccer match against Saudi Arabia's Al Hilal.

A-Z OF THE WORLD'S GREAT PLAYERS

"IN TRAINING, I TRY TO WORK WITH THE SAME INTENSITY I HAD WHEN I FIRST STARTED TO LEARN FOOTBALL, BECAUSE A MAJOR PART OF BEING THE BEST FOOTBALLER I CAN BE IS PRACTICE."
 - CRISTIANO RONALDO, REAL MADRID AND PORTUGAL

"YOU HAVE TO FIGHT TO REACH YOUR DREAM. YOU HAVE TO SACRIFICE AND WORK HARD FOR IT."

LIONEL MESSI, FC BARCELONA AND ARGENTINA

Choosing the greatest players to have graced the game is a subject that has, and will no doubt continue to cause passionate debate. From the terraces around the world - to the armchair expert; and playgrounds to politicians, everyone has an opinion - and every list will have detractors and supporters. Here, we have compiled a comprehensive list of players who have, without doubt, made a huge impact on the beautiful game.

"SUCCESS IS NO ACCIDENT. IT IS HARD WORK, PERSEVERANCE, LEARNING, STUDYING, SACRIFICE AND MOST OF ALL, LOVE OF WHAT YOU ARE DOING OR LEARNING TO DO. "

PELÉ

"BEHIND EVERY KICK OF THE BALL THERE HAS TO BE A THOUGHT."

DENNIS BERGKAMP

Sergio AGÜERO

BORN: 1988, POSITION: STRIKER
NATIONAL TEAM: ARGENTINA, CAPS/GOALS: 71/32
CLUBS: INDEPENDIENTE, ATLÉTICO MADRID, MANCHESTER CITY
CLUB APPEARANCES: 377, CLUB GOALS: 256

In 2003 Agüero became the youngest player to debut in the Argentine Primera División at 15 years and 35 days, breaking the record previously held by Diego Maradona. After 2 seasons he had the highest goals-per-minutes ratio (1:109) in Premier League history.

Flórián ALBERT

BORN: 1941, DIED: 2011, POSITION: FORWARD
NATIONAL TEAM: HUNGARY, CAPS/GOALS: 75/31
CLUBS: FERENCVÁROS
CLUB APPEARANCES: 351, CLUB GOALS: 256
SENIOR PLAYING CAREER: 1958-1974

Nicknamed "The Emperor," Albert has been described as one of the most elegant footballers of all time. He spent his entire career with Ferencváros, and was named European Footballer of the year in 1967. Joint top-scorer in the 1962 World Cup.

Carlos ALBERTO

BORN: 1944, POSITION: DEFENDER
NATIONAL TEAM: BRAZIL, CAPS/GOALS: 53/8
CLUBS: FLUMINENSE, SANTOS, FLAMENGO, NEW YORK COSMOS, CALIFORNIA SURF
CLUB APPEARANCES: 743, GOALS: 64

Carlos Alberto is regarded as one of the finest Brazilian footballers of all time. He captained Brazil to victory in the 1970 World Cup, scoring the fourth goal in the Final against Italy.

Roberto BAGGIO

BORN: 1967, POSITION: FORWARD
NATIONAL TEAM: ITALY, CAPS/GOALS: 56/27
CLUBS: VICENZA, FIORENTINA, JUVENTUS, MILAN, BOLOGNA, INTERNAZIONALE, BRESCIA
CLUB APPEARANCES: 488, GOALS: 218

Baggio scored for Italy in three World Cups (1990, 94, 98), and was the second highest scorer in the 1994 tournament with five goals. In 1993 he was named FIFA World Player of the Year.

Gareth BALE

BORN: 1989, POSITION: WINGER
NATIONAL TEAM: WALES, CAPS/GOALS: 54/19
CLUBS: SOUTHAMPTON, TOTTENHAM HOTSPURS,
REAL MADRID, CLUB APPEARANCES: 263
GOALS: 90

Gifted with tremendous speed, great crossing ability, and exceptional physical qualities, Bale's transfer from Spurs to Madrid saw him become the world's most expensive player. He was voted the PFA Player's Player of the Year in 2011 and 2013.

Gordon BANKS

BORN: 1937, POSITION: GOALKEEPER
NATIONAL TEAM: ENGLAND, CAPS/GOALS: 73/0
CLUBS: CHESTERFIELD, LEICESTER CITY, STOKE
CITY, CLEVELAND STOKERS, HELLENIC, FORT
LAUDERDALE STRIKERS, ST PATRICK'S ATHLETIC

Gordon Banks was FIFA Goalkeeper of the Year on six occasions, and was in goal for England's winning 1966 World Cup campaign. His 1970 reflex save from Pelé is one of the greatest World Cup saves.

Franco BARESSI

BORN: 1960, POSITION: DEFENDER
NATIONAL TEAM: ITALY, CAPS/GOALS: 81/1
CLUBS: INTER MILAN
CLUB APPEARANCES: 531, GOALS: 16
SENIOR PLAYING CAREER: 1977-1997

Baresi spent his entire 20-year career with Inter Milan, where he established a reputation as one of the greatest defenders of all time. He was runner up for the Ballon d'Or in 1989, and in 1999, he was voted Milan's Player of the Century.

Sergio BATISTA

BORN: 1962, POSITION: MIDFIELD
NATIONAL TEAM: ARGENTINA, CAPS/GOALS: 39/0
CLUBS: ARGENTINOS JUNIORS, RIVER PLATE,
NUEVA CHICAGO, TOSU FUTURES, ALL BOYS
CLUB APPEARANCES: 484, CLUB GOALS: 33

Sergio Batista, "El Checho" (The Czech), was at the core of the Argentina sides that won the 1986 World Cup and were runners-up in 1990. A strong player, he fed the ball through to Diego Maradona.

Gabriel BATISTUTA

BORN: 1969, POSITION: FORWARD
NATIONAL TEAM: ARGENTINA, CAPS/GOALS: 78/56
CLUBS: NEWELL'S OLD BOYS, RIVER PLATE, BOCA
JUNIORS, FIORENTINA, ROMA, INTERNAZIONALE,
AL ARABI, CLUB APPEARANCES: 430, GOALS: 245

"El Ángel Gabriel" is Argentina's all-time leading goalscorer, and is the eleventh top scorer of all-time in the Italian Serie A league. He spent most of his career at Fiorentina, who erected a life-size statue of him in 1996, in recognition of his performances.

Franz BECKENBAUER

BORN: 1945, POSITION: SWEEPER
NATIONAL TEAM: GERMANY, CAPS/GOALS: 103/14
CLUBS: BAYERN MUNICH, NEW YORK COSMOS,
HAMBURGER SV, NEW YORK COSMOS
CLUB APPEARANCES: 572, GOALS: 83

Franz Beckenbauer is one of the greats of German football, twice European Footballer of the Year (1972, 1976). He led West Germany to World Cup victories in 1974 (player) and 1990 (manager).

David BECKHAM

BORN: 1975, POSITION: MIDFIELDER
NATIONAL TEAM: ENGLAND, CAPS/GOALS: 115/17
CLUBS: MANCHESTER UNITED, PRESTON NORTH END,
REAL MADRID, LA GALAXY, MILAN, PARIS SAINT-
GERMAIN, CLUB APPEARANCES: 523, GOALS: 97

Won league titles in 4 countries: England, Spain, USA and France. Known for his range of passing, crossing ability and free-kicks, was twice runner-up for FIFA World Player of the Year, and is England's most-capped outfield player.

Ilhor BELANOV

BORN: 1960, POSITION: ATTACKING MIDFIELDER
NATIONAL TEAM: SOVIET UNION, CAPS/GOALS: 33/8
CLUBS: SKA ODESSA, CHORNOMORETS ODESSA,
DYNAMO KYIV, BORUSSIA MÖNCHENGLADBACH +4
CLUB APPEARANCES: 404, GOALS: 111

Belanov made a name for himself at Dynamo Kyiv, winning five major titles and being named European Footballer of the Year in 1986. In 2011, he was named as the "legends of Ukrainian football" at the Victory of Football awards.

Karim BENZEMA

BORN: 1987, POSITION: STRIKER
NATIONAL TEAM: FRANCE, CAPS/GOALS: 81/27
CLUBS: LYON B, LYON, REAL MADRID
CLUB APPEARANCES: 342,
CLUB GOALS: 166

An immensely talented striker, Benzema is strong and powerful and a potent finisher. He has been named French Player of the year three times for his performances in 2011, 2012 and 2014. He has won 14 major trophies to date.

Dennis BERGKAMP

BORN: 1969, POSITION: FORWARD
NATIONAL TEAM: NETHERLANDS, CAPS/GOALS: 79/37
CLUBS: AJAX, INTERNAZIONALE, ARSENAL
CLUB APPEARANCES: 552, CLUB GOALS: 201
SENIOR PLAYING CAREER: 1986–2006

One of the greatest players of his generation, described as having the finest technique of any Dutch international. He finished third twice in the FIFA World Player of the Year award and was selected as one of the FIFA 100 greatest living players

George BEST

BORN/DIED: 1946–2005, POSITION: WINGER
NATIONAL TEAM: N. IRELAND, CAPS/GOALS: 37/9
CLUBS: MANCHESTER UNITED, STOCKPORT
COUNTY, CORK CELTIC, LOS ANGELES AZTECS,
FULHAM, FORT LAUDERDALE STRIKERS, plus 9.

The Manchester United legend made his debut aged 17 and scored 137 goals in 361 appearances during his time there. He was named European Footballer of the Year in 1968. Brazilian icon Pelé has stated, "George Best was the greatest player in the world."

Oleg BLOKHIN

BORN: 1952, POSITION: FORWARD
NATIONAL TEAM: SOVIET UNION, CAPS/GOALS: 112/42
CLUBS: DYNAMO KYIV, VORWÄRTS STEYR, ARIS
LIMASSOL. CLUB APPEARANCES: 495, CLUB GOALS:
225 SENIOR PLAYING CAREER: 1969-1990

Blokhin is the overall top goalscorer in the history of the Soviet Top League. He holds Dynamo's appearance record with 582 appearances during his 18-year spell at the club. In 1975, he won European Footballer of the Year, winning the Ballon d'Or.

Zbigniew BONIEK

BORN: 1956, POSITION: FORWARD
NATIONAL TEAM: POLAND, CAPS/GOALS: 80/24
CLUBS: WIDZEW ŁÓDŹ, JUVENTUS, ROMA
CLUB APPEARANCES: 329 CLUB GOALS: 81
SENIOR PLAYING CAREER: 1975–1988

Zbigniew "Zibi" Boniek is one of the greatest Polish players of all time. He appeared in three World Cups (1978, 1982, 1986), and inspired Poland to their best finish (third place) in the 1982 Finals.

Andreas BREHME

BORN: 1960, POSITION: LEFT-BACK
NATIONAL TEAM: GERMANY, CAPS/GOALS: 86/8
CLUBS: HSV BARMBEK-UHLENHORST, FC SAARBRÜCKEN, FC KAISERSLAUTERN, BAYERN MUNICH, INTER MILAN, ZARAGOZA

Brehme was a free-kick specialist. He famously scored a late penalty that gave West Germany victory in the 1990 World Cup Final, scoring with his right foot despite being a natural left-footer.

Paul BREITNER

BORN: 1951, POSITION: LEFT BACK
NATIONAL TEAM: W. GERMANY, CAPS/GOALS: 48/10
CLUBS: BAYERN MUNICH, REAL MADRID, EINTRACHT BRAUNSCHWEIG
CLUB APPEARANCES: 369, CLUB GOALS: 103

One of the greatest German players of all time, Breitner was named in the FIFA World Cup All-Time Team, and was named by Pelé one of the top 125 greatest living footballers.

Gianluigi BUFFON

BORN: 1978, POSITION: GOALKEEPER
NATIONAL TEAM: ITALY *CAPS: 154
CLUBS: PARMA, JUVENTUS
*CLUB APPEARANCES: 617
* at time of printing

Buffon has been described as the greatest goalkeeper ever. He has played in five World Cup tournaments and won the Golden Glove award in 2006 for the best goalkeeper at the Finals.

Cha BUM-KUN

BORN: 1953, POSITION: FORWARD
NATIONAL TEAM: S. KOREA, CAPS/GOALS: 135/58
CLUBS: SV DARMSTADT 98, EINTRACHT FRANKFURT, BAYER LEVERKUSEN
CLUB APPEARANCES: 308, CLUB GOALS: 98

Nicknamed Tscha Bum in Germany ("Cha Boom") because of his thunderous ball striking ability, Bum-Kun was given the title Asia's Player of the Century. He is the all-time leading goal scorer for the South Korean national team.

Antonio CABRINI

BORN: 1957, POSITION: LEFT-BACK
NATIONAL TEAM: ITALY, CAPS/GOALS: 73/9
CLUBS: CREMONESE, ATALANTA, JUVENTUS, BOLOGNA, CLUB APPEARANCES: 416
CLUB GOALS: 38,

Cabrini is one of the best defenders in the history of Italian football, with great technical, defensive, athletic, and physical qualities. He won the Best Young Player Award at the 1978 World Cup, and won all UEFA Club competitions.

Opposite page: Juventus goalkeeper Gianluigi Buffon in action.

CAFU

BORN: 1970, POSITION: RIGHT-BACK
NATIONAL TEAM: BRAZIL, CAPS/GOALS: 142/5
CLUBS: SÃO PAULO, REAL ZARAGOZA, JUVENTUDE,
PALMEIRAS, ROMA, AC MILAN
CLUB APPEARANCES: 452, CLUB GOALS: 16

Marcos Evangelista de Morais, known as Cafu, holds the record as the first player to appear in three successive World Cup Finals (1994, 1998, 2002), and is Brazil's most capped player.

Fabio CANNAVARO

BORN: 1973, POSITION: CENTER-BACK
NATIONAL TEAM: ITALY, CAPS/GOALS: 136/2
CLUBS: NAPOLI, PARMA, INTER MILAN, JUVENTUS,
REAL MADRID, JUVENTUS, AL-AHLI
CLUB APPEARANCES: 531, CLUB GOALS: 16

Cannavaro is regarded as one of the greatest defenders of all time. He captained Italy to World Cup victory in 2006, was named 2006 World Player of the Year, and won the 2006 Ballon d'Or.

Eric CANTONA

BORN: 1966, POSITION: FORWARD
NATIONAL TEAM: FRANCE, CAPS/GOALS: 45/20
CLUBS: AUXERRES, MARTIGUES, MARSEILLE,
BORDEAUX, MONTPELLIER, NIMES, LEEDS, MAN
UNITED. CLUB APPEARANCES: 369, GOALS: 131

Cantona is regarded as having played a key role in the revival of Man United in the 1990s, winning four Premier League titles in five years. Combining technical skill and creativity with power and goal-scoring ability, he enjoys iconic status at the club.

Roberto CARLOS

BORN: 1973, POSITION: LEFT-BACK
NATIONAL TEAM: BRAZIL, CAPS/GOALS: 125/11
CLUBS: UNIÃO SÃO JOÃO, ATLÉTICO MINEIRO,
PALMEIRAS, INTER MILAN, REAL MADRID, +3
CLUB APPEARANCES: 579, CLUB GOALS: 66

Roberto Carlos, known as the "Bullet Man" due to his powerful bending free kicks (measured at over 105 miles per hour), was a key part of Brazil's 2002 World Cup winning side.

Iker CASILLAS

BORN: 1981, POSITION: GOALKEEPER
NATIONAL TEAM: SPAIN, CAPS/GOALS: 165/0
CLUBS: REAL MADRID, PORTO
CLUB APPEARANCES: 560

Iker Casillas, Spain's goalkeeper-captain, led his side to victory in the 2008 and 2012 European Championship, and the 2010 World Cup, in which he won the Golden Glove award.

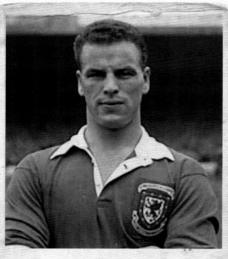

John CHARLES

BORN: 1931, DIED: 2004, POSITION: CENTER
BACK, CENTER FORWARD
NATIONAL TEAM: WALES, CAPS/GOALS: 38/15
CLUBS: LEEDS UNITED, JUVENTUS, ROMA, +3.
CLUB APPEARANCES: 715, CLUB GOALS: 370

Rated by many as the greatest all-round British footballer ever, Charles was equally adept in defense and attack. He excelled in the air and was a prolific goalscorer with his feet, with a powerful accurate shot. He took third place in the 1959 Ballon d'Or.

Bobby CHARLTON

BORN: 1937, POSITION: FORWARD
NATIONAL TEAM: ENGLAND, CAPS/GOALS: 106/49
CLUBS: MANCHESTER UNITED, PRESTON NORTH END, WATERFORD UNITED
CLUB APPEARANCES: 647, CLUB GOALS: 208

Bobby Charlton, regarded as one of the greatest midfielders, was a key member of England's 1966 World Cup winning team, won the Ballon d'Or that year, and is a Manchester United legend.

Hector CHUMPITAZ

BORN: 1943, POSITION: DEFENDER
NATIONAL TEAM: PERU, CAPS/GOALS: 105/3
CLUBS: DEPORTIVO MUNICIPAL, UNIVERSITARIO, ATLAS, SPORTING CRISTAL, CLUB APPEARANCES: NOT KNOW, CLUB GOALS: NOT KNOWN

Nicknamed El Capitan de America, Chumpitaz is one of the greatest ever South American defenders. He was the captain of the Peruvian national team that won Copa America 1975, and was named to the list of best ever World Cup players by Terra.com.

Mario COLUNA

BORN/DIED: 1935¬–2014, POSITION: MIDFIELDER
NATIONAL TEAM: PORTUGAL, CAPS/GOALS: 57/8
CLUBS: BENFICA, LYON, ESTRELA PORTALEGRE
CLUB APPEARANCES: 383, CLUB GOALS: 91
SENIOR PLAYING CAREER: 1954–1972

Coluna was one of the most talented Portuguese players of all time. He played with the outstanding Benfica sides of the 1960s, and in the Portugal side that reached the 1966 World Cup semi-final.

Johan CRUYFF

BORN: 1949, POSITION: ATTACKING MIDFIELDER
NATIONAL TEAM: PERU, CAPS/GOALS: 81/26
CLUBS: ALIANZA LIMA, BASEL, PORTO, FORT LAUDERDALE STRIKERS, SOUTH FLORIDA SUN, MIAMI SHARKS, CLUB APPEARANCES: 506, GOALS: 297

Cruyff is regarded as Holland's greatest ever player. He won the Ballon d'Or three times (1971, 73, 74), led Holland to the 1974 World Cup Final, and with Ajax won the European Cup three times.

Teofilo CUBILLAS

BORN: 1949, POSITION: ATTACKING MIDFIELDER
NATIONAL TEAM: PERU, CAPS/GOALS: 81/26
CLUBS: ALIANZA LIMA, BASEL, PORTO, FORT LAUDERDALE STRIKERS, SOUTH FLORIDA SUN, MIAMI SHARKS, CLUB APPEARANCES: 506, GOALS: 297

Cubillas was selected as Peru's greatest ever player in an IFFHS poll, in which he was also included in the world's Top 50. He was renowned for his technique and free kick ability. He was part of the Peru national team that won the 1975 Copa América.

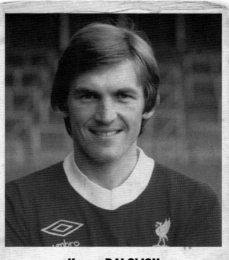

Kenny DALGLISH

BORN: 1951, POSITION: FORWARD
NATIONAL TEAM: SCOTLAND, CAPS/GOALS: 102/30
CLUBS: CELTIC, LIVERPOOL
CLUB APPEARANCES: 559, CLUB GOALS: 230
SENIOR PLAYING CAREER: 1969–1990

Kenny Dalglish is Scotland's most capped player and equal highest scorer (with Denis Law), and won the Ballon d'Or Silver Award in 1983. He had a glittering career with Celtic and Liverpool.

Following page: Action during the league match between Charlton and Manchester United, 1957. Bobby Charlton rises above United teammate Liam Whelan and Charlton keeper Willie Duff on his way to a first hat-trick in league football.

Rinat DASAYEV

BORN: 1957, POSITION: GOALKEEPER
NATIONAL TEAM: SOVIET UNION, CAPS/GOALS: 91/0
CLUBS: VOLGAR ASTRAKHAN, SPARTAK MOSCOW,
SEVILLA, CLUB APPEARANCES: 420
SENIOR PLAYING CAREER: 1976–1991

Rinat Dasayev, the "Iron Curtain," played in goal for the Soviet Union in three World Cups (1982, 1986, 1990), and was awarded the title World's Best Goalkeeper in 1988.

Frank DE BOER

BORN: 1970, POSITION: DEFENDER
NATIONAL TEAM: NETHERLANDS, CAPS/GOALS: 112/13
CLUBS: AJAX, BARCELONA, GALATASARY,
RANGERS, AL RAYYAN, AL-SHAMAL
CLUB APPEARANCES: 519, CLUB GOALS: 43

De Boer is the Netherlands' most capped outfield player. He spent most of his playing career with Ajax, winning five Eredivisie titles and the UEFA Champions League. He later spent five years at FC Barcelona, where he won the 1998–99 La Liga title

Alessandro DEL PIERO

BORN: 1974, POSITION: FORWARD
NATIONAL TEAM: ITALY, CAPS/GOALS: 91/27
CLUBS: PADOVA, JUVENTUS, SYDNEY FC, DELHI
DYNAMOS, CLUB APPEARANCES: 585, GOALS: 234
SENIOR PLAYING CAREER: 1991-2014

Del Piero is regarded as one of the greatest players of his generation, and as one of the best Italian players ever, winning the Italian Footballer of the Year award in 1998 and 2008. He is currently the 2nd-highest-ever Italian top-scorer in all competitions.

Alfredo DI STÉFANO

BORN/DIED: 1926–2014, POSITION: FORWARD
NATIONAL TEAM: ARGENTINA, COLOMBIA, SPAIN
CAPS/GOALS: 6, 4, 31 / 6, 0, 23. CLUBS: RIVER
PLATE, HURACÁN, MILLONARIOS, REAL MADRID,
ESPANYOL. CLUB APPEARANCES: 522, GOALS: 376

Di Stéfano, the "Blond Arrow," was one of the greats of world football—"the most complete footballer in the history of the game"—leading Real Madrid to victory in the first five European Cup Finals (1956–60), and winning the Ballon d'Or in 1957 and 1959.

DIDI

BORN/DIED: 1928/2001, POSITION: MIDFIELDER
NATIONAL TEAM: BRAZIL, CAPS/GOALS: 68/20
CLUBS: AMERICANO, LENCOENSE, MADUREIRA,
FLUMINESE, BOTAFOGO, REAL MADRID, +3
CLUB APPEARANCES: NOT KNOWN

Waldyr Pereira, or "Didi," played in three World Cups ('54, '58, and '62), winning the latter two and named the best player in 1958. He is considered to be one of the greatest midfielders in the sport, renowned for his range of passing, stamina and technique.

Landon DONOVAN

BORN: 1982, POSITION: FORWARD
NATIONAL TEAM: USA, CAPS/GOALS: 157/57
CLUBS: BAYERN LEVERKUSEN, SAN JOSE
EARTHQUAKES, LA GALAXY, BAYERN MUNICH,
EVERTON. CLUB APPEARANCES: 392. GOALS: 155

Donovan is Major League Soccer's all-time leading scorer, and all-time assists leader, and won the Honda Player of the Year Award seven times. In 2015 he was named the Greatest Male American Player of All Time by The Guardian newspaper.

Didier DROGBA

BORN: 1978, POSITION: STRIKER
NATIONAL TEAM: IVORY COAST, CAPS/GOALS: 104/63
CLUBS: LE MANS, GUINGAMP, MARSEILLE,
CHELSEA, SHANGHAI SHENUA, GALATASARY, +1.
CLUB APPEARANCES: 457, CLUB GOALS: 189

Didier Drogba has been named African Footballer of the Year twice, winning the accolade in 2006 and 2009. He spent most of his career at Chelsea, where he is their fourth highest goalscorer of all time, winning the Premier League Golden Boot twice.

Samuel ETO'O

BORN: 1981, POSITION: STRIKER
NATIONAL TEAM: CAMEROON, CAPS/GOALS: 118/54
CLUBS: REAL MADRID, MALLORCA, BARCELONA, INTER
MILAN, ANZHI MAKHACHKALA, CHELSEA, EVERTON,
+2. CLUB APPEARANCES: 515, GOALS: 255

Eto'o is the most decorated African player of all time, having won the African Player of the Year award a joint-record four times between 2003 and 2010. He was third in the World Player of the Year award in 2005, and is Cameroon's all-time leading goal scorer.

EUSÉBIO

BORN/DIED: 1942–2014, POSITION: STRIKER
NATIONAL TEAM: PORTUGAL, CAPS/GOALS: 64/41
CLUBS: SPORTING DE LOURENÇO MARQUES,
BENFICA, BOSTON MINUTEMEN, MONTERREY, +5
CLUB APPEARANCES: 431, CLUB GOALS: 423

Eusébio, born in Mozambique, was the first world-class African player. He made his reputation with Portugal and Benfica, won the Ballon d'Or award in 1965, and was top scorer in the 1966 World Cup.

Giacinto FACCHETTI

BORN: 1942, POSITION: LEFT-BACK
NATIONAL TEAM: ITALY, CAPS/GOALS: 94 / 3
CLUBS: INTER MILAN
CLUB APPEARANCES: 476
CLUB GOALS: 59

Giacinto Facchetti started as a striker but switched to left-back on joining Inter Milan, a position from which he mounted goalscoring attacks. He captained Italy in the final of the 1970 World Cup.

Luís FIGO

BORN: 1972, POSITION: WINGER
NATIONAL TEAM: PORTUGAL, CAPS/GOALS: 127 / 32
CLUBS: SPORTING LISBON, BARCELONA, REAL
MADRID, INTER MILAN
CLUB APPEARANCES: 577, CLUB GOALS: 93

Luís Figo's transfer in 2000 from Barcelona to rivals Real Madrid set a then world record fee of £37 million. On the international stage he represented Portugal at three European Championships and two World Cups.

Elías FIGUEROA

BORN: 1946, POSITION: CENTRAL DEFENDER
NATIONAL TEAM: CHILE, CAPS/GOALS: 47 / 2
CLUBS: SANTIAGO WANDERERS, UNION LA CALERA,
PEÑAROL, INTERNACIONAL, PALESTINO, +2
CLUB APPEARANCES: 791, CLUB GOALS: 38

Regarded as Chile's greatest footballer, as well as one of the best defenders in the history of the sport. He was South American Footballer of the Year three times. He was noted for his elegant style, and for his calmness in the center of defense.

THE WORLD'S GREAT PLAYERS A-Z

Just FONTAINE

BORN: 1933, POSITION: STRIKER
NATIONAL TEAM: FRANCE, CAPS/GOALS: 21/30
CLUBS: US CASABLANCA, NICE, REIMS
CLUB APPEARANCES: 248, CLUB GOALS: 227
SENIOR PLAYING CAREER: 1950–1962

Just Fontaine was the star striker of the 1958 World Cup, scoring 13 goals in six games for France – a record for one player in a single tournament that still stands and which is unlikely to be beaten.

GARRINCHA

BORN/DIED: 1933–1983, POSITION: WINGER
NATIONAL TEAM: BRAZIL, CAPS/GOALS: 50/17
CLUBS: BOTAFOGO, CORINTHIANS, PORTUGUESA CARIOCA, ATLÉTICO JUNIOR, FLAMENGO, OLARIA
CLUB APPEARANCES: 688, CLUB GOALS: 276

Manuel Francisco dos Santos, known as Garrincha ("Little Bird"), ranked alongside teammate Pelé in the 1960s. He led Brazil to World Cup victory in 1962, and was the tournament's leading goalscorer.

Paul GASCOINE

BORN: 1967, POSITION: MIDFIELDER
NATIONAL TEAM: ENGLAND, CAPS/GOALS: 57/10
CLUBS: NEWCASTLE UNITED, TOTTENHAM HOTSPURS, LAZIO, RANGERS, +5
CLUB APPEARANCES: 388, CLUB GOALS: 83

Described by the National Football Museum as "the most naturally gifted English midfielder of his generation," Gascoine was a member of the FIFA World Cup All-Star Team in 1990. He was inducted into the English Football Hall of Fame in 2002.

Claudio GENTILE

BORN: 1953, POSITION: DEFENDER
NATIONAL TEAM: ITALY, CAPS/GOALS: 71/1
CLUBS: ARONA, VARESE, JUVENTUS, FIORENTINA, PIACENZA
CLUB APPEARANCES: 441, CLUB GOALS: 14

Claudio Gentile was one of the best defenders of his generation, whose physical man-marking skills helped Italy to triumph in the 1982 World Cup Final, and Juventus to club success in Europe.

Francisco GENTO

BORN: 1933, POSITION: LEFT-WING
NATIONAL TEAM: SPAIN, CAPS/GOALS: 43/5
CLUBS: RACING SANTANDER, REAL MADRID
CLUB APPEARANCES: 438, CLUB GOALS: 130
SENIOR PLAYING CAREER: 1952–1971

Francisco Gento, known as "El Supersonico" for his lightning-fast bursts of speed down the wing, won a record six European Championships with Real Madrid between 1956 and 1966.

Ryan GIGGS

BORN: 1973, POSITION: MIDFIELDER
NATIONAL TEAM: WALES, CAPS/GOALS: 64/12
CLUBS: MANCHESTER UNITED
CLUB APPEARANCES: 674 (CLUB RECORD)
CLUB GOALS: 114

Giggs spent his entire career at Manchester United. He was the only player to play (and also to score) in each of the first 21 seasons of the Premier League. He has the most assists in Premier League History. He was elected into the PFA Team of the Century.

Opposite page: Italy's Claudio Gentile (R) in action with Brazil's Roberto Dinamite at the 1978 FIFA World Cup

Ruud GULLIT

BORN: 1962, POSITION: FORWARD
NATIONAL TEAM: HOLLAND, CAPS/GOALS: 66/17
CLUBS: HAARLEM, FEYENOORD, PSV EINDHOVEN,
AC MILAN, SAMPDORIA, CHELSEA
CLUB APPEARANCES: 465, CLUB GOALS: 175

Ruud Gullit captained Holland to victory in the
1988 European Championship, the national
team's first major trophy. He won the 1987 Ballon
d'Or ("Golden Ball") award and was twice World
Player of the Year (1987, 1989).

Arie HAAN

BORN: 1948, POSITION: MIDFIELDER
NATIONAL TEAM: HOLLAND, CAPS/GOALS: 35/6
CLUBS: AJAX, ANDERLECHT, STANDARD LIÈGE, PSV
EINDHOVEN, SEIKO
CLUB APPEARANCES: 419, CLUB GOALS: 71

Arie Haan was known for his long-range goals
and was a member of the Ajax side that won the
European Cup for three consecutive years (1971–
1973), plus other silverware in the 1970s.

Gheorghe HAGI

BORN: 1965, POSITION: MIDFIELDER
NATIONAL TEAM: ROMANIA, CAPS/GOALS: 125/35
CLUBS: STEAUA BUCUREŞTI, REAL MADRID,
BRESCIA, BARCELONA, GALATASARAY +2
CLUB APPEARANCES: 516, CLUB GOALS: 257

Gheorghe Hagi, the "Maradona of the
Carpathians," is regarded as the greatest
Romanian footballer ever, known for his dribbling
and passing skills. He played in three World Cups
(1990, 1994, 1998).

Hao HAIDONG

BORN: 1970, POSITION: STRIKER
NATIONAL TEAM: CHINA, CAPS/GOALS: 107/41
CLUBS: BAYI FC, DALIAN SHIDE, SHEFFIELD UNITED
CLUB APPEARANCES: 178, CLUB GOALS: 97,
SENIOR PLAYING CAREER: 1986–2007

Haidong is generally regarded as the best striker in
the history of Chinese football, and is currently the
record top goalscorer for the Chinese national team.
He was the Chinese Player of the Year in 1997 and
1988, and was the A-leagues top goalscorer thrice.

Thierry HENRY

BORN: 1977, POSITION: STRIKER
NATIONAL TEAM: FRANCE, CAPS/GOALS: 123/51
CLUBS: MONACO, JUVENTUS, ARSENAL,
BARCELONA, NEW YORK RED BULLS
CLUB APPEARANCES: 581, CLUB GOALS: 284

Thierry Henry is the record goalscorer for France,
with whom he won the 1998 World Cup and 2000
European Championship. At club level, he is
Arsenal's top goalscorer with 228 goals.

Nándor HIDEGKUTI

BORN/DIED: 1922–2002, POSITION: FORWARD
NATIONAL TEAM: HUNGARY, CAPS/GOALS: 69/39
CLUBS: ELEKTROMOS, HERMINAMEZEI, HUNGÁRIA,
BUDAPESTI TEXTILES, BUDAPESTI BÁSTYA, +1
CLUB APPEARANCES: 381, CLUB GOALS: 265

Nándor Hidegkuti was a key player of the
outstanding Hungary team of the 1950s, winning
Olympic gold in 1952 and scoring a hat-trick in
the historic 6–3 win over England at Wembley in
1953.

Opposite page: Ruud Gullit in action for Sampdoria 1995

Geoff HURST

BORN: 1941, POSITION: STRIKER
NATIONAL TEAM: ENGLAND, CAPS/GOALS: 49/24
CLUBS: WEST HAM UNITED, STOKE CITY, CAPE
TOWN CITY, WEST BROMWICH ALBION, CORK +2
CLUB APPEARANCES: 561, CLUB GOALS: 228

Geoff Hurst played first-class cricket for Essex, but made his name as goalscorer for club and country, becoming the only player to score a hat-trick in a World Cup Final, for England in 1966.

Andrés INIESTA

BORN: 1984, POSITION: MIDFIELDER
NATIONAL TEAM: SPAIN, *CAPS/GOALS: 107/13
*CLUBS: BARCELONA
*CLUB APPEARANCES: 378
*CLUB GOALS: 34

Andrés Iniesta made his international debut in 2006, scored the winning goal for Spain in the 2010 World Cup Final, and helped Spain to victory in the 2012 European Championship.

JAIRZINHO

BORN: 1944, POSITION: WINGER
NATIONAL TEAM: BRAZIL, CAPS/GOALS: 81 / 33
CLUBS: BOTAFOGO, MARSEILLE, KAIZER CHIEFS,
CRUZEIRO, PORTUGUESA, NOROESTE, FAST CLUB
CLUB APPEARANCES: 465, CLUB GOALS: 221

Jair Ventura Filho, known as Jairzinho, was a member of Brazil's outstanding 1970 World Cup winning team, in which he scored in each round of the tournament with seven goals in six games.

Jimmy JOHNSTONE

BORN/DIED: 1944–2006, POSITION: RIGHT-WING
NATIONAL TEAM: SCOTLAND, CAPS/GOALS: 23/4
CLUBS: CELTIC, SAN JOSE EARTHQUAKES,
SHEFFIELD UNITED, DUNDEE, SHELBOURNE, +1
CLUB APPEARANCES: 359, CLUB GOALS: 86

Jimmy Johnstone rose from ballboy at Celtic Park to be one of the stars of the Celtic side that won the 1967 European Cup, plus a haul of domestic silverware in the 1960s and 1970s.

Oliver KAHN

BORN: 1969, POSITION: GOALKEEPER
NATIONAL TEAM: GERMANY, CAPS/GOALS: 86/0
CLUBS: KARLSRUHER, BAYERN MUNICH
CLUB APPEARANCES: 630, CLUB GOALS: 0
SENIOR PLAYING CAREER: 1987–2008

Oliver Kahn was the first goalkeeper named best player at a World Cup (2002), twice German Footballer of the Year (2000, 2001), and holds the record for the most clean sheets in the Bundesliga (196).

Raymond KOPA

BORN: 1931, POSITION: ATTACKING MIDFIELDER
NATIONAL TEAM: FRANCE, CAPS/GOALS: 45/18
CLUBS: ANGERS, REIMS, REAL MADRID
CLUB APPEARANCES: 541, CLUB GOALS: 123
SENIOR PLAYING CAREER: 1949–1967

Kopa was part of the legendary Real Madrid team of the 1950s, winning three European Cups. Kopa was a free-role playmaker who was quick, agile and known for his love of dribbling. Kopa won the Ballon d'Or in 1958.

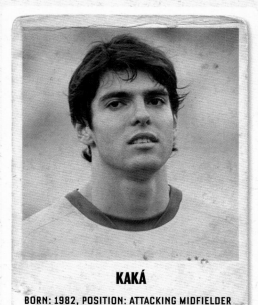

KAKÁ

BORN: 1982, POSITION: ATTACKING MIDFIELDER
NATIONAL TEAM: BRAZIL, CAPS/GOALS: 91/29
CLUBS: SÃO PAULO, MILAN, REAL MADRID,
ORLANDO CITY,* CLUB APPEARANCES: 435
*CLUB GOALS: 131

Kaká received the FIFA World Player of the Year and Ballon d'Or awards in 2007. He made his debut for the Brazil national team in 2002, and was selected for their victorious World Cup squad that year, as well as the 2006 and 2010 tournaments.

Roy KEANE

BORN: 1971, POSITION: MIDFIELDER
NATIONAL TEAM: REP. OF IRELAND, CAPS/GOALS: 67/9
CLUBS: COBH RAMBLERS, NOTTINGHAM FOREST,
MANCHESTER UNITED, CELTIC
CLUB APPEARANCES: 473, CLUB GOALS: 57

Roy Keane is considered among the best defensive midfielders, and one of the hardest players of his generation, renowned for his fearless tackling. He led Manchester United to glory at home and in Europe.

Kevin KEEGAN

BORN: 1951, POSITION: FORWARD
NATIONAL TEAM: ENGLAND, CAPS/GOALS: 63/21
CLUBS: SCUNTHORPE UNITED, LIVERPOOL,
HAMBURG, SOUTHANPTON, NEWCASTLE UTD, +1
CLUB APPEARANCES: 592, CLUB GOALS: 204

After winning three league titles and the European Cup with Liverpool he moved to Hamburg, where he won the Bundesliga and was twice named European Footballer of the Year in 1978 and 1979.

Mario KEMPES

BORN: 1954, POSITION: STRIKER
NATIONAL TEAM: ARGENTINA, CAPS/GOALS: 43/20
CLUBS: INSTITUTO, ROSARIO CENTRAL, VALENCIA
RIVER PLATE, HÉRCULES, FIRST VIENNA, +4
CLUB APPEARANCES: 552, CLUB GOALS: 300

Mario Kempes was a prolific goalscorer for club and country, scoring twice in the 1978 World Cup Final, in which Argentina beat Holland, and was named best player of the tournament.

Jürgen KLINSMANN

BORN: 1964, POSITION: STRIKER
NATIONAL TEAM: WEST GERMANY, GERMANY
CAPS/GOALS: 28, 108/9, 47. CLUBS: INTER MILAN,
MONACO, TOTTENHAM HOTSPUR, BAYERN MUNICH,
SAMPDORIA +3. CLUB APPEARANCES: 506, GOALS: 228

Jürgen Klinsmann was one of Germany's leading strikers of the 1990s, helping West Germany win the 1990 World Cup, and the unified Germany to success in the 1996 European Championship.

Sándor KOCSIS

BORN/DIED: 1929–1979, POSITION: STRIKER
NATIONAL TEAM: HUNGARY, CAPS/GOALS: 68 / 75
CLUBS: KŐBÁNYAI, FERENCVÁROS, ÉDOSZ,
HONVÉD, YOUNG FELLOWS ZÜRICH, BARCELONA
CLUB APPEARANCES: 325, CLUB GOALS: 272

Sándor Kocsis played for Hungary in the 1950s – the national side's golden decade. He was the top goalscorer in the 1954 World Cup (11 goals), and was three times the top scorer in the Hungarian league.

Hans KRANKL

BORN: 1953, POSITION: STRIKER
NATIONAL TEAM: AUSTRIA, CAPS/GOALS: 69/34
CLUBS: RAPID WIEN, BARCELONA, WIENER SPORT-CLUB, KREMSER SC, AUSTRIA SALZBURG
CLUB APPEARANCES: 518, CLUB GOALS: 392

Krankl was named Austrian Player of the Year a record five times, and was voted the most popular Austrian player of the last 25 years. A prolific striker, he was the top scorer in the Austrian league five times.

László KUBALA

BORN/DIED: 1927–2002, POSITION: FORWARD
NATIONAL TEAM: CZECHOSLOVAKIA, HUNGARY, SPAIN, CAPS/GOALS: 6, 3, 19 / 4, 0, 11
CLUBS: PRO PATRIA, HUNGÁRIA, BARCELONA, ESPANYOL +6, CLUB APPEARANCES: 379, GOALS: 217

László Kubala defected to the West in 1949, preventing him from playing for the Mighty Magyars during their golden decade in the 1950s. A star at Barcelona, he scored 194 goals, winning La Liga four times between 1951 and 1960.

Philipp LAHM

BORN: 1983, POSITION: RIGHT-BACK
NATIONAL TEAM: GERMANY, CAPS/GOALS: 113/5
*CLUBS: BAYERN MUNICH, STUTTGART
*CLUB APPEARANCES: 414
*CLUB GOALS: 16

Philipp Lahm, able to play on either flank in defense, captained Germany to victory in the 2014 World Cup and has enjoyed considerable home and European success with club side Bayern Munich.

Michael LAUDRUP

BORN: 1964, POSITION: MIDFIELDER
NATIONAL TEAM: DENMARK, CAPS/GOALS: 104/37
CLUBS: KJØBENHAVNS BOLDKLUB, BRØNDBY, LAZIO, JUVENTUS, BARCELONA, REAL MADRID, +2
CLUB APPEARANCES: 479, CLUB GOALS: 130

Michael Laudrup starred in the Denmark sides of the 1980s and scored on his international debut. At Barcelona he won nine domestic and European trophies, including four league titles.

Dennis LAW

BORN: 1940, POSITION: FORWARD
NATIONAL TEAM: SCOTLAND, CAPS/GOALS: 55/30
CLUBS: HUDDERSFIELD, MANCHESTER CITY, TORINO, MANCHESTER UNITED
CLUB APPEARANCES: 602, CLUB GOALS: 303

Law spent 11 years at Manchester United, where his 171 goals place him third in the club's history, behind Bobby Charlton and Wayne Rooney. Nicknamed The King, he is the only Scottish player to have won the Ballon d'Or award, which he achieved in 1964.

LEONARDO

BORN: 1969, POSITION: MIDFIELDER
NATIONAL TEAM: BRAZIL, CAPS/GOALS: 55/7
CLUBS: FLAMENGO, SÃO PAULO, VALENCIA, KASHIMA ANTLERS, PARIS SAINT-GERMAIN, AC MILAN, CLUB APPEARANCES: 371, GOALS: 70

Leonardo Nascimento de Araújo, known as Leonardo, played in Brazil's 1994 World Cup winning side, and the runners-up team in 1998, and was a leading player with AC Milan.

LEÔNIDAS

BORN/DIED: 1913–2004, POSITION: CENRE FORWARD
NATIONAL TEAM: BRAZIL, CAPS/GOALS: 19/21
CLUBS: ...BONSUCCESSO, PEÑAROL, VASCO DA GAMA, BOTAFOGO, FLAMENGO, SÃO PAULO
CLUB APPEARANCES: 574, CLUB GOALS: 516

Known as the "Rubber Man" due to his agility, Leônidas is regarded as one of the most important players of the first half of the 20th century. Da Silva played for Brazil in two World Cups, and was the top scorer of the 1938 World Cup.

Nils LIEDHOLM

BORN/DIED: 1922–2007, POSITION: MIDFIELDER
NATIONAL TEAM: SWEDEN, CAPS/GOALS: 23/12
CLUBS: VALDEMARSVIKS, SLEIPNER, NORRKÖPING, AC MILAN
CLUB APPEARANCES: 467, CLUB GOALS: 127

Nils Liedholm helped Sweden win gold in the 1948 Olympic Games after which he joined AC Milan for whom he scored 60 goals. Known throughout his career for his passing and crossing skills.

Gary LINEKER

BORN: 1960, POSITION: STRIKER
NATIONAL TEAM: ENGLAND, CAPS/GOALS: 80 / 48
CLUBS: LEICESTER CITY, EVERTON, BARCELONA, TOTTENHAM HOTSPUR, NAGOYA GRAMPUS EIGHT
CLUB APPEARANCES: 466, CLUB GOALS: 238

Gary Lineker is one of England's all-time leading goalscorers, and was top scorer in the 1986 World Cup (six goals), the only time the Golden Boot award has gone to an England player.

Sepp MAIER

BORN: 1944, POSITION: GOALKEEPER
NATIONAL TEAM: W. GERMANY, CAPS/GOALS: 95/0
CLUBS: BAYERN MUNICH
CLUB APPEARANCES: 536, CLUB GOALS: 0
SENIOR PLAYING CAREER: 1962–1980

Sepp Maier is regarded as one of Germany's greatest ever goalkeepers, winning the 1974 World Cup with West Germany and the European Cup three times with club side Bayern Munich.

Paolo MALDINI

BORN: 1968, POSITION: DEFENDER
NATIONAL TEAM: ITALY, CAPS/GOALS: 126 / 7
CLUBS: AC MILAN
CLUB APPEARANCES: 647, CLUB GOALS: 29
SENIOR PLAYING CAREER: 1985–2009

Paolo Maldini was one of the game's finest defenders, whose 24-year career at AC Milan saw him collect 26 domestic and European trophies and reach the Final of the 1994 World Cup.

Diego MARADONA

BORN: 1960, POSITION: FORWARD
NATIONAL TEAM: ARGENTINA, CAPS/GOALS: 91/34
CLUBS: ARGENTINOS JUNIORS, BOCA JUNIORS, BARCELONA, NAPOLI, SEVILLA, +2
CLUB APPEARANCES: 491, CLUB GOALS: 259

Diego Maradona was the world's greatest player in the 1980s and early 1990s, named best player at the 1986 World Cup and scoring what has been called the "goal of the century" in the same tournament.

Following page: Diego Maradona in action against Scotland, 1979.

Josef MASOPUST

BORN: 1931, POSITION: MIDFIELDER
NATIONAL TEAM: CZECHOSLOVAKIA, CAPS/GOALS: 63/10
CLUBS: TECHNOMAT TEPLICE, DUKLA PRAGUE,
CROSSING MOLENBEEK
CLUB APPEARANCES: 483, CLUB GOALS: 98

Josef Masopust played in midfield for
Czechoslovakia, helping them reach the 1962 World
Cup Final where he scored the opening goal. He was
named 1962 European Footballer of the Year.

Lothar MATTHÄUS

BORN: 1961, POSITION: MIDFIELDER
NATIONAL TEAM: W. GERMANY, CAPS/GOALS: 150/23
CLUBS: BORUSSIA MÖNCHENGLADBACH, BAYERN
MUNICH, INTER MILAN, METROSTARS
CLUB APPEARANCES: 595, CLUB GOALS: 161

Lothar Matthäus, the most capped German player,
was renowned for his passing and tackling skills.
He led West Germany to victory in the 1990 World
Cup and won the Ballon d'Or that year.

Stanley MATTHEWS

BORN/DIED: 1915–2000, POSITION: WINGER
NATIONAL TEAM: ENGLAND, CAPS/GOALS: 83/13
CLUBS: STOKE CITY, BLACKPOOL
CLUB APPEARANCES: 697, CLUB GOALS: 71
SENIOR PLAYING CAREER: 1932–1965

One of the greatest players of the English game,
Matthews was the first winner of the European
Footballer of the Year award. "The wizard of the
dribble" played at the top level until he was 50. He
is the only player to be knighted while still playing.

Giuseppe MEAZZA

BORN/DIED: 1910–1979, POSITION: FORWARD
NATIONAL TEAM: ITALY, CAPS/GOALS: 53/33
CLUBS: INTER MILAN, AC MILAN, JUVENTUS,
VARESE, ATALANTA
CLUB APPEARANCES: 463, CLUB GOALS: 271

Giuseppe Meazza was a prolific goalscorer who
played in Italy's first two World Cup victories (1934,
1938) and won domestic honors with Inter Milan
and rivals AC Milan.

Lionel MESSI

BORN: 1987, POSITION: FORWARD
NATIONAL TEAM: ARGENTINA, *CAPS/GOALS: 105/49
*CLUBS: BARCELONA
*CLUB APPEARANCES: 335
*CLUB GOALS: 301

Lionel Messi's record for Argentina and club side
Barcelona single him out as one of the best – if not
the best – players of the present day, renowned
for his pace, dribbling and shooting skills, and an
astonishing goals-per-game ratio.

Roger MILLA

BORN: 1952, POSITION: STRIKER
NATIONAL TEAM: CAMEROON, CAPS/GOALS: 63/37
CLUBS: MONACO, BASTI, SAINT-ÉTIENNE,
MONTPELLIER, SAINT-PIERROISE, TONNERRE, +5
CLUB APPEARANCES: 666, CLUB GOALS: 405

Roger Milla was one of the first African players to
be a major international talent, scoring four goals
for Cameroon at the 1990 World Cup and helping
them reach the quarter-finals.

Luis MONTI

BORN/DIED: 1901–1983, POSITION: MIDFIELDER
NATIONAL TEAM: ARGENTINA, ITALY
CAPS/GOALS: 16, 18/5, 1. CLUBS: HURACÁN,
BOCA JUNIORS, SAN LORENZO, JUVENTUS. CLUB
APPEARANCES: 225 (JUVENTUS), GOALS: 20

Luis Monti was an attacking center-half who played in the first two World Cup Finals, for different nations. He was a key figure for Juventus in the 1930s, picking up four league titles.

Bobby MOORE

BORN/DIED: 1941–1993, POSITION: DEFENDER
NATIONAL TEAM: ENGLAND, CAPS/GOALS: 108 / 2
CLUBS: WEST HAM UNITED, FULHAM, SAN ANTONIO
THUNDER, SEATTLE SOUNDERS, HERNING FREMAD
CLUB APPEARANCES: 708, CLUB GOALS: 26

Bobby Moore was captain of the England team that won the 1966 World Cup, whose 108 caps (90 as captain) was a long-standing national record. He was one of the greatest defenders of all time.

José Manuel MORENO

BORN/DIED: 1916–1978, POSITION: FORWARD
NATIONAL TEAM: ARGENTINA, CAPS/GOALS: 34/19
CLUBS: RIVER PLATE, ESPAÑA, UNIVERSIDAD
CATÓLICA, BOCA JUNIORS, DEFENSOR, +2
CLUB APPEARANCES: 489, CLUB GOALS: 224

José Manuel Moreno was one of Argentina's greatest players, regarded as an all-rounder whose years with club side River Plate in the 1940s saw them dominate Argentine football.

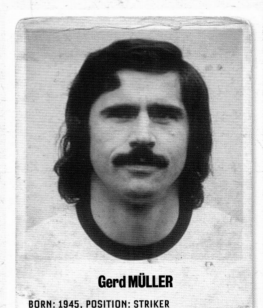

Gerd MÜLLER

BORN: 1945, POSITION: STRIKER
NATIONAL TEAM: W. GERMANY, CAPS/GOALS: 62/68
CLUBS: NÖRDLINGEN, BAYERN MUNICH, FORT
LAUDERDALE STRIKERS
CLUB APPEARANCES: 555, CLUB GOALS: 487

Gerd Müller, a prolific striker renowned for his clinical finishing, is the all-time top scorer in the Bundesliga (365 goals), a Ballon d'Or (1970) and World Cup winner (1974).

Thomas MÜLLER

BORN: 1989, POSITION: FORWARD
NATIONAL TEAM: GERMANY, CAPS/GOALS: 70/31
CLUBS: BAYERN MUNICH
CLUB APPEARANCES: 224
CLUB GOALS: 90

In 2014, Müller was ranked the fifth-best footballer in the world by The Guardian newspaper. He scored 5 goals in 6 appearances at the 2010 World Cup, winning the Golden Boot. At the 2014 World Cup he sored 5 goals and received the Silver Boot.

Hong Myung-Bo

BORN: 1969, POSITION: SWEEPER
NATIONAL TEAM: N. KOREA, CAPS/GOALS: 136/10
CLUBS: POHANG STEELERS, BELLMARE HIRATSUKA,
KASHIWA REYSOL, LA GALAXY
CLUB APPEARANCES: 281, CLUB GOALS: 21

Considered one of the greatest Asian footballers of all time and was the first Asian player to play in four consecutive World Cup finals. He was known as the "Korean Libero" due to his ability to play deep into the midfield and strike a long distance ball.

Following Page: Barcelona's Lionel Messi celebrates with teammates Luis Suárez and Neymar after scoring his second goal for Barcelona against Rayo Vallecano.

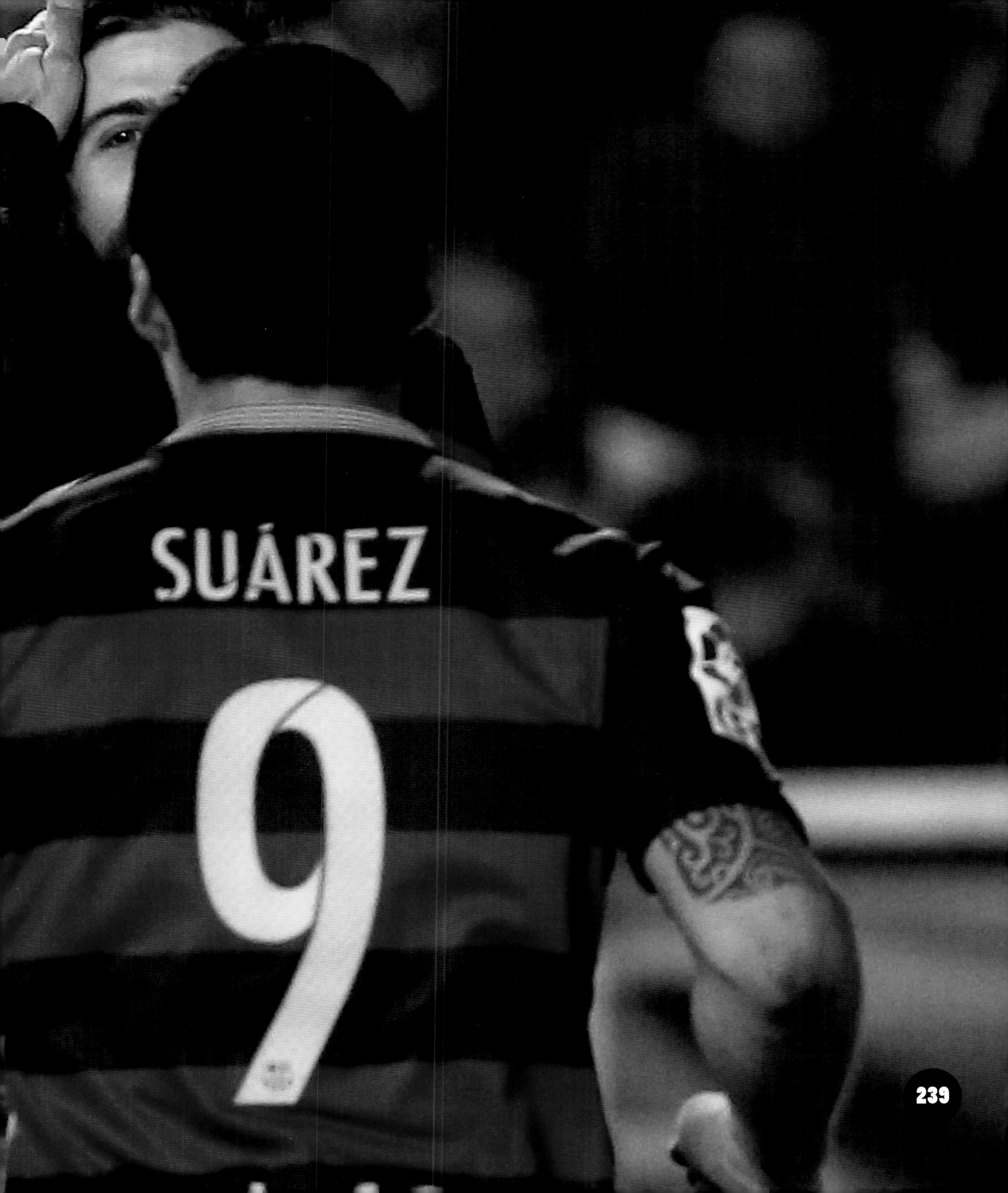
SUÁREZ
9

Hidetoshi NAKATA

BORN: 1977, POSITION: MIDFIELDER
NATIONAL TEAM: JAPAN, CAPS/GOALS: 288 / 41
CLUBS: BELLMARE HIRATSUKA, PERUGIA, ROMA, PARMA, FIORENTINA, BOLTON WANDERERS
CLUB APPEARANCES: 288, CLUB GOALS: 41

Nakata is widely considered to be one of the best Asian footballers of his generation, and one of the greatest Japanese players of all time. In March 2004, Pelé named Nakata in his FIFA 100, a list of the top living footballers at the time.

Pavel NEDVĚD

BORN: 1972, POSITION: WINGER
NATIONAL TEAM: CZECH REPUBLIC, CAPS/GOALS: 91/18
CLUBS: DUKLA PRAGUE, SPARTA PRAGUE, LAZIO, JUVENTUS
CLUB APPEARANCES: 501, CLUB GOALS: 110

One of the best footballers of his generation, Nedvěd is also regarded as one of the most successful players to emerge from the Czech Republic, winning domestic and European success with Italian clubs Lazio where he won the Cup Winners Cup, and Juventus.

Johan NEESKENS

BORN: 1951, POSITION: MIDFIELDER
NATIONAL TEAM: HOLLAND, CAPS/GOALS: 49/17
CLUBS: RACING CLUB HEEMSTEDE, AJAX, BARCELONA, NEW YORK COSMOS, GRONINGEN, +2
CLUB APPEARANCES: 480, CLUB GOALS: 92

Johan Neeskens was one of the greatest midfielders of the 1970s, part of the Holland sides in two World Cup Finals (1974, 1978), and winning silverware with club sides Ajax and Barcelona.

Manuel NEUER

BORN: 1986, POSITION: GOALKEEPER
NATIONAL TEAM: GERMANY, CAPS: 64
CLUBS: SCHALKE 04, BAYERN MUNICH
CLUB APPEARANCES: 337

Regarded by many as the best goalkeeper in the world, Neuer is considered by some in the sport to be the best keeper since Lev Yashin. He won the 2014 World Cup with Germany as well as the Golden Glove award.

NEYMAR

BORN: 1992, POSITION: FORWARD
NATIONAL TEAM: BRAZIL, *CAPS/GOALS: 69/46
*CLUBS: SANTOS, BARCELONA
*CLUB APPEARANCES: 184,
*CLUB GOALS: 103

With 46 goals in 70 matches for Brazil, Neymar is the fifth highest goalscorer for his national team at the age of 24. He has twice won the South American Footballer of the Year award (2011, 2012), and was third leading goalscorer in the 2014 World Cup.

Thomas N'KONO

BORN: 1956, POSITION: GOALKEEPER
NATIONAL TEAM: CAMEROON, CAPS: 525
CLUBS: CANON YAOUNDÉ...ESPAÑOL, SABADELL, CLUB BOLIVAR
CLUB APPEARANCES: 525

Probably the greatest goalkeeper Africa has ever produced, N'kono played for Español for almost a decade appearing in more than 300 games. N'Kono appeared for Cameroon in three World Cups, and four Africa Cup of Nations tournaments.

Jay-Jay OKOCHA

BORN: 1973, POSITION: ATTACKING MIDFIELDER
NATIONAL TEAM: NIGERIA, CAPS/GOALS: 75/14
CLUBS: FENERBAHÇE, PARIS S-G, BOLTON
WANDERERS, QATAR SC, HULL CITY, +2
CLUB APPEARANCES: 454, CLUB GOALS: 85

"So good that they named him twice," Okocha was a quick and skilful playmaker, who is widely regarded as the best Nigerian player of his generation and one of the greatest African players of all time. He was twice named the BBC African Footballer of the Year.

Marc OVERMARS

BORN: 1973, POSITION: WINGER
NATIONAL TEAM: HOLLAND, CAPS/GOALS: 86/17
CLUBS: GO AHEAD EAGLES, WILLEM, AJAX,
ARSENAL, BARCELONA
CLUB APPEARANCES: 399, CLUB GOALS: 78

Marc Overmars' speed down the wing earned him a formidable reputation. He was a key member of Ajax in the 1990s, winning three Dutch titles and the Champions League with them.

Michael OWEN

BORN: 1979, POSITION: STRIKER
NATIONAL TEAM: ENGLAND, CAPS/GOALS: 89/40
CLUBS: LIVERPOOL, REAL MADRID, NEWCASTLE
UNITED, MANCHESTER UNITED, STOKE CITY
CLUB APPEARANCES: 362, CLUB GOALS: 163

Aged 17 in his first full season in the Premier League, Owen was Liverpool's joint top scorer with 18 goals. He repeated this the next year and was their top goal scorer from 1997–2004, winning the Golden Boot in '97 and '98. In 2001 he won the Ballon d'Or.

Darko PANCĚV

BORN: 1965, POSITION: FORWARD
NATIONAL TEAM: YUGOSLAVIA, MACEDONIA
CAPS/GOALS: 33/18. CLUBS: VARDAR, RED STAR
BELGRADE, INTERNAZIONALE, +2.
CLUB APPEARANCES: 290, CLUB GOALS: 175

Darko Pancěv was the highest scorer in European football in the 1990–91 season with 34 goals, for which he was eventually awarded the European Golden Boot award 15 years later. He was runner up for the Ballon d'Or in 1991.

Jean-Pierre PAPIN

BORN: 1963, POSITION: STRIKER
NATIONAL TEAM: FRANCE, CAPS/GOALS: 54/30
CLUBS: ...MARSEILLE, MILAN, BAYERN MUNICH,
BORDEAUX, GUINGAMP, SAINT-PERROISE
CLUB APPEARANCES: 438, CLUB GOALS: 228

Papin achieved his greatest success while playing for Marseille between 1986 and 1992—he was named the European Footballer of the Year in 1991. He was known for his goalscoring, and especially for volleys, which fans nicknamed Papinades in his honor.

Daniel PASSARELLA

BORN: 1953, POSITION: CENTER BACK
NATIONAL TEAM: ARGENTINA, CAPS/GOALS: 70/22
CLUBS: SARMIENTO, RIVER PLATE, FIORENTINA,
INTERNAZIONALE
CLUB APPEARANCES: 447, CLUB GOALS: 140

One of the greatest defenders of all time, Passarella was also one of the most prolific defenders, at one point he was football's top scoring defender, with 134 goals in 451. He was captain of the Argentina team that won the 1978 World Cup.

PELÉ

BORN: 1940, POSITION: FORWARD
NATIONAL TEAM: BRAZIL, CAPS/GOALS: 91/77
CLUBS: SANTOS, NEW YORK COSMOS
CLUB APPEARANCES: 694
CLUB GOALS: 650

Edson Arantes do Nascimento, known as Pelé, is regarded as the greatest player of all time. He is Brazil's leading goalscorer (77 goals) and won the World Cup three times (1958, 1962, 1970).

Silvio PIOLA

BORN: 1913, POSITION: STRIKER
NATIONAL TEAM: ITALY, CAPS/GOALS: 34/30
CLUBS: PRO VERCELLI, LAZIO, TORINO, JUVENTUS, NOVARA
CLUB APPEARANCES: 619, CLUB GOALS: 333

Piola won the 1938 FIFA World Cup with Italy, scoring two goals in the final. He is also the highest goalscorer in Italian 1st league history, with 290 goals. The only player to have the honor of being the all-time Serie A top scorer of three different teams.

Andrea PIRLO

BORN: 1979, POSITION: MIDFIELDER
NATIONAL TEAM: ITALY, CAPS/GOALS: 116/13
CLUBS: BRESCIA, INTERNAZIONALE, MILAN, JUVENTUS, NEW YORK CITY
CLUB APPEARANCES: 525, CLUB GOALS: 60

The epitome of the deep-lying playmaker—widely regarded as one of the greatest ever exponents of this position, with his vision, control and passing ability. He is the fourth-most capped player in the history of the Italian national team with 116 caps.

Michel PLATINI

BORN: 1955, POSITION: MIDFIELDER
NATIONAL TEAM: FRANCE, CAPS/GOALS: 72/41
CLUBS: NANCY, SAINT-ÉTIENNE, JUVENTUS
CLUB APPEARANCES: 432
CLUB GOALS: 224

Michel Platini, a superb passer of the ball and prolific goalscorer, won the Ballon d'Or three times (1983, 1984, 1985) and is the second highest scorer for France with 41 goals

Paul POGBA

1993, POSITION: MIDFIELDER
NATIONAL TEAM: FRANCE, CAPS/GOALS: 29/5
CLUBS: MANCHESTER UNITED, JUVENTUS
CLUB APPEARANCES: 122
CLUB GOALS: 27

"Powerful, skilful, and creative with an eye for goal and a penchant for the spectacular," Pogba won the Golden Boy award for 2013, as the best under-21 player in Europe, and in 2014 was on The Guardian's list of the ten most promising players in Europe.

Gheorghe POPESCU

BORN: 1967, POSITION: SWEEPER
NATIONAL TEAM: ROMANIA, CAPS/GOALS: 11/16
CLUBS: PSV EINDHOVEN, TOTTENHAM HOTSPUR, BARCELONA, GALATASARAY, LECCE, +4
CLUB APPEARANCES: 467, CLUB GOALS: 68

Gheorghe Popescu, six times Romanian Footballer of the Year in the late 1980s and 1990s, was a key part of the Romania national team, and is one of his country's most capped players.

Ferenc PUSKÁS

BORN/DIED: 1927–2006, POSITION: STRIKER
NATIONAL TEAM: HUNGARY, SPAIN
CAPS/GOALS: 85, 4/84, 0
CLUBS: BUDAPEST HONVÉD, REAL MADRID
CLUB APPEARANCES: 521, CLUB GOALS: 508

Ferenc Puskás was captain and star striker for Hungary during the team's golden decade of the 1950s, scoring an incredible 84 goals in 85 matches for the "Mighty Magyars."

Helmut RAHN

BORN/DIED: 1929–2003, POSITION: FORWARD
NATIONAL TEAM: W. GERMANY, CAPS/GOALS: 40/21
CLUBS: ROT-WEISS ESSEN, KÖLN, ENSCHEDE, MEIDERICHER
CLUB APPEARANCES: 418, CLUB GOALS: 145

Helmut Rahn scored twice in the 1954 World Cup Final, his second goal securing Germany's first World Cup victory. He was equal second highest scorer with Pelé in the 1958 tournament.

Thomas RAVELLI

BORN: 1959, POSITION: GOALKEEPER
NATIONAL TEAM: SWEDEN
CAPS/GOALS: 143/0
CLUBS: ÖSTER, GÖTEBORG, TAMPA BAY MUTINY
CLUB APPEARANCES: 461

Thomas Ravelli's career coincided with Sweden's growing international stature. His two saves in a quarter-final penalty shoot-out helped Sweden reach the semi-finals of the 1994 World Cup.

Frank RIJKAARD

BORN: 1962, POSITION: MIDFIELDER
NATIONAL TEAM: HOLLAND, CAPS/GOALS: 73/10
CLUBS: AJAX, SPORTING LISBON, REAL ZARAGOZA, AC MILAN
CLUB APPEARANCES: 540, CLUB GOALS: 98

Frank Rijkaard made his debut for Holland aged 19 and played a key role in the side that won the 1988 European Championship. He won European club honors with AC Milan and Ajax.

RIVALDO

BORN: 1972, POSITION: MIDFIELDER
NATIONAL TEAM: BRAZIL, CAPS/GOALS: 74/35
CLUBS: CORINTHIANS, PALMEIRAS, DEPORTIVO LA CORUÑA, BARCELONA, AC MILAN, CRUZEIRO, +8
CLUB APPEARANCES: 636, CLUB GOALS: 291

Rivaldo Vitor Borba Ferreira, known as Rivaldo, was an attacking midfielder. He was 1999 World Player of the Year and won the Ballon d'Or, and was in Brazil's 2002 World Cup winning team.

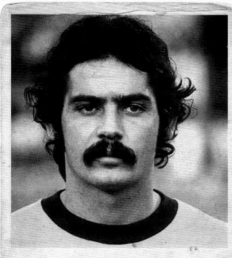

Roberto RIVELINO

BORN: 1946, POSITION: MIDFIELDER
NATIONAL TEAM: BRAZIL, CAPS/GOALS: 92/26
CLUBS: CORINTHIANS, FLUMINENSE, AL HILAL
CLUB APPEARANCES: 686
CLUB GOALS: 217

Roberto Rivellino was a key member of Brazil's 1970 World Cup winning team, often referred to as the greatest-ever World Cup team. He was renowned for swerving free kicks.

Following Page: The legendary Pelé celebrates scoring.

Gianni RIVERA

BORN: 1943, POSITION: MIDFIELDER
NATIONAL TEAM: ITALY, CAPS/GOALS: 63/15
CLUBS: ALESSANDRIA, AC MILAN
CLUB APPEARANCES: 527
CLUB GOALS: 166

Gianni Rivera, the Bambino d'Oro (Golden Boy) of the Italian press, made his Serie A debut aged 15, won the Ballon d'Or in 1969 and scored the goal that put Italy in the 1970 World Cup Final.

ROMÁRIO

BORN: 1966, POSITION: STRIKER
NATIONAL TEAM: BRAZIL, CAPS/GOALS: 70/55
CLUBS: VASCO DA GAMA, PSV EINDHOVEN, BARCELONA, FLAMENGO, VALENCIA, FLUMINENSE,+4
CLUB APPEARANCES: 448, CLUB GOALS: 309

Romário de Souza Faria, known as Romário, star of Brazil's 1990s attacking play, scored more than 1,000 goals for club and country and was player of the tournament at the 1994 World Cup.

Bryan ROBSON

BORN: 1957, POSITION: MIDFIELDER
NATIONAL TEAM: ENGLAND, CAPS/GOALS: 90/26
CLUBS: WEST BROMWICH ALBION, MANCHESTER UNITED, MIDDLESBOROUGH
CLUB APPEARANCES: 571, CLUB GOALS: 115

Bobby Robson once stated that Robson was the best British player he ever worked with. In 2011, Robson was voted as the greatest ever Manchester United player from a poll of ex-Manchester United players. He captained his country 65 times.

RONALDINHO

BORN: 1980, POSITION: FORWARD
NATIONAL TEAM: BRAZIL, CAPS/GOALS: 97/33
CLUBS: GRÊMIO, PARIS SAINT-GERMAIN, BARCELONA, AC MILAN, FLAMENGO, +3
CLUB APPEARANCES: 443, CLUB GOALS: 168

Ronaldo de Assis Moreira, known as Ronaldinho, was a key player in Brazil's 2002 World Cup winning team, renowned for his dribbling skills, overhead kicks, quick passes and free kicks.

RONALDO

BORN: 1976, POSITION: STRIKER
NATIONAL TEAM: BRAZIL, CAPS/GOALS: 98/62
CLUBS: CRUZEIRO, PSV EINDHOVEN, BARCELONA, INTER MILAN, REAL MADRID, AC MILAN, CORINTHIANS
CLUB APPEARANCES: 343, CLUB GOALS: 247

Ronaldo Luís Nazário de Lima, known as Ronaldo, is second only to Pelé as Brazil's leading goalscorer, winner of the Ballon d'Or (1997, 2002) and World Player of the Year (1996, 1997, 2002).

Cristiano RONALDO

BORN: 1985, POSITION: FORWARD
NATIONAL TEAM: PORTUGAL, *CAPS/GOALS: 125/56
*CLUBS: SPORTING LISBON, MANCHESTER UNITED, REAL MADRID
*CLUB APPEARANCES: 451, *CLUB GOALS: 340

Cristiano Ronaldo, one of the best players of the present day, is Portugal and Real Madrid's leading goalscorer, winner of the Ballon d'Or (2008, 2013, 2014) and World Player of the Year (2008).

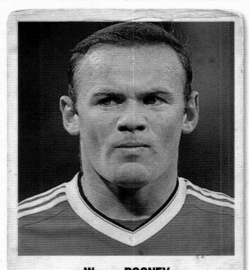

Wayne ROONEY

BORN: 1985, POSITION: FORWARD
NATIONAL TEAM: ENGLAND, CAPS/GOALS: 109/51
CLUBS: EVERTON, MANCHESTER UNITED
CLUB APPEARANCES: 429
CLUB GOALS: 192

With 51 goals in 109 internationals, Rooney is England's all-time record goalscorer and 4th most-capped player. In 2013, Rooney scored his 200th goal for Manchester United. Currently on 244 goals, making him the club's second top goalscorer.

Paolo ROSSI

BORN: 1956, POSITION: STRIKER
NATIONAL TEAM: ITALY, CAPS/GOALS: 48/20
CLUBS: JUVENTUS, COMO, VICENZA, PERUGIA, JUVENTUS, AC MILAN, HELLAS VERONA
CLUB APPEARANCES: 251, CLUB GOALS: 103

Paolo Rossi is one of the greatest Italian strikers of all time, who won a hat-trick of awards in the 1982 World Cup – winner's medal, Golden Boot (top goalscorer) and Golden Ball (best player).

Karl-Heinz RUMMENIGGE

BORN: 1955, POSITION: FORWARD
NATIONAL TEAM: W. GERMANY, CAPS/GOALS: 95/45
CLUBS: BAYERN MUNICH, INTER MILAN, SERVETTE
CLUB APPEARANCES: 424
CLUB GOALS: 220

Karl-Heinz Rummenigge was a striker for West Germany when the national side won the 1980 European Championship and finished runners-up in the World Cup (1982, 1986).

Matthias SAMMER

BORN: 1967, POSITION: DEFENSIVE MIDFIELDER
NATIONAL TEAM: E. GERMANY, GERMANY
CAPS/GOALS: 74 / 14
CLUBS: INTERNAZIONALE, BORUSSIA DORTMUND, +2
CLUB APPEARANCES: 291, CLUB GOALS: 84

With Borussia Dortmund, Sammer won the Bundesliga and DFL-Supercup in 1995, the Bundesliga, DFL-Supercup, and European Footballer of the Year in 1996, and the UEFA Champions League and Intercontinental Cup in 1997.

Hugo SÁNCHEZ

BORN: 1958, POSITION: FORWARD
NATIONAL TEAM: MEXICO, CAPS/GOALS: 58/29
CLUBS: UNAM, ATLÉTICO MADRID, REAL MADRID, AMÉRICA, RAYO VALLECONA, ATLANTE, LINZ...
CLUB APPEARANCES: 684, CLUB GOALS: 400

A prolific goalscorer known for his spectacular strikes and volleys, Sánchez is widely regarded as Mexico's greatest-ever footballer, and one of the greatest players of his generation. In 1999, the IFFHS voted Sánchez the 26th best footballer of the 20th century.

José SANTAMARIA

BORN: 1929, POSITION: CENTER-HALF
NATIONAL TEAM: URUGUAY, SPAIN
CAPS/GOALS: 20, 16/0
CLUBS: NACIONAL, REAL MADRID
CLUB APPEARANCES: NOT RECORDED, 227
CLUB GOALS: NOT RECORDED, 2

José Santamaria was at the center of the Real Madrid defense in the 1950s and 1960s, winning European and Spanish silverware. He was a key player for Uruguay at the 1954 World Cup.

Djalma SANTOS

BORN/DIED: 1929–2013, POSITION: RIGHT-BACK
NATIONAL TEAM: BRAZIL, CAPS/GOALS: 98/3
CLUBS: PORTUGUESA, PALMEIRAS, ATLÉTICO PARANAENSE
CLUB APPEARANCES: 964, CLUB GOALS: 23

Djalma Santos is considered one of the greatest right-backs of all time and was outstanding in defense for the Brazil teams that won back-to-back World Cups (1958, 1962).

Dejan SAVIĆEVIĆ

BORN: 1966, POSITION: ATTACKING MIDFIELDER
NATIONAL TEAM: YUGOSLAVIA, CAPS/GOALS: 5 19
CLUBS: BUDUĆNOST TITOGRAD, RED STAR BELGRADE, MILAN, RAPID VIENNA
CLUB APPEARANCES: 347, CLUB GOALS: 96

Savićević was a part of the Red Star Belgrade team that won the 1991 European Cup before joining A.C. Milan in '92. With Milan, he won three Serie A titles and the '94 UEFA Champions League. He represented Yugoslavia at the '90 and '98 World Cups.

Peter SCHMEICHEL

BORN: 1963, POSITION: GOALKEEPER
NATIONAL TEAM: DENMARK, CAPS/GOALS: 129/1
CLUBS: …BRONDBY, MANCHESTER UNITED, SPORTING CP, ASTON VILLA, MANCHESTER CITY
CLUB APPEARANCES: 648, CLUB GOALS: 9

Regarded as one of the greatest goalkeepers of all-time, the IFFHS ranked Schmeichel among the top 10 keepers of the 20th century in 2000. Unusually for a goalkeeper, Schmeichel scored 11 goals during his career, including one for the national team.

Karl-Heinz SCHNELLINGER

BORN: 1939, POSITION: LEFT-BACK
NATIONAL TEAM: W. GERMANY, CAPS/GOALS: 47/1
CLUBS: KÖLN, MANTOVA, ROMA, AC MILAN, TENNIS BORUSSIA BERLIN
CLUB APPEARANCES: 387, CLUB GOALS: 13

Ever-dependable in defense for West Germany and one of the few players to have played in four World Cup tournaments (1958, 1962, 1966, 1970). In his prime he was usually considered one of the best leftbacks in the world in his era.

Paul SCHOLES

BORN: 1974, POSITION: MIDFIELDER
NATIONAL TEAM: ENGLAND, CAPS/GOALS: 66/14
CLUBS: MANCHESTER UNITED
CLUB APPEARANCES: 499
CLUB GOALS: 107

Scholes is one of the most successful footballers in history, having won a total of 25 trophies, including 11 Premier League titles and 2 Champions League titles. Widely lauded, Xavi called him "the best central midfielder I've seen in the last 15, 20 years."

Uwe SEELER

BORN: 1936, POSITION: STRIKER
NATIONAL TEAM: W. GERMANY, CAPS/GOALS: 72/43
CLUBS: HAMBURG, CORK CELTIC
CLUB APPEARANCES: 477
CLUB GOALS: 406

Uwe Seeler is one of only three players to have scored in four World Cups (1958, 1962, 1966, 1970), the others being Pelé (Brazil) and fellow countryman Miroslav Klose. In 2004, he was named as one of FIFA's 125 greatest living players.

Salvatore SCHILLACI

BORN: 1964, POSITION: STRIKER
NATIONAL TEAM: ITALY, CAPS/GOALS: 417/154
CLUBS: MESSINA, JUVENTUS, INTERNAZIONALE, JUBILO IWATA
CLUB APPEARANCES: 417, CLUB GOALS: 154

Schillaci was the star of the 1990 World Cup, where he scored six goals, claiming the Golden Boot as the leading goalscorer, and received the Golden Ball as player of the tournament. That year he would also place second in the 1990 Ballon d'Or.

Andriy SHEVCHENKO

BORN: 1976, POSITION: STRIKER
NATIONAL TEAM: UKRAINE, CAPS/GOALS: 111/48
CLUBS: DYNAMO KIEV, MILAN, CHELSEA
CLUB APPEARANCES: 446
CLUB GOALS: 219

Shevchenko is the fifth-top goalscorer in all European competitions with 67 goals, and is the all-time top scorer for the Ukrainian national team (48 goals). He won the UEFA Champions League in 2003 with Milan, and won the Ballon d'Or in 2004.

Alan SHEARER

BORN: 1970, POSITION: STRIKER
NATIONAL TEAM: ENGLAND, CAPS/GOALS: 63/30
CLUBS: SOUTHAMPTON, BLACKBURN ROVERS, NEWCASTLE UNITED
CLUB APPEARANCES: 559, CLUB GOALS: 283

Shearer scored 283 league goals in his career, including a record 260 in the Premier League with a record 11 Premier League hat-tricks, and a total of 422 in all competitions. He had a remarkable goals to game ratio of 0.667

Peter SHILTON

BORN: 1949, POSITION: GOALKEEPER
NATIONAL TEAM: ENGLAND, CAPS: 12
CLUBS: LEICESTER, STOKE, NOTTINGHAM FOREST, SOUTHAMPTON, DERBY, PLYMOUTH ARGYLE, +5.
CLUB APPEARANCES: 1,001, CLUB GOALS: 1

Shilton holds the record for playing more games for the England men's team than anyone else, earning 125 caps, as well as the record for the most competitive appearances in world football. He shares the record of keeping 10 clean sheets in World Cup finals.

Allan SIMONSEN

BORN: 1952, POSITION: STRIKER
NATIONAL TEAM: DENMARK, CAPS/GOALS: 55/20
CLUBS: VEJLE DK, BORUSSIA MÖNCHENFLADBACH, BARCELONA, CHARLTON ATHLETIC
CLUB APPEARANCES: 500, CLUB GOALS: 202

Arguably the most influential player in the history of Danish football, Allen Simonsen was named 1977 European Footballer of the Year. Simonsen is the only footballer to have scored in the European Cup, UEFA Cup, and Cup Winners' Cup finals.

Matthias SINDELAR

BORN: 1903, POSITION: CENTER-FORWARD
NATIONAL TEAM: AUSTRIA, CAPS/GOALS: 43/26
CLUBS: FK AUSTRIA VIENNA
CLUB APPEARANCES: UNKNOWN
CLUB GOALS: UNKNOWN

Known as "The Mozart of football" Sindelar was renowned as one of the finest pre-war footballers for his fantastic dribbling ability and creativity. He was voted the best Austrian footballer of the 20th century in a 1999 poll by the IFFHS.

Omar SÍVORI

BORN: 1935, POSITION: STRIKER
NATIONAL TEAM: ARGENTINA/ITALY
CAPS/GOALS: 28/17
CLUBS: RIVER PLATE, JUVENTUS, NAPOLI
CLUB APPEARANCES: 341, CLUB GOALS: 176

An acclaimed Argentinian striker, and winner of the coveted European Footballer of the Year in 1961, Sívori played for Argentina and Italy at national level, winning the Copa América with Argentina, and appearing at the 1962 World Cup with Italy.

Wesley SNEIJDER

BORN: 1984, POSITION: MIDFIELDER
NATIONAL TEAM: HOLLAND, *CAPS/GOALS: 121/29
*CLUBS: AJAX, REAL MADRID, INTER MILAN, GALATASARAY
*CLUB APPEARANCES: 346, *CLUB GOALS: 97

Wesley Sneijder is Holland's second-most capped player, after goalkeeper Edwin van der Sar. He made his international debut aged 18 and is a midfield playmaker with a skill for free kicks.

Nilton SANTOS

BORN: 1925, POSITION: LEFT BACK
NATIONAL TEAM: BRAZIL, CAPS/GOALS: 75/3
CLUBS: BOTAFOGO
CLUB APPEARANCES: 723
CLUB GOALS: 11

Regarded as one of the greatest defenders in the history of the game, Santos is a member of the World Team of the 20th Century, and was named by Pelé one of the top 125 greatest living footballers at a FIFA Awards ceremony in 2004.

Hristo STOICHKOV

BORN: 1966, POSITION: FORWARD
NATIONAL TEAM: BULGARIA, CAPS/GOALS: 84/38
CLUBS: HEBROS, CSKA SOFIA, BARCELONA, PARMA, AL-NASSR, KASHIWA REYSOL, CHICAGO FIRE, D.C. UNITED
CLUB APPEARANCES: 473, CLUB GOALS: 243

Hristo Stoichkov made his name as one of Europe's leading goalscorers. At the 1994 World Cup he inspired Bulgaria to third place, scoring six goals and winning the Golden Boot.

Dragan STOJKOVIĆ

BORN: 1965, POSITION: MIDFIELDER
NATIONAL TEAM: YUGOSLAVIA, CAPS/GOALS: 84/15
CLUBS: RADNICKI NIŠ, RED STAR BELGRADE, MARSEILLE, HELLAS VERONA, NAGOYA GRAMPUS 8,
CLUB APPEARANCES: 422, CLUB GOALS: 125

Dragan Stojkovic was captain of Yugoslavia and club side Red Star Belgrade, and is one of his country's most capped players. He led Yugoslavia to the quarter finals of the 1998 World Cup.

Luis SUÁREZ

BORN: 1987, POSITION: FORWARD
NATIONAL TEAM: URUGUAY, *CAPS/GOALS: 83/45
*CLUBS: NACIONAL, GRONINGEN, AJAX, LIVERPOOL, BARCELONA
*CLUB APPEARANCES: 331, *CLUB GOALS: 212

Luis Suárez, widely regarded as one of the world's greatest strikers, is the all-time leading goalscorer for Uruguay, and has been just as prolific for the clubs he has played for.

Davor ŠUKER

BORN: 1968, POSITION: STRIKER
NATIONAL TEAM: YUGOLSAVIA / CROATIA
CAPS/GOALS: 79/52. CLUBS: ...DINAMO ZAGREB,
SEVILLA, REAL MADRID, ARSENAL, WEST HAM, +1
CLUB APPEARANCES: 448, CLUB GOALS: 203

Sukor, a strong, quick-footed striker, is
remembered most for a high loop over Peter
Schmeichel to round out Croatia's 3-0. His
hardware includes UEFA 2003 Golden Player, 1998
World Cup top goal scorer, Golden Boot and Silver
Ball, and is the only Croatian in the FIFA 100.

Marco TARDELLI

BORN: 1954, POSITION: MIDFIELDER
NATIONAL TEAM: ITALY, CAPS/GOALS: 81/6
CLUBS: PISA, COMO, JUVENTUS, INTER MILAN, ST.
GALLEN
CLUB APPEARANCES: 393, CLUB GOALS: 43

Marco Tardelli was a powerful defensive
midfielder who won World Cup glory with Italy in
1982, along with a host of domestic and European
trophies with club side Juventus.

Lilian THURAM

BORN: 1972, POSITION: DEFENDER
NATIONAL TEAM: FRANCE, CAPS/GOALS: 142/2
CLUBS: MONACO, PARMA, JUVENTUS, BARCELONA
CLUB APPEARANCES: 503
CLUB GOALS: 10

Lilian Thuram is France's most-capped player,
playing in the teams that won the 1998 World
Cup and the 2000 European Championship. He
was known for his pace and ability to read the
game.

TOSTÃO

BORN: 1947, POSITION: ATTACKING MIDFIELDER
NATIONAL TEAM: BRAZIL, CAPS/GOALS: 54/32
CLUBS: AMÉRICA, CRUZEIRO, VASCO DE GAMA
CLUB APPEARANCES: 449
CLUB GOALS: 270

Considered one of the best players in the world in
his prime. He represented Brazil in two World Cups,
and winning it in 1970, forming a lethal partnership
with Pelé. He had to retire early, suffering from a
detached retina after being hit by a ball.

Yaya TOURÉ

BORN: 1983, POSITION: MIDFIELDER
NATIONAL TEAM: IVORY COAST, CAPS/GOALS: 100/19
CLUBS: ...OLYMPIACOS, MONACO, BARCELONA,
MANCHESTER CITY
CLUB APPEARANCES: 422, CLUB GOALS: 72

Touré was voted African Footballer of the Year
for 2011, 2012, 2013 and 2014—only Touré and
Samuel Eto'o have won it four times. He helped
Manchester City earn its first league title in 44
years, and has over 100 caps for the Ivory Coast.

Marco VAN BASTEN

BORN: 1964, POSITION: STRIKER
NATIONAL TEAM: HOLLAND, CAPS/GOALS: 58/24
CLUBS: AJAX, AC MILAN
CLUB APPEARANCES: 280
CLUB GOALS: 218

Marco van Basten's five goals in the 1988
European Championship helped Holland win the
tournament. World Player of the Year (1992) and
winner of the Ballon d'Or (1988, 1989, 1992).

Edwin VAN DER SAR

BORN: 1970, POSITION: GOALKEEPER
NATIONAL TEAM: HOLLAND, CAPS/GOALS: 130/0
CLUBS: AJAX, JUVENTUS, FULHAM, MANCHESTER UNITED
CLUB APPEARANCES: 605, CLUB GOALS: 1

Edwin van der Sar is Holland's most capped player. He set a world goalkeeping record of 1,311 minutes without conceding a goal, and was voted Best European Goalkeeper (1995, 2009).

Obdulio VARELA

BORN: 1917, POSITION: HOLDING MIDFIELDER
NATIONAL TEAM: URAGUAY, CAPS/GOALS: 45/9
CLUBS: DEPORTIVO JUVENTUD, MONTEVIDEO WANDERERS, PEÑAROL. CLUB APPEARANCES: UNKNOWN, CLUB GOALS: UNKNOWN

Regarded as one of the greatest holding midfielders, Varela was adept in defense and was renowned for his tenacity and leadership. He was the captain of the Uruguayan national team that won the 1950 World Cup after beating Brazil in the decisive final.

Velibor VASOVIĆ

BORN/DIED: 1939–2002, POSITION: SWEEPER
NATIONAL TEAM: YUGOSLAVIA, CAPS/GOALS: 32/2
CLUBS: PARTIZAN, RED STAR BELGRADE, PARTIZAN, AJAX
CLUB APPEARANCES: 286, CLUB GOALS: 23

Velibor Vasović was a versatile sweeper known for his defensive skill. A star with Partizan Belgrade, he went on to captain Ajax, leading them to European Cup success in 1971.

Fritz WALTER

BORN/DIED: 1920–2002, POSITION: FORWARD
NATIONAL TEAM: GERMANY, CAPS/GOALS: 61/33
CLUBS: KAISERSLAUTERN
CLUB APPEARANCES: 364
CLUB GOALS: 357

Fritz Walter was captain of the West Germany side that won the 1954 World Cup – the first time Germany had won. Walter was a national hero, and the biggest star in German football.

George WEAH

BORN: 1966, POSITION: STRIKER
NATIONAL TEAM: LIBERIA, CAPS/GOALS: 60/22
CLUBS: ...TONNERE YAOUNDÉ, MONACO, PSG, MILAN, MANCHESTER CITY, MARSEILLE, AL-JAZIRA
CLUB APPEARANCES: 411, CLUB GOALS: 193

One of the greatest African players ever, in 1995 he was named World Player of the Year and won the Ballon d'Or— the first African player to win it. In '89, '94 and '95 he was the African Footballer of the Year, and in '96, African Player of the Century.

Billy WRIGHT

BORN: 1924, POSITION: CENTER HALF
NATIONAL TEAM: ENGLAND, CAPS/GOALS: 105/3
CLUBS: WOLVERHAMPTON WANDERERS
CLUB APPEARANCES: 490
CLUB GOALS: 0

The first footballer ever to earn 100 international caps, Wright appeared 105 times for England, captaining them a record 90 times. Under his captaincy Wolves won the First Division three times between 1954 and 1959 and the FA Cup in 1949.

XAVI

BORN: 1980, POSITION: MIDFIELDER

NATIONAL TEAM: SPAIN, CAPS/GOALS: 133/13

*CLUBS: BARCELONA, AL SADD

*CLUB APPEARANCES: 579

*CLUB GOALS: 63

Xavier Hernández Creus, known as Xavi, a Barcelona star for 17 years, has won more trophies (28) than any other Spanish player, including a World Cup winner's medal (2010).

Lev YASHIN

BORN/DIED: 1929–90, POSITION: GOALKEEPER

NATIONAL TEAM: SOVIET UNION, CAPS: 78

CLUBS: DYNAMO MOSCOW

CLUB APPEARANCES: 326

CLUB GOALS: 1

Lev Yashin is regarded as the greatest goalkeeper of all time, known for his reflex saves. He won Olympic gold (1956), the Ballon d'Or (1963), and saved more than 150 penalties.

Ricardo ZAMORA

BORN: 1901, POSITION: GOALKEEPER

NATIONAL TEAM: SPAIN, CAPS/GOALS: 46/0

CLUBS: ESPANYOL, BARCELONA, REAL MADRID, NICE. CLUB APPEARANCES: UNKNOWN

CLUB GOALS: 0

Regarded as one of the greatest goalkeepers of all time, the award for the best goalkeeper in La Liga, the Ricardo Zamora Trophy, is named in his honor, and he was voted one of the greatest players of the 20th century by World Soccer magazine.

ZICO

BORN: 1953, POSITION: MIDFIELDER

NATIONAL TEAM: BRAZIL, CAPS/GOALS: 71/48

CLUBS: FLAMENGO, UDINESE, KASHIMA ANTLERS

CLUB APPEARANCES: 332

CLUB GOALS: 192

Arthur Antunes Coimbra, known as Zico, was a free kick specialist with the Brazil teams of the late 1970s and 1980s. He is one of his country's all-time leading goalscorers.

Zinédine ZIDANE

BORN: 1972, POSITION: MIDFIELDER

NATIONAL TEAM: FRANCE, CAPS/GOALS: 108/31

CLUBS: CANNES, BORDEAUX, JUVENTUS, REAL MADRID

CLUB APPEARANCES: 506, CLUB GOALS: 95

Zinédine Zidane is hailed as the greatest ever player for France, and among the best the world has seen. His two goals in the 1998 World Cup final helped win the trophy for France.

Dino ZOFF

BORN: 1942, POSITION: GOALKEEPER

NATIONAL TEAM: ITALY, CAPS: 112

CLUBS: UDINESE, MANTOVA, NAPOLI, JUVENTUS

CLUB APPEARANCES: 642

CLUB GOALS: 0

Dino Zoff was outstanding in goal for Italy, and led his side to World Cup glory in 1982. He holds the record for the longest time between conceding international goals (1,142 minutes).

MANAGERS, COACHES AND REFEREES

"I WOULDN'T SAY I WAS THE BEST MANAGER IN THE BUSINESS...BUT I WAS IN THE TOP ONE."

- BRIAN CLOUGH

MANAGERS AND COACHES

A manager or head coach of either a club or national team has a great variety of tasks and duties to perform, from setting the tone at press conferences to analyzing the opposition and their key threats, assessing in training whether a player is looking sharp enough to justify selection and poring over his or her optimal starting formation and tactics to nullify opponents and secure victory. All coaches know that should their team triumph, the players will garner most of the glory whilst should they fail, it is they, as the person who selects the team and tactics, who will be held most responsible.

Preparation And Selection

Managers and coaches prepare for a forthcoming game assiduously, leaving no stone unturned in their search for an advantage. They will discuss with their assistant coaches which formation to adopt, who to select and who to place on the bench to potentially deploy later in the game. Analysis of video footage of opponents may force a coach to alter his preferred style of play and personnel to devise a system to counter the rival team's biggest threats whilst, with between 15 and 30% of all goals coming from set pieces (corner kicks, throw-ins and free kicks), set piece moves may be devised and drilled over and over again.

During a game, the ability to react to game events, change the shape of the side and deploy substitutions effectively can be crucial to success. Yet, however much control a coach or manager may have over team selection, formations and substitutions, he or she is often powerless during the game as the action unfolds. Tactical plans can be shredded after a moment of madness or a major error by the manager's charges or a moment of brilliance from the opposition. In contrast, some tactical decisions can exceed a coach's expectations and appear a tactical masterstroke

such as when US men's national team coach Bruce Arena decided to bring on Eddie Johnson in a 2004 qualifying match for the 2006 FIFA World Cup versus Panama. Johnson went on to score a hat-trick in only his second game for the US team. At the 2014 FIFA World Cup, an unusual substitution was made by Dutch coach Louis Van Gaal who brought on Tim Krul as a substitute goalkeeper just for the penalty shootout versus Costa Rica. It could have backfired but proved successful as Krul saved two penalties and the Netherlands were victorious.

Coaching Casualties / Managerial Merry-Go-Round

Tenure is precarious when managing a top club where success is demanded by the board and fans. More than half of all the 92 league teams in the four professional English leagues changed their manager during the 2015-16 season, for example, Sevilla coach Antonio Álvarez was the first casualty in the 2015-16 La Liga season, sacked after only five games. More extreme, was the case of Serie A club, Palermo who parted company with their head coach Beppe Iachini, in November 2015 only to re-hire

him as coach three months later after Palermo owner, Maurizio Zamparini had appointed and dismissed four successive coaches (Davide Ballardini, Guillermo Barros Schelotto, Giovanni Tedesco and Giovanni Bosi).

In this context, long-serving club managers such as Arsène Wenger, who has completed 20 years and over 1,100 matches in charge of Arsenal and Thomas Schaaf who managed Werder Bremen from 1999 to 2013, are a rarity today, although in the past, some clubs gave managers such as Bill Shankly, Jock Stein and Valeriy Lobanovskiy more time to build a successful dynasty. Few, though, can compete with Auxerre legend, Guy Roux who first took charge of French club, Auxerre, in 1961 when the club was in the fifth tier of French football and finally retired in 2005 (with three short breaks in 1962, 2000 and 2001) after gaining promotion to Ligue 1 in 1980, coaching the side in 894 Ligue 1 games and winning the Ligue 1 title in 1996 as well as four Coupe de France competitions.

Whilst most national team coaches stay in charge for one competition cycle, for example a four year spell to take a country to the next FIFA World Cup, Morten Olsen is unusual. Appointed head coach of Denmark in 2000 and planning to retire after the EURO 2016 tournament, the Dane became the first person to achieve a century of caps as a player followed by 100 matches as coach of the same national team. In women's football, former Real Madrid trainee, Ignacio Quereda embarked on an exceptionally lengthy term in charge of the Spanish national women's team from 1988 to 2015 which included a record-breaking 17-0 victory over Slovenia in 1994, in European Champions qualifying - still the joint largest margin of victory in a senior UEFA competition fixture.

Coaching Success

Many coaches are rightly revered for their role in reviving a club or, like Brian Clough at Nottingham Forest, taking it to domestic prominence for the first time. Repeating the success at other clubs and in other leagues cements a top coach's status as a serial winner. Ottmar Hitzfeld is one example. He won two Swiss Super League titles with Grasshopper Club Zurich before becoming the Bundesliga's most successful coach, by first guiding Borussia Dortmund to two championships before taking Bayern Munich to five more German league titles between 1998-99 and 2007-08.

Some club coaches or managers can be extraordinarily successful within their borders, presiding over a period of dominance yet unable, with the resources given, to conquer their continental rivals. This was the case with Walter Smith who coached Rangers to ten Scottish Premier League titles and 21 domestic trophies in total yet could not win a European competition. Others, have won European competitions, but their legacy lies outside of the trophies won. Hungarian Béla Guttmann worked all over the world, finding most success with Benfica who he coached to two European Cups in 1960 and 1961, but it was his coaching philosophy, favoring a short pass and move style and the introduction of the 4-2-4 formation which proved influential especially after the formation was adopted by Brazil when they won both the 1958 and 1970 FIFA World Cup.

Pages 256-57: Nottingham Forest manager Brian Clough holds the European Cup 1980. Opposite Top Left: Manchester City manager Manuel Pelligrini and Kevin De Bruyne. Bottom: Spain's coach Vicente del Bosque with players during a training session. Top: Pep Guardiola and Marcello Lippi chat post match. Above: Arsenal manager Arsène Wenger on the touchline. Right: Chelsea Manager José Mourinho during press conference.

TOP MANAGERS AND COACHES I

Sir Alex Ferguson

Born: 1941
Nationality: Scottish

A masterful man manager with an enormous will to win and the Scottish League's top goalscorer whilst playing for Dunfermline in the 1965-66 season, Ferguson is so synonymous with Manchester United that it is sometimes forgotten that he had already enjoyed great success with Aberdeen before his appointment at Old Trafford in 1986. He took Aberdeen to three Scottish league titles, four Scottish Cups and in 1983, coached them to their first European trophy, the UEFA Cup Winners Cup. He also managed the Scottish national team for a short spell before joining United.

In an era where few managers of top clubs last more than two seasons, Ferguson's 27 year, 1,500 game reign at United has already passed into folklore. The club became England's most powerful team under his tutelage, winning a staggering 13 Premier League titles, five FA Cups, four League Cups and the Champions League twice in 1999 and 2008, the latter year also including a FIFA World Club Cup triumph. Ferguson's eye for a transfer saw some stunning deals from Eric Cantona and Peter Schemichel to a young Cristiano Ronaldo, bought for £12.24 million and sold on to Real Madrid for a record £80 million. Arguably, Ferguson's greatest legacy was the development of a clutch of talented players who in the cases of Ryan Giggs, Gary Neville and Paul Scholes spent their entire playing careers at the club whilst more than a dozen of Ferguson's former players at Aberdeen and Manchester United, from Alex McLeish and Gordon Strachan to Mark Hughes and Ole Gunnar Solskjær, have entered football management themselves.

Carlo Ancelotti

Born: 1959
Nationality: Italian

A former midfielder for Serie A clubs, Parma, AC Milan and Roma, Ancelotti began his coaching career at Reggiana who he took to promotion to Serie A in 1995. The following year, he left to manage his former club, Parma who under his calm, assured guidance obtained a runners-up finish in Serie A and a place in the UEFA Champions League – a competition that Ancelotti had twice won as a player with AC Milan. After a short, unsuccessful spell at Juventus, Ancelotti took the helm at his former club in 2001 and guided AC Milan to two UEFA Champions League titles, the first in 2002-03 especially sweet as it involved defeating Juventus in the final. Whilst he won league titles at his next two clubs – Chelsea (2009-2011) and Paris Saint-Germain (2011-13), it was at Real Madrid that he added a third Champions League crown, defeating Atlético Madrid 4-1 in the final and making Ancelotti the second coach to have won the competition three times (after Liverpool's Bob Paisley) and the only three-time winner to have also won the competition as a player. In December 2015, it was confirmed that Ancelotti would replace Pep Guardiola as head coach of Bayern Munich.

Josep "Pep" Guardiola

Born: 1971
Nationality: Spanish

A former midfielder for Barcelona as well as Brescia and Qatar club Al Ahli, Guardiola became the hottest managerial prospect in world football after four extraordinary seasons in charge of Barcelona from 2008-09 onwards. Jettisoning former stars such as Samuel Eto'o, Ronaldinho and Deco in favor of new signings

and promoting from reserve and youth teams, Guardiola became Barcelona's most successful manager in just four seasons. The team, with Lionel Messi at its helm, played sparkling football as they won 14 trophies including three La Liga titles and two UEFA Champions League crowns. Under Guardiola, Barcelona won 178 and lost only 21 of their 246 games scoring 633 goals as they lit up Spanish and European football. After taking a sabbatical from football, Guardiola signed up to replace Jupp Heynckes at Bayern Munich and took the German giants to the Bundesliga title in each of his three seasons in charge before news emerged in early 2016 that at the end of the 2015-16 season, he was moving to England to take charge of Manchester City.

Brian Clough

Born: 1935 Died: 2004
Nationality: English

An outstanding goalscorer in English football, Clough scored 251 goals in just 274 games for Middlesbrough and Sunderland before anterior cruciate ligament damage cut his playing career short at the age of 29. Forming a highly profitable management partnership with Peter Taylor, first at Hartlepool, the pair moved on to Derby and transformed them from second division makeweights to league champions in 1972 in only five years. Clough and Taylor had brief spells at Brighton and Leeds United before moving to another second division side, Nottingham Forest. It took just four seasons for the abrasive, unpredictable but talented Clough to win the English league with Forest. Consisting mainly of veteran journeyman and discarded or unproven talents, Clough's forest side played a patient passing game and hit their peak in 1979 and 1980 when they won back-to-back European Cups. A brilliant motivator and the most outspoken of English managers, Clough was rarely far from the headlines, a trait which is believed to be the reason why he was never appointed England manager.

Rinus Michels

Born: 1928 Died 2005
Nationality: Dutch

Sometimes, a coach's trophy cabinet and individual honors only tell part of the story of their great influence and impact. This was certainly the case with Marinus "Rinus" Michels who introduced his brand of free-flowing, creative tactics and play known as "Total Football" whilst coaching an outstanding Ajax side from 1965 to 1971 and the Dutch national team that captivated neutrals at World Cups in the 1970s. Under Michels, who had given Johan Cruyff his club debut at the age of 17, Ajax won four Dutch league titles and the first of three European Cups in a row, before he moved to Spain to become Barcelona manager where he won La Liga in 1972-73 and then took the Dutch national team to the final of the 1974 FIFA World Cup. Spells in Germany and coaching the Los Angeles Aztecs in the short-lived North American Soccer League (NASL) followed before Michels was appointed Dutch head coach for a second spell in 1984. Presiding over a team packed with talent including Marco van Basten, Frank Rijkaard and Ruud Gullit, Michels guided the team to win the 1988 UEFA European Championship. The following year, FIFA named Michels as their Coach of the Century.

Giovanni Trapattoni

Born: 1939
Nationality: Italian

One of the great European managers, Trapattoni has coached nine different clubs in Portugal, Germany, Austria and Italy. He has won league championships in all four countries at least once (with Bayern Munich in Germany, Red Bull Salzburg in Austria and Benfica in Portugal) In Italy, he is considered one of the country's most successful coaches, winning Serie A seven times as a manager (six with Juventus and one with Inter Milan) as well as two Coppa Italia competitions and a complete haul of continental trophies – the European Cup, Cup Winners' Cup, UEFA Cup and European Supercup – all with Juventus. The unflappable Italian has also managed the Republic of Ireland team to EURO 2012 and the Italian team between 2000 and 2004.

Opposite Top Left: Sir Alex Ferguson in his legendary Fergie time pose. Bottom: Guardiola giving instructions to Messi. Top Right: Rinus Michels (R) with his assistant manager Nol de Ruiter. Above: Nottingham Forest Manager Brian Clough (R) celebrates victory with his assistant Peter Taylor.

TOP MANAGERS AND COACHES II

Guus Hiddink

Born: 1946
Nationality: Dutch

One of football's great globetrotting coaches, the highly-experienced Hiddink has coached a large number of club and national teams with equal aplomb over a long managerial career. It began in his native Netherlands as he stepped up from his assistant coach role at PSV Eindhoven to take charge of the Dutch club and lead them to three Eredivisie titles in a row (1986-87 to 1988-89). He would return to the club in 2002 and gain two more Dutch league titles, but in between coached Fenerbahçe in Turkey, Spanish clubs Valencia, Real Betis and Real Madrid as well as getting his first taste of international management as head coach of the Netherlands (1994-98) and South Korea (2001-02). He led both countries to fourth places at successive FIFA World Cups and in South Korea was particularly celebrated for the achievement, becoming the first person to be made an honorary South Korean citizen. Four further national team jobs have followed with Australia, Russia, Turkey and a second spell in charge of the Dutch side whilst Hiddink has re-entered club management twice with Chelsea as interim manager, the latest in 2015 following the departure of José Mourinho.

Diego Simeone

Born: 1970
Nationality: Argentinean

A combative midfielder with Vélez Sarsfield, Simeone debuted for the Argentina national team at the tender age of 18 and appeared in three FIFA World Cups, retiring in 2006 as his country's most-capped player with 106 caps. He entered management with Racing

Club of Argentina before quickly moving to Estudiantes and then River Plate winning league titles with both of these clubs before returning to Europe and Atlético Madrid, a club he had played for in two spells. At Madrid, he became famed for an impressive transfer record of buying cheaply and selling at a great profit. Stars such as Sergio Agüero, Radamel Falcao, David De Gea and Thibaut Courtois have all passed through the club during his reign which has seen just 41 losses from his first 247 games in charge. Simeone has twice been awarded La Liga coach of the year as his club have sought to overturn the dominance of Real Madrid and Barcelona with some success, winning the Europa League, the Copa Del Rey and the 2013-14 Spanish league title.

Valeriy Lobanovskiy

Born: 1939 Died: 2002
Nationality: Soviet / Ukrainian

A talented left winger himself for Dynamo Kiev and other Soviet clubs, Lobanovskiy earned a degree in thermal engineering during his playing career and is remembered for being amongst the first managers to apply scientific methods to training and preparation. His meticulous planning included collecting and analyzing data and statistics on both his own players and opponents as well as enlisting the assistance of Olympic athletics coach, Valentin Petrovski to increase player's sprint performances. In three separate spells in charge of Dynamo Kiev, Lobanovskiy helped establish the club as a powerful force. He won five league titles in his first period (1974-82) as well as the European Cup Winner's Cup and in total would lead the club to 13 league championships including five Ukraine league titles. In his final stint with Kiev from 1997 to 2002, the team recorded an outstanding tally of 110 wins from 138 league matches. He also guided the Soviet Union national team to a bronze medal at the 1976 Olympics and to the final of the 1988 UEFA European Championships where they were narrowly defeated by the Netherlands.

Jürgen Klopp

Born: 1967
Nationality: German

Emotional, passionate and a firm favorite with fans, Klopp coached FSV Mainz 05 for seven years during which period the club reached the Bundesliga for the very first time in 2004. At this point, he had spent over 18 years at the club, debuting for Mainz as a striker but from 1995, playing as a defender. Klopp was appointed Borussia Dortmund head coach in May 2008 and hauled the underachieving side up the Bundesliga table, finishing sixth and fifth in his first two seasons before embarking on a serious challenge to unseat German champions Bayern Munich. Klopp's unusual training methods and motivational techniques, which have seen him take the squad out training in public parks, bore fruit in the 2010-11 and 2011-12 seasons as Dortmund won the Bundesliga twice, making it a double in 2011-12 by winning the DFL-Pokal. The following season saw Klopp mastermind Borussia Dortmund's UEFA Champions League campaign defeating Ajax, Manchester City and Real Madrid, amongst others, to reach the final where they suffered defeat to rivals, Bayern. In 2015, Klopp left Dortmund on a sabbatical but was back in management by the end of the year, replacing Brendan Rodgers as Liverpool manager.

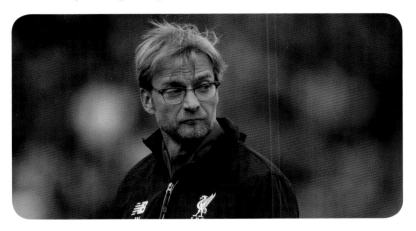

José Mourinho

Born: 1963
Nationality: Portuguese

Controversial and outspoken, Mourinho is nevertheless one of the most successful and tactically astute coaches working in club football. Starting out as a scout and coach for local teams, such as Estrela da Amadora, he became employed as a Portuguese-English translator in 1992 for Bobby Robson when he worked at Sporting CP. Mourinho followed Robson, first to Porto, and then Barcelona as an assistant coach, where he also worked with Robson's successor, Louis van Gaal. After short stints in charge of Benfica

and União de Leiria, Mourinho secured the job of Porto head coach in 2002. He took the Portuguese club to a brief but dazzling spell of success with two league titles, the 2002-03 UEFA Cup and in 2003-04, became UEFA Champions League champions. It was the start of an astonishing run of 150 unbeaten home games in charge for Mourinho at four different clubs (Porto, Chelsea, Inter Milan and Real Madrid) between 2002 and 2011. All four clubs became league champions during his time in charge, with Inter Milan also collecting the 2009-10 UEFA Champions League and Coppa Italia whilst Real Madrid, under Mourinho, won the Copa del Rey. A return to Chelsea in 2013-14, brought another league title the following season - his eighth in just 13 seasons, but a disastrous start to the following season saw Mourinho and Chelsea part company leaving many potential suitors from all over Europe interested in offering the charismatic Portuguese his next job in management.

Jock Stein

Born: 1922 Died: 1985
Nationality: Scottish

When he retired as a player for Celtic in 1957, the former center half was put in charge of coaching Celtic's reserve team before moving to Dunfermline in 1960 to get his first taste of club management. The club were facing a relegation struggle and had not won a game in four months yet under Stein carried out a remarkable turnaround, winning their first six games with him in charge, capturing the 1960-61 Scottish FA Cup (defeating Celtic in the final) and the following year, reaching the quarter finals of the European Cup Winners' Cup. After a short spell managing Hibernian, Stein was installed as Celtic boss and from 1965 to 1978 won a staggering 10 league titles, 8 Scottish Cups and the 1966-67 European Cup – the first by a British club. Stein left Celtic in 1978 for an unsuccessful spell at Leeds United before becoming Scotland team manager. Whilst masterminding Scotland's attempt to qualify for the 1986 World Cup, Stein suffered a fatal heart attack at the end of an away match versus Wales.

Mauricio Pochettino

Born: 1972
Nationality: Argentinean

After a long playing career, beginning at Newell's Old Boys in Argentina but mostly spent at Espanyol in the Spanish leagues, Pochettino turned to management in 2009, leading Espanyol to comfortable La Liga finishes before moving to Southampton in 2013 to replace Nigel Adkins. Pochettino's discipline and rigorous training methods as well as his careful team selections blending experienced players with young, emerging, footballers gave Southampton their highest English Premier League points total in 2013-14, before he moved to Tottenham Hotspur. His impact on developing young players at both Southampton and Spurs has been notable, so much so that ten of the last 18 England debutants – from Luke Shaw to Harry Kane, Dele Alli and Eric Dier – have been developed by Pochettino.

Opposite: Atlético Madrid's Antoine Griezmann celebrates his goal with coach Diego Simeone. Top: New Liverpool manager, Jürgen Klopp. Above: José Mourinho on the touchline.

THE OFFICIALS / REFEREES

Much maligned and showered with ridicule and abuse by managers, chairmen and fans in the ground and on social media, one has to feel sympathy for the referee. Most are huge football enthusiasts looking to give back to the sport they love and without them to control matches and rule on a wide range of contentious decisions from which team should get a throw-in to whether a penalty should be awarded, football matches would simply not go ahead.

The Umpires, The Ref And Their Whistle

Referees were formerly introduced on the pitch in the 1891 reworking of the Laws of the Game. Up until that point, games were officiated by two umpires, one provided by each competing team to which the players of the team could make an appeal. This system proved slow and unwieldy if the two umpires could not agree, so a third official, ideally independent, stood close to but not on the pitch to decide. This figure, the referee, became the sole arbiter of the match and the Laws of the Game, in 1891 by which time their single most valuable tool, the whistle, had supplanted umpires waving a small white flag as the way to halt a game and attract players' attention. The Joseph Hudson Company in the English city of Birmingham (later known as Acme Whistles) began producing whistles for Victorian police forces. These, especially their legendary family of Acme Thunderer whistles, were adopted by football referees worldwide, and by 2014, had sold over 200 million units.

Supporting Officials

The referee is the sole decision maker on the pitch but he or she is assisted by two officials who patrol the sidelines. These referee assistants use flag signals to communicate to the referee whether

the ball has left the field of play and which side should gain possession at the restart (throw-in, goal kick or corner). They also advise on whether a player should be penalized for finding themselves in an offside position and can also alert the referee if they spot misconduct occurring outside of the view of the referee. These two assistants have been augmented in recent times by the arrival of the fourth official. Whilst a named replacement referee was part of some competitions stretching back to the 1960s, the role was not made formal until an International Football Association Board decision in 1991. The fourth official acts as a potential substitute should one of the three match officials suffer an injury. In addition, he or she assists with substitutions and can advise the referee on occasion of any major misconduct. Spectators tend only to notice the fourth official when they display the amount of added time at each end of a half, but at the 2006 FIFA World Cup Final, the fourth official, Luis Medina Cantalejo became the center of attention when he alerted referee, Horacio

Elizondo about Zinédine Zidane's headbutt on Italian defender, Marco Materazzi, resulting in a red card for the French legend.

Super Refs

Whilst some referees are remembered for the controversies they were embroiled in, a number of officials are widely recalled as being excellent officials, skilled at keeping a grip of a game and consistent and accurate with their decisions. Uzbekistan referee, Ravshan Irmatov, for example has been awarded the AFC Referee of the Year five times between 2008 and 2014 whilst Mark Geiger, twice the MLS referee of the year, became in 2014 the first US official to take charge of a knockout match at a FIFA World Cup.

At one time, top-flight referees were forced to retire at 45 years of age, regardless of their physical fitness and recent performances. This saw top referees like Pierluigi Collina and Kim Milton Nielsen retire, arguably at the height of their powers. Nielsen officiated 154 international matches as well as 53 UEFA Champions League fixtures whilst Collina was widely considered one of the finest officials of the modern era, and named World Referee of the Year six times. The mandatory retirement rule was relaxed following a FIFA decision in 2014 and now officials who pass 45 years of age and wish to continue are evaluated closely on an annual basis.

Increasing Innovation

In the past 20 years, the role of top referees has developed with greater professionalism, training and support as well as an increased emphasis on fitness and further technical innovations. FIFA's fitness testing for its top referees is designed to ensure that they can keep up with play no matter how fast the game unfolds. It involves timed stamina runs around an athletics track and periods of high intensity sprinting with the officials performing six timed 40m sprints in succession with short rest periods and a maximum allowed duration of 6.2 seconds per sprint.

The numbers of female referees and assistants is growing with the 2015 Women's World Cup featuring solely female officials and a small but increasing number of female officials officiating men's matches. In 2015, Sanja Rođak Karšić became the first woman to referee a Croatian first division match when she was appointed in charge of the Lokomotiva versus Osijek fixture whilst Bibiana Steinhaus has officiated in Bundesliga 2 matches. One of the pioneers was Nicole Petignat who refereed more than 90 male Swiss League matches, the final of the 2007 Swiss Cup and four years earlier, became the first female referee of a men's UEFA Cup match when AIK Solna played Fylkir.

Technical innovation is gradually coming to the aid of officials. At the 2014 FIFA World Cup, for instance, referees were equipped with GoalControl watches which used 14 high speed cameras to relay speedily whether the ball had crossed the goal line or not. This World Cup was also the first to feature vanishing spray – a can that produces a white shaving foam-like temporary marking that allows referees to delineate clearly the ten yards defenders should stand away from the ball at free kicks. The spray, invented by Brazilian Heine Allemagne in 2000, was first used in Brazilian leagues during the 2000s and debuted at a major international competition at the 2011 Copa América.

Opposite Top: Italian referee Pierluigi Collina shows Chelsea's Mateja Kezman a yellow card. Bottom: Referee Daniele Orsato with assistant referees and ball boy. Top: Tottenham's Ryan Mason appeals to referee Nicola Rizzoli. Top Right: Referee Cüneyt Çakır marks the ground with vanishing spray. Above: FC Basel's Reto Zanni argues with ref Nicole Petignat during the Swiss cup final.

265

FOOTBALL DISCIPLINE

Football is a game both played and watched with passion. The emotion, drama and passion involved in the sport can be amongst its best traits but does sometimes spill over on the pitch into violence and mayhem. Whilst retrospective action is sometimes taken by football authorities, control of the game at the time is in the hands of the referee. He or she must quell flare-ups, warn players regarding their conduct and if needs be, punish players that transgress the Laws of the Game with cautions or sendings off. If a game lurches well and truly out of control, a referee can consider the possibility of abandoning the game. A game can also be abandoned if the referee or his assistants are attacked or injured by players or spectators as was the case in one EURO 2008 qualifying match in 2007 when German referee, Herbert Fandel was assaulted by a Danish fan after awarding Sweden a penalty. UEFA fined the Danish FA around €33,000 and awarded the match as a 3-0 victory to Sweden.

Cautions

Since referees were introduced in 1891, they have been given the power to warn a player about their behavior, cautioning and writing their name down in their notebook, hence the term, 'booking'. A second caution results in the player being dismissed from the game, leaving the pitch and his or her team continuing the game with one player less. Very occasionally, a referee fails to keep count, the most high profile example occurring at the 2006 FIFA World Cup Group F match between Croatia and Australia where English referee Graham Poll booked Josip Šimunić in the 61st minute and then the 90th minute without sending him off. Poll then booked Šimunić for remonstrating with him three minutes later at the end of the game, making the Croatian defender one of the only players to be booked three times in the same game.

Cautions are given for a range of fouls deemed serious enough to warrant a booking by the referee as well as repeated infringements of the Laws of the Game such as persistent timewasting, not retreating ten yards from a free kick, dissent or entering or leaving the pitch without the referee's permission. In 2004, FIFA president Sepp Blatter, lobbied successfully for the removal of shirts by players celebrating a goal to be added to the list of unsporting behavior deserving of a booking. The donning of masks is also a bookable offence under Law 12 of the Laws of the Game as Brazilian attacker, Neymar discovered to his cost in a 2011 Copa Libertadores game when he was shown a second yellow card and sent off for wearing a mask of himself handed to him by a delighted Santos fans after he had scored against Colo Colo.

Communicating Decisions / Red and Yellow Cards

Before 1970, players were booked or sent off but there were no red or yellow cards which are used by referees to communicate their decision to the crowd and even players. This was rarely an issue within early domestic competitions but as player movement between countries increased and at international competitions, the language barrier could lead to confusion and an escalation of on-field problems.

British footballing official Ken Aston had first qualified as a referee in 1936 and had presided over one of the World Cup's most notorious games, the 1962 "Battle of Santiago" – a particularly ill-disciplined and foul-tempered match between Chile and Italy. Rated highly, he was put in charge of all World Cup referees at the 1966, 1970 and 1974 FIFA World Cups. At the first of these tournaments, Aston learned of how England defender, Jack Charlton had been booked by German referee, Rudolf Kreitlein during the England v Argentina quarter final but hadn't been aware of the booking until reading the newspaper the day after. Whilst musing over this state of events as he drove through London in 1966, Aston had the brainwave or using the red and yellow (amber) of traffic lights on cards which could be brandished by a referee to communicate their disciplinary decision.

Yellow and red cards were road-tested at the 1968 Olympics football tournament and then debuted at the FIFA World Cup in 1970. Soviet Union striker, Givi Georgiyevich Nodia, became the first recipient of a yellow card in the tournament's opening match, against hosts, Mexico, but the first red card wasn't shown until the 1974 tournament when Chilean attacker, Carlos Caszely was dismissed in Chile's opening round game versus West Germany.

Sent Off / Dismissed From The Pitch

Red cards may frequently alter the complexion of a game but the team going one player down may not necessarily end up losing the match. Their coach may make one or more substitutions and reshape their team to make up for the reduction in player numbers. On occasion, their opponents may struggle to break down the ten men team or suffer a later red card themselves. Even two sendings off in a game doesn't guarantee defeat. In a 2012 French Ligue 1 match, Stade Rennais were reduced to nine men early in the second half yet still managed to hold Paris Saint-Germain at bay to record a memorable against-the-odds 2-1 victory.

Managers and coaches can also be sent off by the referee for dissent, abuse of the officials, leaving their technical area repeatedly or encroaching on the pitch. In the 2015-16 season high profile managers such as Chelsea's José Mourinho, Valencia's Gary Neville and Bayer Leverkusen's Roger Schmidt have all been dismissed. In Schmidt's case, he refused to leave the field of play causing the game to be postponed for eight minutes, and he later received a stadium ban. This pales in comparison to a chaotic Argentinean lower league match between Victoriano Arenas and Claypole in the fifth tier of the country's leagues in 2011. Referee Damián Rubino eventually brandished 36 red cards as he sent off all 22 onfield players, coaches and substitutes after mass brawls broke out during the game.

Red Card Records

Some red cards have been notable for their cause. In a 2005 English Premier League match against Aston Villa, Newcastle United suffered two red cards when two of their players, Lee Bowyer and Kieron Dyer, were sent off for fighting each other. Eight years later, Argentina's Javier Mascherano was sent off in a World Cup qualifier versus Ecuador for kicking a medic who was carrying him off the pitch on a stretcher. Mascherano's offence occurred in the 87th minute but some red cards have been awarded earlier in the game, few earlier in top flight competition than Giuseppe Lorenzo's red card after just 10 seconds of a 1990 Serie A match between Bologna and Parma.

The most red cards awarded at a single World Cup tournament was 28 at the 2006 competition. Astonishingly one player, Gerardo Bedoya, has eclipsed that figure throughout his career. The Colombian defender received 46 red cards as a player, his 41st accompanied by a 15-match ban for violent conduct. In 2016, he was appointed assistant coach at Colombian club, Independiente Santa Fe whereupon he was sent to the stands in his very first game, versus Junior FC.

Opposite: Newcastle's Jack Colback is shown a yellow card by referee Martin Atkinson. Top Right: Galatasaray and Trabzonspor players in a brawl. Above: Paris Saint-Germain's Zlatan Ibrahimović is shown a red card by referee Paolo Tagliavento Above Right: Referee Graham Poll famously gave out three yellow cards to Croatia's Josip Simunic.

THE WOMEN'S GAME

"I AM A MEMBER OF A TEAM, AND I RELY ON THE TEAM, I DEFER TO IT AND SACRIFICE FOR IT, BECAUSE THE TEAM, NOT THE INDIVIDUAL, IS THE ULTIMATE CHAMPION."

- MIA HAMM

WOMEN'S FOOTBALL: A BRIEF HISTORY

Women have long battled against prejudice and ignorance regarding their participation in sports and football was no exception. Fears that women were not equipped to deal with the rigors of the sport and its collisions and tackles as well as chauvinistic beliefs that football wasn't a "ladylike" endeavor led to the women's game being neglected, underdeveloped and, at times, banned for decades.

The First Wave

In the 1870s onwards, as football played by men captured increasing public interest in England and Scotland, a small number of women began to play. For some, it was a political statement especially at the time when struggles for equality and universal suffrage were being debated and protested. In May 1881, an unofficial international between teams representing Scotland and England was held in Edinburgh with the Scottish team wearing bonnets, blue jerseys, white knickerbockers, red belts and high heeled boots defeating England 3-0. In 1895, The British Ladies Football Club was formed by Mary Hutson who used the pseudonym, Nettie Honeyball. Placing adverts to recruit women players, she gathered together around 30 recruits who were trained in Hornsey in London with some coaching from Tottenham Hotspur center-half J.W. "Bill" Julian. The club split into North and South XIs for its first match in Crouch End in 1895, watched by between 10,000 and 11,000 spectators and embarked on tours, playing some 100 exhibition matches in the following two years.

The Munitions Teams

Women's football was established but not particularly well-received in much of British society before World War I. That changed with the outbreak of the "War to End all Wars." With vast numbers of men enlisted to fight in the armed forces during World War I, the English Football League suspended all of its sanctioned matches at the end of the 1914-15 season. New women's teams formed predominantly from women working in munitions factories and attracted greater public interest than before. The Alfred Wood Munition Girls Challenge Cup (commonly known as the Munitionettes' Cup) was founded in August 1917 and the following year, its first winners were Blyth Spartans who defeated Bolckow Vaughan at Ayresome Park in front of a crowd of approximately 22,000. The year, 1917, also saw the most famous munitions team founded in Preston, managed by Alfred Frankland and featuring female employees from the Dick, Kerr & Co works.

Dick, Kerr Ladies FC's first match drew a crowd of 10,000 at Preston's Deepdale ground and interest in the talented team of players didn't abate with the war's end. In 1920, their Boxing Day match against St Helen's ladies saw an estimated 14,000 spectators locked out of the ground, Goodison Park, home of Everton, whilst a record 53,000 were crammed inside to witness the team which included Alice Woods and the remarkable Lily Parr who, according to the National Football Museum, scored more than 1,000 goals in a playing career that spanned three decades. In France, the Federation des Societies Feminine Sportives de La

Fédération des sociétés féminines sportives de France had been formed to promote female sports participation by Alice Milliat, a strong advocate of women playing football. Contacted by Alfred Frankland, Milliat traveled with a French team to play four matches against Dick, Kerr Ladies in England in 1920, the first, attracting a crowd of 25,000 and raising over £3000 for charity.

Cut Off In Its Prime

"Complaints having been made as to football being played by women, Council felt impelled to express the strong opinion that the game of football is quite unsuitable for females and should not be encouraged." With these words from the English Football Association's Consultative Committee in 1921, the authorities cut off the first wave of women's football in its prime. Women's matches were prohibited from being held at Football League venues and women's football effectively went underground.

Dick, Kerr Ladies vowed to continue and embarked on a famous tour of North America. Arriving in Canada, only to find they were refused permission to play, they headed into the United States and played a clutch of matches against all-male opposition winning three matches including one against the New Bedford Whalers and drawing

three other games against male teams in the form of the Washington Stars, J&P Coats of Pawtucket and the Fall River Marksmen. The team changed their name to Preston Ladies in 1926 and continued to attract interest, but increasingly found it hard to find teams to play against. The FA ban would remain in place until 1969 and stifled the women's game in Britain. With its lifting came the Establishment of the Women's Football Association the same year and the first national cup competition, the Mitre Cup (which later became the Women's FA Cup) which attracted 71 entrants including clubs from Scotland and Wales in its inaugural season of 1970-71.

Increasing Interest

In many other countries, women's football was also treated with suspicion, disinterest or saw similar bans instituted to that of the English FA. In 1931 a women's football team in Floya were barred from organizing charity football matches by the Norwegian Football Associations whilst in 1955, the Deutscher Fußball-Bund (DFB) which ran football in West Germany forbid all women's football at its affiliated clubs. The ban would stay in force until 1970. The 1960s, though, saw increasing interest in the women's game and in 1969, the Coppa Europa per Nazioni was held with the final in Turin with Italy beating Denmark 3-1. This tournament and a second, held in 1979 were precursors to the Women's European Championships whilst an unofficial 1970 seven-team tournament, also held in Italy, and called the Coppa del Mondo (World Cup) featured England, Denmark, Germany, Mexico, Austria, Switzerland and Italy and was won by Denmark in the Stadio Communale in front of a crowd of approximately 40,000. In the United States, the first known women's competition, the Craig Club Girls Soccer League in St Louis, Missouri, played its first seasons in 1950 and 1951 but soccer mostly developed in colleges and universities especially after Title IX legislation banned discrimination in education. Across the Pacific, the Asian Ladies Football Confederation (ALFC) formed in 1968 and in 1975 the first AFC Women's Asian Cup competition was held. This official, confederation-approved, international tournament would be followed by continental competitions for all regions, an official FIFA World Cup in 1991 as well as semi-professional and professional leagues in a number of countries.

Opposite Top Left: The North London side that played the first official match, 1895. Nettie Honeyball is second from the left in the top row. Bottom: French women's football 1920s. Top: Dick, Kerr's Ladies F.C. Above: North Korea's Kim Chung-sim (L) tussles with Australia's Heather Ann Garriock during the AFC Women's Asian Cup 2010 final. Above Right: Michelle Akers of the US (C) holds the World Championship trophy, 1991, with teammates Julie Foudy (L) and Carin Jennings.

WOMEN'S CLUBS

Many women's football clubs have enjoyed illustrious if short histories. Teams like the Washington Freedom and the Boston Breakers had success in Women's United Soccer Association (WUSA) competition before the league closed after just three seasons whilst successful Brazilian women's side Santos, were twice winners of the Copa Libertadores Femenina before being closed down in 2012 due to funding issues, only to be restarted in 2015. Some leagues may have been beset with financial difficulties whilst others, such as the Swedish Damallsvenskan and the Japan Women's Football League running since 1989 have been long-standing operations. Clubs have emerged to top these and other leagues and establish spells of success and dominance.

FFC Frankfurt

Founded: 1998: Germany
Competes In: Frauen-Bundesliga (Women's Bundesliga)

In the late 1990s, the women's team of SG Praunheim broke away to form their own club which have become one of Germany's most successful sides. A total of seven women's Bundesliga titles have come along with a record nine women's DFB-Pokal cup competitions giving the club memorable league and cup doubles on six occasions (1998-99, 2000-01, 2001-02, 2002-03, 3006-07 and 2007-08). Whilst struggling domestically more in recent times with the rise of teams like VFL Wolfsburg and Frankfurt's great rivals, FFC Turbine Potsdam, they have enjoyed significant success continentally. The side has won a record four UEFA Women's Champions League titles, the latest in the 2014-15 season when 14 goals in the competition from Célia Šašić (eight more than any other player) including one in the final, saw the German side defeat Paris Saint-Germain Féminines to take the title again.

Olympique Lyonnais Féminin

Founded: 1970 as FC Lyon: France
Competes In: Championnat de France de Football Féminin

A powerhouse in French women's football, the club has been part of Olympique Lyonnais since 2004 by which time they had won four league championships. Swooping to the title again in 2006-07, the club has utterly dominated domestic rivals winning every league title since as well as seven Coupe de France Féminine and made it to the final of the UEFA Women's Champions League on four occasions, winning twice. The club has been home to a succession of foreign stars from US goalkeeper Hope Solo and midfielder, Megan Rapinoe to Norway's Ada Hegerberg who arrived in 2014 and scored 55 French league goals in her first 40 starts. The club's Swedish star, Lotta Schelin, was the league's top goalscorer in 2012-13 with 24 goals and in 2014-15, eclipsed that tally with a stunning 34 goals. The club completed a remarkable clean sweep in the league that season, winning all 22 of their games, conceding just six goals and ending the season with an incredible +141 goal difference as they won their 13th league title.

ASD Torres Femminile Sassari

Founded: 1980: Italy
Competes In: Serie A

Commonly known as Torres by fans, the team was founded as A.C.F. Delco Costruzioni of Sassari and entered their local division of Serie C in 1981. Rising up through the ranks, the club enjoyed back to back promotions in 1989 and 1990 to reach Serie A where, propelled by the stunning form of Italian legend, Carolina Morace, they won their first league title in the 1993-94 season. A further six would follow, the latest in 2012-13 as the team became rated the strongest in Italy, winning seven Supercoppa Italiana competitions between 2000 and 2013 and eight Coppa Italia trophies as well. Perennial Round of 16 or quarter finalists in the UEFA Women's Champions League, Torres were looking to mount a serious challenge for European glory but financial issues

caused the departure of the club's president and its head coach in 2014 and the following year, with debts believed to be in excess of €90,000, the club was refused a licence to compete in the 2015-16 Serie A season.

Nippon TV Beleza
Founded: 1981: Japan
Competes In: Japan Women's Football League
Starting out as Yomiuri SC Ladies Beleza, the team won its first Japan Women's Football League title in the competition's second season (1990) and won the next three titles in a row. They have been a constant top of the table threat ever since with only two finishes outside of the league's top two (in 1995 and 1996) and a record 13 league championships to their name including the 2015 title. The team who play their home matches in Tokyo's Inagi Central Park, have been equally successful in the Empress's Cup with 11 victories and have also won five Nadeshiko League Cup competitions. Long-serving defender, Azusa Iwashimizu who joined the club in 2001, is the current club captain and has seen Japanese stars arrive and depart the club including free-scoring striker Shinobu Ohno and Japanese captain Homare Sawa. The club also is the only member of the league never to have been relegated.

Arsenal L.F.C.
Founded: 1987: England
Competes In: Women's Super League
Founded by the kit man for the Arsenal men's team, Vic Akers, who served as manger until his retirement in 2009, Arsenal Ladies have been England's most successful women's club. The side has featured some of England's best-known female footballers including Casey Stoney, Rachel Yankey and Kelly Smith who returned in 2012 from the Boston Breakers for her third spell at the club and now captains the side. The club has won an unparalleled 12 Women's Premier League titles between 1993

and 2010 and were champions in the first two Women's Super League seasons in 2012 and 2013. Between October 2003 and March 2009, the team went on an extraordinary unbeaten run in the league, going 108 games without defeat. In addition to their league success, the team's bulging trophy cabinet contains 13 FA Women's Cups, and a prestigious UEFA Women's Cup in 2007 when they defeated Umeå IK 1-0 on aggregate over the two game final, the first time a British club had won the competition.

Umeå IK
Founded: 1985: Sweden
Competes In: Damallsvenskan
The women's section of the general sports club founded in Umeå in 1917 took its time to make its mark in the Swedish top flight. The club were promoted into the Damallsvenskan in 1996, relegated the following year but bounced back in 1998 and have remained a top flight presence ever since. Featuring predominantly Swedish players such as Hanna Ljungberg, mixed with a sprinkling of foreign players such as Brazilian great, Marta and Japan's Mami Yamaguchi, the club enjoyed a sparkling first decade of the 21st century, winning seven league championships and four Swedish Cups. They also proved a potent force in continental competition, reaching the final of the UEFA Women's Cup five times and winning on two occasions, in 2003 and 2004.

FC Kansas City
Founded: 2012: United States
Competes In: National Women's Soccer League
The Blues played their first match at the Shawnee Mission District Stadium against the Portland Thorns in the first match played in the NWSL. Assisted by 12 goals and 9 assists from the league's top scorer Lauren Holiday, Kansas City finished their first season on 38 points, tied with the Thorns and Western New York Flash but lost in the play-offs. They rallied the following season with a seven game winning streak to again finish in the top four but this time prevail in the play-offs and defeat Seattle Reign in the final. The same pair of teams met and contested the final of the 2015 season where victory gave Kansas City back-to-back NWSL titles.

Opposite Left: FFC Frankfurt's team players pose with trophy after winning their UEFA Women's Champions League final, 2015. Right: ASD Torres Femminile Sassari team shot. Above: Kelly Smith of Arsenal Ladies in a match against Leeds. Right: FC Kansas City's Lauren Holiday (R) in action.

TOP WOMEN PLAYERS I

Mia Hamm
Born: 1972
Nationality: American
Position: Striker
Caps: 275   **Goals:** 158

Women's football first global superstar, Mariel Margaret Hamm became the United States' youngest international player when she made her debut at the age of 15. Playing for the North Carolina Tar Heels, alongside Kristine Lilly, she quickly grew to become women's football most lethal attacker. Hamm used her vision and eye for space to quickly ghost into excellent goalscoring positions where she could exploit opponents via her exquisite dribbling and feinting skills to unleash sharp shots to devastating effect. Quickly racking up the goals in international competitions, it became lore that if Hamm scored, the US national team would win – as was the case 64 times out of 68 games during the 1990s. By 1999, Hamm was an Olympic gold medalist and two time World Cup winner and in that year also became the world record goal scorer with her 108th versus Brazil. She even once played in goal during a 1995 World Cup match versus Denmark after Briana Scurry was red-carded. Retiring after the 2004 Olympic games, Hamm formed a charitable foundation but has also stayed involved in football becoming an ambassador for Spanish side, Barcelona whilst in 2014, she was appointed to the board of directors of Serie A club, Roma.

Birgit Prinz
Born: 1977
Nationality: German
Position: Striker
Caps: 214   **Goals:** 128

A phenomenal goalscorer and three times awarded FIFA's World Player of the Year, Prinz began her career at SV Dörnigheim FC followed by FC Hochstadt before entering the women's Bundesliga with FSV Frankfurt and from 1998, FFC Frankfurt. Save for a short spell playing in WUSA for the Caroline Courage, Prinz stayed in Germany where she won an astonishing eight German Player of the Year awards, seven Bundesliga titles and eight DFB-Pokal for women's cup competitions. On the international stage, Prinz had a major impact. At times, unplayable with her imposing physique, Prinz's eye for an angle, a powerful shot and good aerial prowess saw her crowned the Bundesliga's top scorer on four seasons and Germany's all-time leading scorer. With the national team, Prinz won five UEFA European Championships and two Women's World Cups (2003, 2007) as well as three Olympic bronze medals. She is also the second highest goalscorer at Women's World Cups with 14 goals. In 2011, she announced her retirement, a year after receiving her masters degree in psychology and now works as a sports psychologist at German club, TSG 1899 Hoffenheim and in 2014 began heading a long term FIFA study into mental health and sports.

Marta
Born: 1986
Nationality: Brazilian
Position: Striker
Caps: 101   **Goals:** 100

Discovered as a footballing talent at the age of 14 and joining Brazilian club, Vasco da Gama, Marta Vieira da Silva moved to

Sweden as an 18 year old to play for Umeå IK in the Swedish women's top league, the Damallsvenskan. With rapid feet and an exceptional touch, the diminutive attacker often led opponents for dead and scored over 100 competitive goals for Umeå and winning four league titles before moving to professional leagues in the United States in 2009 and playing for the Los Angeles Sol followed by FC Gold Pride, spells at Brazilian club, Santos, before finally returning to Sweden and joining Tyresö FF in 2012. By this time, Marta had won five FIFA World Player of the Year titles in a row (2006-10). She would also finish runner-up on a further four occasions, such was her pre-eminence and high profile. In 2014, she switched clubs to FC Rosengård and was named as one of six ambassadors for the men's 2014 FIFA World Cup alongside Brazilian legends such as Mario Zagallo and Ronaldo. The following year at the Torneio Internacional de Brasilia, Marta scored twice against Mexico to reach a century of goals for her national team.

Carli Lloyd
Born: 1982
Nationality: American
Position: Midfielder
Caps: 220   **Goals:** 86

Lloyd's sensational hat-trick in the final of the 2015 FIFA Women's World Cup cemented her place as one of the most exciting and

effective attacking talents in women's football. The former Rutger University's Scarlet Knights footballer who made her national team debut in 2005 versus Ukraine, showed a poacher's instinct to nip in to score; her first two goals in the 2015 final followed were off an audacious strike from the halfway line over the head of stumbling Japanese goalkeeper, Ayumi Kaihori to complete only the second hat-trick in any World Cup final (after Geoff Hurst for England in 1966). In the same year, Lloyd moved clubs to the Houston Dash, her ninth club in 16 years after spells with teams including the New Jersey Wildcats, Chicago Red Stars and Atlanta Beat. The following year, she struck her sixth hat-trick for the US national women's team, another rapid-fire effort in 22 minutes, this time against the Republic of Ireland.

Sun Wen
Born: 1973
Nationality: Chinese
Position: Forward
Caps: 152   **Goals:** 106

A legend in Asian football, Sun Wen took up football at the age of 10 and within seven years was playing for the Chinese national team. Small at 1.62m (5'3") yet packing significant goal threat with sudden bursts of acceleration and excellent ball control skills, Wen appeared at four Women's World Cups and helped China win four Asian Cups in 1991, 1993, 1995 and 1997.

She was at her peak at the 1999 FIFA Women's World Cup where she was the tournament's top scorer and was also awarded the Golden Ball as the competition's best player. The following year, she was jointly awarded FIFA's World Women's Player of the Century alongside the United States' Michelle Akers and was first pick in the player draft for the inaugural season of the Women's United Soccer Association (WUSA) in 2002-03.

Opposite Top Left: USA player Mia Hamm kisses her Gold Medal at the 2004 Olympic Games. Bottom: Brazil's Marta clashes with Britain's Sophie Bradley. Top Right: Sue Wen in action. Above: US midfielder Carli Lloyd takes a penalty kick against Mexico.

TOP WOMEN PLAYERS II

Christie Rampone

Born: 1975
Nationality: American
Position: Central defender
Caps: 311   **Goals:** 4

Relatively short for a central defender at 1.68m (5'5") Rampone has made up for her lack of stature through skill, excellence at reading the game and sheer will to win. Graduating from Monmouth University, Rampone played for the Central Jersey Splash in 1997, the same year as her international debut. She later switched clubs to the New York Power in 2001 and in 2009 moved to Sky Blue FC, becoming player-coach later that year. A stalwart of the US women's team which has enjoyed enormous success, Rampone has won three Olympic gold medals and two Women's World Cups, the second in 2015 at the age of 40. When she came on as an 86th minute substitute in the 2015 final versus Japan, she became the oldest player to appear in the final of either the men's or women's World Cup.

Homare Sawa

Born: 1978
Nationality: Japanese
Position: Midfielder
Caps: 204   **Goals:** 83

A footballing prodigy who joined the Japanese adult L. League at the age of 12, Sawa made her international debut at the age of 15, stunning spectators with four goals in the match versus the Philippines. Small but combative when challenging for possession, Sawa proved highly composed on the ball and one of the world's great playmaking midfielders, capable of making a telling pass or fashioning chances for teammates to score. Sawa also had an eye for goal herself, as shown by the five she scored at the 2011 World Cup where she was both the leading scorer and won the most valuable player award as she became a World Cup winner. To cap a glorious year, she was later voted FIFA World Player of the Year and the following year captained Japan to a silver medal at the 2012 Olympics. Playing her club football both in the United States for teams like the Washington Freedom and Atlanta Beat, and for NTV Beleza (formerly Yomiuri Beleza) and INAC Kobe Leonessa in Japan, Sawa was twice awarded AFC Women's Player of the Year (2004, 2008).

Nadine Angerer

Born: 1978
Nationality: German
Position: Goalkeeper
Caps: 146   **Goals:** 0

A brave, acrobatic and highly effective goalkeeper, Angerer played for FC Nürnberg, Wacker Munich and Bayern Munich before embarking on seven seasons with 1.FFC Turbine Potsdam winning two Bundesliga titles and the UEFA Women's Cup before joining FFC Frankfurt. Forced to remain understudy to Silke Rottenberg for most of a decade, Angerer took her chance at the

2007 Women's World Cup where she did not concede a goal all tournament and saved a penalty kick in the final which Germany won. Following the retirement of Birgit Prinz in 2011, Angerer was made German captain and led the side to EURO 2013 glory, saving two penalties in the final as Germany managed to secure a 1-0 victory. The following year, she was named the 2013 FIFA World Player of the Year, the first time that either the men's or women's award had been won by a goalkeeper. In 2015, she announced her retirement from competitive football and later in the year joined the Portland Thorns as goalkeeping coach.

Christine Sinclair

Born: 1983
Nationality: Canadian
Position: Striker, attacking midfielder
Caps: 230   **Goals:** 161

Canada's most famous female footballer, Sinclair starred for Canada's under-18 team before making her senior debut at age 16 at the 2000 Algarve Cup where she immediately made her mark by becoming tournament top scorer. A complete forward who has good skills on the ground and in the air, she is adept at leading the line or playing in a slightly withdrawn role as an advanced attacking midfielder. A fixture in the Canadian national team since the early 2000s, Sinclair has appeared at four World Cups and has been nominated for FIFA World Player of the Year six times. Playing club football for a variety of Canadian and American teams, she has won three professional league championships in 2010 (with the FC Gold Pride), 2011 (with Western New York Flash) and in 2012 (with the Portland Thorns FC). As captain, she led Canada to the CONCACAF Women's Championship in 2010 and the Pan American gold medal in 2011. In February 2016, Sinclair struck two goals against Costa Rica which guaranteed Canada's qualification for the 2016 Olympics.

Kristine Lilly

Born: 1971
Nationality: American
Position: Midfielder
Caps: 352   **Goals:** 130

A veteran of three Olympic games and five FIFA Women's World Cups, Kristine Lilly began her career at Wilton High School where she was still studying when she was first selected for the US women's national team in 1987. Moving to the University of North Carolina, she played for the Tar Heels women's team there winning four National Collegiate Athletic Association (NCAA) championships (1989-92) and in 1991, became a world champion as the US team won the 1991 World Cup. Moving to Sweden to play for Tyresö FF in 1994, Lilly joined the Washington Warthogs in the short-lived Continental Indoor Soccer League the following year where she was the league's only female player. She would later play for the Boston Breakers in two separate spells (2001-03 and 2009-11) as well as another stint in Sweden with KIF Örebro DFF. Whilst her clubs changed, appearances for the national team remained a constant and Lilly, indispensable to the team, quickly became a record breaker. She reached 300 caps for her country in 2006, against Norway and scored her 105th goal for her country. She finally retired in 2011, becoming the only US footballer to have played national team football in four different decades.

Opposite: Germany goalkeeper Nadine Angerer in action. Top Right: USA's Kristine Lilly (R) tackles China's Liu Ying. Above: Canada forward Christine Sinclair challenges Switzerland goalkeeper Gaelle Thalmann.

TOP WOMEN PLAYERS III

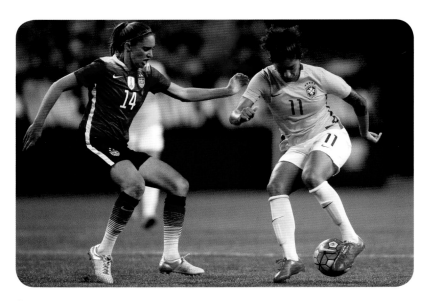

Cristiane

Born: 1985
Nationality: Brazilian
Position: Attacking midfielder, Striker
Caps: 117   **Goals:** 83

Cristiane Rozeira de Souza Silva started out playing for local clubs such as Clube Atlético Juventus in her native city of São Paulo. The talented forward has since become a truly globetrotting footballer enjoying spells for clubs in Germany, Sweden, Russia, South Korea and the United States and in 2015 moved from Brazilian club, Centro Olimpico to France to play for Paris Saint-Germain. An explosive attacker with sudden changes of pace and a strong shot, Cristiane has been joint or outright topscorer at two Olympic games (2004, 2008) and also scored the fastest hat-trick in Olympic history – a 14-minute flurry of three goals against Nigeria in 2008. Her five goals at the 2007 FIFA Women's World Cup helped propel Brazil to the final for the first time. She also scored the first hat-trick in WPS (Women's Professional Soccer) for the Chicago Red Stars in 2009 and at the 2015 Pan American Games which Brazil won, scored five goals in a single game, versus Ecuador.

Louisa Nécib

Born: 1987
Nationality: French
Position: Midfielder
Caps: 136   **Goals:** 34

Starting out by playing for two hometown clubs, Union Sportive de Marseille and Celtic de Marseille, Nécib was spotted and signed by Clairefontaine and helped her gain promotion to Division 2 in 2004, and after a short spell at Montpellier, was signed by Lyon in 2007.

The combination of Nécib and Lyon proved unstoppable as they romped to the Division 1 title and succeeded in capturing two UEFA Women's Champions League titles (2010-11, 2011-12). Nécib has been nicknamed, "the female Zidane" partly for her part-Algerian ancestry and early football career in Marseille (just like Zinédine Zidane) but mostly for superb technical skills, vision and passing range similar to the French maestro. After her international debut in 2005, Nécib has become a vital cog in the French national team and was picked in the 2011 World Cup All-Star Team after playing a full part in securing a top four finish for France.

Abby Wambach

Born: 1980
Nationality: American
Position: Striker
Caps: 255   **Goals:** 184

The world-leading women's international goalscorer, Wambach started out at Florida University setting numerous scoring records for the Florida Gators before moving to Washington Freedom in 2002 to compete in the WUSA professional league where she scored ten goals and made ten assists in her first season. She also scored her first international goal, against Finland, that year. The U.S. Soccer Federation's Soccer Athlete of the Year on six occasions (2003, 2004, 2007, 2010, 2011, 2013), Wambach proved tough, tenacious and tireless. Her physical presence and aerial threat regularly provided the US national team with an outlet in attack and a focal point for attacking crosses and set pieces. Her last Women's World Cup goal was the winner in a close 1-0 match versus Nigeria in 2015 and later that year, her 184th and final goal for the US women's team came against Costa Rica in 2015 before she announced her retirement later that year.

Lotta Schelin

Born: 1984
Nationality: Swedish
Position: Striker, winger
Caps: 154   **Goals:** 80

Schelin started out playing alongside her sister, Camilla, at local club, Kållereds SK, before signing for professional side Göteborg FC at the age of 17. She would resist overtures to play in North America and stay with the Swedish side for seven seasons, bouncing back from career-threatening injuries, to become the league top scorer in 2007. In the following year she moved to French side, Lyon. Forming a strong understanding at Lyon with players like Louisa Nécib and Amandine Henry, Schelin has won seven French women's league titles and four French cups as well as two UEFA Women's Champions League titles. Internationally, her consistently strong performances have aided Sweden to third place finishes at both the 2011 FIFA Women's World Cup and EURO 2013; at the latter tournament, she was the Golden Boot winner as its top scorer. It was only a matter of time before Schelin broke the Swedish all-time goalscoring record of 72 goals by Hanna Ljungberg, a feat which occurred in 2014 when she scored her 73rd goal for Sweden in a match versus Germany.

Kelly Smith

Born: 1978
Nationality: English
Position: Striker
Caps: 117   **Goals:** 46

Smith's father formed a team, Pinner Ladies, to allow his daughter to play after she was thrown out of a local boy's team after complaints from teammates' parents. She joined Wembley Ladies in 1994 and the following year won player of the match on her international debut on the left wing against Italy. Just over two weeks later, she scored her first goal for England in a 5-0 thrashing of Croatia and in 1996, began the first of three spells playing for Arsenal Ladies punctuated by periods playing for fully professional teams in the United States including the New Jersey Lady Stallions, the Philadelphia Charge and the Boston Breakers. Although dogged by injuries at different times throughout her career, the quick-footed Smith always possessed a natural eye for goal and scored freely for both club and country, becoming England's record national team goalscorer with two hat-tricks versus Hungary and the Netherlands in 2007 World Cup qualifying matches and her last goal came in a thrilling 4-4 draw with Scotland in 2013.

Hope Solo

Born: 1981
Nationality: American
Position: Goalkeeper
Caps: 193   **Goals:** 0

A two time Olympic gold medalist and 2015 FIFA Women's World Cup champion, Solo started out playing collegiate football at the University of Washington before joining the Philadelphia Charge in the Women's United Soccer Association (WUSA). The much-traveled keeper played for seven further clubs including Lyons in France and the Atlanta Beat before joining National Women's Soccer League club, Seattle Reign in 2013. Solo made her national team debut versus Iceland in 2000 but had a long wait as understudy to Briana Scurry before becoming first choice keeper for the US side. Voted the best goalkeeper of both the 2011 and 2015 Women's World Cup, Solo has kept 96 clean sheets, a record in women's international football.

Opposite Top Left: Brazil forward Cristiane shields the ball back from United States midfielder Morgan Brian. Opposite Bottom: France midfielder Louisa Neçib scores against Germany at the FIFA 2015 Women's World Cup. Above: England's Kelly Smith (R) in action against Ukraine. Above Right: United States goalkeeper Hope Solo makes a save against Germany.

The Women's World Cup

After much lobbying from players, coaches and officials in women's football, FIFA trialed a global women's tournament featuring 12 invited teams in China in 1988. The tournament saw Brazil finish third with Norway triumphing over Sweden in an all-Scandinavian final. Its success gave FIFA the impetus to introduce an official Women's World Cup starting in 1991. The six editions of the tournament since that time has seen the competition grow at an impressive rate as more teams entered qualifying, the quality of play and matches soared, and media and public interest rose. The 2015 tournament was watched by over 1.3 million live spectators and, according to FIFA, the global TV audience measured in hundreds of millions with a further 86 million following matches online or via a mobile device.

1991 Women's World Cup

Hosts: China
Games: 26   Goals: 99
Final: USA 2 Norway 1

Some 510,000 live spectators came to witness history at the inaugural Women's World Cup where the host's defender, Ma Li, scored the first goal in the opening game - a 4-0 victory over Norway, one of the twelve team tournament's favorites. China would progress from their four-team group only to be knocked out by a Sweden team who recorded the tournament's highest scoreline — an 8-0 defeat of Japan — but were knocked out at the semi-final stage by Norway who had bounced back from their opening defeat. The Norwegian side faced the US in the final for whom Michelle Akers was in prime form. Her two goals in the 20th and 78th minute of the final made the US champions and her the Golden Shoe winner as the most prolific goalscorer with 10 goals overall.

1995 Women's World Cup

Hosts: Sweden
Games: 26   Goals: 99
Final: Norway 2 Germany 0

The 1995 tournament saw Japan's Homare Sawa and Brazilian midfielder, Formiga make their World Cup debuts. Both players would appear at the five tournaments that followed, an incredible long service record. The tournament followed the same format as before with three groups of four teams from which the top two sides in each group qualified plus the next two teams with the highest points tally – in this case, Denmark and Japan. Germany had finished top of Group A and cruised past England and China in the knockout stages to reach the final where they faced a Norwegian team who exacted revenge on the US for their 1991 final defeat via Ann Kristin Aarønes' sixth goal of the tournament. Whilst she didn't score in the final, player of the tournament, Hege Riise and Marianne Pettersen did, to make Norway both European and World champions.

1999 Women's World Cup

Hosts: United States
Games: 32   Goals: 123
Final: United States 0 (5) China 0 (4) penalties after extra time

The tournament expanded with 16 teams playing in four groups. Whilst two teams qualified from each group, the four group winners (USA, China, Brazil and Norway) proved the standout teams as all four made it unbeaten to the semi-finals. There China, propelled by the prowess of players such as Sun Wen, Liu Ailing and Gao Hong, overpowered the defending champions Norway 5-0 and became the highest scorers in the tournament with 19 goals in total. Neither they nor the US team could find a way past each other's defense in the final which was witnessed by a world record attendance for a female sports event of 90,185 in Pasadena's Rose Bowl. The final went to a shootout with Briana Scurry the heroine as she saved China's third penalty to give the US their first Women's World Cup and the only one so far won by a host country.

2003 Women's World Cup

Hosts: United States
Games: 32   Goals: 107
Final: Germany 2 Sweden 1

The SARS epidemic in Asia saw the tournament moved from China to the United States. China kept their automatic qualification status whilst some 99 teams battled it out in qualification for the remaining 15 places, with Argentina, France and South Korea all making their tournament debuts. Canada recovered well from a Group C defeat to Germany to beat Japan, Argentina and knock out China in the quarter finals (their first victory over China in 12 matches) but lost to Sweden at the semi-final stage. Germany, with top scorer Birgit Prinz in prime form, bestrode the tournament scoring 25 goals, 11 more than any other team as they powered through the group and knockout stages and defeated the hosts and defending champions 3-0 in the semi-finals. In the final, Sweden struck first via Hanna Ljungberg's 41st minute goal but Germany hit back five minutes later and the game went into extra time. There, Nia Künzer, an 88th minute substitute, scored the winning golden goal for Germany ten minutes later.

Opposite: US midfielder Carli Lloyd celebrates after beating Japan in the final of the FIFA 2015 Women's World Cup. Top Left: Heidi Mohr (L) in action in the 1991 Women's World Cup. Top Right: USA's Michelle Akers slots away a penalty scores against Brazilian goalie Maravilha in their Women's World Cup semi-final match.

The Women's World Cup contd.

2007 Women's World Cup

Hosts: China
Games: 32   **Goals: 111**
Final: Germany 2 Brazil 0

Over 1.1 million spectators attended the tournament, the first Women's World Cup to feature prize money bonuses dependent on progression. Many were Chinese fans hoping for success but their side struggled, beaten 4-0 by Brazil in their group and knocked out in the quarter finals by Norway. Elsewhere, Germany smashed Argentina 11-0, contended with a rare goal-less draw (versus England) but then cruised through the latter stages, astonishingly failing to concede a single goal in the tournament. In the other half of the draw, it was Brazil who emerged as their biggest threat, especially after Marta, Cristiane and Osborne all struck to defeat the US team 4-0 in the semi-final. Whilst Brazil's key attacking force, Marta, would be awarded the Golden Shoe as top goalscorer (with 7 goals) and the Golden Ball as the tournament's best player, it was Germany who came away as champions and the first team to defend the trophy successfully.

2011 Women's World Cup

Hosts: Germany
Games: 32   **Goals: 86**
Final: Japan 2 (3) USA 2 (1) penalties after extra time

Germany won the bid process contested by six nations – from Australia to Peru – to host the fifth edition of the tournament. But on the pitch, there was to be no three-in-a-row triumph for their team as they were sensationally knocked out of the tournament by an extra-time goal from diminutive striker Karina Maruyama, taking Japan into the semi-finals for the very first time. China had failed to qualify for the tournament for the first time but Colombia and Equatorial Guinea made their Women's World Cup debuts whilst Australia qualified ahead of Norway out of their group and England topped their group but were knocked out in the quarter finals by France after a tense penalty shootout. Japan, for whom Homare Sawa proved hugely influential as well as becoming the tournament top scorer, faced a strong US team in the final which went to extra time and then a shootout. There, Shannon Boxx, Carli Lloyd and Tobin Heath all missed penalties for the US as Japan emerged triumphant.

2015 Women's World Cup

Hosts: Canada
Games: 52   **Goals: 146**
Final: USA 5 Japan 2

The first Women's World Cup to feature 24 teams, the tournament was played on artificial turf at six stadia and provided some captivating entertainment. A record 134 women's national teams entered qualifying which resulted in eight new debutantes at the tournament (Netherlands, Spain, Switzerland, Thailand, Ecuador, Ivory Coast, Cameroon and Costa Rica) and a newly-instituted Round of 16 before the quarter final stage. During the group states, occasional mismatches in team quality resulted in thrashings such as Germany's 10-0 defeat of Ivory Coast and Switzerland's 10-1 victory over Ecuador. Yet, many games were tense and close with 75% of the Round of 16 and quarter final games decided by a single goal. Old foes Germany, the US and Japan made it to the semi-finals where they were joined by England who knocked out the hosts, 2-1 with goals from Jodie Taylor and Lucy Bronze, fell to Japan by the same scoreline in the semi-finals but defeated Germany to finish the tournament in third place. The final saw Carli Lloyd score the fastest Women's World Cup hat-trick with stunning strikes in the third, fifth and 16th minutes, the third a memorable effort from the halfway line, confirmed the US team as champions and Lloyd as joint top scorer along with Germany's Célia Šaši, both on six goals.

Above: German players celebrate victory of the World Cup final 2003 amid dejected Swedish players. Opposite Top: Homare Sawa of Japan lifts the trophy after winning the FIFA Women's World Cup. Bottom: Germany's team celebrates after defeating Brazil in the final of the 2007 FIFA Women's World Cup.

CHAMPIONS

Women's International Competitions

Football associations were slow to offer meaningful competitions for women's international football but today, all confederations have at least one major competition for the elite teams from the confederation's continent or region. The boost given by the establishment of the **FIFA Women's World Cup** led to other continental or invitational tournaments being established for women's national teams or, in the case of competitions already founded before the arrival of the World Cup, gave them the impetus to expand and increase team numbers.

UEFA Women's European Championship

Starting out as the unofficial UEFA European Competition for Representative Women's Teams in 1984, the inaugural tournament was played with a smaller, size 4, ball and featured halves lasting just 35 minutes each. Sweden won the competition, defeating England in the final and would learn what being beaten finalists was like in the subsequent competition held in 1987 and, additionally in 1995 and 2001. By this time, the tournament had been given full, official status and had been renamed the Women's European Championship in time for the 1991 competition in Denmark. This tournament marked the first time a unified Germany competed and won the competition. It would not be the last as successive German sides ran rampant at the Women's EUROs, winning all bar one of the competitions, including six in a row from 1995 to 2013. Early editions only featured four teams at the finals but this was expanded to eight in 1997, twelve in 2009 and sixteen for the forthcoming 2017 competition to be held in the Netherlands.

The Olympics

After much lobbying, a women's football competition at the Olympics finally became a reality at the 1996 games held in Atlanta, Georgia. With no time to organize and stage qualifying matches globally, the inaugural tournament featured the eight nations that finished in the top eight places at the 1995 FIFA World Cup. Unlike the men's tournament, there are no age restrictions on players and national teams field their full strength squads for the chance of winning a precious Olympic medal. Eight women's teams so far have stood on the Olympic medal podium, Japan and Canada both gaining their first women's football medals at London 2012, the first to feature a team containing Scottish and English players competing under the banner of Great Britain. This team topped their group but were knocked out by Canada who despite an epic hat-trick from tournament leading scorer Christine Sinclair in the semi-final versus the United States lost 4-3 in the semi-finals. The American team, as has been the case at all bar one of the women's Olympic tournaments, were unstoppable and defeated Japan in the final to win their fourth Olympic title. Only a final defeat to Norway in 2000 blemishes their perfect record.

CONMEBOL Competitions

The Copa América Femenina (formerly known as the Campeonato Sudamericano de Fútbol Femenino) was first held in 1991, featured just three teams (Brazil, Chile and Venezuela) and acted as qualifying for the 1991 FIFA Women's World Cup. Subsequent tournaments have also provided World Cup attending teams from South America although the competition format has extended to ten teams in 2014 who contest a league with round robin matches. Brazil have been the most successful side taking part, winning six of the first seven tournaments with Argentina the other victors. In recent editions, though, Colombia have reached two finals and finished third in the last four tournaments. In 2009, with the burgeoning interest in women's football in the region, CONMEBOL establish a continental competition for clubs in 2009. As in the Copa América Femenina, the Copa Libertadores de Fútbol Femenino has been dominated by Brazil with Santos beating Universidad Autónoma in the first final in 1991, by a record 9-0 margin whilst fellow Brazilian club, São José have won the competition three times (2011, 2013, 2014).

Opposite: Germany celebrate their UEFA Women's European Championship win in 2009. Above: US midfielder Tobin Heath (17) and Canada's Ashley Lawrence fight for possession during the 2016 CONCACAF women's Olympic soccer tournament. Top Right: Carli Lloyd of the US heads in past Japan goalkeeper Miho Fukumoto in the women's final at the London 2012 Olympic Games. Bottom: North Korea's Kim Kyong Hwa on her knees as Sweden's players celebrate a Charlotta Schelin goal.

Women's International Competitions contd.

African Women's Championship

The Confederation of African Football first organized a continent-wide eight team tournament for female teams in 1991 to act as a qualifier for the 1991 Women's World Cup. Nigeria and Cameroon contested the final and these two teams are the only ones to qualify for and attend all 11 championships so far, although Cameroon did withdraw from the 1995 competition at the quarter final stage. Nigeria have dominated the competition and in 2014, when they again met and defeated their old rivals Cameroon in the final, it would be their ninth championship title. Nigeria's leading striker throughout the 2000s, Perpetua Nkwocha, was four times the tournament's top scorer (2002, 2004, 2006, 2010) and in 2010 scored a record 11 goals in a competition which saw Nigeria defeat Equatorial Guinea, the only other team besides Nigeria to win the competition (2008, 2012). South Africa and Ghana are the competing teams who have got close the most times; South Africa have reached the semi-final stage at eight championships and the final at four, whilst Ghana have been runners-up three times. In 2015, CAF decided to rename the competition, which will be held in Cameroon in 2016, as the Africa Women Cup of Nations.

AFC Women's Asian Cup

Asia can lay claim to the oldest surviving continental tournament for national women's teams as the Women's Asian Cup was first played for in 1975 in Hong Kong. The inaugural tournament was won by invited side, New Zealand who defeated Thailand in the final. Held mostly biannually ever since, Far Eastern and Pacific Rim nations have tended to predominate in the competition with China embarking upon a run of seven successive triumphs between 1986 and 1999 as well as a further victory in 2006. In more recent times, however, the competition has been more open and has seen North Korea win a trio of titles (2001, 2003, 2008) and Australia emerge as a force in the competition with "the Mathildas" reaching their first final in 2006, winning the competition in 2010 and becoming losing finalists for the second time in 2014 when Japan won the competition for the first time. Thirteen different nations have reached the semi-final stage of the Women's Asian Cup including Malaysia, India and Singapore.

CONCACAF Women's Tournaments

First held in 1991, tournaments are organized by CONCACAF as a way of determining qualifiers for the FIFA Women's World Cup. Two of the tournaments, in 1993 and 2000 were not held in a World Cup cycle and as a result also featured teams invited from other confederations such as China from the AFC. In both competitions, an invitee made it to the final (Brazil in 1993, New Zealand in 2000) but lost to the United States who have dominated the competition, winning seven of the nine tournaments so far, the latest in 2014 when they defeated Costa Rica 6-0 in the final. The US dominance was knocked in 2010 when Verónica Pérez-Murillo's 26th minute goal gave Mexico victory and knocked the US out of the competition which was eventually won by Canada for a second time. Their first victory had also came against Mexico, but in the 1998 tournament.

OFC Women's Championship

Oceania has held a women's competition since 1983 which has been dominated by Australia and New Zealand although invited guest side, Chinese Taipei (Taiwan) won both the 1986 and 1989 editions of the competition. The 2014 competition hosted by Papua New Guinea involved the top four teams after qualifying playing each other in round robin fashion. New Zealand were in imperious form, overpowering the Cook Islands 11-0 and thrashing Tonga 17-0 to win their third consecutive title.

Left: Nigeria's Olaitan Yusuf is challenged by Ghana's Rosemary Konadu in their African Women's Soccer Championship game, 2000. Opposite Top: North Korea's Song Jong-sun in action with Australia's Elise Kellond-Knight during their AFC Women's Asian Cup 2010 final. Right: Brazil celebrate with the Copa América Femenina trophy, 2014.

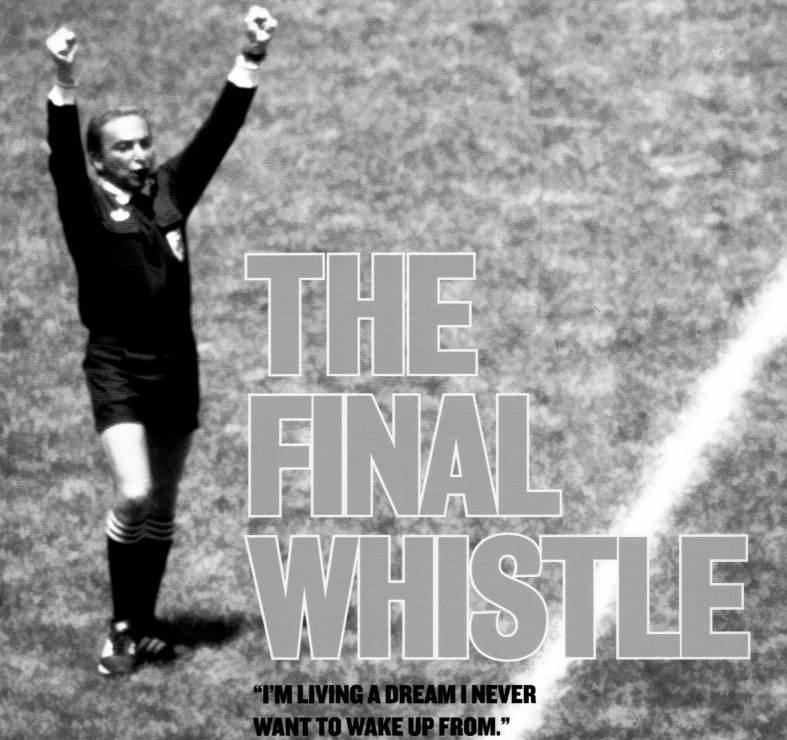

THE FINAL WHISTLE

"I'M LIVING A DREAM I NEVER WANT TO WAKE UP FROM."
CRISTIANO RONALDO

WORST EVER STADIUM DISASTERS

Football doesn't just make headlines on the back page – it lights up the front page too, and usually for all the wrong reasons. Wherever large crowds gather, accidents can, and do, happen, with tragic results.

1. Lima football disaster

Where: Estadio Nacional, Lima, Peru
When: 24 May 1964
Fatalities: 328

It's a record that no-one would want to have, the worst disaster in the history of football, and like so many others it could so easily have been prevented.

It happened in an Olympic qualifier, when Argentina played Peru at Peru's national stadium in the capital Lima. In the closing minutes the home side scored what seemed to be the equalizer, only for the referee to disallow it. Angered, Peru's fans got onto the pitch and challenged the official, and the police responded with tear gas. The crowd panicked and ran down flights of steps to the exits, only to find them locked as the game was not yet over. As the fleeing crowd swelled and tried to push forwards, those at the back were unaware of the disaster unfolding at the front, where people were crushed and suffocated against the closed exits.

2. Accra Sports Stadium disaster

Where: Accra Sports Stadium, Accra, Ghana
When: 9 May 2001
Fatalities: 127

Ghana's two most successful football teams, Accra Hearts of Oak Sporting Club and Asante Kotoko, faced each other at Accra Sports Stadium. Trouble had been anticipated, and extra security measures had been taken, and when the home side scored two late goals to defeat Kotoko 2–1, the visiting fans began throwing plastic seats and bottles onto the pitch. The police responded with tear gas and rubber bullets, causing the crowd to panic. In the stampede to leave the stadium, 127 people were crushed to death and asphyxiated, making it Africa's worst stadium disaster.

3. Hillsborough Stadium disaster

Where: Hillsborough Stadium, Sheffield, England
When: 15 April 1989
Fatalities: 96

Liverpool and Nottingham Forest supporters made their way to neutral territory in the city of Sheffield for the semi-final of the FA Cup, to a stadium that was ill-prepared for those that made the journey.

Thousands of Liverpool fans were directed to one end of Hillsborough Stadium, to a stand set aside for them away from opposition fans. With the turnstiles unable to cope with the influx of so many people, the exit gates were opened in an attempt to reduce the congestion outside the ground. Fans rushed through, eager to find a place on an already packed stand, and as the numbers increased those at the front were pushed forward until they were crushed up against a fence. In chaotic scenes, fans tried to escape from the overcrowded stand by climbing over the fence, or hauling themselves up into the upper tier. The worst disaster in English football claimed the lives of 96 people, and brought an end to standing terraces at English stadiums.

Opposite Bottom Left: Scenes from the Lima diaster. Opposite Top Right: Friends and relatives look down the stairwell where so many sustained injury and fatalities at Accra. Top Right: Hillsborough Stadium - Sheffield - 15/4/89 An injured fan is treated by a St John Ambulance worker and his friend after being crushed by overcrowding. Above: Fans climb out of the Leppings Lane terrace into the West Stand to escape the crush as supporters continued to pour into the ground.
Right: A memorial to the 96 who lost their lives at Hillsborough.

WORST EVER STADIUM DISASTERS Contd.

4. Kathmandu Stadium disaster

Where: Dashrath Stadium, Kathmandu, Nepal
When: 12 March 1988
Fatalities: at least 93

Dashrath Stadium is Nepal's national football stadium, in
the capital, Kathmandu. In a match between Nepalese and
Bangladeshi teams in 1988, a sudden hailstorm forced supporters
in the stadium's three open stands to run for cover in the west,
covered, stand.

On seeing a crush developing, police began to beat the crowd,
causing panic and a rush toward tunnels leading to the exits, which
were locked as the game was underway. In the surge that developed,
people at the back of the tunnels pushed those in front, crushing to
death those trapped at the exit barriers.

5. Mateo Flores National Stadium disaster

Where: Mateo Flores National Stadium, Guatemala City, Guatemala
When: 16 October 1996
Fatalities: 84

Such was the interest to see the 1998 World Cup qualifying
match between Guatemala and Costa Rica, a huge crowd had
turned up at Guatemala's National Stadium. Designed for 37,500,
some estimates claim that 50,000 fans pushed their way into the
stadium, some of whom had come with counterfeit tickets.

In the inevitable surge as fans pushed their way inside, many
were crushed to death against the fence separating the stands and
the pitch.

6. Port Said Stadium disaster

Where: Port Said Stadium, Port Said, Egypt
When: 1 February 2012
Fatalities: 74

Kick-off for the game was delayed thirty minutes because El Masry
(Port Said) fans repeatedly stormed the pitch, as they did during
half-time and after each of the three second-half goals for El
Masry. At the end of the match, thousands of spectators ran onto
the playing field. El Masry fans threw bottles and fireworks at the
visiting El Ahly players, who fled to their changing rooms under
police protection. The Masry fans, armed with clubs, swords, knives,
fireworks and rocks, attacked the El Ahly (Cairo) fans, who tried to
flee, but were unable to do so, as at least some of the stadium gates
were locked. In the riot that followed, the police were ineffective
and may actually have made matters worse by opening barricades
between the two groups of supporters. The riot only ended when the
Egyptian military was called in. As a result of the riot, 74 people
were killed and more than 500 were injured. Some were stabbed
and clubbed, while others were thrown off the stands or died in the
stampede as they were trying to escape through a closed stadium
gate in the back of the stands. Eyewitnesses said that the police "did
nothing to stop it," and "refused to open the closed gates" to allow
the crowds to escape. The Egyptian army airlifted in soldiers by
helicopter to rescue the players, who were stranded in their locker
rooms. Seventy-three defendants, including 9 police officers and
2 officials from Port Said's Al-Masry club, were charged in the
killing of 74 Ahly football club fans. On 26 January 2013, Port
Said Criminal Court, convening at the Police Academy in New
Cairo for security reasons, issued preliminary death sentences
to 21 defendants. A verdict against the other 52 defendants was
postponed. The Egyptian government shut down the domestic
league for two years.

7. Puerta 12 disaster

Where: El Monumental (River Plate Stadium), Buenos Aires, Argentina
When: 23 June 1968
Fatalities: 71

Disaster struck at the end of the match between home side River Plate and arch-rivals Boca Juniors, when River Plate supporters in the upper tier set light to flags and newspapers and dropped them onto the Boca fans below.

As they rushed to escape from the burning debris, the Boca fans made for the nearest exit – Puerta 12 (Gate 12) – only to find it was locked. Unable to get out, many were crushed to death at this gate, which was at the center of the tragedy.

8. Lenin Stadium disaster

Where: Lenin Stadium (Luzhniki Stadium), Moscow
When: 20 October 1982
Fatalities: 66

Due to the weather in Moscow being snowy and extraordinarily cold for the middle of October, a crowd of some 16,500 fans (despite 82,000 match tickets being available) had braved the bitter weather to watch the 1982–83 UEFA Cup clash between Spartak Moscow and Dutch side Haarlem. As the match neared the end, the cold spectators started to leave the stadium. Many were headed for the exit closest to the underground metro station, hoping to get away quickly.

With so many people in a hurry, it takes only one person to fall to cause a pile-up – which is what happened. According to the interviewed witnesses, one of the fans fell at the lower steps of Stairway 1. According to some, it was a young woman who had lost her shoe on the stairs and stopped, trying to retrieve it and put it back on. Some people also stopped, trying to help, but the moving dense crowd on the stairs, limited by metal banisters, began crushing those in front and below. They began to stumble over the bodies of those who were crushed and a domino effect followed. More and more mostly teenage fans were joining the crowd on the stairs, trying to push their way through, unaware of the tragedy unfolding below, which caused a massive chain-reaction pile-up of people. A total of 66 people died. All of the deceased victims died of compressive asphyxia.

Opposite Bottom Left: Mateo Flores National Stadium disaster aftermath. Opposite Top: Al Ahli Soccer players try to leave the stadium as chaos erupts at the end of the game. Above Left: A man holds a lit flare at Tahrir Square in Cairo January 18, 2013, during a protest demanding justice for 74 people killed in the stadium stampede in Port Said. Above Right: People react after hearing the final verdict of the massacre, in Port Said, January 26, 2013. An Egyptian court sentenced 21 people found guilty of involvement to death.

WORST EVER STADIUM DISASTERS Contd.

9. 1971 Ibrox disaster

Where: Ibrox Park, Glasgow, Scotland
When: 2 January 1971
Fatalities: 66

Glasgow's two great football teams – Rangers and Celtic, together known as The Old Firm are bitter rivals, and any meeting between them is a guaranteed sell-out match. And so it was when the Old Firm clashed at Ibrox Park, the home of Rangers FC, in January 1971.

The game was almost over, and with only minutes left on the clock fans began leaving the ground. As hundreds made their way down Stairway 13, someone at the front fell, starting a domino-like reaction in the people behind who stumbled and fell.

In the resulting mass pile up, 66 people were asphyxiated and crushed to death, and more than 200 were injured.

10. Bradford City stadium fire

Where: Valley Parade Stadium, Bradford, England
When: 11 May 1985
Fatalities: 56

It should have been a day to celebrate – the day that Bradford City FC were presented with the Third Division Trophy and

promotion to what was then the second tier of English football. Instead, the match against Lincoln City FC turned to tragedy. The home crowd was in good spirits, and Bradford's old wooden stand was filled to capacity. Just before half-time, smoke could be seen coming from the stand, and within minutes it was ablaze, the windy conditions fanning the fire.

In the panic, fans spilled out onto the pitch. Others ran for the turnstiles, but found themselves trapped, unable to escape. As was the practice at the time, the turnstiles had been locked once the game

began. By the time the flames were out, 56 were dead and more than 250 were injured.

The inquiry that followed found that rubbish that had been allowed to build up under the stand was the likely seat of the blaze – perhaps ignited by a discarded match or cigarette.

Left: The Bradford City Stadium fire starts. Top: The fire rapidly turned into an inferno. Above: A memorial for the 56 who perished.

WORST STADIUM DISASTERS

Year	Stadium	What happened
1902	Ibrox Park, Glasgow, Scotland	25 died and 517 injured when a stand collapsed during an international between England and Scotland.
1946	Burnden Park, Bolton, England	33 died and 500 injured when a wall collapsed during a match between Bolton and Stoke.
1955	Estadio Nacional, Santiago, Chile	6 died when 70,000 people crammed into the stadium for the final of the South American soccer tournament.
1964	Estadio Nacional, Lima, Peru	328 died in a riot during a match between Argentina and Peru.
1967	Atatürk Stadium, Kayseri, Turkey	43 died and 300 injured after a disallowed goal caused a riot.
1968	El Monumental Stadium, Buenos Aires, Argentina	71 died and 150 injured when fans tried to escape burning newspaper being thrown down from an upper tier, and were trapped due to a closed exit.
1971	Ibrox Park, Glasgow, Scotland	66 died and 200 injured in a crowd crush near the end of a match between Old Firm rivals Celtic and Rangers.
1974	Zamalek Stadium, Cairo, Egypt	At least 48 died and 50 injured as crowds broke barriers and smashed through a wall to gain entry to the stadium.
1981	Karaiskakis Stadium, Piraeus, Greece	21 died and at least 55 injured in a stampede to leave the ground.
1982	Lenin Stadium (Luzhniki Stadium), Moscow, Russia	At least 66 died and more than 300 were injured when fans tried to re-enter the stadium after a last-minute goal.
1982	Estadio Olímpico Pascual Guerrero, Cali, Colombia	24 died and 250 injured in a stampede.
1982	Algiers, Algeria	10 died when a concrete stadium roof collapsed.
1985	Valley Parade, Bradford, England	56 died and 250 injured when fire swept through an antiquated wooden stand.
1985	Heysel Stadium, Brussels, Belgium	39 died and 600 injured in a pre-match riot at the European Cup Final between Liverpool and Juventus.
1988	Dasarath Stadium, Kathmandu, Nepal	At least 93 died and more than 100 injured in a stampede at Nepal's national football stadium.
1989	Hillsborough, Sheffield, England	96 died and at least 200 injured in a crush caused by overcrowding of a stand.
1992	Armand Cesari Stadium, Bastia, Corsica	18 died and 400 injured when a crowded temporary stand collapsed.
1996	Independence Stadium, Lusaka, Zambia	At least 15 died and 50 injured in a stampede following Zambia's victory over Sudan.
1996	Mateo Flores National Stadium, , Guatemala	84 died and 150 injured in a stampede before a match between Guatemala and Costa Rica.
2000	National Sports Stadium, Harare, Zimbabwe	13 died after police fired tear gas into the crowd causing a stampede as fans ran for the exits.
2001	Ellis Park Stadium, Johannesburg, South Africa	43 died and 155 injured as fans pushed their way inside an already overcrowded stadium.
2001	Accra Sports Stadium, Accra, Ghana	127 died after police fired tear gas at fans who were tearing up seats, causing a stampede.
2007	Konkola Stadium, Chililabombwe, Zambia	12 died and 50 injured in a stampede to leave the ground.
2009	Felix Houphouet-Boigny Stadium, Abidjan, Ivory Coast	At least 19 died in a stampede.
2012	Port Said Stadium, Port Said, Egypt	At least 74 died and 500 injured in a riot at the end of a match.

MUNICH AIR DISASTER

On a snowy night in Munich, a plane attempted to take off for a flight to England. On board were the Manchester United football team, nicknamed the "Busby Babes," supporters and journalists, returning home from an away match.

Refueling stop

The date was 6 February 1958, and the rising stars of Manchester United were homeward bound after the previous day's 3–3 draw against Red Star Belgrade in a European Cup match in Belgrade, Yugoslavia (now Serbia). It was a good result for manager Matt Busby, as his young team had claimed a place in the semi-finals, winning 5–4 on aggregate.

The take-off from Belgrade was delayed for an hour after outside right Johnny Berry lost his passport. At 1:15pm the Airspeed Ambassador, carrying six crew and 44 passengers, touched down to refuel at Munich-Riem Airport, West Germany, as the flight from Belgrade to Manchester was beyond the aircraft's range. Refueling wouldn't take long, so everyone stayed on board.

Failed take-offs

A little over an hour later, after refueling, pilots James Thain and Kenneth Rayment were ready to resume the flight, but the first attempt to take-off was abandoned when the pilot became aware the left engine sounded odd while accelerating. A second attempt was made, and that too was abandoned as the engine was over-accelerating. The plane returned to its gate, and the passengers disembarked, expecting to stay in Munich and fly home the next day, but after just fifteen minutes they were called back. Fearing they would get too far behind schedule, Captain Thain rejected an overnight stay in Munich in favor of a third take-off attempt, only this time he would accelerate down the runway at a slower speed to avoid the problems he'd had with the left engine on the previous attempts. Munich had a long runway (2km / 1.2 miles), and the pilot was confident he'd reach take-off speed before the runway ran out.

Manchester United team photo - The 1957 league champions, who were involved in the Munich air disaster of February 6th 1958. Seven of the team died, the rest were injured. Photo shows: (back row L-R) Webster (not on plane); McGuinness (not on plane); Blanchflower (injured); Doherty (not on plane); Colman (dead); (middle row L-R) T. Curry (trainer, dead); Foulkes (injured); Charlton (injured); Goodwin (not on plane); Wood (injured); Whelan (dead); Jones (dead); Edwards (injured); Inglis (trainer, not on plane); (front row L-R) Viollet (injured); Berry (injured); Matt Busby (manager, critically injured); Byrne (captain, dead), Murphy (assistant manager, not on plane); Taylor (dead); Pegg (dead).

Fatal third attempt

By the time of the third attempt at just after 3:00pm, snow was falling, and there was a layer of slush at the end of the runway. The plane headed off down the runway, but failed to reach take-off speed, plowed through the slush and a fence at the end of the runway and crashed into a house, home to a family of six. The father and eldest daughter were away and the mother and the other three children escaped as the house caught fire. Part of the plane's tail was torn off before the left side of the cockpit hit a tree. The right side of the fuselage hit a wooden hut, inside which was a truck filled with tires and fuel, which exploded. Seeing flames around the cockpit, Thain feared that the aircraft would explode and told his crew to evacuate. The stewardesses, Rosemary Cheverton and Margaret Bellis, were the first to leave through an emergency window in the galley, followed by radio officer Bill Rodgers. Rayment was trapped in his seat and told

Thain to go without him. Thain clambered out of the galley window. On reaching the ground, he saw flames growing under the starboard wing, which held 500 gallons (2,300 L) of fuel. He shouted to his crew to get away and climbed back into the aircraft to retrieve two handheld fire extinguishers, stopping to tell Rayment he would be back when the fires had been dealt with.

Meanwhile, regaining consciousness in the cabin, goalkeeper Harry Gregg was thinking that he had died. He felt blood on his face and "didn't dare put his hand up. Thinking the top of his head had been taken off, like a hard boiled egg." Just above him, light shone into the cabin, so Gregg kicked a hole wide enough for him to escape. He also managed to save some passengers.

Cause of the crash

An investigation by West German authorities originally blamed the pilot, Captain James Thain, saying he had not de-ice the aircraft's

Opposite Top Left: An Airspeed Ambassador similar to the one involved in the crash. Opposite Top Right: Emergency crews arrive at the scene. Opposite Bottom Left: The plane wreckage.

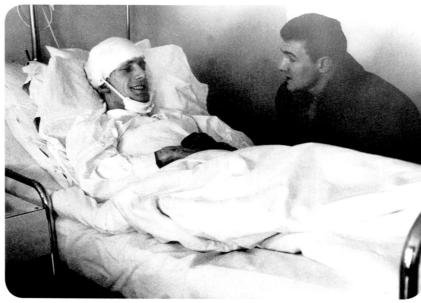

wings, despite eyewitness statements saying he had. Proceedings against Thain dragged on until 1968, when he was finally cleared of any responsibility for the crash. As the official cause, British authorities recorded a build-up of melting snow on the runway which prevented the "Elizabethan" from reaching the required take-off speed. During take-off, the aircraft had reached 117 knots (217 km/h), but, on entering the slush, dropped to 105 knots (194 km/h), too slow to leave the ground, with not enough runway to abort the take-off. Thain, having been dismissed by British European Airways shortly after the accident and never re-engaged, retired and returned to run his poultry farm in Berkshire. He died of a heart attack at the age of 53 in August 1975.

Aftermath

At the time of the crash, Manchester United were trying to become the third club to win three successive English league titles; they were six points behind League leaders Wolverhampton Wanderers with 14 games to go. They also held the Charity Shield and had just advanced into their second successive European Cup semi-final. The team had not been beaten for 11 matches. The crash not only derailed their title ambitions that year but also virtually destroyed the nucleus of what promised to be one of the greatest generations of players in English football history.

The crash claimed the lives of 23 people (20 were killed at the scene), eight of whom were Manchester United players. Seven of Manchester United's players died immediately, and Duncan Edwards

died from his injuries on 21 February at the Rechts der Isar Hospital in Munich. Johnny Berry and Jackie Blanchflower were both injured so severely that they never played again. Matt Busby was seriously injured and had to stay in hospital for more than two months after the crash, and was read his Last Rites twice. After being discharged from hospital, he went to Switzerland to recuperate in Interlaken. At times, he felt like giving up football entirely, until he was told by his wife Jean, "You know Matt, the lads would have wanted you to carry on." That statement lifted Busby from his depression, and he

returned by land to Manchester to begin the slow and painful job of rebuilding his team.

Meanwhile, there was speculation that the club would fold, but a threadbare United team completed the 1957–58 season, with Busby's assistant Jimmy Murphy standing in as manager; he had not traveled to Belgrade as he was in Cardiff managing the Welsh national team at the time. A team largely made up of reserve and youth team players beat Sheffield Wednesday 3–0 in the first match after the disaster. The program for that match showed simply a blank space where each United player's name should have been.

United only won one league game after the crash, causing their title challenge to collapse and they fell to ninth place in the league. They did manage to reach the final of the FA Cup, however, losing 2–0 to Bolton Wanderers, and even managed to beat Milan at Old Trafford in the semi-finals of the European Cup, only to lose 4–0 at the San Siro.

Busby resumed managerial duties the next season (1958–59), and eventually built a second generation of Busby Babes, including George Best and Denis Law, that ten years later won the European Cup, beating Benfica. Bobby Charlton and Bill Foulkes were the only two crash survivors who lined up in that team.

Opposite Top Left: Manchester United star Bobby Charlton lays injured and heavily bandaged in a hospital bed. Opposite Top Right: Dennis Viollet is visited by Bill Foulkes in the Munich hospital. Opposite Bottom: Fans pay their last tribute to Roger Byrne, Manchester United's international captain, as the funeral procession passes. Top: 1958 Duncan Edwards of Manchester United takes to the field for the European Cup Quarter Final against Red Star Belgrade. Above: Old Trafford - 2/2/16 Manchester United fans hold up tributes for the survivors and injured of the Munich Air Disaster before their game against Stoke.

MAD MASCOTS

What is it about football clubs and mascots? The game has enough real characters as it is, without having to invent some bizarre over-stuffed creature with a weird head (invariably a big one) which someone has to dress up as. Get it right, and a mascot will connect the club (or nation) to the fans and inspire support, but get it wrong and an unloved mascot will be quickly sidelined and soon forgotten.

Usually fuzzy and charming with a penchant for mischief, mascots have proven time and time again to be decisive factors for their team's performance. The impact of a positive and powerful mascot cannot be understated.

Mascots come in a variety of shapes, sizes, species and historic time periods, but typically remain relatively straightforward. For example, a team mascot's could be an eagle or a Roman soldier, but nine times out of 10, there will be very little crossover of what they represent.

The word mascot can be traced back to 1867 in Provence and Gascony, France, where it was used to describe anything bringing luck. The French word "mascotte" means talisman, charm, and is derivative of the word "masco" meaning sorceress. In 1880, French composer Edmond Audran wrote a popular comic operetta titled La Mascotte. It was translated into English as The Mascot, thus introducing into the English language a word for any animal, person, or object that brings good luck.

AC Milan's Milanello

Pepe Zorillo, Real Valladolid

FA Cup mascot Billie. Bille was designed by 12-year-old girl, who won a Blue Peter competition

Jünter the Foal, Borussia Mönchengladbach's mascot

Opposite, Clockwise from Top Left: 1966 England's Bobby Charlton pictured with World Cup Willie, official mascot for the 1966 World Cup tournament. Club Tijuana's Xolo Mayor is anything but your normal "fuzzy friend" with a muscular build closer to "club bouncer" than "friend to children.". Moonchester (Manchester City) with girlfriend "Moonbeam". Hammerhead (West Ham) A semi-robotic character, the storyline behind his creation says he was forged when a bolt of lightning struck the Thames Ironworks and Shipbuilding Company, where West Ham were formed over 100 years ago.

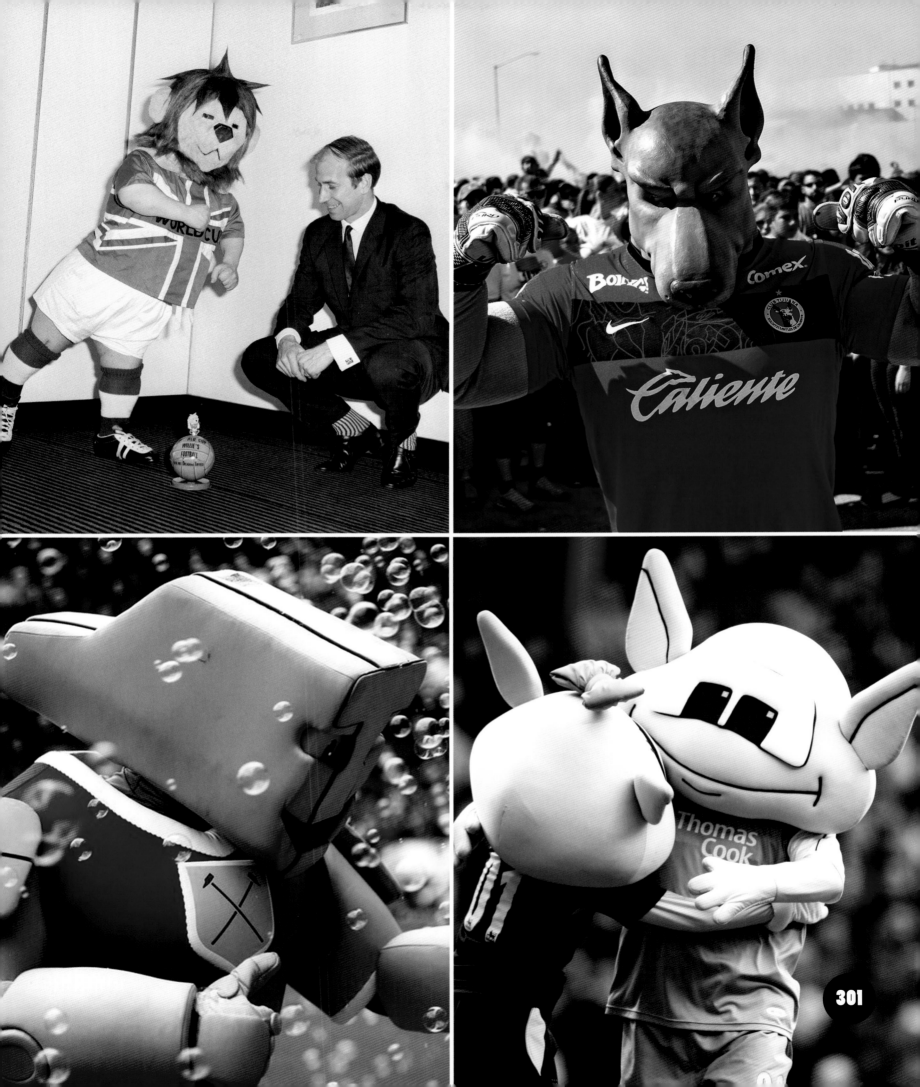

IT'S A FUNNY OLD GAME

Football is an unpredictable game. No one knows what's going to happen, and sometimes the oddest things make us stop and smile. It is, as they say, a funny old game.

TWO GOALS FOR THE PRICE OF ONE

The record books show the 1994 Caribbean Cup qualification match ended Barbados 4 Grenada 2. But the story behind the goals reveals one of football's strangest matches ever.

Barbados needed to beat Grenada by two goals in order to reach the final, and a draw after 90 minutes would result in extra time, which would be decided by a golden goal – the first to score would win. For some reason the organizers had decided that the golden goal would count as two goals. Towards the end of normal time, Barbados, leading 2–0, seemed to be coasting to the final. They had the two goal difference they needed, and that was it. Or so they thought.

With the clock ticking toward 90 minutes, Grenada pulled one back, and Barbados were out of the final. Rather than try to score a third goal to restore their two-goal lead, Barbados did the opposite and scored a deliberate own goal to level the score at 2–2. It forced the match into extra time, and the prospect of scoring a "two-goal golden goal" – which Barbados did after just four minutes, stopping the match and seeing them through to the final!

RED CARD FOR THE REFEREE

The referee is the one who usually shows the red card, but in 2007 Belarusian referee Sergei Shmolik was shown one. In a 1–1 match between Vitebsk and Naftan, he didn't move from the center circle for the entire 90 minutes, other than to wobble precariously around it. Voted the best referee in Belarus, was he trying out a new method of refereeing at a distance? Did he have back trouble and was unable to run, as some suggested? Or was the real reason more to do with a pre-match vodka binge? Escorted from the field at the end of the game, it was straight to the medics and a blood test, which revealed a high level of alcohol in his system, and a red card from the Belarusian FA who suspended him from refereeing.

PITCH INVADERS

There's a long, and not always happy, history of supporters invading the pitch – sometimes in celebration, sometimes in anger, and sometimes for a laugh (though not everyone will see the funny side).

And then there are those pitch invasions entirely beyond the control of the match and stadium officials, when animals stop the game and give hapless players and marshals the runaround.

Dogs are the main culprits. In Brazil, in 2011, a tail-wagging police dog interrupted the game between Ituiutaba and Uberlândia, chasing after the ball just as it would in the park. The playful hound was collared by his embarrassed owner and escorted from the field.

The stray that ran the length and breadth of the field during a 2014 game between Argentina's River Plate and Rosario Central didn't go so quietly. With players and stewards trying to grab it, the stressed animal legged it to the far end of the pitch, and proceeded to poo near the goal, before being caught and carried off the field. It was a clear foul in the box!

In England, in 2012, the Premier League match between Liverpool and Tottenham Hotspur was stopped when a grey and white tabby cat strolled across the pitch, much to the amusement of the 44,000 fans inside Anfield. The homeless moggy had been seen outside the stadium for years, but this was the first time it had found its way inside, instantly becoming an internet sensation known as the "Anfield Cat," complete with thousands of Twitter followers!

FAKE PLAYER

Some people will do just about anything to get onto the pitch. Take Ali Dia, a player from Senegal so desperate to play in the English league he persuaded a friend to make a hoax phone call to Southampton manager Graeme Souness. The friend claimed to be Liberian international and former World Player of the Year, George Weah, and that Dia, his cousin, had played for Senegal and for Paris Saint-Germain, and was looking to move to an English club. Without even seeing him in action, Souness signed the "African international" on a one-month contract. Dia made just one appearance for Southampton, against Leeds United on 23

November 1996, coming on as substitute before being substituted himself. His performance was embarrassing to watch, and Dia was promptly released from his contract. He regularly features in lists of all-time bad players, usually near the top.

PHOTO BOMBER

Eleven players in a football team, right? Not when Manchester United lined up for their team photo in the 2001 Champions League match against Bayern Munich (Below). Standing on the left of the back row was a twelfth man, who'd strolled onto the Munich turf in full United kit, and was promptly snapped by the press photographers. He was Karl Power, a notorious prankster from Manchester, who was soon spotted and led away, but not before he'd claimed his place in football's footnotes.

Power's pranks didn't stop here. He walked out to bat for England against Australia

at Headingley in 2001, beat Michael Schumacher to the podium at the British Grand Prix in 2002, and in 2003 hit a few tennis balls over the net on the Centre Court at Wimbledon, and on the Old Trafford pitch he re-enacted a goal scored by Diego Forlán against Liverpool at Anfield earlier that season. This stunt saw Power banned for life by Manchester United.

FACTS & FIGURES

From earning the minimum of £4 per week in 1901 to multi-millionaire Premier League footballers earning £1m a month - or more, a lot has changed in the financial landscape of the national sport.

After the First World War, professional footballers received a maximum weekly wage of £10. In 1920 the Football League Management Committee proposed a reduction to £9 per week maximum. Players called for the AFU (Association Footballers' Union) to resort to strike action. However, large numbers of players resigned from the union and the Football League was able to impose the reduction. The following year it was reduced to £8 for a 37 weeks playing season and £6 for the 15 weeks close season.

Despite the efforts of the Players' Union, there was no other change until 1945 when the maximum close season wage was increased to £7 per week. Two years later a National Arbitration Tribunal was established. It decided that the maximum wage should be raised to £12 in the playing season and £10 in the close season. The minimum wage for players over 20 was set at £7.

The maximum wage was increased to £14 (1951), £15 (1953), £17 (1957) and £20 (1958). The union argued that in 1939 the footballers' £8 was approximately double the average industrial wage, by 1960 the gap had narrowed to £5 with these figures standing at £20 and £15 respectively.

Further wage demands were called for in 1960 and backed by a threat to strike on 14th January, 1961. The Football League responded by abolishing the maximum wage. Johnny Haynes, the England captain, became the first £100 per-week player.

The average footballer's wage in England's top division has climbed from £20 per week in 1961 to £33,868 per week or thereabouts 50 years later.

Today however, The "superstars" (players and managers alike!) of world football, earn mind-blowing sums of money. Barcelona superstar Lionel Messi banked almost £1million-a-week last year - making him the highest-paid footballer in the world. The Argentine earns over £26million in his basic salary before bonuses - and almost the same again in commercial deals with the likes of Adidas and Turkish Airlines. According to France Football's annual survey of wages, Messi's total income is around a staggering £47.8 million!

TOP 15 FOOTBALLERS WITH HIGHEST SALARY IN 2015-16 SEASON

NO#	PLAYER	WEEKLY	YEARLY
1	Cristiano Ronaldo (Real Madrid)	£288,000*	£15 million*
2	Lionel Messi (FC Barcelona)	£275,000*	£14.5 million*
3	Wayne Rooney (Man United)	£250,000	£13 million
4	Zlatan Ibrahimović (PSG)	£250,000	£13 million
5	Yaya Touré (Man City)	£230,000	£11.9 million
6	Sergio Agüero (Man City)	£230,000	£11.9 million
7	Asamoah Gyan (Shanghai SIPG)	£227,000	£11.8 million
8	Neymar (Barcelona)	£220,000	£11.4 million
9	David Silva (Man City)	£210,000	£10.9 million
10	Luis Suárez (Barcelona)	£205,000	£10.66 million
11	Gareth Bale (Real Madrid)	£200,000	£10 million
12	David De Gea (Man United)	£200,000	£10 million
13	Bastian Schweinsteiger (Man Utd)	£200,000	£10 million
14	Thiago Silva (PSG)	£185,000	£9.6 million
15	Eden Hazard (Chelsea)	£185,000	£9.6 million

* indicates salary after tax
(Basic Salary, not including bonuses and endorsements)

HIGHEST PAID FOOTBALL MANAGERS AROUND THE WORLD

NO#	MANAGER	TEAM	SALARY
1	Pep Guardiola (New)	Manchester City	£15m
2	Pep Guardiola	Bayern Munich	£14.8m
3	Arsène Wenger	Arsenal	£8.30m
4	Zinédine Zidane	Real Madrid	£8m
5	Louis Van Gaal	Manchester United	£7.3m
6	Jürgen Klopp	Liverpool	£7m
7	José Enrique	FC Barcelona	£7m
8	Rafael Benítez	Newcastle United	£4.5m
9	Roberto Mancini	Inter Milan	£4.30m
10	Antonio Conte	Italy	£3.95m
11	Manuel Pellegrini	Manchester City	£4.2m
12	Massimiliano Allegri	Juventus	£3.50m
13	Laurent Blanc	PSG	£3.45m
14	Jorge Jesus	Benfica	£3.34m
15	Roberto Martínez	Everton	£3m
16	Slaven Bilić	West Ham United	£2.95m
17	Roy Hodgson	England	£2.95m
18	Joachim Low	Germany	£2.80m
19	Dunga	Brazil	£2.50m
20	Ronald Koeman	Southampton FC	£2.30m

(Basic Salary, not including bonuses and endorsements)

WORLD'S TOP 20 RICHEST FOOTBALL CLUBS IN 2016

NO#	CLUB	VALUE	REVENUE	2015
1	Real Madrid	$3.26 billion	$746m	1st
2	FC Barcelona	$3.17 billion	$657m	2nd
3	Manchester United	$3.10 billion	$703m	3rd
4	Bayern Munich	$2.34 billion	$661m	4th
5	Manchester City	$1.37 billion	$562m	7th
6	Chelsea	$1.36 billion	$526m	6th
7	Arsenal	$1.30 billion	$486m	5th
8	Liverpool	$982 million	$415m	10th
9	Juventus	$837 million	$379m	9th
10	AC Milan	$775 million	$339m	8th
11	Borussia Dortmund	$700 million	$355m	11th
12	Paris Saint-Germain	$634 million	$645m	15th
13	Tottenham Hotspurs	$600 million	$293m	13th
14	FC Schalke	$572 million	$290m	12th
15	Inter Milan	$439 million	$222m	14th
16	Atlético Madrid	$436 million	$231m	17th
17	Napoli	$353 million	$224m	New
18	Newcastle United	$349 million	$210m	New
19	West Ham United	$309 million	$186m	New
20	Galatasaray	$294 million	$220m	16th

TRANSFER RECORDS

There's money in football, and when the £100 transfer barrier was broken in 1893 with the transfer of Willie Groves from West Bromwich Albion to Aston Villa there must have been some mutterings in the stands. Since then, of course, transfer fees have risen to almost unimaginable heights.

The first £100 transfer fee for a player was Scottish striker Willie Groves when he made the switch from West Bromwich Albion to Aston Villa in 1893, eight years after the legalization of professionalism in the sport. Twelve years later the figure would become £1000, when Sunderland striker Alf Common moved to Middlesbrough. It wasn't until 1928 that the first five-figure transfer took place with David Jack of Bolton Wanderers courted by Arsenal, and in order to negotiate the fee down, Arsenal manager Herbert Chapman got the Bolton representatives drunk. As a result, David Jack was transferred for a world record fee when Arsenal paid £10,890 to land their man.

The first player from outside Great Britain to break the record was Bernabé Ferreyra, a player known as La Fiera for his powerful shot. His 1932 transfer from Tigre to River Plate cost £23k. In 1961, Luis Suárez Miramontes was sold by FC Barcelona to Inter Milan for £152k, becoming the first ever player sold for more than £100k.

2013 Gareth BALE (Wales) £85,300,000

2009 Christiano RONALDO (Portugal) £80,000,000

1999 Christian VIERA (Italy) £32,100,000

1987 Ruud GILLIT (Holland) £6,000,000

1976 Paolo ROSSI (Italy) £1,750,000

1968 Pietro ANASTASI (Italy) £500,000

1957 Enrique OMAR SÍVORI (Argentina) £93,000

1949 Eddie QUIGLEY (England) £26,500

1932 Bernabé FERREYRA (Argentina) £93,000

1914 Percy DAWSON (England) £2,500

1905 Alf COMMON (England) £1,000

1893 Willie GROVES (Scotland) £100

1st: Gareth Bale, Tottenham to Real Madrid, £86m

2nd: Cristiano Ronaldo, Man United to Real Madrid, £80m.

3rd: Luis Suárez, Liverpool to Barcelona, £75m.

4th: Neymar, Santos to Barcelona, £71.5m

FOOTBALLERS' INJURIES

Playing football should come with a health warning. Professional footballers know they are at risk of picking up an occupational injury, the worst of which can end a career in an instant. Fortunately, such injuries are rare. More common are the ones that force a player to miss a few games.

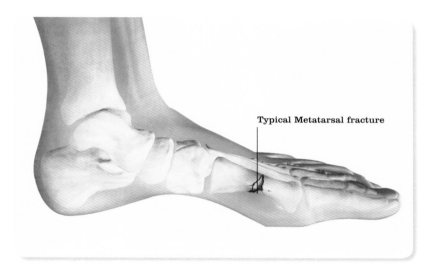

Typical Metatarsal fracture

Metatarsal fracture

The metatarsal bones are a group of five long bones in the midsection of the foot, numbered first to fifth metatarsal, starting with the big toe. These fragile bones are easily damaged. A metatarsal fracture is one of the most common footballing injuries, especially a fracture of the fifth metatarsal (the bone connecting to the little toe).

Metatarsal fractures are treated with anti-inflammatory medication and the wearing of a cast, which keeps weight and pressure off the damaged bone and helps to realign it. In severe cases surgery may be required, involving the insertion of a screw into the bone. It can take up to eight weeks before the cast comes off, after which the player can start light training, until gradually a full recovery is made and he is back to full strength.

Sprained ankle

Given the fast-paced nature of football, with players constantly twisting, turning and tackling, ankle sprains are particularly common injuries. They occur when the ligaments surrounding the ankle joint are damaged or stretched further than their limit.

Mild ankle sprains are relatively minor injuries, from which players quickly recover. Severe injuries can involve dislocation of the ankle joint and painful swelling, from which it can take several weeks to recover and a course of physiotherapy.

Groin strain

When a player stretches to reach the ball, his adductor muscles, located in the inner thigh, are at full stretch. It's when he over-stretches those muscles that painful groin strains occur, inhibiting movement and often resulting in a bruise.

Treatment for groin strain is straightforward – ice packs and rest. A player usually recovers quickly from a mild strain, but a severe strain may leave him in need of physiotherapy and several weeks of enforced rest.

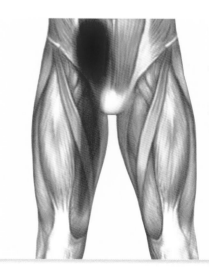

Sprinting, changing directions, jumping for the ball, and landing after a jump are all examples of actions that could trigger the injury. Inadequate warm-ups, poor technique and taking a blow to the groin area are also possible causes.

Hamstring injury

When a player running at full speed comes to a sudden stop, clutching his thigh in obvious pain, chances are he's damaged his hamstrings – tendons at the back of the thighs that attach the thigh muscle to the bone. Hamstring injuries are very common in football and occur if the tendons are stretched beyond their limit. Recurring injury is common if there's a history of injury.

A hamstring injury varies from a mild muscle strain to a complete muscle tear. For a mild strain, treatment involves rest, ice packs and anti-inflammatory medication, and full recovery usually takes a few days. But, if a player has torn the muscle he will be left unable to walk. He'll be off for weeks or months, and will have to keep his damaged leg elevated, apply ice regularly and receive physiotherapy.

Cruciate ligament injury

The anterior (front) and posterior (back) cruciate ligaments of the knee joint prevent the lower and upper leg bones from sliding forward and backwards on each other. They can become damaged when a player twists his leg awkwardly, or as the result of a tackle.

A cruciate ligament injury is painful, requires surgery to repair the damage, and can take up to a year to recover from. During recovery, a player will need extensive physiotherapy to bring his quadricep (front of leg) and hamstring (back of leg) muscles back to full strength.

Opposite Top Right: Didier Drogba over-stretches for the ball in a move that often results in a groin strain. Above: Blackburn Rover's Morten Gamst Pedersen holds his hamstring as his picks up an injury. Above Right: England defender John Terry sits in an ice bath at the national squad's EURO 2004 Lisbon training camp in Portugal, to assist his recovery from a recent hamstring injury. Bottom Right: Bayern Munich defender Holger Badstuber twists his knee as he challenges Mario Götze of Borusia Dortmund. Badstuber had to undergo surgery after suffering a torn cruciate ligament in his right knee that ruled him out for five months.

GLOSSARY

0–9

2–3–5: common 19th- and early 20th-century formation consisting of two defensive players (previously known as full backs), three midfield players (half-backs), and five forward players. Also known as the pyramid formation.

4–4–2: common modern formation used with four defenders, four midfielders, and two attacking players.

4–5–1: common modern formation used with four defenders, five midfielders and one striker.

4th place trophy: The achievement of qualifying for the UEFA Champions League by finishing in the top four places in the English Premier League. The term was coined by Arsène Wenger, who said that "For me, there are five trophies, the first is to win the Premier League... the third is to qualify for the Champions League."

6+5 rule: proposal adopted by FIFA in 2008. Designed to counter the effects of the Bosman ruling, which had greatly increased the number of foreign players fielded by European clubs. The rule required each club to field at least six players who are eligible to play for the national team of the country of the club. The European Parliament prevented the rule from coming into effect in the European Union, declaring it incompatible with EU law – its future remains uncertain.

12th man: expression used to describe fans present at a football match, especially when they make such noise as to provide increased motivation for the team. The metaphor is based on the fact that a team numbers 11 active players at the start of a game. The term can also be used where a referee is perceived to be biased in favor of one team. "They had a 12th man on the pitch" is a complaint made by fans.

A

Academy: model used by some professional clubs for youth development. Young players are contracted to the club and trained to a high standard, with the hope that some will develop into professional footballers. Some clubs provide academic as well as footballing education at their academies. Also known as a youth academy.

Administration: legal process where a business unable to pay its creditors seeks temporary legal protection from them, while it attempts to restructure its debt. Clubs going into administration usually incur a points deduction.

Advantage: decision made by the referee during a game, where a player is fouled, but play is allowed to continue because the team that suffered the foul is in a better position than they would have been had the referee stopped the game.

AFC: acronym for either the Asian Football Confederation, the governing body of the sport in Asia, or association football club, used by teams such as Sunderland AFC. Also used for "athletic football club," for instance AFC Bournemouth.

Against the run of play: describes a goal scored, or a win or draw achieved, by a side that was being clearly outplayed.

Armband: worn by a team's captain, to signify that role. Black armbands are occasionally worn by an entire team in commemoration of a death or tragic event.

Assist: pass that leads to a goal being scored.

Assistant referee: one of a number of officials who assist the referee in controlling a match.

Attacker: usually refers to a striker, but can be used to describe any player close to the opposing team's goal line.

Away goals rule: tie-break applied in some competitions with two-legged matches. In cases where the scores finish level on aggregate, the team that has scored more goals away from home is deemed the winner.

B

Back-pass rule: rule introduced into the Laws of the Game in 1992 to help speed up play, specifying that goalkeepers are not allowed to pick up the ball if it was intentionally kicked back to them by a teammate.

Backheel: pass between teammates, in which one player uses their heel to propel the ball backwards to another player. Sometimes spelled back heel.

Ball: spherical object normally kicked around by football players. Balls used in official matches are standardized for size, weight, and material, and manufactured to the specifications set in the Laws of the Game.

Ball boy: one of several youth, male or female, stationed around the edge of the pitch, whose role is to help retrieve balls that go out of play.

Ballon d'Or: may refer to the current FIFA Ballon d'Or, awarded to the player voted the best in world football, or a previous award, which recognized the best player in European football.

Behind closed doors: matches in which spectators are not present. May be imposed as a form of sanction for clubs whose supporters have behaved inappropriately.

Bench: area on the edge of the pitch where a team's substitutes and coaches sit, usually consisting of an actual covered bench or a row of seats. More formally known as the substitutes' bench. Also sometimes called a dugout.

Booking: act of noting the offender in a cautionable offense, which results in a yellow card.

Boot boy: young player who, in addition to his football training, is expected to perform menial tasks such as cleaning the boots of first-team players.

Bosman ruling: ruling by the European Court of Justice related to player transfers that allows professional football players in the European Union to move freely to another club at the end of their term of contract with their present team. Handed down in 1995, it also banned the restricted movement of EU members within the leagues of member states. Named after Jean-Marc Bosman, the plaintiff in that court case.

Brace: when a player scores two goals in a single match.

Break: attacking maneuvre in which several members of a defending team gain possession of the ball and suddenly counter-attack into their opponent's half of the pitch.

Bung: secret and unauthorized payment, used as a financial incentive to help a transfer go through.

C

CAF: acronym for the Confederation of African Football, the governing body of the sport in Africa.

Cap: a player's participation in a game for a national team. Originates from the traditional presentation of a cap to British players who made international appearances.

Cap-tied: a term used when a player has represented a national team and as a consequence is ineligible to play for another.

Captain: player chosen to lead a team, and in a match to participate in the coin toss before the start of play. Also known as a skipper.

Caretaker manager: person chosen to perform managerial duties when no permanent manager is installed.

Center circle: 10-yard radius circle around the center spot.

Center spot: mark in the center of the pitch from which play is started at the beginning of each half, and restarted following the scoring of a goal.

Channel: empty space between the fullback and the central defender when a defense is playing with a back four. Wide-playing strikers are said to operate "in the channels."

Champions League: annual confederation-wide tournament involving the champions and other successful teams from that confederation's domestic leagues. The term can refer to the tournaments held in the AFC, CAF, CONCACAF or OFC, but is most commonly used in reference to the competition held by UEFA. The CONMEBOL equivalent is the Copa Libertadores.

Chance: situation where an attacking player can shoot at goal with a realistic prospect of scoring. Also known as an opportunity.

Chip: high trajectory shot, hit with the intention of the ball going over the goalkeeper and into the goal.

Clean sheet: when a goalkeeper or team does not concede a single goal during a match.

Clearance: when a player kicks the ball away from the goal they are defending.

Club: collective name for a football team, and the organization that runs it.

Co-ownership: system whereby two football clubs own the contract of a player jointly, although the player is only registered to play for one club.

CONCACAF: acronym for the Confederation of North, Central American and Caribbean Association Football, the governing body of the sport in North and Central America and the Caribbean; pronounced "kon-ka-kaff."

CONMEBOL: acronym for the South American Football Association, the governing body of the sport in South America; pronounced "kon-me-bol."

Corner flag: flags are placed in each of the four corners of the pitch to help mark the boundaries of the playing area.

Corner kick: kick taken from within a one-yard radius of the corner flag; a method of restarting play when a player puts the ball behind their own goal line without a goal being scored.

Cross: delivery of the ball into the penalty area by the attacking team, usually from the area between the penalty box and the touchline.

Crossbar: horizontal bar across the top of the goal.

Cup (~ competition, ~ format, ~ -tie): a single-elimination tournament, as opposed to a league (round-robin tournament); named after England's FA Cup and Football League, respectively. Depending on the competition, cup-ties may be a single match or a two-legged tie; often the "cup final" is a single match at a predetermined venue.

Cup run: a series of wins in a cup competition, usually applied to teams from lower division.

Cup-tied: where a player is ineligible to play in a cup competition because they have played for a different team earlier in the same competition.

D

D: semi-circular arc at the edge of the penalty area used to indicate the portion of the 10-yard distance around the penalty spot that lies outside the penalty area.

Dead ball: situation when the game is restarted with the ball stationary, such as a free kick.

Deep: used to describe the positioning of a player (or a line of players, such as the defense or midfield) who is playing closer to their own goal than they traditionally would.

Defender: one of the four main positions in football. Defenders are positioned in front of the goalkeeper and have the principal role of keeping the opposition away from their goal.

Derby: match between two, usually local, rivals.

Designated player rule: rule in Major League Soccer that allows teams to nominate players who are paid either partially or completely outside the salary cap.

Direct free kick: awarded to fouled team following certain listed "penal" fouls. A goal may be scored directly without the ball having first touched another player.

Dirty work: the type of play undertaken by a defensive midfielder – such as making tackles in midfield, playing short passes to the wing, and breaking up opponent's attacking moves. Necessary for a team to be successful, but rarely receives recognition or acclaim, and is not considered "glamorous."

Diving: form of cheating, sometimes employed by an attacking player to win a free kick or penalty.

Double: most commonly used when a club wins both its domestic league and its country's major cup competition in the same season. Also used to describe a pair of victories, home and away, by one club over another in the same league season.

Dribbling: when a player runs with the ball at their feet under close control. Dribbling on a winding course past several opponents in close proximity without losing possession is sometimes described as making a mazy run or mazy dribble.

Drop ball: method used to restart a game, sometimes when a player has been injured accidentally and the game is stopped while the ball is still in play.

Dummy: skill move performed by a player receiving a pass from a teammate. The player receiving the ball will angle their body in such a way that the opponent thinks they are going to play the ball. The player will then intentionally allow the ball to run by them to a teammate close by without touching it, confusing the opponent.

E

El Clásico: derby fixtures in Spanish-speaking countries such as Argentina and Mexico. In Spain, and countries where Spanish is not a primary language, it is commonly understood as the name of the derby between Spanish clubs Real Madrid and Barcelona.

Equalizer: goal that makes the score even.

European night: night-time game in a UEFA club competition.

Extra time: additional period, normally two halves of 15 minutes, used to determine the winner in some tied-cup matches.

F

FA Cup: English knockout competition – the oldest cup tournament in the world.

Fan: dedicated follower of a football team or someone who simply enjoys watching the game. Also known as supporter.

Fans' favorite: player that is extremely popular with fans of a club or nation.

Favorite: team that is expected to win a particular match or tournament.

FC: acronym for football club, used by teams such as Watford FC.

Feeder club: club whose role is to provide first-team experience for younger players with a formal or informal agreement that successful ones can move on to the bigger club.

Fergie time: the idea that Manchester United, when managed by Sir Alex Ferguson, got what rival fans considered to be generous and/or excessive added time when Ferguson's team were losing, particularly at home.

FIFA: acronym for Fédération Internationale de Football Association (International Federation of Association Football), the world governing body of the sport.

Fifty-fifty: a challenge in which two players have an equal chance of winning control of a loose ball.

First eleven: the eleven players who, when available, would be the ones usually chosen by the team's manager to start a game.

First team: the most senior team fielded by a club.

First touch: skill attribute for a player which signifies their ability to bring the ball completely under control immediately upon receiving it.

Fixture: scheduled match which has yet to be played.

Flag: small rectangular flag attached to a handle, used by an assistant referee to signal that they have seen a foul or other infraction take place. One assistant referee's flag is a solid color (often yellow), and the other assistant referee has a two-color (often red and yellow) in a quartered pattern. Some flags have buttons on the handle, which will activate an alarm worn by the referee to attract their colleagues' attention. Can also refer to the corner flag.

Flat back four: defensive positioning system, in which the primary first position of each member of a four-man defense is in a straight line across the pitch; often used in conjunction with an offside trap.

Flick-on: when a player receives a pass from a teammate and, instead of controlling it, touches the ball with their head or foot while it is moving past them, with the intent of helping the ball reach another teammate.

Football: a widely used name for association football. Can also refer to the ball.

Football League: English league competition founded in 1888, the oldest such competition in the world.

Football program: also known as match program; booklet purchased by spectators prior to a football match containing information relevant to it, including lists of players, short articles penned by commentators, and the like.

Football pyramid: also known as league system; a hierarchy of leagues in which teams can be promoted or relegated, depending on finishing positions or play-offs. They are often referred to as "pyramids" due to their tendency to have an increasing number of divisions further down the tiers (or "steps"), thus leading to a pyramid-like structure.

Formation: how the players in a team are positioned on the pitch. The formation is often denoted numerically (see 0-9 above), with the numbers referring to the corresponding number of players in defensive, midfield and attacking positions.

Foul: breach of the Laws of the Game by a player, punishable by a penalty or a free kick by the fouled player. Such acts can lead to yellow or red cards, depending on their severity.

Fourth official: additional assistant referee, who has various duties and can replace one of the other officials, in case of injury.

Free kick: the result of a foul outside the penalty area, given against the offending team. Free kicks can be either direct (shot straight toward the goal) or indirect (the ball must touch another player before a goal can be scored).

Friendly: match arranged by two teams with no competitive value, such as a player's testimonial or a warm-up match before a season begins.

Full-time: the end of the game, signaled by the referees whistle (also known as the final whistle).

Fullback: position on either side of the defense, whose job is to try to prevent the opposing team attacking down the wings. Also spelled full back or full-back.

G

Game of two halves: expression used by commentators to describe a close match where one team dominates each half.

Giant-killing: cliché used to describe a lower division team defeating another team from a much higher division in that country's league.

Goal: the only method of scoring in football; for a goal to be awarded the ball must pass completely over the goal line in the area between the posts and beneath the crossbar.

Goal average: number of goals scored divided by the number of goals conceded. Used as a tie-breaking method before the introduction of goal difference.

Goal difference: net difference between goals scored and goals conceded. Used to differentiate league positions when clubs are tied on points.

Goalkeeper: player closest to the goal a team is defending. A goalkeeper has the job of preventing the opposition from scoring. They are the only player on the pitch that can handle the ball in open play, although they can only do so in the penalty area. Known informally as a keeper or a goalie.

Goal kick: method of restarting play when the ball is played over the goal line without a goal being scored.

Goal line: line at one of the shorter ends of the pitch, spanning from one corner flag to another, with the goalposts situated at the halfway point; sometimes used to refer to the particular section of the goal line between the two goalposts Also known as goal-line.

Goal-line clearance: when a player performs a clearance of the ball right off the goal line.

Goal-line technology or GLT: a system to determine whether the ball has crossed the line for a goal or not. Sometimes referred to as a goal decision system or GDS.

Goal poacher: type of striker, primarily known for excellent scoring ability and movement inside the penalty area.

Goalmouth: the section of the pitch immediately in front of the goal.

Goalmouth scramble: when multiple players from both teams attempt to gain control of a loose ball in the goalmouth. This often results in a short period of chaotic play involving attackers shooting toward goal and defenders blocking shots.

Goalside: when a player is located closer to the goal than his opponent.

Golden goal: method of determining the winner of a match which is a draw after 90 minutes of play. Up to an additional 30 minutes are played in two 15-minute halves, the first team to score wins and the match ends immediately.

Grand Slam: achieved by a club that wins all official international competitions.

Group of death: group in a cup competition that is unusually competitive because the number of strong teams in the group is greater than the number of qualifying places available for the next phase of the tournament.

H

Half-back: position employed in a 2–3–5 formation, half-backs would play in front of the full-backs and behind the forwards. The middle half-back was known as a center-half; those on either side were known as wing-halves.

Half-time: break between the two halves of a match, usually lasts 15 minutes.

Half-volley: pass or shot in which the ball is struck just as, or just after, it touches the ground.

Handbags: colloquialism, especially in the United Kingdom, used to describe an event where two or more players from opposing teams square up to each other in a threatening manner, or push and jostle each other in an attempt to assert themselves, without any actual violent conduct taking place.

Handball or hand ball: when a player (other than a goalkeeper inside their penalty area) deliberately touches the ball with their hand in active play. A foul is given against the player if spotted.

Hat-trick: when a player scores three goals in a single match.

Header: using the head as a means of playing or controlling the ball.

Hold up the ball: when a player, usually a forward, receives a long ball from a teammate, and controls and shields it from the opposition, with the intent of slowing the play down to allow teammates to join the attack.

Holding role or Holding midfielder: central midfielder whose primary role is to protect the defense.

Hole: space on a pitch between the midfield and forwards. In formations where attacking midfielders or deep-lying forwards are used, they are said to be "playing in the hole."

Home and away: a team's own ground and their opponent's, respectively. The team playing at their own stadium are said to have "home advantage."

Hooligans: fanatical supporters known for violence.

Hospital ball: sometimes referred to as hospital pass; when a player plays a slightly under-strength pass to a teammate, to such an extent that it becomes likely that both the teammate and an opposing player will come into contact with the ball simultaneously, therefore increasing the likelihood of one or both players suffering an injury while challenging for the ball.

Howler: glaring and possibly amusing error made by a player or referee during a match.

Humdinger: Used to describe a highly anticipated or thrilling match.

GLOSSARY

I

IFAB: acronym for the International Football Association Board, the body that determines the Laws of the Game of association football.

Indirect free kick: type of free kick awarded to the opposing team following "non-penal" fouls, certain technical infringements, or when play is stopped to caution or dismiss an opponent without a specific foul having occurred. Unlike in a direct free kick, a goal may not be scored directly from the indirect kick.

Inside forward: position employed in a 2–3–5 formation. The inside forwards played just behind the center forward, similar to the modern attacking midfielder or second striker.

Intercept: to prevent a pass from reaching its intended recipient.

International break: period of time set aside by FIFA for scheduled international matches per their International Match Calendar. Also known as FIFA International Day/Date(s).

J

Journeyman: player who has represented many different clubs over their career. Opposite of one-club man.

Jumpers for goalposts: informal name for a version of street football where players lay down items of clothing to mark out the two goals. ("Jumper" is a sweater or similar in British English.) The term also has a nostalgia factor, especially in England, intended to invoke memories of a more "innocent" and "pure" type of football from previous generations.

K

Keepie-uppie: the skill of juggling a football, keeping it off the ground using the feet, the knees, the chest, the shoulders or the head. The phrases are sometimes spelled as two separate words, for instance keepie uppie.

Kick-off: method of starting a match; the ball must be played forwards from the center spot with all members of the opposing team at least 10 yards from the ball. Also used to restart the match when a goal has been scored.

Kit: football-specific clothing worn by players, consisting of a jersey with full sleeves, shorts, knee-high socks, shin guards, adequate footwear and (for goalkeepers) specialized gloves. Also known as a uniform or a strip.

Kop: British colloquial name for terraced stands in stadiums, especially those immediately behind the goals. Most commonly associated with Liverpool FC, they are so named due to their steep nature, which resembles a hill in South Africa that was the scene of the Battle of Spion Kop in January 1900 during the Second Boer War.

L

Last man: situation where an attacking player is in possession, with only one opposing defender between the ball and the goal. If the defender commits a foul on the attacker, a red card is usually shown.

Laws of the Game: codified rules that help define association football. These laws are published by the sport's governing body FIFA, with the approval of the International Football Association Board, the body that writes and maintains the laws. The laws mention: the number of players a team should have, the game length, the size of the field and ball, the type and nature of fouls that referees may penalize, the frequently misinterpreted offside law, and many other laws that define the sport.

Lay-off pass: short pass, usually lateral, played delicately into the space immediately in front of a teammate who is arriving at speed from behind the player making the pass. The player receiving the pass will then be able to take control of the ball without breaking stride or (if they are close enough to the goal) attempt to score with a first-time shot.

League: form of competition in which clubs are ranked by the number of points they accumulate over a series of matches. Often structured as round-robin tournaments.

Linesman: see Assistant referee.

Loan: when a player temporarily plays for a club other than the one they are currently contracted to. Such a loan may last from a few weeks to one or more seasons. This often occurs with young players who are commonly loaned to lower league clubs in order to gain valuable experience. The loaning club often takes over the responsibility of paying the player's wages, so it can also occur when the originating club seeks to cut down expenses.

Long ball: attempt to send the ball a long distance down the field via a cross, without the intention to pass it to the feet of the receiving player. Often used to speed up play, the technique can be especially effective for a team with either fast or tall strikers.

Lost the dressing room: where a team's manager is deemed to have lost control and support of the players.

M

Magic sponge: sponge filled with water which has a seemingly miraculously reviving effect on injured players.

Man of the Match: award, often decided by pundits, sponsors and sometimes fans, given to the best player in a game.

Man on!: warning shout uttered by players (and fans) to a teammate with the ball to alert him of the presence of an opposing player behind him.

Man-to-man marking: a system of marking in which each player is responsible for an opposing player rather than an area of the pitch. Compare with zonal marking.

Manager: the individual in charge of the day-to-day running of the team. Duties of the manager usually include overseeing training sessions, designing tactical plays, choosing the team's formation, picking the starting eleven, and making tactical switches and substitutions during games. Some managers also take on backroom administrative responsibilities such as signing players, negotiating player contracts. Sometimes these tasks are also undertaken by two separate individuals: a Head coach for on-field tasks, and a General manager or Director of Football for off-field administrative duties.

Marking: defensive strategy aimed at preventing an attacker from receiving the ball from a teammate. See man-to-man marking and zonal marking.

Match fixing: expression used to describe the situation when a match is played to a completely or partially pre-determined result motivated by financial incentives paid to players, team officials or referees in violation of the rules of the game.

Medical: mandatory procedure undertaken by a player prior to signing for a new team which assesses the player's fitness and overall medical health. Usually the procedure includes muscle and ligament/joint examinations, cardiovascular tests to identify potential heart problems, respiratory tests, and neurological tests to identify possible concussions or other such problems.

Mexican wave: self-organized crowd activity in which spectators stand up, raise their hands in the air, and sit down in sequence, creating a ripple effect that moves around the stadium's stands. Despite having been carried out in stadia for many years previously, it was first brought to worldwide attention during the 1986 FIFA World Cup in Mexico, hence its name.

Mickey Mouse cup: cup, league, or other competition considered of a lower standard, importance, or significance.

Midfielder: one of the four main positions in football. Midfielders are positioned between the defenders and strikers.

N

Near post/Far post: notional concept referring to the position of a goalkeeper in relation to the posts. When an attacker scores a goal by placing the ball between the goalkeeper and the post to which they are closest, the goalkeeper is said to have been beaten at the near post.

Neutral ground: venue for a match that belongs to neither team.

Nutmeg: when a player intentionally plays the ball between an opponent's legs, runs past the opponent, and collects their own pass.

O

Obstruction: illegal defensive technique, in which a defensive player who does not have control of the ball positions their body between the ball and an attacking opponent, or otherwise blocks or checks an opponent, in order to prevent that opponent from reaching the ball.

OFC: acronym for the Oceania Football Confederation, the governing body of the sport in Oceania.

Offside: Law 11 of the laws of football, relating to the positioning of defending players in relation to attacking players when the ball is played to an attacking player by a teammate. In its most basic form, a player is offside if they are in their opponent's half of the field, and is closer to the goal line than both the second-last defender and the ball at the moment the ball is played to them by a teammate.

Offside trap: defensive tactical maneuver, in which each member of a team's defense will simultaneously step forward as the ball is played forward to an opponent, in an attempt to put that opponent in an offside position. An unsuccessful performance of this maneuver results in the opponent "beating the offside trap."

Olympic goal: goal scored directly from a corner kick.

One touch: style of play in which the ball is passed around quickly using just one touch. Also used for the same type of training which aims to improve the speed of players' reaction when receiving the ball.

One-club man: player who spends their entire professional career at one club.

One-on-one: situation where the only player between an attacking player and the goal is the opponent's goalkeeper.

One-two: skill move between teammates to move the ball past an opponent. Player One passes the ball to Player Two and runs past the opponent, whereupon they immediately receive the ball back from Player Two, who has received, controlled, and passed the ball in one movement.

Open goal: where no player is defending the goal.

Outfield player: any player other than the goalkeeper.

Outside forward: position used in a 2–3–5 formation, in which the players are the main attacking threat from the flanks. Similar to modern wingers.

Overlap: move between teammates. An attacking player (who has the ball) is shadowed by a single defender; the attacker's teammate runs past both players, forcing the defender to either continue to shadow the player on the ball, or attempt to prevent the teammate from receiving a pass. The first player can either pass the ball or keep possession, depending on which decision the defender makes.

Own goal: where a player scores a goal against their own team.

P

Panenka: skill move used when taking a penalty kick wherein the player taking the penalty delicately chips the ball over a diving goalkeeper, rather than striking the ball firmly, as is the norm. Named after Antonín Panenka, who famously scored such a penalty for Czechoslovakia against West Germany in the final of the 1976 UEFA European Football Championship.

Parachute payment: series of payments made for four years by the Premier League to every club relegated from that league.

Paralympic football: consists of adaptations made to the sport of association football for athletes with a disability.

Parking the bus: expression used when all the players on a team play defensively, usually when the team is intending to draw the game or when defending a narrow margin. The term was coined by Chelsea FC manager José Mourinho, referring to Tottenham Hotspur FC during a game against Chelsea in 2004.

Pass: when a player kicks the ball to one of their teammates.

Passive offside: exception to the offside rule, wherein play may continue if a player in an offside position makes no attempt to involve himself in the game at the moment an offside call would usually be made, and allows an onside player to win control of the ball instead.

Penalty area: rectangular area measuring 44 yards (40.2 meters) by 18 yards (16.5 meters) in front of each goal and where a foul by a defender is punishable by a penalty kick.
Penalty kick: kick taken 12 yards (11 meters) from goal, awarded when a team commits a foul inside its own penalty area, and the infringement would usually be punishable by a direct free kick.
Penalty shootout: method of deciding a match in a knockout competition that has ended in a draw after full-time and extra-time. Players from each side take it in turns to attempt to score a penalty against the opposition goalkeeper. Sudden death is introduced if scores are level after five penalties have been taken by either side. Also spelled penalty shoot-out.
Perfect hat-trick: when a player scores three goals in a single match, one with the left foot, one with the right foot and one with a header.
Phoenix club: club which has been created following the demise of a pre-existing club. Phoenix clubs usually take on the same colors and fan base as those of the defunct club and may even be established by fans themselves.
Pitch: playing surface for a game of football; usually a specially prepared grass field. Referred to in the Laws of the Game as the field of play.
Pitch invasion: when a crowd of people who are watching run onto the pitch to celebrate, protest about an incident or confront opposition fans. Known as rushing the field in the United States.
Play to the whistle: an informal phrase used to instruct players to keep on playing until the referee blows their whistle.
Play-acting: similar to diving, play-acting is deceiving the officials that a player is injured to try to gain an advantage or force the referee to punish the "aggressor." Also known as feigning injury or Diving.
Play-off: series of matches toward the end of the season that determine which clubs are promoted and/or relegated, tied league positions or qualifiers for continental competitions.
Playmaker: attacking player whose job is to control the flow of their team's play.
Points deduction: method of punishing clubs for breaching the rules of a tournament by reducing the number of accumulated points during a league season. Points deductions can be applied for offenses such as going into administration, financial irregularities, fielding ineligible players, match fixing, or violent conduct amongst club staff or supporters. The offending team may also lose one or more titles and temporarily be barred from play.
Pozna: celebration which involves fans turning their backs to the pitch, joining arms and jumping up and down in unison. It takes its name from Polish club Lech Poznań, whose fans are thought to be the first to celebrate in this way.
Pre-season: period leading up to the start of a league season. Clubs generally prepare for a new season with intensive training, playing friendlies, and signing new players.
Premier League: name of the top division of English football since 1992. The phrase can also be used generically, or as a translation for leagues in other countries.
Pressing: A tactic where defending players move forward toward the ball, rather than remaining in position near their goal. They may pressure the player that has the ball or get close to other opponents in order to remove passing options. A successful press will recover the ball quickly and further up the pitch, or force the opponents to make an inaccurate long kick. However, if the opponents are able to pass the ball forward, fewer defending players are protecting the goal, making pressing a high-risk, high-reward strategy.
Professional: player who is engaged by a club under a professional contract and who is paid a wage by the club to focus on their sport in lieu of other employment.
Professional foul: foul committed by a player who is aware that they are about to intentionally commit the foul, and who does so having calculated the risk, and determined that committing the foul and taking a yellow card or even a red card will be more beneficial to their team than if the player allowed their opponent to continue unimpeded.
Promotion: when a club moves up to a higher division in the league hierarchy as a result of being one of the best teams in their division at the end of a season.
Pyramid: may refer to the 2–3–5 formation, or to a football pyramid, a hierarchical structure of leagues.

R

Rabona: method of kicking the football whereby the kicking leg is wrapped around the back of the standing leg.
Red card: awarded to a player for either a single serious cautionable offense or following two yellow cards. The player receiving the red card is compelled to leave the game for the rest of its duration, and that player's team is not allowed to replace him with another player.
Referee: the official who presides over a match, with the help of assistant referees and the fourth official.
Relegation: when a club moves down to a lower division in the league hierarchy as a result of gaining the least number of points in their division at the end of a season.
Reserve team: team which is considered supplemental to the club's senior team. Matches between reserve teams often include a combination of first team players that have not featured in recent games, as well as academy and trial players.
Retired number: squad number which is no longer used as a form of recognizing an individual player's loyal service to the club. Sometimes a number is retired as a memorial after their death.
Round-robin tournament: competition in which each contestant meets all other contestants in turn. A competition where each team plays the other teams twice is known as a double round-robin.
Rounding the 'keeper: attacking move in which a player attempts to dribble the ball around the goalkeeper, hoping to leave an open goal.
Route one: attacking style of football which generally involves taking the most direct route to goal.
Roy of the Rovers stuff: an event during a game or an entire game in which a player or team is victorious despite extreme adversity, or secures victory in an overtly spectacular or dramatic fashion, especially against a team generally considered to be "stronger." The term originates from the long-running football-themed English comic strip Roy of the Rovers, in which such events were commonplace.
Row Z: term used by commentators to describe the hypothetical destination of a forceful clearance, on the assumption that rows in which spectators are seated are ordered alphabetically so that row Z is the furthest from the pitch. Also used to describe a shot which goes a long way over the crossbar.

S

Save: when a goalkeeper prevents the football from crossing the goal line between the goalposts.
Scorpion kick: acrobatic kick of the type first notably performed as a save by René Higuita in 1995 while playing for Colombia against England at Wembley Stadium.
Scrimmage: a term used in the 19th century for what would now be called a goalmouth scramble. In the early days of newspaper coverage of the sport, reporters were often unable to identify the scorer of a goal under such circumstances and would report simply that the goal had been scored "from a scrimmage." For this reason, the scorers of several goals in early FA Cup finals are unknown.
Seal dribble: type of dribble, in which a player flicks the ball up from the ground onto their head and then proceeds to run past opponents whilst bouncing the ball on top of their forehead, somewhat imitating a seal.
Season: the time period during which primary competitions in a certain country are played. In most European countries the season starts around September and ends in May, with a winter break in December and January. In other countries the season is played within a single calendar year. It is often customary to use the Super Cup to mark the beginning of a season while the Cup final usually marks its end.
Second season syndrome: phrase sometimes used by commentators in English football used to describe a downturn in fortunes for a football club two seasons after its promotion to the Premier League.
Set piece: dead ball routine that the attacking team has specifically practiced, such as a free kick taken close to the D.
Shielding: defensive technique, in which a defensive player positions their body between the ball and an attacking opponent, in order to prevent that opponent from reaching the ball. At all times while shielding the ball, the defender must maintain control of the ball within a nominal playing distance, otherwise the technique becomes obstruction, and a foul is called.
Shin pads or Shin guards: mandatory piece of equipment, usually made of plastic or rubber, worn underneath the socks in order to protect the shins.
Shoot: specialized kicking technique mainly used by forwards. The purpose of shooting is to get the ball past the goal line (usually beating the goalkeeper in the process), though some shots may be made in order to win corners or force the keeper to deflect the ball into the path of a teammate - this will only be the case if scoring directly from the shot seems unlikely.
Side netting: outside of the net part of the goal, which stretches back from the goalpost to the stanchion.
Silver goal: rule which was briefly in use between 2002 and 2004 in some UEFA competitions, when elimination matches were level after 90 minutes. In extra time, the match would end if one team was winning after 15 minutes of extra time. Unlike the golden goal, the game did not finish the moment a goal was scored.
Silverware: slang for the trophies teams receive for winning, and players for performance
Six-pointer: game between teams both competing for a title, promotion or relegation, whereby the relative difference between winning and losing can be six points.
Slide tackle: type of tackle where the defending player slides along the ground to tackle their opponent.
Soccer: alternative term for football in countries where other codes of play are prominent, e.g., soccer in the United States and Canada, and Australian rules football. However, these countries also participation in some association football conferences. Originating in Britain, and derived from the "s-o-c" in "association" the 1970s.
Squad numbers: numerical markings on players' shirts used to distinguish individual players in a game of football. First used in 1928, and initially assigned to distinguish positions in a formation, they gradually became associated with individual players, irrespective of where they are positioned on the pitch. This gave rise to the custom of retiring numbers.
Squad rotation system: managerial device, whereby the manager selects from a large number of players in first team games, rather than having a regular first eleven.
Square ball: when a ball is passed between teammates laterally, across the field of play.
Squeaky-bum time: tense final stages of a league competition, especially from the point of view of the title contenders, and clubs facing promotion and relegation. Coined by Manchester United manager Alex Ferguson.
Stanchion: part of the framework of the goal which holds the upper rear part of the net in the air and away from the crossbar.
Stepover: skill move performed by an attacking player in which the player with the ball will move their foot over the ball without making contact with it. The intent of the move is to confuse a defender into thinking that the attacking player is moving with the ball in a certain direction; when the defender changes direction in response, the attacker will quickly change direction.
Stoppage time: an additional number of minutes at the end of each half, determined by the match officials, to compensate for time lost during the game. Informally known by various names, including injury time and added time.
Straight red: a penalty given by the referee in punishment for a serious offense that is deemed to be worse than a booking and results in immediate sending off of a player
Street football: informal variations of the sport. Games often forego many requirements of

a formal game of football, such as a large field, field markings, goal apparatus and corner flags, eleven players per team, or match officials (referee and assistant referees).

Striker: one of the four main positions in football. Strikers are the players closest to the opposition goal, with the principal role of scoring goals. Also known as forward or attacker.

Studs: small points on the sole of a player's boots to help prevent slipping. A tackle in which a player directs their studs toward an opponent is referred to as a studs-up challenge, and is a foul punishable by a red card.

Subbed: A player who is withdrawn from the field of play and replaced by a substitute is said to have been subbed or subbed off. An oncoming substitute may be referred to as being subbed on.

Substitute: a player who is brought on to the pitch during a match in exchange for an existing player.

Sudden death: feature of penalty shootouts. If scores are level after each side has taken five penalties, the shootout continues until one side misses.

Super Hat-trick: when a player scores four goals in a single match.

Suspension: players are forced to miss their team's next game(s) if they pick up an allotted number of bookings in league or tournament matches, or are sent off in a previous fixture.

Sweeper: defender whose role is to protect the space between the goalkeeper and the rest of the defense by "sweeping up" the ball out and away. Also called the libero, from the Italian "free".

T

(to) Take a touch: to control the ball with a legal part of the body before passing or shooting.

(it) Takes a touch: when the ball, often unintentionally, takes a deflection off a player to alter its intended trajectory.

Tackle: method of a player winning the ball back from an opponent, either by using a leg to wrest possession from the opponent, or making a slide tackle to knock the ball away. A tackle in which the opposing player is kicked is punishable by either a free kick or penalty kick. Dangerous tackles may also result in a yellow or red card.

Target man: type of striker. Usually tall, with a strong build and good heading ability, capable of controlling or attacking balls in the air. Target men give the forward line different options in how to attack the goal, and are often used to hold up the ball or play layoff passes to their teammates.

Technical area: area within which the manager must remain while coaching their team during a match, marked by white lines at the side of the pitch.

Telstar: match ball designed by Adidas for the 1970 FIFA World Cup. The first ball to use a truncated icosahedron design, with 12 black and 20 white patches intentionally used to improve visibility on black-and-white TV sets. The design remains common in club crests and decorations, even though modern match balls look considerably different. Known as bubamara (ladybug) in countries where Serbo-Croatian is spoken.

Terrace: standing area of a stadium, consisting of a series of concrete steps which are erected for spectators to stand on. Often occupied by ultras. Terraces have been phased out in some countries, due to safety concerns.

Testimonial match: friendly match organized in honor of a player with long service, usually 10 years at a single club.

Three points for a win: point system in which three points are awarded to the team winning a match, with no points to the losing team. If the game is drawn, each team receives one point. Replacing the previous convention of two and one points awarded for wins and draws respectively, the system is intended to encourage teams to attack in search of a win, rather than settle for a draw.

Through-ball: pass from the attacking team that goes straight through the opposition's defense to a teammate. Invariably the teammate will run onto the ball – standing behind the defenders when the ball was played would result in offside being called.

Throw-in: method of restarting play. Involves a player throwing the ball from behind a touchline after it has been kicked out by an opponent.

Tiki-taka: style of play characterized by short passing and movement, working the ball through various channels and maintaining possession. The style is primarily associated with Spanish club FC Barcelona and the Spanish national team.

Toe punt: method of kicking the ball with the tip of the foot. Also known as a toe poke.

Too good to go down: the belief, often misguided, that the ability within a team will preclude it from relegation.

Top corner: the parts of the goal immediately below the two 90° angles where the crossbar and posts intersect. Generally considered the most difficult part of the goal for a goalkeeper to reach.

Top flight: the league at the highest level of a league system.

Total Football: tactical theory in which any outfield player can take over the role of any other player in a team. Invented by the Dutch coach Rinus Michels, Total Football was popularized by AFC Ajax and the Netherlands national team in the early 1970s.

Touch-line: markings along the side of the pitch, indicating the boundaries of the playing area. Throw-ins are taken from behind this line.

Tracksuit manager: phrase used by commentators to describe a manager who has a hands-on approach, meaning that they have a tendency to work with players on the training ground, spending a significant amount of time on improving players' abilities.

Transfer window: period during the year in which a football club can transfer players from other countries into their playing staff.

Trap: skill whereupon the player uses their foot (or, less commonly, chest or thigh) to bring an airborne or falling ball under control.

Traveling army: expression used by commentators for any set of away fans – that is, fans who traveled to the match to support their team. Often a team's traveling army are referred to as the 12th man.

Treble: achieved by a club that wins three major trophies in a single season. Competitions generally considered as part of a treble include the top tier domestic league, domestic cup and continental cup. Trebles achieved without winning a continental competition are known as domestic trebles. UEFA defines a European Treble as the feat of winning all three seasonal club confederation competitions.

Two-footed tackle: where a player, often a defender, tackles their opponent with both feet. Such tackles often result in a foul being called, if the tackling player is deemed not to be in control of his or her body.

U

UEFA: acronym for Union of European Football Associations, the governing body of the sport in Europe; pronounced "you-eh-fa."

Ultras: type of football fans predominantly found in Europe renowned for their fanatical support and elaborate displays at football matches. These displays often include the use of flares, vocal support in large groups, displays of banners at stadium terraces and other forms of tifo choreography. Tifo is Italian for the phenomenon of supporting a sport team.

Under the cosh: a team's defense experiences a period of concerted or unrelenting attacking play.

Underdog: the team that is not expected to win a particular game or competition.

Upset: game in which the underdog defeats a higher ranked team.

Utility player: player who can be used in different positions or for different roles transcending the traditional division of outfield players into defenders, midfielders and strikers.

V

Vanishing spray: short-lasting aerosol paint applied to the grass by the referee to mark the 10-yard exclusion area in a free kick.

Video technology: long-campaigned for method of determining close decisions, such as whether a ball crosses the goalline, using instant replays provided by television cameras. It is yet to be introduced by FIFA, though they are testing it.

Volley: pass or shot in which the ball is struck before it touches the ground.

Vuvuzela: horn-shaped plastic instruments popularized by supporters at the 2010 FIFA World Cup in South Africa. FIFA has since banned them, along with fireworks, megaphones and hooters.

W

Wall: row of defensive players who line up 10 yards away from a free kick, covering a portion of the goal to make it more difficult for an attacking player to have a shot on goal direct from the free kick.

Want-away: player who has made public their intentions to leave their current club.

War chest: the amount of money a manager has been given by a club's chairman, owner or investors to acquire new players.

Webster ruling: The 2006 court case stipulated that players are able to unilaterally walk away from a contract after a fixed period, regardless of the duration of the contract itself. Named after Andy Webster. Compare Bosman ruling.

Wing: area of the pitch that runs parallel to the sidelines.

Winger: wide midfield player whose primary focus is to provide crosses into the penalty area. Alternatively known as a wide midfielder.

Winter break: period between December and January in which competitive football is suspended and which cuts some national or continental seasons in half. Known as "year-end" or "summer break" in the Southern Hemisphere.

Withdrawn: A forward or attacking midfielder who plays deeper than the name of their conventional position suggests. A forward or attacking midfielder who drops deep may be described as playing in a withdrawn role. Withdrawn may also be used to refer to a player who has been substituted: "the injured midfielder was withdrawn on the hour mark."

Woodwork: common description of the posts and the crossbar, as in "the ball came back off the woodwork," meaning a shot at goal struck either the post or the crossbar and remained in play. The expression is still widely used even though goals are no longer made of wood.

Work rate: the extent to which a player contributes to running and chasing in a match while not in possession of the ball.

World Cup: Associated with the women's FIFA Women's World Cup, men's FIFA World Cup, international tournaments for youth football, (such as the FIFA U-20 World Cup), and also the FIFA Club World Cup.

Worldie: Used to refer to a goal which is considered to be world class, e.g. "he scored with a worldy." Also used to describe what is considered to be a world-class performance by a player not well known in the game, playing at a lower level.

X

X-rated challenge: malicious tackle when a player has possible motivation to injure an opponent.

Y

Yellow card: shown by the referee to a player who commits a cautionable offense. If a player commits two cautionable offenses in a match, they are shown a second yellow card, followed by a red card, and are then sent off. Also known as a caution or a booking.

Yo-yo club: club that is regularly promoted and relegated between higher and lower league levels.

Youth: a player (or team of players) contracted under the youth system, generally under the age of 18 and not playing professionally although youth players can appear for the first-team.

Z

Zonal marking: system of play, in which each player is responsible for an area of the pitch, rather than an opposing player.

INDEX

INDEX

INDEX

INDEX